Sitcoms
AND CULTURE

COMEDY & CULTURE

Nick Marx and Matt Sienkiewicz

Sitcoms

AND CULTURE

JAMES SHANAHAN

INDIANA UNIVERSITY PRESS

This book is a publication of

Indiana University Press
Herman B Wells Library 350
1320 East 10th Street
Bloomington, Indiana 47405 USA

iupress.org

© 2025 by James Shanahan

All rights reserved
No part of this book may be reproduced or utilized in any form or by any means, electronic or mechanical, including photocopying and recording, or by any information storage and retrieval system, without permission in writing from the publisher.

First printing 2025

Cataloging information is available from the Library of Congress.
ISBN 978-0-253-07300-6 (hdbk.)
ISBN 978-0-253-07301-3 (pbk.)
ISBN 978-0-253-07303-7 (ebook)
ISBN 978-0-253-07302-0 (web PDF)

CONTENTS

Acknowledgments vii

1. Cultural Indicators 2
2. A Brief History of Situation Comedies 34
3. "Sitlit": Sitcoms and Their Images, Content, and Effects 78
4. *Family, Life, Love, Good, House*: The Universe and Demography of Sitcoms 120
5. Textual Analysis 155
6. Sitcoms, Cultural Indicators, and Social Change 188

Afterword 222
Appendix A: Situation Comedies Referenced 230
Appendix B: Sitcom Syllabus 239
Bibliography 279
Index 299

ACKNOWLEDGMENTS

The basis and inspiration for the work reported in this book comes from George Gerbner (1919–2005). He developed a research approach called cultural indicators that has inspired hundreds of studies. I don't know if he would approve of what I've done in this study, but he was very gracious about and supportive of my efforts when I was able to talk to him personally. This book also could not have been done without building on the many studies by Gerbner's collaborators: Larry Gross, Nancy Signorielli, and Michael Morgan. Each of them has made many, many key contributions to the study of media effects over the years. I thank Nancy in particular for allowing me to use the data that she spent years curating. The fact that the television data used in this book stretch over a fifty-year period is due to all of their efforts, with Nancy in particular carrying the ball to the very end. Michael Morgan has been a constant mentor and collaborator over a thirty-five-year period. Larry, Nancy, and Michael are inspirational all in their own ways. They bear no responsibility for any errors in the book and should share some credit for anything of value that builds on their scholarship.

At Indiana University, I'm fortunate to have some fine grad students. Two in particular helped a lot with data analysis and collection: Yaojun Harry Yan and Seung Woo Chae. I appreciate all of their work and hope that they in some way will be able to continue the research traditions found in this book. I also thank Ayush Sekhsaria and Kartheek Janapati; they helped to collect new sources of data that required computational techniques. My appreciation also goes to the Media School at IU for granting two research leaves that helped in the completion of this book.

I thank series editors Nick Marx and Matt Sienkiewicz for their confidence that a boundary-crossing book could work. Thanks are also due to Gary Dunham and Allison Chaplin at IU Press for their help in producing the book and navigating all the potential pitfalls.

One of the intended messages of the situation comedy is how to have a happy family. I'm lucky in that regard. My thanks to Lisa, Isabel, and James for their continued best wishes, and to my mom, Casey, Steve, Jeannette, and Luke.

Sitcoms
AND CULTURE

Chapter 1 Frontis. Carroll O'Connor and Mike Evans in a scene from *All in the Family*, "Archie Gives Blood" (S1E4).

1

Cultural Indicators

> There are several kinds of stories, but only one
> difficult kind—the humorous.
> —*Mark Twain*

IN THE EARLY '70S, our family sat around the television most evenings, much like any other American family. Despite our faithful television viewing habits, it was not necessarily a TV-supportive household. My father was someone who regularly criticized television as a "boob tube" or "idiot box"—with some justification, looking back on the shows we watched.

What we watched was mostly whatever came on. On a Wednesday night in 1973, we might have watched *The Sonny and Cher Comedy Hour*, fulfilling CBS's intention to grab younger viewers, but we brought our parents along (though not without objection from our father; although he had acquired some mod-ish tendencies in dress by the mid-'70s, the silliness of *Sonny and Cher* was a little too much for his sensibilities). On a Friday night, we could choose from *The Flip Wilson Show* or *The Brady Bunch* (1969–74).[1] My parents did not participate too much in the Friday night viewing, so my sisters and I were equally likely to pick one as the other, depending on our whim.

Saturday night proved most interesting, though, because the main (and becoming near unanimous) choice among Americans was *All in the Family* (1971–79). We watched it, as shocked as anyone by some of the very direct and explicit uses of racial terms. In all honesty, we had already heard a lot of them, either at school or from our own father. He used bad words frequently. But hearing them on television was a different experience. We were given to understand that the character of Archie Bunker was being criticized and that the overall point of the show was that we should all move away from this sort of behavior.

Not everyone in the family had that reaction, though. Over time, I realized that my father was in fact kind of a version of Archie Bunker. He was not quite so working class but also not so far from working-class roots that he couldn't see where Archie was coming from. He became one of those viewers who *liked* Archie. He was an example of a controversy that emerged around the program: that *All in the Family* was encouraging and strengthening racism among some viewers, perhaps because the Archie character was too likable. (We look at some of the studies on this issue below.)

We grew up in an area that was racially homogenous. Therefore, programs like *All in the Family* were important in sensitizing us to the social problems that were emerging in the '70s. These shows were much different from those we had watched in the '60s, when, without TV, we would have had no idea that things like race riots were happening or that there was a war in Vietnam. Only through TV programs that showed people different from us did we have any sense about what those differences might mean. Not that minorities were portrayed especially realistically in any of those '70s "relevance" sitcoms, but at least they were in fact portrayed.

In the early '70s at John Read Middle School, we had debates about the Nixon/McGovern election. I knew from my family that I was supposed to support Nixon and couldn't really understand why other kids were aligned with McGovern. I did not know too much about politics, and sitcoms were one of my few clues. Later in the '70s, when I went to college, I was exposed to whole groups of people who were quite the opposite from my father. Having viewed *All in the Family* and the other liberally oriented sitcoms earlier in the decade, I had some context about where my new friends were coming from. Not perfect context, not wholly accurate context, but *some* context about narratives that would work in such a thought community. A simple formula: "These are people who disagree with Archie Bunker. They are more like Mike Stivic."[2] The shows were important parts of my stock of knowledge going into this new world; they had an effect. Whether they made me more liberal or more accepting was a complicated question, difficult to prove, but it was indisputable that their existence was relevant to my thought process.

This book is about a simple and specific question: Do situation comedies, as an important component of the larger television ecosystem, matter in how we see the world? The question is simple; the answers are more complex. It is a question about *media effects*. The book also looks at another related question: Do situation comedies indicate anything to us about how life *is* in the real world, or are they mere entertainment, with scant connection to how we live our lives? For this type of research, we are interested in what we call *cultural indicators*.

*

In Bhutan, the government measures gross national happiness. In the US, the Gallup organization has developed a measurement of well-being. Nobel Prize winner Daniel Kahneman (1999) conceived of something he called a national well-being account. These efforts were and are manifestations of a fifty-plus-year history of research into social indicators, empirical measures of social welfare and progress that go beyond raw quantification of economic states. They are intended to be measures that reveal benefits for individuals.

We are, of course, well acquainted with economic indicators, as we use them in our life on a regular basis. The Dow Jones Industrial Average provides a daily snapshot of one kind of economic health, and almost every news program that we see features some sort of weekly or monthly indicator tracking economic reality. Along with economic indicators, social indicators—things like marriage rates—are also used fairly frequently. But apart from these, measures of *cultural* states are hardly discussed at all. While Bhutan's King Wangchuck may have seen a strong national culture as indicative of a healthy and happy people, most social scientists have been less enthusiastic about including cultural indicators in the arsenal of measurement tools that can be used to make policy decisions—with one notable exception.

Fifty years ago, George Gerbner (1969, 1970) conceived cultural indicators as empirical measures of meaning that would complement other types of indicators, primarily economic and social, that were employed by social scientists and policymakers (Shanahan & Morgan, 1999; Shanahan, 2004, 2021). Other dimensions of Gerbner's research program, especially his theories of media effects, soon eclipsed the idea of cultural indicators, but the original work retains its relevance. Gerbner's work was foundational, but apart from it, there are few existing programs for systematically gathering and reporting data that go beyond simple indices of social welfare to reflect cultural states in which *meaning* is embedded. In this book, we build heavily on the work that Gerbner started, to see whether media messages can be used as cultural indicators. Adding onto much existing scholarship that answers this question affirmatively, we focus especially on one genre of television: the situation comedy. Our main purpose in looking at the question of cultural indicators,

6 SITCOMS AND CULTURE

and at situation comedies in particular, is to assess three possibilities: (1) whether media messages act as a mirror on the culture, as some have claimed; (2) whether they might act as a causal force in making or producing social change; or (3) whether they are simply entertainment, without much impact on or relation to social and cultural reality.

In this chapter, we first look at some history and theory about indicators. Next, we discuss some conceptual and theoretical questions about using sitcoms as cultural indicators. Finally, we turn our attention to an initial look at what we can learn from situation comedies.

The Role of Indicators[3]

Why do we collect indicator data? In both the economic and the social spheres, data are needed to describe current situations, prescribe future policies, and evaluate past policy action. A similar condition arguably holds for culture, with a need for assessing cultural realities, evaluating cultural change, and prescribing measures for cultural management. Cultural indicator data can be used to perform the same functions as in the economic and social spheres, at the cultural level itself.

Indicators of Social Change

Social indicators have a more recent history than economic indicators, even though examples of data collection efforts in social arenas such as health, crime, and family can be found as far back as the mid-nineteenth and early twentieth centuries. For example, in 1854, Snow used the home addresses of over five hundred people killed in the first few days of a cholera epidemic and a map of London to determine that the source of the disease outbreak was a public well. Durkheim's classic treatment of suicide rates offers another early example of social indicator data (see Jones, 1986). In 1927, the International Association of Chiefs of Police began an effort to create a consistent system of crime reporting across law enforcement jurisdictions in order to compile comparative and national crime statistics on an annual basis. This effort was eventually taken over by the Federal Bureau of Investigation (FBI) in 1930 and became the basis for the FBI's Uniform Crime Reports (UCR) that are still used today.

However, though collected and applied to social management, these measures of social change and phenomena were not systematically integrated within a common framework, as happened with economic indicators. Still, some early attempts were made. For example, in his theoretical volume entitled *Social Change*, Ogburn (1922) argued "that social change was best explained by the development and evolution of culture, and that this could best be studied by developing reliable measures [quantitative time series] of change" (cf. Carley, 1981, p. 16). Following his theoretical work, Ogburn directed and promoted a compendium of social indicators and trends published in 1933 by the US government called *Recent Social Trends*.

After Ogburn's work, the idea of systematically collecting social indicators to measure social trends languished until the 1960s. In the latter period, the social indicators movement was formed in response to the earlier successful creation of national accounts and economic indicators for use in economic policymaking and evaluation (Carley, 1981; Duncan, 1969; Land, 1983, 2000). Guided by the same philosophy of social engineering and interventionism that led to the development of national accounts and economic indicators, the goal of the social indicators movement was to create a conceptual framework and methodology for a "system of social indicators—statistics, statistical series, and other forms of evidence—with which to detect and anticipate social change and evaluate specific programs and determine their impact" (Land, 2000, p. 2682).

From this work, we see three types of commonly used social indicators. These have been used in the domains of health, crime, family, education, and so forth. The first type of social indicator is what may be termed policy indicators, criterion indicators, or normative welfare indicators. These are used to design and enact public policymaking as part of a system of public collection and reporting of social statistics (Land, 1983, 2000; MacRae, 1985). Such a social indicator is "a direct measure of [public] welfare and is subject to the interpretation that if it changes in the 'right' direction while other things remain equal, things have gotten better or people are better off" (Land, 2000, p. 2683).

A second type of social indicator is the descriptive indicator that tracks social trends and social changes over time, as Ogburn (1922) originally proposed (Land, 2000). These indicators are used by social scientists to describe changes within society and how social phenomena may be interrelated. Descriptive social indicators do not necessarily inform normative policy goals. Nor do they measure commonly agreed on public goods, as absolute changes in these indicators do not necessarily signal a decrease or increase in public welfare, though in some cases normative welfare indicators may also act as descriptive indicators (Land, 2000). Examples of descriptive social indicators may be the number of criminals incarcerated or the number of nurses and doctors within a community.

Life satisfaction or happiness indicators (more recently, wellness) are the third type. They focus on the idea that "direct monitoring of key socio-psychological states (attitudes, expectations, feelings, aspirations, and values) in the population is necessary for an understanding of social change and the quality of life" (Campbell & Converse, 1972; Land, 2000). The goal of these indicators is to establish measures and indicators of subjective states and perceptions among populations to complement social indicators of objective states and determine how each may interact. One example of this type of approach is the 1995 collaboration between the Bureau of Justice Statistics and the US Bureau of the Census, which conducted a survey of fifty thousand households on the public's perception of crime and criminal activity within their neighborhoods to compare with reported criminal incidents from the National Crime Victimization Survey and the UCR.

In spite of all this, an integrated and standardized system of social accounts and indicators akin to the system of national accounts and economic indicators was never established. Funding and enthusiasm for such an endeavor dissipated, though social indicators and indices in such social arenas as health, education, child welfare, family planning, and crime continue to be measured and tracked by a plethora of public and private organizations.

Beyond Social Indicators, toward Culture

If there are difficulties integrating social indicators, it is even more difficult to achieve theoretical and practical consistency with cultural indicators. We recognize that measuring culture is not a straightforward task. No matter what definition we take on for the term, it proves to be difficult, and impossible by some standards, to measure it successfully. Vazquez (2014) defined *cultural indicators* as "sets of measures used to quantify the amount of creative and/or cultural expression in a geographic area. Typical sets of indicators include economic (e.g., organizations, revenues) and behavioral measures (e.g., ticket buyers, activities)." In limiting himself to things that are latently observable, he noted, "Cultural and creative activities are critical for improving quality of life in communities. Culture helps members of communities feel connected to one another by maintaining and expressing their society's beliefs; creativity promotes new ways of thinking, which helps individuals and societies better adapt to changing conditions and build their capacity to address problems. But creativity and culture, like love and compassion, are themselves impossible to measure. Creativity happens every day. Culture is expressed everywhere. But what can be measured are outputs, economic activities, participation, and levels of support" (Vazquez, 2014, p. 1396).

Not everyone accepts Vazquez's limits, but most of the larger-scale efforts to index culture do tend to stick to types of data that can be gathered and collated from secondary sources. International cultural organizations have made steps toward proposing cultural inventories or accounts that can provide indicators of cultural health and progress. The United Nations Educational, Scientific and Cultural Organization (UNESCO), in a variety of projects and with varying success, has developed approaches that assess the role of culture in development, with the idea that cultural diversity and freedom are important attributes that can be overlooked when development is defined from a solely economic perspective. Most recently, culture has been factored into the UN's 2030 agenda for sustainable development, with one specific indicator meant to capture a country's cultural health: "SDG [Sustainable Development Goal] Target 11.4 calls on countries to 'strengthen efforts to protect and safeguard cultural and natural heritage.' The SDG Indicator 11.4.1, developed by the UIS, is defined as the: *Total expenditure per capita spent on the preservation, protection and conservation of all cultural and natural heritage, by source of funding (public, private), type of heritage (cultural, natural) and level of government (national, regional and local/municipal).* This indicator is part of global efforts to gauge the overall magnitude of investment in heritage."[4]

Clearly the indicator lines up with Vazquez's observation that culture itself may be difficult to measure but that economic behavior with respect to culture can be more easily and reliably assessed. The UNESCO Institute for Statistics (UIS) has been collecting some data of this type, but the data are spotty and their usefulness has not yet manifested. There are voluminous sources of data that pertain to cultural industries (e.g., television penetration, revenue from filmed entertainment, number of music albums produced per year, etc.), but again, these don't get much beyond the economic aspect of culture that economists, those most likely to be interested in indicators, are comfortable measuring.

Content Analysis and the Measurement of Meaning

Culture is a semantic, syntactic, and linguistic construct that militates against its measurability. One wonders which aspects of culture lend themselves to numeration in ways that go beyond the simply economic. Within the field of communication research, this is the question that has typically been undertaken by content analysis, which has been under development since the early twentieth century. In content analysis, the idea is to examine texts quantitatively to unearth aspects of their meaning, especially aspects that might be less reliably discovered by subjective processes of human interpretation (Krippendorf, 2018).

Early examples tended to focus on texts that could be gathered in large numbers across time, such as newspaper articles, which could then be used in a myriad of ways to reach conclusions about social, political, economic, and cultural trends. As we will see below, most of the studies using this method are in fact a form of cultural indicator, deriving or attempting to derive statistical meaning from cultural products.

Albig (1937) provided an early example of the aims of such a project and the pitfalls that could be experienced. He analyzed radio schedules to gain some idea of the distribution of types of content that Americans were exposed to across the years 1925–35. He began by noting that "latterly, methods for recording some of the more subtle aspects of culture change have been tentatively put forward" (338). Building from studies that had begun with newspaper content, Albig sought to extend that type of analysis into electronic media. Early studies such as this often were limited to examining types of content that were offered, which can lead to some meaningful cultural assessment but can go only so far. Albig ended up with detailed data about the *genre* of programming to which Americans were exposed (music, women's, weather, news, etc.). But he could not offer much more about the content of those programs in a way that would provide a truly meaningful cultural indicator: "For definitive accounts, however, such observations should provide but suggestions as to problems to be examined in an organized way. Such studies of contemporary programs could be made by 'listening in.' Past programs could not be so satisfactorily dealt with, but a detailed analysis could be made from the accumulated scripts of past programs which are filed by some of the larger stations. It would be a laborious procedure" (348).

Other researchers were learning about the work (the "laborious procedure," the "listening in") that would go into trying to obtain true cultural indicator data from media content. Actually watching, listening to, or reading media content meant long hours of human effort to code it into meaningful categories. Well before the era in which computers could even attempt to classify and understand media content (and it is still an inexact science), any meaningful analysis of what content was telling us culturally was possible only with ample resources and time.

Another early example, the well-known Payne Fund Studies (Jowett et al., 1996), looked at early films as cultural indicators, focusing mostly on their violence. A significant effort was devoted to the systematic viewing and coding of material from the examined films. But the Payne Fund researchers were not able to track filmed culture over time, which would be another key aspect of a successful cultural indicator.

The Project

As television emerged, no one doubted that it was a key cultural force, for better or worse. In the 1960s, Gerbner began his project designed to examine the social role of television. The project included a call for the development of indicators to measure culturally important shifts in society that complemented established social and economic indicators. Gerbner (1973) believed that the traditional way of taking stock of society using only economic and social indicators could be improved with the addition of cultural indicators and would result in better informed policy decisions. According to him, "The social and cultural transformations of our society have made economic and labor statistics and census information less than adequate to meeting our national needs with knowledge and reason" (1973, p. 177). Michael Morgan, a major participant in the projects that Gerbner began, noted the importance of gathering these indicators over time: "Whereas most social research projects tend to be one-shot deals, often undertaken in response to some immediate crisis or fad or isolated question, he [Gerbner] argued for a long-term coordinated program of Cultural Indicators research that would yield a more coherent base of knowledge allowing comparative analysis of trends in the symbolic cultural environment over time" (Morgan, 2012, p. 56). This is exactly what happened as the data collection begun by Gerbner in the '60s continued well into the 2010s.

For Gerbner, television presented itself as a repository of images, narratives, conceptions, and cultural presentations that could be measured. In his work, "cultural indicator" proved to be a useful but also a variable concept. The proximate reason for Gerbner's analysis was to count instances of violence as part of the widespread social concern at the time that televised violence (the culture) was affecting real social levels of violence. His well-known finding from the time was that television's overrepresentation of violence may or may not have affected real social levels of violence, but there were clearer effects in terms of people's fear reaction in relation to portrayed violence (Gerbner & Gross, 1976). He called this the Mean World Syndrome. The cultural indicator (television violence) was disjunct with the social indicator (real-world violence), but actual social fear was more closely related to the disjunction. In this way, culture can influence social reality. Thus, having information from both indicators is useful toward a greater policy understanding of the problem.

Gerbner's content analyses went well beyond violence, though, and could say many other useful things from a cultural perspective. He coded data about gender, occupation, age, race, and many other categories. When we look at such data and how they evolve over time, television tells us, in a broad way, about aspects and dimensions of the cultural mainstream. By the 1960s, television had usurped the past ways of representing and understanding the world through interpersonal communication, disseminating widely shared messages that could shape perceptions or recognitions of power distributions. Television is not just an aspect of culture; it is also a producer and disseminator of culture. The policies governing television—and maybe policy in general—would be better informed if television's messages (representing culture writ large) were tracked in the same manner that economic and social issues were tracked. Cultural indicators were thus meant both to monitor the message system, particularly in the context of short-term policy debates about issues such as violence, and to track changes in the broader production of culture.

Gerbner offered a well-developed program for carrying out cultural indicator (CI) work. He claimed that a system of cultural measurement should begin with an Institutional Process Analysis to answer questions about how messages are produced and selected. He outlined a scheme to analyze the power relationships of those who oversee message production, those involved with message production, those who finance message production, and those exposed to the messages produced. However, this aspect of the CI project received less actual research attention.

The second prong of Gerbner's research program was message system analysis, which is a large-scale analysis of television messages focusing on popular fiction. The content analysis looks at the system of messages rather than at any single program or genre. In the areas of violence, gender, sex roles, occupational perceptions, and others, this aspect of the research has been carried out consistently over the years (by researchers once affiliated with Gerbner and many others—e.g., Bryant, Carveth, and Brown 1981; Carveth and Alexander 1985; Kwak, Zinkhan, and Dominick 2002; Morgan 1983, 1984; Signorielli 1990; Weaver and Wakshlag 1986). For violence, Gerbner developed a detailed coding scheme resulting in a violence index that factored in

Cultural Indicators 13

the percentage of programs containing violence, the number of violent acts per program, the number of violent acts per hour, the percentage of main characters involved in acts of violence, and the percentage of main characters involved in homicides. In that it was collected over a fifty-year period (Signorielli, 2003; Signorielli et al., 2019), it represents the most consistently gathered cultural indicator that is available. Later, we will see some of the details about how this project worked.

Unlike many content analyses that have been, over the years, criticized for being descriptive and atheoretical, Gerbner's analyses were very much part of an active program of cultural analysis and criticism. The research program was one of the most influential of its time in terms of actually reflecting on policy discourse and decisions. The data collection, while following the very best scientific standards of content analysis at the time, was also very much informed by a critical take on media industries and their motivations. More than most content analyses of the time, and perhaps since, the CI efforts were oriented toward describing a narrative (a metanarrative, really) rather than just a fixed set of demographic characteristics or anodyne countings of violence. Empirical findings were interpreted in terms of larger theoretical assumptions about power and its use within the television medium.

The third area of study in the CI project was cultivation analysis. This uses survey data to link television exposure (time spent watching television) to beliefs about the real world. This work has been connected so strongly with the term *cultural indicators* (see Shanahan & Morgan, 1999 for a summary) that it tends to overshadow the actual collection and interpretation of indicator data. As well, the frequency of discussion and critique of cultivation as a method has tended to detract from the conceptual origins of cultural indicators. In this book, we don't deal much with cultivation until the end, focusing mainly on media content as indicators.

Integration of Indicators

Thinking about cultural indicators raises some interesting problems. Some cultural indicators could be more exactly described as indicators of phenomena that are *portrayed in* cultural products such as television, movies, novels, and so forth. For instance, data about TV violence is cultural in that it comes from television, a cultural product, but it is social in that it deals with a social issue. Other cultural indicators could be conceived as indicators that are *about* culture, whether or not they come from cultural artifacts. Economic data about cultural spending would be such an indicator.

The three main types of indicators (economic, social, and cultural) can be integrated into a framework that differentiates between *indicators* and *indicated*. For any indicator, there is a medium used to signal phenomena. Such a medium can be economic, social, or cultural. At the same time, that which the indicator indicates can fall into the same three domains.

The traditional use of indicators is to measure conditions within their own domain. For example, economic indicators such as gross domestic product (GDP) measure economic conditions while also existing as economic data. Social indicators, such as health and family well-being, are derived from observations of social groups and indicate conditions in the social domain. Cultural indicators have been a little more flexible in terms of what they represent, such as the portrayal of social issues—for example, violence (see Gerbner et al., 1980; Gerbner et al., 1994; Signorielli, 2003) or the more culturally contingent portrayal of homosexuality on television (see Gross, 1984; Shanahan & Morgan, 1999). Both indicators are derived from media (cultural products) while indicating social conditions.

Of potentially equal interest, however, is the possibility of using indicators from one domain to measure conditions in another, resulting in an integrated framework that provides a broader spectrum of indicators than has been heretofore considered by most social scientists. Economic data on unemployment and poverty rates are examples of economic indicators of social conditions. In the cultural domain, financial, sales, and advertising data on various types of cultural industries (e.g., book publishing, newspaper, television) or specific cultural products (crime novels, advertising spending in the gay press, types of music albums, etc.) are examples of economic indicators of cultural phenomena.

While the integration of economic and social indicator data is not a new idea, the integration of cultural indicators in addition to economic and social indicators has, as of yet, not been fully realized. Gerbner's (1969) original call for cultural indicators, apart from his own efforts and as continued by those who originally worked with him, resulted in little sustained attention to the challenge of developing cultural indicators and little effort to integrate these indicators across a broader spectrum. Still, the theoretical integration of economic, social, and cultural indicators could allow social scientists to create a clearer picture of the underlying societal challenges in any of the three areas. Cultural indicator data in particular can add meaning to what is already measured through the other indicators. For instance, data on average household income levels can tell us *how many* people are impoverished. Social indicators can provide evidence about what people *think* or *feel* about such impoverishment. Cultural indicators data can tell us more about *what it means* to be impoverished and the extent to which impoverishment is *visible* within cultural products. Taken together, such data would give a more complete picture of how policy should be framed, discussed, and planned.

Overall, the indicator is nothing more than a sign, and therefore it may be treated theoretically within the field of semiotics, or the study of signs (Eco, 1979). This field examines signs for their structure and function, with the eventual goal of providing a comprehensive explanation of how signs function in all communicative domains. While verbal signs have been most extensively studied and understood within the domain of linguistics, semioticians have proposed methods that could be used to study any form of symbolic communication, from the nonverbal to the mediated and other domains.

One of the most widely accepted notions in semiotics is that a sign consists of two parts: the *signifier* and the *signified*. Barthes (1967) has argued that we often tend to confuse the sign with its signifier, without realizing that the sign exists only when there is a conventionally mutually understood relation between the actual symbol and that which it signifies. "The sign is therefore a compound of signifier and signified. The plane of signifiers constitutes the plane of expression and that of the signifieds constitutes the plane of content" (39).

Applying this seemingly simplistic but useful concept to indicators, we can easily see that there are two parts to any indicator: the actual symbol or symbolic medium used to represent something and that which it stands for. In the case of GDP, for instance, the symbols used are aggregations of dollar units attached to economic activity. These are combined into one symbolic representation. The overall signified, in this case, is *productivity*. While one can imagine many ways to represent the productivity of a people or nation, GDP uses dollar aggregations as a conventionally mutually understood way to stand for the idea. This is a case in which both the signifier and its signified stand within the economic domain. With much use, GDP has thus become a well-understood sign that is used internationally. Of course, the acceptance of GDP as a measure of economic health also takes attention away from other things that could be used as measures.

With social indicators, we may again examine both sides of the conventionally used sign. The essence of a social indicator, as we noted above, is that it is about people and their social states. This is differentiated from purely economic indicators by the fact that we are gathering observations from or about people beyond their simple transactions in the economic sphere. While it is possible to argue that economic activity is also social in nature, economic activity does not capture everything there is to say about social reality. Thus, in some sense, social indicators sit over and above economic indicators, capturing the aspects of human life that are not purely economic.

For instance, marriage and divorce rates are social indicators that tell us something about social reality in a given nation. While such rates may have economic implications, they also indicate noneconomic facts about a society that are of interest. In the case of marriage rates, the signifier is in the social domain in that it is derived from observations of people in noneconomic social transactions, or practices. Similarly, the signified is social because the content of the indicator is itself a social situation.

Again, though, it is possible to imagine indicators in which the signifier and the signified cross domains. For instance, consumer confidence, though typically thought of as an economic indicator, actually has a social signifier in that it is derived from the collected reports of people. Its signified is economic, and thus we have a hybrid social/economic indicator.

An economic signifier per se means that the symbols are generated from transactions of people in the marketplace or economic sphere. In order to gather these data, the people do not need to be consulted; their behavior is merely recorded as a currency transaction. A social signifier means that some human activity must be recorded, going beyond mere economic transactions. To record a valid marriage, for instance, the participants must engage in a particular ceremony, consent according to accepted laws and traditions, and so on. Social indicators may often be demographic in nature. Opinion or attitude surveys are basically social in nature in that they require respondents to answer particular questions; their thoughts cannot be recorded automatically without the people themselves giving responses. Thus, a social signifier requires that people have been observed in social activity, or they have given responses that are cumulated into indicators.

Following this reasoning, we can look at cultural indicators as data that come from cultural interactions. *Culture* generally means the activity of people together, at a broad macro level, establishing unified *meanings* around coexistence. The places where we interact as individuals, often under socially guided rules and norms, constitute the areas where we enact our culture, where we maintain it, where we re-create it, and within which we can all find meaning at the individual level. Of course, it is also the place where we can contest each other, as in the case of "culture wars." It is ultimately a communicative space

Cultural Indicators

in which expression and understanding are two sides of the coin that create something eventually understood as a culture. Although it is not as simple as with economic and social indicators, we *can* gather data from this scene as part of a broader overall attempt to understand the various dimensions of human life. Thus, we can propose that cultural indicators, gathered from any site where culture is enacted and maintained, sit over and above both economic and social indicators in that they can be seen as harvesting measurements from the human space(s) where meaning is finally assigned to events.

Within the scope of this one volume, we cannot achieve the complete integration of indicators as described theoretically above. However, an awareness of the fact that economic, social, and cultural phenomena are quite interweaved and connected, and that we can see these connections empirically and quantitatively, can be enormously helpful to understand questions about media effects that are posed at the macro level.

Sitcoms as Cultural Indicators

Why Sitcoms?

For some, a situation comedy is television's most disposable product, created on a three-jokes-per-page assembly line meant to appeal to lowest-common-denominator audiences for nothing but commercial gain. Undoubtedly this is true for many and maybe even most of television's sitcoms. In a medium as voracious as television with respect to the need for content creation, it would be surprising if most of its products were able to meet the quality standard seen in, say, feature films (even though many films, if not most, also fade into history and are motivated by the same commercial needs as the TV medium). Regarding the sitcom, most observers would have to agree with veteran TV producer Bob Shanks: "Television is used mostly as a stroking distraction from the truth of an indifferent, silent universe, and the harsh realities just out of sight and sound" (Genzlinger, 2020). One does not expect high art. It is easy to compile a list of lowbrow sitcoms that achieved commercial success (e.g., *The Beverly Hillbillies* [1962–71], *Three's Company* [1977–84], or *Married with Children* [1987–97]) to support this point.

On the other hand, not everything is bad. Certainly there are beloved sitcoms from every decade that transcended the limitations of the medium. They help us to remember how we thought in those decades, and in some cases they formed an important part of the cultural fabric of that time. In the '50s, *I Love*

Lucy (1951–57) was appreciated for its comic genius, for the way it revolutionized the television industry, and as a commentary on the "battle of the sexes" that was an important precursor to the sexual revolution of the '60s and '70s. In the 1970s, a move toward quality sitcoms—a recognition that some sitcoms could do something other than entertain for half an hour—was noticeable. *All in the Family* drew attention in a mass-mediated way to cultural tensions that still needed to be resolved after the civil rights movements of the '50s and '60s, in relation to prejudice and bigotry. And it was funny. A bit later, *M*A*S*H* (1972–83) brought antiwar themes into American living rooms with a comedic patina that allowed it to come before the more serious cinematic treatments. The '70s have been identified as the period of "relevance" sitcoms, when series production guru Norman Lear (*All in the Family, The Jeffersons* [1975–85], *Maude* [1972–78]) launched an era in which sitcoms intentionally—rather than accidentally—attempted to influence collective understanding of social issues.

Between these poles, we find the majority of sitcoms. Neither artistically enlightening nor actively horrifying, they were the result of a competitive market-oriented process in which writers, actors, and producers vied for America's attention through the relatively narrow gate of the three (and later four, five, and six) main television networks. These sitcoms are as interesting to us as the memorable ones because they constituted the bulk of viewing. With any of them, one could expect a high level of technical professionalism across the board in the creative product, though with the recognition that the product needed to appeal to an extremely large and heterogeneous audience. From this, in looking at the totality of American sitcoms, we have a mass-produced artifact that is interesting at least (if not more) from the anthropological and sociological standpoint of telling us what people were watching and what they thought was worth their time. And of course, it tells us as well what corporate interests thought that their audiences would find worthwhile to watch.

In Mass Communication Research, What Is It to Study Culture?

Understanding the number of hours that humans have devoted to watching sitcoms (perhaps billions if we account for all of them) provides an important insight into why we should study them.[5] Regardless of what we think of their quality, there is no doubt that it is reasonable to hypothesize that their content makes a difference in some way. For that reason alone, and for others that will be adumbrated below, we set out to look at sitcoms from a variety of viewpoints, but especially from a data-oriented standpoint.

In communication research, there are many avenues leading toward the study of television and television as culture. Gray and Lotz (2019) identify three broad approaches: social science, humanities, and cultural studies. In the social science vein, the focus is on media as persuasion (Shanahan, 2021). Humanists deal with television as art or as art-like (Newcomb, 1976). In cultural studies, the focus has most often been on power.

Obviously, as we approach sitcoms in this book from a cultural perspective, one might suppose that our own endeavor should be placed in that cultural studies box. However, this would be somewhat misleading. Often, when we employ a cultural approach, we look at data gathered through interpretive, qualitative, interview, or ethnographic methods. These methods are held to be the best way to assess the reality of a cultural experience by attempting, as much as possible and within a research approach, to live within the data, to be in the culture itself, and hopefully to make an accurate reading of it. It is less common, at least until recently, to see empirical techniques applied along with the claim that something cultural is being understood. More commonly, survey and content analyses are used within an institutional approach, or from a straight *media effects* perspective.

In the media effects (social science) perspective, data are usually deployed to demonstrate effects at an individual level, often focusing on how individuals retain specific pieces of communication from media messages and campaigns. What the retained items might *mean* to the recipients within a larger cultural context is sometimes difficult to fathom. The original (and oft-criticized) research question posed by mass media effects researchers was "Who says what in which channel to whom with what effects?" (Bryson et al., 1940; Lasswell, 1948, p. 37). This question, as interpreted by most researchers, led to a perspective on media that can be seen as informational. "Media messages are usually seen as pieces or streams of information that can be absorbed by recipients. The questions of Lasswell lend themselves quite easily to this outlook; the methods of social science like to be able to boil things down to single quantifiable variables. Across hundreds and even thousands of studies, the goal of this kind of media effects research (even still) is to determine to what degree these absorptions are effective. Media effects has been, in many ways, a vast elaboration of the basic ideas of persuasion research" (Shanahan, 2021, p. 24).

The many studies focused on media-as-information have been quite informative in some ways, but often they are also seen as inconclusive, temporizing, or even tautological with common sense. They yield a paradox wherein media effects studies often find "limited effects" (Lang, 2013).

Gray and Lotz identify Gerbner's Cultural Indicators work with the social science label, as many have done. But Gerbner actually brought aspects of both social science and cultural studies, and even a little bit from humanities. True, Gerbner wanted to use all of the analytic tools of social science to gain a broad perspective on that which could not be observed by a single individual watching an idiosyncratically selected suite of programs and then reaching judgment. Gerbner was originally operating under the expectation of his funders that television, and important aspects of it such as violence, could be reliably and systematically "counted."[6] So, he wanted to be systematic. At the same time, he felt very strongly that television should be observed critically and that the rampant commercialization and domination of the storytelling function by institutional interests had profound cultural ramifications. He was also a *critical* theorist. Morgan (2012) pointed out how Gerbner crossed the disciplines:

> In order to resolve this paradox, it is essential to recognize that "qualitative versus quantitative" and "critical versus administrative" are two completely independent dimensions. Whether a research project uses qualitative or quantitative methods (or both) says nothing about whether the research at hand is critical or administrative. Indeed, the qualitative-quantitative distinction made little difference to Gerbner at that time.... The choice of research methods is not the issue. Rather, since mass media content is seen as "expressive of social relationships, and as formative of social patterns" (Gerbner, 1958, p. 88), the task of the critical scholar is to illuminate these by any means possible. (Morgan, 2012, p. 23)

Morgan's point emphasizes an important challenge for this book. Media scholars are accustomed to assuming common worldviews and research practices within their own subdisciplines, violations of which are normally thought to be committed by outsiders. Gerbner's work often suffered attacks from many sides; in fact he faced three-way criticism: on humanistic grounds for his work (Newcomb, 1978), on the nuts and bolts of the survey work he did (Hirsch, 1980), and even from the television industries of which he was critical.[7]

These kinds of thought divisions have been recognized by scholars since the work of Snow (1959). Gerbner appropriately sought to bridge intellectual cultures (Snow termed them "literary" and "scientific") in his critical pursuit of understanding culture. Despite the noise and attacks, his work has been influential. In the present study, we aspire to capture some of the spirit of boundary crossing that Gerbner embodied by triangulating empirical data with cultural criticism.

Triangulation can bring its own epistemological dangers. One might be slighting the depth of understanding that could come from an unadulterated cultural studies approach or a rigorous straight media effects study. In the realm of studying sitcoms, both fields can lay claim to addressing some important questions wholly within their own domain. Cultural studies has quite a lot to say about the representation of women and minority groups in sitcoms, which are seen to be patriarchally motivated and generally repressive on behalf of racial majorities (e.g., Brunsdon & Spigel, 2007; Means Coleman, 1998). We will see much of that criticism in this book. Media effects research normally partakes of this critical spirit as well; many of its studies are focused on topics of representation, but they are also geared toward understanding whether their messages ultimately make any difference in terms of attitude and belief, and they sometimes run in contradictory directions to what critical theory would predict. Empirical research often muddies the picture. A great example would be the study by Vidmar and Rokeach (1974) on variable attitudes toward the character of Archie Bunker, which will be addressed further below.

Recognizing that it may be difficult for one scholar to master the literatures and techniques that cross these historical divides and that both continue to produce valuable insight within their own traditions, there is also the between-the-cracks tradition of media research that takes what it needs from where it can be found. The tools of the cultural indicator worker are at the macro level, but they can be applied across questions of media effects as well as in the cultural domain. The archetypical topic that cultural indicator theorists are interested in, after depicting the cultural landscape and its relationship to media, is in relation to questions of social change. *Do media depictions mirror society? Do media messages maintain the status quo? Do they reflect social change after it happens? Or do they sometimes precede or lead to social change?* These are the ultimate questions we look at in this book.

In the cultural domain, even Gerbner would agree that there is no substitute for rich descriptions of cultural experience, the likes of which can't always be achieved in content analysis and surveys. But while recognizing that those could also lead us astray, adding a macro perspective and embedding that within a data-driven theory-testing approach can provide much-needed breadth to our understanding of the meaning of things culturally.

What Are the Inherent Tensions in Studying
Culture through the Lens of Data?

Gerbner's investigations were a kind of forerunner to what we now think of as *big data*. In his field, the work that he did, and that which follows it well into the 2020s, comprised the largest and most consistent accumulation of data about television that had ever been accrued. It is still yielding studies today (e.g., Signorielli et al., 2019).

Yet now, technical and procedural means for gathering data are improving well beyond the capacities that Gerbner could have marshaled. His years of investigation created a dataset that finally accumulated information about 3,468 programs and 12,635 characters within those programs. These early big data could easily fit onto a single thumb drive today. Gerbner's team accumulated boxes of videotapes that were at one time the largest collection of such programming; now, these are dwarfed by any single day's output on YouTube. As computer processing and natural language analytics improve, it is possible to gather data many orders of magnitude larger, with much less of the human cost that Gerbner and associates incurred. *Big data* means something entirely new now.

Scholars from a wide range of disciplines can harvest media data, which accumulate by the terabyte every day, to answer a variety of questions about society and culture. Computational methods invade communication research—for example, Vargo, Guo, and Amazeen's (2018) uses of big data to test traditional agenda-setting questions. Computer scientists increasingly deal with media effects questions (e.g., Lazer et al.'s [2018] analysis of "fake news"). Computer techniques to parse natural language data, though by no means perfect, offer more avenues to analyze media where such media can be turned into text—for instance, as with captioning media dialogue. It's not clear what recent introductions of widely available artificial intelligence platforms will mean for the field. While there is still a role for human coding in content analysis, and perhaps there will always be (Paolillo, 2019), the efflorescence of new techniques for harvesting data from large corpora of texts offers new ways to understand culture. There is also a lot going on in the area of "digital humanities" (Berry, 2012), where data analysis intersects with criticism and interpretation, that is relevant to our study of television.

At the same time, we should recognize that these changes and advances have been a long time coming, evolving incrementally. From the '70s onward, each new advance (such as developments in computer-aided content analysis) has been optimistically thought to bring revolutions in what we could do with content. The ability to do things with words and phrases (such as creating concordances or lists of keywords in context) has been available for quite some time to most researchers, at an affordable cost. Proprietary packages such as Diction (Hart, 2022) could analyze text according to preset dictionaries in a way that was a precursor to modern approaches such as topic modeling. These efforts were important, as they brought systematic quantitative techniques to fields that had previously been solely humanistic in method.

All of this newness, though, could mask difficulty. Even since the beginning of content analysis, those doing the labor were hoping that computers could take over for them. Still, even through the 2000s, most of the content analyses that were influential in the field of communication research were based on human coding. The still-ineffable aspects of human communication that could not be taught to a computer had to be done by us, even as we always manifested some degree of unreliability in doing it. One could not avoid interpretation. While big data is often heralded as a cure-all for a variety of social science problems, brute force alone, the specialty of big data, still can't carry the ball all the way to the end zone. In that respect, automated big data for cultural indicators might simply become the latest instantiation and advance of content analysis, which will still include a lot of handwork.

So, what can cultural indicators tell us? We can learn "how many" about lots of things, especially types of people who appear in programs. We can learn about "what happens," as shown by the way that the CI project coded instances of violence over the years. We can learn whether characters are "good" or "bad" based on subjective but reliable codings from trained viewers. We can learn the occupations they are involved in and whether those seem segregated by race, gender, and so forth. We can answer many similar questions, most them ultimately oriented toward trying to discover what the meta-narrative of a medium is telling us. Is there finally a moral or lesson from all of the media images and our never-ending exposure to them?

Comedy as a Site to Study Culture?

In the original CI project, the focus was on *all* of television (though operationally, what was measured was normally scripted prime-time programming). The importance of specific programs was counted, and specific genres were seen as meaningful. In spite of this, though, the idea was that viewers tended to expose themselves to everything; the more they watched of one thing, the more they watched of everything else. Therefore, CI researchers looked for patterns across the totality of programming, focusing on anything that

24 SITCOMS AND CULTURE

was storytelling (leaving out news, sports, and other nonfictional types of programs).

This approach tended to blur comedy, drama, and action together. Because any of the specific genres were often treated as generic (in the worst sense of the word), with little attention to their artistic or redeeming social values, the lessons that could come from an episode of *Baywatch* (action) were not seen as that much different from lessons that could come from other commercially mass-produced genres, whether it be a drama (like *Marcus Welby, MD*) or a sitcom (such as *The Andy Griffith Show* [1960–68]). Ultimately, all programs were seen as part and parcel of the larger message system, with individual differences tending to wash away as hours of exposure to generically produced programming accumulated.

There is good evidence that this is still a valuable approach (i.e., Morgan, Shanahan & Signorielli, 2015). But even as the CI research began in the '70s, other researchers were adducing the importance of genres. Most commonly, it was argued that exposure to violent programs should be most relevant to social and cultural experiences of violence (Wilson et al., 1998). While Gerbner argued that violence was found across all programming (and it is), there was a certain common sense to the notion that increased exposure to a specific genre should also matter. From a media effects researcher's perspective, Gerbner's views about genre actually tended to be in the minority.

Also, as we will see below, comedy makes up a huge portion of scripted prime-time TV—around a third. So, there is ample reason to believe that heavy viewers of TV are also heavy viewers of comedy. Sitcoms are an important part of the four-legged stool that has come to dominate TV (sitcom, drama, action, reality). An average person consuming three hours a day for a year will have been exposed to over four hundred hours of sitcoms in that time—certainly enough for the large-scale cultural patterns that Gerbner was interested in to emerge, especially when one looks at a lifetime of program viewing.

Another reason to consider genre more in cultural indicators work is that television itself has undergone enormous change. We should recall that the earliest CI researchers were studying the three-network system. This system persisted from the '50s well into the 2000s, but it was under threat from other sources as early as the '80s. Clearly, it is now possible for viewers to specialize their programming by genre (or even more specifically than that, if they want). One can watch as much of a specific genre as one wants (or even binge a specific program) and do this in the same amount of time that one used to be able to devote only to all of television. Early heavy viewers used to watch

Cultural Indicators

25

all genres by definition; now one can be much more picky. For some viewers, the choice will be comedy.

Sitcoms, by their sheer number, are thus a very viable genre-place in which to mine for cultural indicators. Another feature of the sitcom recommends it. Sitcoms have most often been produced with a single goal: to be funny enough to attract viewers and generate profit. This is not to deny the artistic or social aspirations of some producers and some shows, but taken as a whole, it means that sitcoms are produced relatively quickly and meant to appeal to the most heterogeneous audiences. Therefore, they must incorporate relatively commonplace ideas about social situations that matter to people, about rules of engagement in the community that are understandable, and about social roles that people inhabit that can be accepted by broad audiences. It doesn't mean that sitcoms can't push against these for comic effect, but normally such conflicts have to be resolved *toward* the cultural mainstream. All of these rules, norms, and institutional structures on display are thus an anthropological treasure trove for the cultural indicators researcher.

Another factor that can attract us to sitcoms is that we normally understand them as comedy and not really as making any sort of cultural, social, or political point. Unlike news, with its specific point of view and persuasive intent, a sitcom shows us all sorts of things about culture with our defenses down. When we are in such a state, persuasion is potentially greater, as shown in research about entertainment-education programs, which are seen to be more effective than those that take a straight informational approach (Moyer-Gusé, 2008). Comedy minimizes "reactance," the psychological state in which we turn away from information because we perceive that it is trying to persuade us (Dillard & Shen, 2005).

Ultimately, we can see sitcoms—at least most of them—as places where television has deposited its most banal and quotidian images, and it is precisely these characteristics that make them valuable to us: "Indeed the sitcom cannot totally escape the 'obligation' which marks television in general to address and incorporate changing cultural standards and a sense of its own 'development' as a medium. The charges of conservatism, excessive stereotyping of racial, class, sexual and regional differences, and so on, which are often levelled at the sitcom, seem to pinpoint not so much to the total imperviousness of the form but rather the particular way in which it operates as a *site of negotiation* of cultural differences" (Neale & Krutnik, 2018, pp. 137–38).

Unlike a work of art that aspires to last forever, these mass-produced artifacts cannot avoid inscribing important features of the culture into them, even if they are not attempting to do so. Especially as we gain distance from them—and cultural indicators research allows us to do that—we can begin to see the role that sitcoms play in reflecting the culture, in showing what the culture was like at a specific time, and, in rare cases, how the sitcom itself actually influenced cultural development.

Irony, Ambiguity, Comedy, and Data

One of the difficulties with computer data analysis techniques such as natural language processing, or any form of computer-aided content analysis, is teaching computers how to understand ambiguities in human language (Wallace 2015). Computers are good at doing things like counting words and figuring out parts of speech, and they can even create texts that seem humanlike within certain parameters. But attempts to make computers understand, let alone produce, ironic or comedic communications that seem human are quite rudimentary. There is a long way to go before computers pass this particular version of the Turing test.[8]

Given this, the field of cultural indicators needs to proceed along several routes. Human-coded content analysis will still be needed, especially if we are dealing with texts, such as sitcoms, that are heavily ironic and where almost any statement has a double meaning leading toward a joke. The downside of this technique is the human cost; it is laborious. Yet, big data and natural language processing can give us tools to go along with these analyses. A typical research path might look like this:

1) Researcher reflection, interpretation, and criticism lead to hypotheses to be tested about the body of content.

2) Initial hypothesis testing is done with human-coded content analysis, leading to possible revision of hypotheses (return to phase 1) or confirmation.

3) If hypotheses are confirmed in phase 2, big data and automated examinations can be conducted across much larger corpora, where techniques such as word counts and language analysis make sense at a wider scale.

4) If these analyses confirm what we found in phase 2, we can return to phase 1 to interpret and reconsider what our findings mean at the level of culture.

Suppose we are interested in using sitcoms as a corpus to test whether culture has become "coarser" over the decades. We might start with the casual observation that words that were formerly considered taboo in public media dialogue are starting to appear more. Words like *suck* (as in *this sucks*), *ass*, and other words that were explicitly proscribed on TV (the so-called "seven dirty words") seem to be appearing with more frequency. This goes along with our observation that programs seem to deal much more often with sexual themes, that clothing is becoming more suggestive, and other indicators of coarsening.

All of this could be true, or it could simply be a result of our idiosyncratic take on things; maybe others wouldn't see it that way. A content analysis along the lines of a typical CI project would establish guidelines along which multiple viewers (coders) could reliably code the body of programs and thus establish some numerical realities about the frequencies that we hypothesized in the first phase of thinking about the problem. Our coders could be assigned to determine when there is an episode within a program that deals with sexual themes (or other themes that might indicate coarsening), or perhaps they could be instructed to evaluate the program as a whole. They may also count instances of language that people would normally construe as coarse. If we find that coders can do this task reliably, we can interpret their results as something additional to and useful along with our initial interpretations.

Keeping in mind that human coders can look at only so much content, we can then move toward looking at our corpus in a different way. Given that we might have all dialogue from specific programs available to us from databases of TV closed-captioning, perhaps we can simply count the frequency of words that we consider coarse. We can fairly easily obtain an analysis that looks like what we see in figure 1.1, which confirms that the proportional frequency of coarse language has indeed gone up. It doesn't mean that we know what happened each and every time a coarse word was used. Maybe *ass* referred to a donkey in one episode and to the human anatomy in another episode; undoubtedly, it was used in innumerable different ways and contexts across the history of the dataset. But if trends are consistent with what we see in our human-coded content analysis, adding the two together allows us to triangulate something useful about our understanding of cultural history from the cultural indicator.

Twenge, VanLandingham, and Campbell (2017) did something similar in their analysis of "swear words" in American books. They did indeed find increasing use of the terms, which they connected to a rise in "individualism"

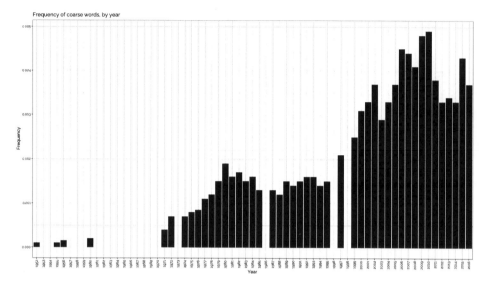

Figure 1.1. Frequency of coarse words in American sitcoms.

in American culture. In developing their reasons for examining cultural products, they offered rationales for cultural indicators in general: "First, culture includes the context as well as the person, and cultural products capture culture 'outside the head.' Second, cultural products are not subject to the biases that plague self-report measures, such as reference group and social desirability effects. Third, and perhaps most important, cultural products shape individuals' ideas of cultural norms and 'common sense'" (2).

Science and Sitcoms?

Can we study sitcoms scientifically? At this juncture, probably not in the way that most people think about science. We won't be able to hypothesize laws, and truly causal assertions will be difficult; we must be honest that such goals would remain far in the future, if they are ever achieved. However, there is no desire at this point to move on from the vital tasks of interpretation, criticism, and evaluation that are so needed in regard to all media products.

Still, cultural indicator theorists, coming as they do from the critical research tradition, can work hand in hand with those doing cultural studies, particularly by providing descriptive data at the broadest possible macro level to indicate the sometimes seismic, sometimes glacial shifts that seem to happen in the cultural sphere. For most of the shifts that we care about, whether

Cultural Indicators

they be in terms of demographic representation, in terms of themes dealt with in media, or in terms of important issues like violence in culture, our ever-increasing ability to harvest and analyze cultural data means profitable future potential partnerships in the fields of media and cultural studies generally. This book seeks to develop and extend some ideas about these potential partnerships. While we focus here on one very limited domain, that of the television sitcom, we should expect to see that advancements in areas as varied as digital humanities, computer-assisted content analysis, and artificial intelligence can help establish academic convergence on clearer understandings of the impacts of cultural products.

Also, a note about *big data*. Studies that now are truly using big datasets are often simply enormous in their size. Those types of studies will likely become more common in future media effects research. In this book, though, we are not using datasets of such enormous magnitude. We are making more use of computational tools than was typical in Cultural Indicators research, and this has allowed us to go beyond the limitations of traditional human coding. We can honestly say that in some ways we are doing bigger or big-ish data in comparison to earlier analyses, though not approaching, for instance, the scale of studies that log millions of interactions on social media platforms such as X.

Plan of the Book

In the remainder of this book, we move toward trying to answer a larger question about the role of sitcoms in social change. We can understand sitcoms in different ways:

1) as *reflecting* social change that is occurring for other reasons;

2) as *causing* social change by bringing new images to public accessibility;

3) as *retarding* social change by moving more slowly than the pace of actual social change;

4) as *playing no role* in social change whatsoever; sitcoms are simply *entertainment*.

Although it is a bit of a spoiler, most readers will likely understand that sitcoms can be seen as playing these roles in multiple ways; there is more than one way to look at the issue. Nevertheless, we will try through this book to make an assessment that fairly judges sitcoms' role in the movement and progress of American culture.

In chapter 2, we provide some background on the history of situation comedies. This will add to some work that has been done admirably by others, although it remains true that sitcoms are understudied compared to many genres and still viewed pejoratively in many contexts. Here, we simply try to understand them for what they were and are and appreciate them as well when they deserve it.

In chapter 3, we look at the critical and scholarly literature on sitcoms (*sitlit*, we call it), especially across major issues of analysis such as family, class, race, and gender. These are the issues other authors have most commonly identified as social and cultural sites that are possibly affected by sitcom portrayals.

In chapter 4, we look at the demography of sitcoms from a Cultural Indicators perspective. We draw from the CI database (1967–2015) to give a very detailed look at who populated sitcoms and how they represented the US. Variables analyzed include gender, age, race, and marital status as well as some variables relating to character qualities. We also compare our analyses to actual US demography and provide quantitative analysis and metadata about the universe of sitcoms. Drawing from secondary data sources, we have large amounts of information about the many sitcoms that were broadcast from the early days of TV onward: their casts, their gender compositions, and a few other variables.

In chapter 5, we look into how textual analysis can be used to understand sitcoms. Our example is the program *Seinfeld* (1989–98). Using a database of all dialogue in every episode, we look at how different kinds of characters express themselves, with an eye toward the major questions (class, race, gender) under analysis in this book.

In chapter 6, we synthesize our analyses to present some theories about the role of sitcoms in social change. These theories are developed along with more extended thought about how television cultivates viewers and about how society changes both in spite of these cultivations and, sometimes, because of them.

The arrangement of the chapters is meant to help readers navigate through the different levels of analysis in the book, none of which may be seen in typical media studies or media effects texts. The chapters fit within a scheme that is quite consistent with the idea developed by cultural indicators researchers of starting with "institutional process analysis" (see more in chap. 6). The history and analysis of chapters 2 and 3 are meant to lay out and make clear

Cultural Indicators
31

the assumptions about media institutions and programming that form the basis for cultural indicator work. These assumptions can be very much at the macro level and sometimes susceptible to overgeneralization. But they are later subject to empirical test. After such analysis, the scholar then needs to show systematically what is *in* the media content. That is our chapter 4. Chapter 5 adds more about content, with textual data, than what has been done previously with cultural indicators approaches to content data. Only after these steps does the cultural indicators researcher begin to feel comfortable about coming back to make critical conclusions about media content, which are in our chapter 6.

Two appendices are also provided. Appendix A is a list of all sitcoms discussed in the book, with dates and a short description of each show. Appendix B is a sitcom syllabus, with suggested episode viewing for every year from 1950 to 2020, along with some relevant readings. Readers who are not very familiar with sitcoms might start with or scan appendix B to get a sense of the kinds of stories that are told.

NOTES

1. For each sitcom referenced in the text, please see appendix A for a brief description of the show.

2. Rob Reiner played the character of Mike Stivic, Archie's liberal grad student son-in-law. They were always at odds politically.

3. Some material in this section was originally presented in Shanahan, J., E. Nisbet, J. Diels, B. Hardy, and J. Besley. 2005. *Cultural Indicators: Integrating Measures of Meaning with Economic and Social Indicators*. New York: International Communication Association.

4. UNESCO Institute for Statistics (2024).

5. Imagine a single half-hour episode of a sitcom in the '70s that was watched by 50 million people. There are 26 episodes in a season, meaning that 650 million person hours would have been devoted to that single show ($26 \times 50,000,000 \div 2$). Accounting for reruns, the total number becomes difficult to calculate.

6. Gerbner's work began during the episode of enormous social concern around TV violence that led to national examinations and a report from the surgeon general.

7. "Though in general respected within his field, Gerbner is misunderstood, misrepresented, and even mocked outside it. Network executives make what sound like common-sense dismissals of his Cassandra-esque claims," wrote Scott Stossel in an *Atlantic* piece in 1997. See https://www.theatlantic.com/magazine/archive/1997/05/the-man-who-counts-the-killings/376850.

8. The advances can be startling, however. Asking ChatGPT, a recent evolution in AI, to define "situation comedy" gives this answer: "A situation comedy, also known as a sitcom, is a genre of comedy that focuses on the lives of a group of characters who are usually friends or family members and who find themselves in humorous situations. Sitcoms are typically filmed in front of a live studio audience and often feature a laugh track to enhance the comedic effect. They are typically aired on television and can be either a single episode or a serialized show with multiple episodes. Some popular examples of situation comedies include *The Big Bang Theory*, *Friends*, and *Seinfeld*." Not bad! Examples of AI doing content analysis were emerging as this book was being finalized.

Chapter 2 Frontis. Jackie Gleason, Art Carney, and Audrey Meadows in a scene from *The Honeymooners*, comedic tales of working-class New York.

2

A Brief History of Situation Comedies

A SITUATION COMEDY AS we currently know it—and especially in the era of network television that we are studying in this book—is a serial program, usually half an hour in length, with repeating characters in similar scenes or environments. Most often the context is a family, but workplaces are also common, and there are miscellaneous other situations in which characters can find themselves. The important thing is that the situation makes sense as a recurring context for the repeated episodes of the program. The genre is especially linked to US television, though there are many in the UK and examples from other cultures.

In a situation comedy, what is the situation? It is simply the context into which a group of characters is placed, which creates opportunities for interaction over time. Usually, the characters don't have much choice about being there and who the others are, which means that people of varying character types are forced to interact with each other. *Situation* can also mean the little problems and scrapes that the characters find themselves in from episode to episode.

Any sitcom installment usually establishes a mildly problematic condition (or sometimes two or three) that threatens the harmony of the group. Because we have seen the characters in many episodes before and know them well, we can understand within a minute or so the challenge that threatens the group peace. In the space of about twenty-four minutes, allowing for commercials, the problem is resolved with cohesion intact.

Any sitcom could provide examples that hew very closely to this model because almost all of them do. Here are some samples chosen randomly from across the history of sitcoms:

36   SITCOMS AND CULTURE

- *I Love Lucy*, "Building a Barbecue," April 8, 1957: Ricky is on vacation from work and is always in Lucy's way. Lucy and Ethel decide to start building a barbecue in order to trick Ricky and Fred into taking over what should be a man's job. Unfortunately, Lucy loses her wedding ring in the process.

- *I Dream of Jeannie* (1965–70), "The Birds and the Bees Bit," April 10, 1967: Learning that a genie will lose her powers if she marries a mortal, Tony proposes to Jeannie. After Roger and Jeannie learn that their children might get magical powers, Jeannie keeps Roger away so that Tony won't learn that little fact.

- *The Bob Newhart Show* (1972–78), "Who's Been Sleeping on My Couch?" March 10, 1973: Bob finds out that Jerry has been sleeping on his office couch overnight. Jerry is hurt over a broken romance and does not want to go home to his apartment.

- *Friends* (1994–2004), "The One with the Jellyfish," September 25, 1997: Ross chooses between Rachel and his bald-headed girlfriend, Bonnie; Joey, Chandler, and Monica have a perilous encounter with a jellyfish at the beach.

- *Black-ish* (2014–22), "Black Nanny," March 22, 2016: Bow persuades Dre to hire a nanny, and after several interviews that don't go well, they meet Vivian, who impresses them with her desire to take care of the whole family. Meanwhile, when Diane decides to run for class president, Zoey helps her create a smear campaign to win Diane the vote.[1]

Sometimes a sitcom will delve into more serious territory. Historically, the well-known "very special episode" moniker has been used occasionally to tell viewers that the episode might deal with something weightier, a serious moral issue, but this would normally be an exception.

Roots

All of this is very familiar to most people; we have seen hundreds of these episodes in our lifetime. The sitcom is such a commonly understood format that we are unlikely to question its origins. It is easy to assume that it is simply an endemic or original TV genre. Yet situation comedy, as with any dramatic form, has roots that extend well before the era of TV. Given that we are now more than seventy years out from the advent of television, it is easy to lose sight of the origins of the sitcom, which did not emerge full-blown on television as something entirely new. The genre was well explored in the 1920s through the 1940s in the golden age of radio, and of course radio was drawing from other sources as the sitcom evolved.

Farce

Despite our immediate association of the term with television, *situation comedy* was in use even in the nineteenth century. An 1880 review from the University of Michigan School of Music, Theater, and Dance referred to Rossini's *Barber of Seville* as a situation comedy. A 1920 screenwriting handbook used the term to distinguish slapstick physical comedy from more mannered plots: "The term has come into common use . . . in order to distinguish between the clean-cut, plausible quality of screen humor and what is known as 'slapstick' comedy" (Christie, 1920, p. 3). "In studio parlance the term 'situation-comedy' is applied to the one- and two-reel subjects in which the characters are dressed as they would be in real life, and in which their actions are plausible and based upon human motives" (p. 5).

One of the origins of the modern sitcom can be seen in the theatrical genre of farce, a comedic form with high levels of buffoonery and silliness, perhaps with some physical comedy, in highly improbable situations. In a farce, the comedy is often based on the fact that we can see various misunderstandings that are occurring between characters while the characters cannot. One person learns what another is doing by eavesdropping. Multiple complications make for more riotous farce. After a suitable buildup of tension, there is usually a happy ending, though a foppish or ridiculous character will get a comeuppance.

There were farces in ancient Greek theater and plenty of demand for this whimsical form of entertainment as theater spread throughout the European world. Farces could be alternatives to forms of theater that were more accepted by the church, reflecting a popular need for letting off steam in tightly controlled cultural conditions.

It is important to note that, as with sitcoms, farces were often put down and denigrated. A mere farce was seen as something less than a serious dramatic form, which disguised the fact that farces focused on romantic, family, and community situations were often relevant commentaries (indeed, they functioned as a kind of cultural indicator) on domestic conditions of the time. They reflected the rule that something seen as funny also tells us something about what is considered normal: "The comic spirit of farce delights in taboo-violation, but avoids implied moral comment or social criticism and prefers to debar empathy for its victims. This combination is vital for farce to succeed. The more respectable its victims, and the more successfully it avoids moral implications flowing from their victimization, the funnier farce will be. Its guiding rule is to tread the fine line between offense and entertainment" (Davis, 2014, pp. 6–7).

To violate a taboo is to show what is considered non-taboo; indeed, it is the function of the taboo to do so. Sitcoms, apart from the well-known ones that explicitly focus on white-bread portrayals of "normal" families, often are involved with taboos. Thus, both farces and sitcoms give us clues as to what is considered acceptable in mainstream society.

To be clear, not all sitcoms would be considered true farces, though many of them do inherit elements from the genre. Some more recent sitcoms, such as *Frasier* (1993–2004), intentionally produced whole episodes that were farces in style and form. The *Seinfeld* episode "The Barber" (S5E8) is modeled on farcical Italian operas such as *The Barber of Seville*.

Vaudeville

The sitcom is an American form; the precursors of American electronic media entertainment are found in genres such as vaudeville and minstrelsy. Vaudeville was a form of live-theater variety shows that was dominant in America from the late 1800s to the early 1900s. A typical vaudeville show was an affordable mix of different types of acts: dancers, singers, jugglers, stand-up comedians, specialty acts, comedy sketches, and so forth. "Vaudeville entrepreneurs were the first businesspeople to even attempt to provide amusement on a national scale to the majority of the people" (Monod, 2020, p. 149). Butsch (2000) notes that vaudeville's origins in urban "concert saloons" mostly contained set routines as their comic material; this changed over toward short domestic and comic sketches that Butsch considered to be forerunners of the sitcom.

Two important facets of vaudeville offer us clues to the development of sitcoms. First, there was vaudeville's networked structure. Vaudeville theaters could be found in any city of any size during the period of their popularity. Economically, they were quickly dominated by regional and national "block booking" syndicates that controlled talent and thus functioned as producers for a more or less standardized kind of show that could be seen around the country. It was a forerunner of the truly nationalized entertainment that

Brief History of Situation Comedies

would later be offered simultaneously on electronic broadcast networks. When radio developed, it first turned to vaudeville for its talent, to a pool of performers already in place with proven mass appeal (Monod, 2000).

Second, and perhaps even more strongly in terms of effects on content, was the development of what we now call stand-up comedy, especially as something that emerged from ethnically stereotyped portrayals. The vaudeville era was a time when America was assimilating various ethnic groups, sometimes quite uneasily. In cities especially, this meant exposure to (and cross-pollination by) a variety of character types: Jewish, Italian, Irish, Black. Comedians based routines on these stereotypes; the stand-up comedy material of the time was quite frequently based on ethnic send-ups, to the exclusion of other topics. These influences carried over into the sitcom era on radio. Jewish comedians especially were influential as vaudeville material transferred over to the airwaves. Routines focused on Black life and stereotypes of it also were quite important—something that developed even before vaudeville in the era of minstrelsy.

Monod (2020) notes that vaudeville was successful because of its portrait of modern urban society that was developing in the US. This meant showing an ethnic mix, and it was in fact a channel for ethnic Americans to be employed in the entertainment industry. Inevitably, though, as with farcical forms, it meant a form of stereotyping for comedic effect that, while entertaining, could also affect how people perceived ethnic groups in reality: "Nineteenth century stereotypes, or facets of them . . . continued to exert a baleful influence in entertainment because performers were able to draw usefully from the cultural or emotional associations. Unfortunately, through vaudeville, they now appeared not to be theatrical conventions but expressions and appearances that were 'true'" (Monod, 2020, p. 16). The idea of comedy as affecting (or even infecting) peoples' understanding of racial and ethnic groups became very important as sitcoms developed. This was especially true in the case of the influence of American minstrelsy in sitcoms.

Minstrelsy

By the 1840s, a systematized form of blackface stage entertainment— minstrelsy—would emerge as the rage of American popular culture, the first concerted appropriation and commercial exploitation of a Black expressive form. African-American humor (along with elements of song and dance) was lifted from its original context, transformed and parodied, then spotlighted for the entertainment and amusement of non-Black audiences.

The phenomenon, in a less satiric and consciously malicious form, would be repeated over the years; Paul Whiteman would be promoted as the "King of Jazz," Benny Goodman as the "King of Swing," Elvis Presley as the "King of Rock," and a raft of non-Blacks would achieve popular success by burlesquing supposed Negro performance and lifestyles. But none of these subsequent mimetic excursions into Black cultural life would be as methodically demeaning or as lastingly damaging as minstrelsy. (Watkins, 1994, p. 82)

Minstrelsy was a uniquely American live entertainment product. Its main theme was the portrayal of Black life in the American South. Originating in the 1840s, minstrelsy had a typical structure that would begin with some comic routines followed by a variety segment of singing and dancing (the *olio*) and ending with a final group song-and-dance number or skit. Several characteristics of minstrelsy were important to the early development of sitcoms.

The salient features that most people associate with minstrelsy are the use of blackface by white performers and song and comedy styles that portray lifestyles of Blacks in the American South during the period of slavery. The initial fascination with blackface performance came from the popularity of so-called Negro melodies such as "Jump Jim Crow." Composer Stephen Foster wrote many of the songs that we most characteristically associate with the minstrel genre, such as "Oh! Susanna" and "Camptown Races." These could be considered the first instances of popularly marketed songs in the American culture.

A full examination of all the functions and dysfunctions of blackface in American entertainment is beyond the scope of this book. Butsch (2000) notes that its prominence was a reflection of the overwhelming whiteness of American entertainment. While Northern audiences were fascinated with Black life, the idea that Black performers would themselves provide that portrayal was never considered, at least at first. Even though there were Black audiences for minstrelsy and eventually Black performers, the form was by and for whites. Minstrelsy is the comedic counterpart of the "Tom" theatrical portrayals based on the novel *Uncle Tom's Cabin* (Stowe, 1852), which originated as melodramatic depictions of the undeserved suffering of Blacks. Tom portrayals were then inevitably accompanied by "anti-Tom" portrayals (Williams, 2001), with switched roles such that whites were not villainous, a genre that reached its apotheosis in D. W. Griffith's film *The Birth of a Nation*.

Minstrelsy, while extremely popular for a period, was always based in a racial characteristic that was different from prejudices against other ethnic groups in both quality and quantity. With other groups such as the Irish, Jews,

Brief History of Situation Comedies   41

and Italians, there certainly were corrosive stereotypes and blocks to success. But the inerasable bars of color were not present for those groups. With the white ethnicities, the stereotyping could at least have a more "laughing with you" flavor than "laughing at you." When ethnic sitcoms emerged on radio and then on television, the effect of such stereotypes for these groups was simply less demeaning (in a show like *The Goldbergs* [1949–56], for instance) than it was for Blacks (in a show like *Amos 'n' Andy* [1951–53]).

Though minstrelsy was criticized by the emerging middle class of American Blacks almost from the beginning, the acceptance of minstrel themes by many parts of the mainstream American audience continued long after the actual live entertainment form died out. Brooks (2020) documents the endurance of minstrel elements and materials in all electronic and visual media after the live form had gone away. In film, superstar performers such as Al Jolson made careers built on blackface. In radio, the popularity of *Amos 'n' Andy* was enormous (as an audio form of "blackvoice"), and the success of the show continued from radio into television. In the UK, minstrel shows were very popular on TV and continued even into the 1970s.

The TV scandal of *Amos 'n' Andy* (see discussion below) dealt a final blow to minstrelsy as an acceptable form of entertainment. That did not mean the complete death of minstrel tropes, though. In later years, sensitivity to the damage that minstrelsy caused was cited when any Black character moved toward "jive" or even just authentically Black forms of comedy. Such was the case with *Good Times* (1974–79), which began as a show meant to highlight a somewhat realistic portrayal of working-class Black life, something that had been missing from television. The enormous popularity of Jimmie Walker's character, JJ, a highly stylized low-comedy type of portrayal, was disturbing even to the show's own stars, who eventually left. The echoes of the minstrel era were such that any burlesque or grotesque type of portrayal based on Black dialect was likely to be offensive to Black middle classes, who were looking for more ennobling characterizations. Meanwhile, in the later years of television, other ethnicities were happily stereotyping themselves—for example, lots of Jewish themes appeared without much controversy in shows such as *Seinfeld*. Images of drunk Irishmen, cheap Jews, or criminal Italians seemed much less problematic and were used often.

Radio

Along with farce, vaudeville, and minstrelsy, America was concurrently developing mass media forms that would provide the true home for situation comedy. Gladden (1976) argues that there are newspaper roots for sitcoms, found in the recurrent columns that focused on a single family (such as the Spoopendykes) where husband-versus-wife confrontations over domestic matters formed the bulk of the humor. Comic strips focused on family situations (e.g., *Blondie*, which later became a TV sitcom) eventually took over in popularity from the columns, a development that helped launch the genre of serial family comedy. These forms set the stage for radio to develop the sitcom in its daily, then weekly, form.

The golden age of radio was primarily in the '30s and '40s, with television taking over in the '50s. Radio originally became a force in the life of American entertainment in the 1920s; its rise to mass popularity was quite rapid (Barnouw, 1966). Among the various types of content that were tried as programming on early radio (classical music, dance music, sports, news), it soon became evident that light narrative entertainment worked very well, particularly in a serial format. To craft this entertainment, producers drew from the various roots discussed above, along with genres from film such as screwball comedy, which all found their way in some shape or form into the radio programming mix; they comprised the stream of programming that would become comedy on radio, and then even more popularly on TV.

Amos 'n' Andy was much more than the symbolic death knell of explicit minstrel racism in American entertainment. It began as radio's original hit and one of the first situation comedies. It lampooned American Blacks, drawing straight from the minstrel tradition's blackface origins. Apart from its racism, which dominates most discussion, it had another characteristic that would be important across many more sitcoms in the era of TV. Its ease of production and replication was key: "The *Amos 'n' Andy* series broke new ground in several ways. It established syndication as a mechanism, even though recordings were still of doubtful quality and limited to five-minute lengths. The feasibility of the continued story was also overwhelmingly shown. A basic dilemma continuing for weeks, far from alienating listeners, enmeshed ever-widening rings of addicts. . . . All this would bring a flood of radio serials in coming years" (Barnouw, 1966, pp. 228–29). The importance of "the feasibility of the continued story" cannot be overemphasized.

An example can show us how radio sitcom roots migrated over to television. Fuller-Seeley (2015) provides a narrative of how comedian Jack Benny made the move from variety/vaudeville to radio and then television (*The Jack Benny Program* [1950–65]), negotiating the demands placed by the new medium. A vaudeville comic would typically have a set amount of material, much like today's stand-up comics, and reuse it for audiences that were different each time. With radio, such material was quickly used up; the broadcast comedian had to feed a voracious maw demanding more content. Generating more and more stand-alone jokes in the vaudeville mold would quickly prove impossible. The solution was to create situations and characters within those situations that offered repetitive opportunities for jokes of the same type, with a plot that moved minimally along for novelty and continued audience interest. In Benny's case, the idea was a "show within a show"; other later sitcoms took a similarly meta stance (*The Dick Van Dyke Show* [1961–66], for instance). Within this structure, characters adhered to certain types. Although Benny evolved over the years to a finely honed persona (Fuller-Seeley calls it the "fall guy") that became an international hit, surrounding character types remained constant, providing the comic disturbances that motivated each episode.

The early Benny radio scripts show a corniness that would have been understood well by vaudeville audiences, wherein comic teams dueled each other, also reminiscent of the banter of the "endmen" in minstrel shows. Verbal interlocutions led to frequent punch lines; intercourse was rapid, interlaced with sarcasm and irony, but ultimately any threats and put-downs were harmless. In addition, all of it had to be structured so as to feature the sponsor:

MUSIC: "JELLO" JINGLE

ANNOUNCER (DON): "The Jello Program", starring Jack Benny! With Mary Livingstone, Phil Harris, Dennis Day, and yours truly Don Wilson. The orchestra opens the program with "Philly".

MUSIC: "PHILLY", ESTABLISH, THEN QUIETLY, UNDER

DON: That was "Philly", played by Phil Harris and his Orchestra. And now, ladies and gentlemen, this being the first Sunday in November, we bring you the last rose of summer: JACK BENNY!

JACK: Thank you! Thank you. Jello again! This is Jack Benny talking, and, Don, I've heard you give me some pretty silly introductions in the past, but that one takes the cake. "Last rose of summer" . . . What does that mean, anyway?

DON: It doesn't mean anything. I was just trying to be clever, that's all.

JACK: Don, you just make with the Jello. I'll take care of the clever stuff around here. Anyway, I don't want to start out every broadcast talking about me, me all the time. It's embarrassing!

PHIL: It's a little dull too.

JACK: Oh, it is? Well, Phil, let me ask you something, now that you've established your presence among us. Is this program getting a little too monotonous for you?

44 SITCOMS AND CULTURE

PHIL: Well, it's not exactly—
JACK: I mean, do you find me, personally, so incompatible?
PHIL: Incom-what?
JACK: Incompatible.
PHIL: Would ya mind cuttin' that down where I can get at it?
JACK: Not at all. What I'm trying to get at, Phil, is this. Do I bore you? I mean, do I grate on your nerves?
PHIL: No, not exactly. Why?
JACK: Because, Phil, there's an old Chinese proverb that says: "When orchestra leader unhappy over job, him soon clap hands with joy in breadline." Velly good advice![2]

Later, the TV episode "Jack at the Supermarket" (S11E14) shows how elements of vaudeville and minstrelsy persisted, even as late as the 1961 air date, while the show was also trying to develop a more modern aesthetic. Archaic aspects included Jack dressing up as a maid because he had lost a bet to Rochester, his housekeeper. Rochester used many comic devices that would have been common in minstrelsy (e.g., an exaggerated Black dialect). But Rochester often bested his boss and usually seemed cleverer. Jack had to do the shopping at the supermarket—a nod to modern problems. There, he encountered comic foils such as actor Frank Nelson, whose trademark "eee-YESS?" was a foil for Benny's own catchphrase: "Now stop that!" The Benny program showed that audiences would not punish performers for running gags; in fact, they were expected. There is a narrative pleasure in seeing familiar punch lines deployed in new ways. Yet, vaudeville elements persisted: jokes were at the expense of women (men in drag) and minorities (Chinese costumes used for comic effect, Rochester's dialect). Still, though, Benny developed a cooler modern personality of comic reaction; most of his laughs came from looking bemused at the insanity around him. Later comics such as Bob Newhart also developed this technique in sitcoms, where the star is the calm center around which disturbances fly;[3] Bill Cosby in *The Cosby Show* (1984–92) would be another example.[4] Benny's cooler style worked well on television, showing that not all TV comedy has to be physically slapstick, as with Lucille Ball. The move of the Benny program from New York to LA also emphasized the cooler style that TV seemed to encourage in its sitcoms.

Radio had many other comedies, though not all were sitcoms. Some were of the variety or revue format. Other examples of the radio sitcom format that were popular included:

Fibber McGee and Molly (1935–56). A working-class husband and wife.

Our Miss Brooks (1948–57). A radio sitcom about a teacher seeking love and dealing with fractious students and colleagues. It eventually transitioned to TV and even film.

The Aldrich Family (1939–53). A teen- and school-centered comedy, later on TV.

Blondie (1939–50). A husband-and-wife radio sitcom adaptation of the popular comic strip. Also later on TV.

Father Knows Best (1954–60). A radio sitcom that became a TV standard bearer for conservative family values.

The Adventures of Ozzie and Harriet (1944–54). A family sitcom that eventually transitioned to TV in the 1950s and became a major hit.

TV

Our stereotype of 1950s sitcoms revolves around a nuclear family solving white-bread problems in a suburban environment. But sitcoms were more varied than that, even in the early 1950s, as content transitioned from radio to television. The move from radio was smooth in some senses but very rough in others. The technical capability of television existed well before it was fully commercialized. World War II interrupted the rollout of TV, as technical expertise in the video field was turned to war production. But the concept of what TV content was or could be was well understood and actually much anticipated. Two decades of radio had provided the template, and the very same companies that were dominating radio would control the TV market (Barnouw 1970).

The 1950s

Some of TV's earliest sitcom content transitioned directly from radio. Like the Benny program discussed above, another example of the show-within-a-show format that started on radio was *The George Burns and Gracie Allen Show* (1950–58). Comedians George Burns and Gracie Allen had been working successfully in radio, very much in a vaudeville style (where they had started). Their routine emphasized Gracie as a "dizzy blonde" or a "dumb Dora," with husband George as the straight man. In the television version, we see the homelife of a show business performer and a wife who is always scheming (with her best friend, à la *I Love Lucy*) to get one over on him. The schemes always fail in the end, but George is a somewhat benevolent dictator when it comes to Gracie. Their life is an opulent one in Hollywood, reflecting the TV focus on "gracious living" that was seen in many of the sitcom homes of the 1950s. They do have a child, but nuclear family business is not the only focus of the show, and the Jewish and Irish ethnic roots of the two stars do shine through in many ways. Theirs is a Depression-era ethnic sensibility transferred to California, where they are "making it."

Burns himself (1955) acknowledged the usefulness of the sitcom format in transitioning from vaudeville:

> We were too old for the he-she kind of jokes we were doing at the time. The character Gracie plays was flirting with the announcer, and we were having boy-friend, girl-friend jokes and insulting each other. Now you can insult your girl, but not your wife. Everybody knew we were married, and everybody knew we had growing children. The situation just wasn't true, and you have to have truth in a joke just the way you do in anything else, to make it any good. If it's basically dishonest, it isn't funny. . . . We changed our entire basis of humor to a domestic-situation comedy, which is what we have today. (pp. 173–84)

In 1950s sitcoms, we see some interesting transitions that were happening in American society, focused around where and how we lived. Early sitcoms that were focused on families in urban environments (e.g., *The Goldbergs, The Honeymooners* [1955–56]) had families living in cramped (for TV) urban quarters. Though the actual square footage of TV apartments such as those seen in *The Honeymooners* might have been larger than what many urban tenement dwellers were actually living in (especially when accounting for families with children), the point of *The Honeymooners'* Kramdens was to emphasize a lower-working-class physical environment as part of the comedy.

Figure 2.1 shows how new home sizes were beginning to increase in the US at the same time as household size (in terms of numbers of people) was decreasing, starting a climb that would more than double the size of new US homes by the 2000s. *The Honeymooners* could never hope to escape their urban squalor, but *The Goldbergs* did achieve a move toward the suburbs, where they started to find other 1950s sitcom families. While the Goldberg family was hoping to maintain something of an ethnic identity when they reached suburbia, the other families that were already there were busy leaching out cultural markers and defining a stereotypical whiteness that was as misrepresentative as some of the other ethnic stereotypes. (The white sitcom family still serves as a straw man for culture wars arguments.) A typical problem for the construction of some later sitcoms would become whether urban Jewish comedic sensibilities could be translated to a less urban setting, with less obvious ethnicity, and still remain funny.

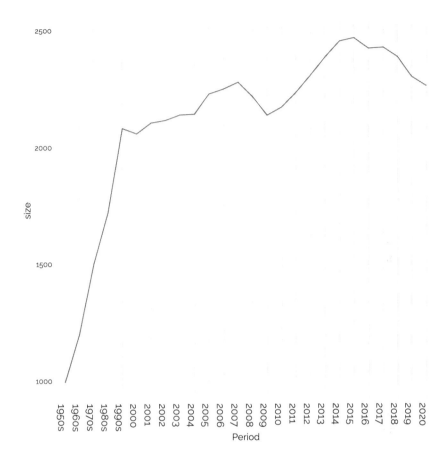

Figure 2.1. Average dwelling size, US new homes, 1950–present.

The domestic example of *The Honeymooners* proved less workable for most sitcoms, despite the comedic quality of the show. Future shows would emphasize Middle-American living styles with professionally decorated homes in a conservative and tastefully done manner. The decade's most popular sitcom, *I Love Lucy*, took place in an urban apartment, but it was spacious and pleasing, much the opposite of that seen on *The Honeymooners*. Later, even the nice apartment proved too cramped, and the Ricardos decamped to a roomier house in Connecticut. Although we could not know the exact square footage of their living quarters, their move was tracking what was happening with house size in the US. Landay (2016) notes that the show's popularity directly affected consumer tastes in the '50s: "One ad proclaiming 'Live Like

48

SITCOMS AND CULTURE

Lucy!' [fig. 2.2] indicates how television brought the world into the home and the home into the world with commodities. Clearly, the vision of domesticity enacted in the Ricardos' apartment was, for Lucy, a commodified one, with many episodes centering on the struggle to get the money to get something for herself or the home" (pp. 35–36).

The *how* of living focused on the emerging materialism that was possible for some families in the postwar period and the explosion of consumer merchandising that TV facilitated. Any television show could be a suitable vehicle for a consumer product, but sitcoms had obvious appeal for sponsors of home products. Carnation and Jell-O sponsored the Burns and Allen show. Lever Brothers, a soap company, sponsored Jack Benny. Shows themselves featured kitchens with the latest appliances, or in the case of *The Honeymooners*, Ralph's failure to provide the latest gadgets and a nice kitchen proved a point of contention (Alice: "I am the only girl in town with an atomic kitchen; the place looks like Yucca Flats after the blast!")

Major sitcom families of the era were living above the median. Lucy, Ozzie, "Beaver," Donna Reed, and others were consuming prolifically, even if it wasn't clear what their source of income was (as in the case of Ozzie Nelson). As *Amos 'n' Andy* ground to a halt over its racism controversy, the rest of the sitcom world reactively focused on white families, often of more-than-average means. The sitcom mode for stereotypically "acceptable" family presentation was thus established from the mid-1950s. A geographic center of gravity seemed to be emerging around the Midwest, or at least it was assumed to be so, for example in cases like *Father Knows Best* where one was not sure of the exact location. A kind of Middletown esthetic, later parodied in *The Simpsons* (1989–), was accepted as the best vehicle for product promotion as it was least likely to raise the eyebrows of censorious types. Best of all, it seemed perfectly acceptable to mass audiences.

Barnouw (1978) shows how sponsors played a key role in the move away from the depiction of home environments on TV:

> Lower-class settings were [a] source of exasperation. The enormous success of Paddy Chayefsky's *Marty*, about the love problems of a butcher in the Bronx, inspired a flood of plays about what Chayefsky called "the marvelous world of the ordinary." Sponsors were meanwhile trying to "upgrade" the consumer and persuade him to "move up to Chrysler," and "live better electrically" in a suburban home, with help from "a friend at Chase Manhattan." The sponsors preferred beautiful people

Figure 2.2. Ad for *I Love Lucy* themed furniture set.[1]
[1] https://commons.wikimedia.org/wiki/File:I_love_lucy_bedroom_set_1953.JPG.

50 SITCOMS AND CULTURE

in mouth-watering décor, to convey what it meant to climb the mobile socio-economic ladder. The commercials looked out of place in the Bronx settings. (pp. 106–7)

The concept of "least objectionable programming" was starting to emerge. TV executive Paul Klein codified the idea in the 1970s based on how television had been programmed from the outset. The idea was that people watched *television*, not programs. Because programs had to be acceptable across the various parts of the country with different regional constituencies, there was a tendency toward conservatism and avoiding controversy (Shales, 1977, p. B1): "One of Klein's most famous operating maxims is the Least Objectionable Program theory—the idea that people do not watch programs, they watch television, and they pick not the shows they like most, but the ones they dislike least. He still subscribes to this particular gospel."

Klein is asked if there is one major abiding misconception that naive people have about television.

"Yes," he says.

What is it?

"That the content matters."

*

The memorability of certain 1950s sitcoms, and their durability in reruns, can lead to the impression that the decade was dominated by sitcoms. This was not the case. As shown in figure 2.3, which shows cumulative ratings points earned by the top twenty shows in different genres during the decade, sitcoms were normally the second or third most popular genre. The 1950s started off with variety programs being the main fare and ended with action (mostly Western) programs becoming the most popular. In between, *I Love Lucy* was unquestionably the dominant *single* program, but some years had only one other sitcom in the top twenty.

Other sitcoms that appeared the top twenty in these years were:

Mama (1949–57). A traditional Norwegian nuclear family assimilating in America.

The Aldrich Family (1949–53). The television continuation of the radio sitcom adventures of American teen Henry Aldrich.

Life with Luigi (1952). An Italian entry in the ethnic comedy genre, canceled due to protests over stereotypes.

Our Miss Brooks. A school- and classroom-focused comedy; a continuation of the radio series.

Brief History of Situation Comedies

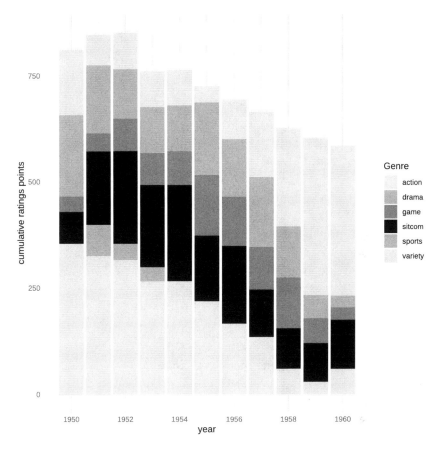

Figure 2.3. Ratings points earned by 1950s TV programs.

Private Secretary, aka *Susie* (1953–57). A secretary to a theatrical agent in a workplace-based comedy.

The Honeymooners. Bus driver Ralph Kramden, ever the loser; his wife, Alice; and their upstairs neighbors deal with working-class concerns in urban squalor.

Father Knows Best (1954–60). A conservative 1950s Midwestern nuclear family.

The Real McCoys (1957–63). An Appalachian family moves to California.

The Danny Thomas Show, aka *Make Room for Daddy* (1953–64). Showbiz dad and his family in 1950s–'60s America.

Dennis the Menace (1959–63). A television version of the popular comic strip. A mischievous boy troubles his neighbor.

The 1960s

The 1950s established that a sitcom could be the dominant prime-time show, but the 1960s proved to be a period in which sitcoms would be the dominant genre (fig. 2.4). In the ecosystem of prime-time television that was emerging, four basic types of programs were workable: action (including crime and Westerns), variety comedy-music programs, drama, and sitcoms. Other genres such as reality were minor players (*Candid Camera* being the main example), with sports and game shows also having relatively minor roles in prime time.

Why did sitcoms become more important in the 1960s? In some ways it is odd, but also perhaps causal, that entertainment choices turned to comedic escapism when other forms of entertainment, and American culture itself, were dealing with increasing levels of civil upheaval that would reach their peak toward the end of the decade. The sitcom decade of the 1960s is notable for at least three trends: its rural focus, its fantasy focus, and its racial homogeneity.

Rural-coms

The rural wave was presaged by *The Real McCoys* in the 1950s but gained steam early in the 1960s with the success of *The Andy Griffith Show*. This was a top-ten show throughout almost the entire decade of the 1960s. The basic plots focused on minor disturbances in a rural Southern American setting, solved by a mild-mannered sheriff, Andy Taylor, who didn't carry a gun. Worland and O'Leary (2016) argue that a show like *Griffith*, which was immediately popular, came out of several programming urges. There was the need to move comedy away from the Jewish/ethnic/urban roots that were redolent of vaudeville and that persisted into the 1950s, allowing broadcasters to serve a larger, more heterogeneous audience as TV became available outside of major cities. The failure of ethnic shows like *Amos 'n' Andy* and *Life with Luigi* augured for a WASPier tone. Churchgoing was not overly emphasized, but a Protestant ethos certainly suffused *Griffith*, with its quietly moralizing star. Almost every episode had a lesson for Opie, the sheriff's young son.

Adding to the rural flavor was the odd success of *The Beverly Hillbillies*. Like *The Real McCoys*, the Hillbillies went to California from the rural South; they were all outrageous stereotypes of mountain people. America had plenty of experience with rural forms of expression in its mass media. Humorists Mark Twain, Joel Chandler Harris, and others had brought dialect comedy to the national literature. Will Rogers delivered folksy rural wisdom in vaudeville, in

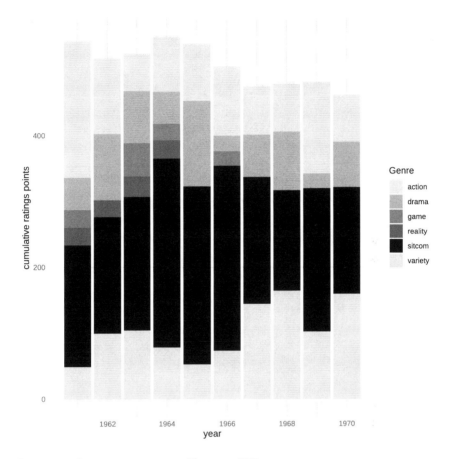

Figure 2.4. Ratings points earned by 1960s TV programs.

movies, and on radio. Radio had its own rural-focused sitcoms, and country music had been emphasizing the "rube" or "hick" persona since the 1920s.

In *Hillbillies*, the main source of comedy was the fact that the family was rich because of an oil strike back home. In Beverly Hills, sophisticated people of means such as bankers were forced to suck up to them because of their wealth. Attalah (2003) observes that the show was mostly a comedy of class reversal, along with characterizations that involved contradictory elements, such as the fact that Ellie May was a nubile female but dressed like a boy, or that Grannie was incredibly old but also very feisty. There was a carnivalesque quality or role-swapping to the entire series. The show rocketed to number one in its first year and stayed in the top twenty throughout the decade.

54 SITCOMS AND CULTURE

Green Acres (1965–71) used the same strategy of class mix-up, with a rich man dropped into a rural farming community. Again, the rubes got the best of the city slicker. *Gomer Pyle, USMC* (1964–69) was spun off from *Griffith*, where Jim Nabors's heavily accented Southern stereotype always frustrated his marine sergeant. Along with the many Westerns that were still popular during the decade, the rural flavor of TV was strong, even as more Americans moved into cities and as inner-city problems dominated the news.

Fantasy Focus

Another unique quality of the decade's sitcoms, again reflecting its turn away from urban problems and international war, was the focus on fantasy-themed sitcoms, also known as "magicoms" (Kenton, 2016). Most notable among these were *Bewitched* (1964–72) and *I Dream of Jeannie* (1965–70). In both shows, very attractive female magical figures (a witch and a genie) created problems for their male counterparts. *Bewitched* showed the problems around which a nuclear family, trying to hide the magical powers of its star, negotiated modern problems. It had some harbingers of feminist themes, as Samantha, the witch, had tremendous powers, but still she only wished to become a "regular housewife." Kenton notes that some aspects of the show reeked of "prefeminist agitation," where the woman was the smarter and more effective partner, even if the husband retained titular privilege and control. In *Jeannie*, the male stars were astronauts, bringing something of a space-age flair. It had few if any harbingers of feminist themes, as the scantily clad Jeannie was basically concerned only with pleasing her "Master," though of course she was always getting him into trouble—an updated magical version of the Dumb Dora character.

Whiteness

"Investigations across a range of disciplines into the powerful positions and discourses that have been afforded to white people have been referred to as the study of whiteness" (Green et al., 2007). The term *whiteness* is very much of the twenty-first century and its identity-based culture wars, but there are solid reasons to look for (some of) its origins in 1960s sitcoms. In chapter 3, we examine scholarly research on sitcom depictions of race in detail, including a review of the literature on whiteness in sitcoms. Here, in the context of 1960s programs, we can point out that only one sitcom featured a Black character in a starring role: *Julia* (1968–71), a show about a Black single mother making her way in a white world. A few other sitcoms had recurring Black characters,

Brief History of Situation Comedies   55

such as Rochester in the Benny show. But the networks had become allergic to ethnic themes after the failures of the 1950s. Even a show featuring a maid as the main character was done with a brassy white woman as the lead (*Hazel* [1961–66]); in the previous decade, it had been standard to cast Black women as maids, even in a starring role (such as in *Beulah* [1950–53]).[5] Not until the 1970s would Black themes be addressed directly, even though Blacks constituted about 10 percent of the population in the 1960s.

Sitcom whiteness in many ways became the accepted stereotype of the cultural aspects of being white that are still so frequently criticized. When a white persona was desired, an unidentifiable standard American accent was used, much as sitcoms had de-ethnicized their collective affect in a bid to be acceptable across the country. Whites were assumed to believe in and propagate myths about the nuclear family, which were so potently symbolized in some early sitcoms. To the extent that it meant anything to be white in postwar America, it often meant the absence of ethnicity, which is what the mass medium of TV was requiring at the time.

Early American comedy had always relied on difference as a source of humor, and ethnicity was often the tool used to achieve the difference. As that tool became less attractive commercially, to develop novelty in characters, sitcoms would turn away from ethnicity and choose other routes, such as in *The Munsters* (1964–66), a family of ghouls for whom race was not the differentiator. A similar strategy was seen in *The Addams Family* (1964–66).

Even the in the rural sitcoms, for those that had semi-serious intentions such as *Andy Griffith*, the Southern white personality (one of the original American ethnic flavors) is divorced from its many cultural complexities and presented in a homogenized and sanitized way. Andy Taylor's down-home virtue signaling, in a non-Gothic version of the South, would work as well in the Springfield of *Father Knows Best* as in his own Mayberry, North Carolina. The sitcom trends of the '60s did well economically, but ultimately they didn't do white people any favors culturally. The rebellion against TV whiteness took a while to start up and then was successful only in fits and starts.

Other shows of note in the 1960s included:

The Flintstones (1960–66). Animated show somewhat reminiscent of *The Honeymooners* in characterization but focusing on a family living in the Stone Age.

The Dick Van Dyke Show. Arguably the best show of the decade, a Camelot-era sitcom about a comedy writer and his beautiful wife living the commuter lifestyle in New Rochelle.

56   SITCOMS AND CULTURE

The Donna Reed Show (1958–66). Archetypical nuclear family sitcom.

My Three Sons (1960–72). An early entry in the motherless family genre; a dad raises three sons with the help of a cantankerous "uncle."

The Patty Duke Show (1963–66). Identical cousins, both played by the star. Capitalized on the teen trends in media production.

Hogan's Heroes (1965–71). Audacious show concept to explore the comedic aspects of life in a Nazi POW camp.

The 1970s

The 1970s in many ways became *the* decade of the sitcom, though it would not have been foreseen at the very start. Some observers classify the first years of the 1970s as a part of what we now call the Sixties. For television, it was when sitcoms began to make halting, then more rapid moves toward updating their take on what American family life might really be like. By the end of the decade, sitcoms were dominating the prime-time lineup numerically, even as a spasm of social relevance was coming to an end as Americans turned toward a Reaganite interlude.

The top sitcom in 1970–71 was *Here's Lucy* (1968–74), which was a fading echo of Lucille Ball's star power. Everything was upended for sitcoms in the next TV season, when *All in the Family* (*AITF*) became a smash surprise number one hit. *All in the Family* focused on a liberal-conservative culture war within a single family. It brought viewers back to prime-time television. It made Archie Bunker a household name—and a symbol for bigotry. It achieved a rating of 34, which was roughly five points higher than the number one show of 1971, *Marcus Welby, MD*. This was unusual because most seasons of network television had tended to show declines in overall ratings. *AITF* managed ratings in the 30s (meaning that 30 percent of households with TVs were watching) until 1977, when it was unseated by *Happy Days* (1974–84).

We have a more extensive analysis of *AITF* in chapter 3. In the context of the 1970s, it can take its place among the three great '70s sitcoms that were issue-focused. *AITF* addressed any social issue that had a liberal-conservative take (race, gender, abortion, Vietnam, many others). *Mary Tyler Moore* (1970–77) was considered an indispensable contribution to the advancement of women in the portrayal of family and work structure on television. *M*A*S*H* was the sitcom that finally dealt with the Vietnam Era from an antiwar perspective, even though it was about the Korean War.

These shows, and others that were spun off from them, are now considered part of the era of "relevance" sitcoms. Rather than turning away from thorny social problems and whitewashing them in the process, these sitcoms showed there was an audience for shows that were more honest, even if they were also more controversial. Who was this audience? CBS started the ball rolling by consciously deciding to kill its stable of rural-focused shows, which drew an older but broadly geographically based demographic, in favor of a younger and more urban audience. As a demographic with a higher spending profile as well as a politically more liberal outlook, this new audience was in fact already waiting for programs like *AITF*; it would be a profitable move.

CBS's gamble proved to resonate culturally with audiences. In one comprehensive study, Smith (1990) found that American society since World War II had been greatly liberalized on a number of issues: "Overall, the post–World War II period has been a time of liberal advance" (p. 502). On the family issues most likely to be dealt with in sitcoms, American opinions had moved since the 1940s in a consistently liberal direction. Americans became less racist, less sexist, more likely to favor abortion, and more likely to support more freedom and tolerance for marginalized groups such as gay and lesbian people. Smith also found that these attitudes were plateauing (becoming the norm) in the 1970s, which is precisely the time when television started to catch up with them—an interesting foretaste of conclusions we can reach about how television is related to social change.[6]

All in the Family was creator and producer Norman Lear's attack on these issues. Cullen (2020) points out that *All in the Family* was an interesting reversal of the blackface minstrelsy approach. All of the worst characteristics of a white bigot were concentrated in one character who frequently used malapropisms in the same way that cork-faced minstrel characters used to, to show how ridiculous such bigotry appeared in the modern liberalized age: "One of the most reliable tactics for eliciting laughter in *All in the Family* was Archie's failed attempts to use formal language, as in his frequent use of the terms 'ipso fatso,' 'present company suspected' and the like. Gynecology became 'groinocology,' and feminism was referred to as 'the women's lubrication movement.' Archie would similarly mangle or splice truisms when making observations like 'we better not kill those chickens before they cross the road,' or noting that 'patience is a virgin'" (Cullen, 2020, p. 21). Whether Archie himself was an unfair characterization of a certain personality type has been considered much less often.

Mary Tyler Moore had already had major success in the 1960s on *The Dick Van Dyke Show*. Her show, *Mary Tyler Moore* (*MTM*), was created as vehicle for the idea that a female star could show independence. Other shows had

58 SITCOMS AND CULTURE

made this move tentatively, notably *That Girl* (1966–71) in the 1960s. *MTM* was produced with Moore's husband, Grant Tinker; the MTM company continued on producing many successful sitcoms through the '90s. *MTM* was in the television top twenty from 1972 to 1976.

The feminism displayed in *MTM* was not aggressive. Mary was usually deferential to her male boss, calling him Mr. Grant. Her place on the totem pole of the newsroom was close to the bottom, especially at the start of the show when she was a low-paid assistant producer. Mary's singleness, and her apparent lack of interest in ending that status, was where most of the more "progressive" content lay. Both men and women were more likely to be single in the US after about 1960, but even in 1972 it was hard to recognize that fact on TV. For men, being single could be treated as a desirable marker of a swinging bachelor or *Playboy*-inspired lifestyle; for women, it was more likely to be seen through a *spinster* or *old maid* lens. Simple statistics showed that there would be an increasingly large audience of single women looking to see themselves represented in ways that would affirm the lifestyle choices they made. Still, though, everyone needs a family, and so the other function of *MTM* was to show that family could be found anywhere. In Mary's case, the family was the other characters in her newsroom, as dysfunctional but ultimately lovable as any real family.

M*A*S*H was the show that arguably did the most to establish a liberal political aesthetic in sitcoms. This is noteworthy because the most well-known sitcoms from the two previous decades were known either for their conservatism (such as *Father Knows Best* or *The Andy Griffith Show*) or for their studied eschewal of political issues (the various fantasy-coms, like *Bewitched*). Norman Lear broke down the barrier, as we have seen, showing that it would also be profitable to move toward more affluent liberal audiences. *M*A*S*H* walked through the door and set up shop well into the 1980s with this same target audience.

There can be some discussion about whether *M*A*S*H* was a true sitcom. Its roots were in director Robert Altman's very dark black-comedy film of the same name. The setting was a mobile army surgical hospital in Korea. Television did not often explore the counterculture world that was going on in films and literature at the time (antiheroes, revisionist Westerns, dystopic science fiction), and so it might have seemed likely that the true spirit of the film and novel would be much watered down for a half-hour comedy with a laugh track. The early years of the show were very much comedically based, with talent that came from the comedy world. As the show evolved, there was more a of

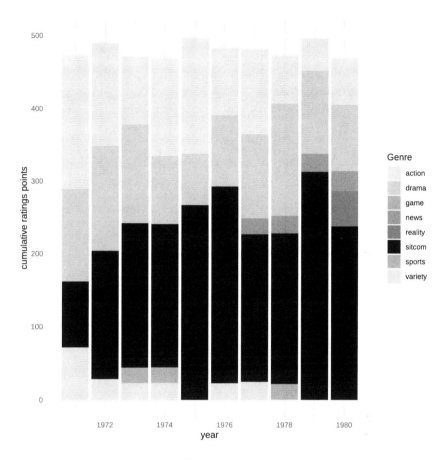

Figure 2.5. Ratings points earned by 1970s TV programs.

a mix, and entire episodes could be totally serious in tone, usually focused on the senseless nature of war. Other shows would later attempt the comedy-drama mix, but it was difficult to pull off without the talent that *M*A*S*H* had. The final episode of *M*A*S*H*, in 1984, was seen by the largest audience that a scripted series had ever drawn on network television up to that point.

Another feature of 1970s sitcoms was that Black families were starting to show up again in prime time. This was mainly due to the Lear output; three of his shows made it into the top twenty. *The Jeffersons*, spun off from *All in the Family*, showed a Black family that was "movin' on up" from economic disadvantage. *Sanford and Son* (1972–77), Lear's take on the British show *Steptoe and Son* (1970–74), was mostly about a grouchy junk dealer arguing with his son.

60 SITCOMS AND CULTURE

And *Good Times* was Lear's attempt to be more realistic about the situation of inner-city Black families. *The Jeffersons* was the most successful of these, lasting well into the 1980s.

Taken together, the Lear shows, *MTM* and its spin-offs, and *M*A*S*H* created a decade of sitcom dominance in the ratings. By the end of the 1970s, about half of the ratings points in the top twenty were being garnered by sitcoms. In 1980, these shows were, along with *M*A*S*H*:

> *Three's Company.* A sitcom in the emerging T & A genre.
> *Alice* (1976–85). A single woman making her way, based on the Scorsese movie.
> *Flo* (1980–81). A spin-off of *Alice*.
> *The Jeffersons.* A spin-off from *AITF*.
> *One Day at a Time* (1975–84). A Lear show about a single woman making her own way with two daughters.
> *Taxi* (1978–83). A sitcom from the producer of *MTM*. The work milieu moves from newsroom to taxi garage.
> *Happy Days* (1974–84). A nostalgic response to relevance sitcoms and the harbinger of the end of the relevance era.

With the exception of *Happy Days*, none of these is a sitcom about a stereotypical nuclear family.

The 1980s

As we will discuss later in this book, the nuclear family did not die so easily and may be an objective preference for many. The 1980s showed a partial reaction to the relevance era. The early part of the decade was a fading of the dominance of sitcoms as the nation headed into a wave of fascination with evening soap operas such as *Dallas* and *Dynasty*. The "Who Shot JR?" episode of *Dallas* became another example of hyper-mass viewing that network TV could still generate.[7] In 1984, only *The Jeffersons*, at the end of its run, and *AfterMASH* (1983–85), a follow-up to *M*A*S*H* that did not last long, made it into the top twenty. Sitcoms were still sprinkled liberally throughout the network lineups, but they were not hitting home runs. "It wasn't so much that sitcoms were dead—they were alive and well and occupied much of the top 20 Nielsen ranking—but that their continuing presence had been put in the shade by the roaring rise of the hour-length and longer drama" (Hilmes, 2013, p. 298). The early 1980s proclamation of the death of the sitcom was one of many. The 1960s wave seemed to be exhausting itself when the relevance era arrived. And future decades

Brief History of Situation Comedies

would see funeral announcements about sitcoms that, like the one for Mark Twain, came too soon.

As the relevance era wore itself out, the Reagan period seemed ripe for something more comfortable. Maybe audiences would be happy enough with a return to shows like *Father Knows Best*, retooled with some of the safer conclusions of relevance now baked into their premises. For those who are skeptical about the power of sitcoms to be progressive in any way, this return to "traditional" nuclear families in the '80s is a prime arguing point: "It is not that sitcoms are incapable of representing progressive values; some certainly do. However, the genre's most frequent creative choices—middle-class domestic settings, deference to white patriarchal authority, subservient women characters—have repeatedly sought to keep things just the way they are" (Sienkiewicz & Marx, 2022, p. 60).

The two outstanding examples are *The Cosby Show*, which became the number one show of the decade, and *Family Ties* (1982–89), where the parents were the liberals and the oldest son was conservative. We have an extensive analysis of *Cosby* in chapter 3. The basic desire of the show, seemingly quite admirable, was to depict an essentially "normal" Black existence from the point of view of the Black upper-middle class. The idea was tremendously successful with audiences and led to the spin-off *A Different World* (1987–93), which made the 1980s something of a golden age for Black shows on network TV. *The Cosby Show* was number one from 1986 to 1990. It also received criticism for not depicting Black life accurately; somehow, the idea that a Black family could "make it" through individual effort and achievement was troubling to some viewers—surely a failure to recognize what would now be called white privilege. However, the show came out of Bill Cosby's own personal philosophy, which prized higher education; he was often critical of Black culture for not hewing to his more middle-class values. *Cosby* focused on family-based comedy, which was not far from the family-based storytelling that had made Bill Cosby such a successful stand-up comedian. Clearly the humor of the show was centered around patriarchal authority, though not white. And, as in many sitcoms, the Cosby character was often posed as somewhat powerless against the zany things his kids did or the strong professional woman who was his wife. Looking back, in critical terms, *Cosby* suffered from the fact that it was the first Black show that was number one, and so it was freighted with all the expectations and hopes for racial depictions on television. In audience terms, it suffered not at all.

Family Ties came from liberal producers. The development of the character of the aforementioned son, Alex Keaton (played by Michael J. Fox), as a

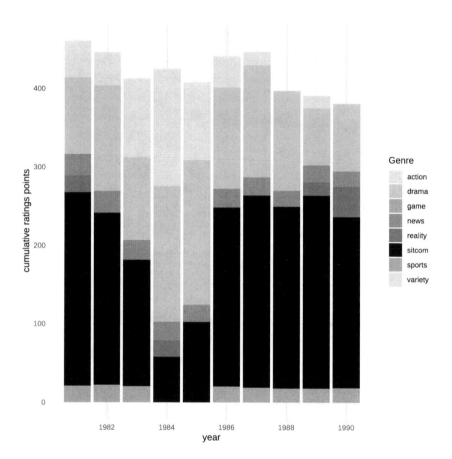

Figure 2.6. Ratings points earned by 1980s TV programs.

blazer-wearing Reaganite was meant as comedy. As with Archie Bunker in the 1970s, though, the character was a breakout hit, and many viewers actually identified with him. In 1986–87, *Family Ties* was the number two show right behind *Cosby*. If any program cemented the idea that Americans wanted a return to traditional sitcoms, this was the one. Both *Family Ties* and *Cosby* were gentler forms of comedy. Audiences seemed happy to have their family dysfunction move from the sitcom world to the nighttime soaps.

A third sitcom of note was *Cheers* (1982–93). As with many sitcom successes in the network period, programmers were calling up those producers who had been successful previously. With *Cheers*, the team that had produced *MTM* and then *Taxi* produced this similarly character-driven

Brief History of Situation Comedies   63

workplace comedy. Unlike *MTM*, and perhaps more like *Taxi*, there was less infusion of social issues. *Cheers* picked up on the barroom as the site par excellence for characters to find family when there was none at home. Sam Malone (as played by Ted Danson) was an unreconstructed male chauvinist. He fit rather closely the "dumb dad" characterization and was regularly outdone intellectually by his love interest, Diane. The show was as focused on romantic comedy and sexual tension between Sam and Diane as typical sitcom plots usually were. The show was in the top ten from 1985 to 1993.

Some of the other sitcoms that were popular in the 1980s were:

ALF (1986–90). An alien puppet.

Amen (1986–91). A deacon in a Black church had comedic adventures. One of very few church-based sitcoms.

Archie Bunker's Place (1979–83). The continuation of *AITF*.

The Golden Girls (1985–92). Four women shared life in retirement.

Newhart (1982–90). Comedian Bob Newhart reprised sitcom success as the proprietor of an inn in Vermont.

The 1990s

In the 1980s, network television underwent various threats, most notably from cable TV and VCRs. But the '90s was gearing up to be a last period of dominance for the network TV era (fig. 2.7), and sitcoms would play the major role. The flavor of the decade can be captured in four sitcoms and a sitcom subgenre that developed outside of the major network ecosystem. It is again of interest that none of the four most popular sitcoms of the decade focused on "traditional" nuclear families; they were all different from tradition in some way.

Roseanne (1988–97) depicted a nuclear family but unlike any usually seen on TV. Their very working-class milieu was emphasized in a way that had not been seen since *The Honeymooners*. Roseanne Barr's comedic persona proved to be a stirring antidote to the anodyne '80s comedies. *Roseanne* tapped into a raunchy reality of underpaid, overworked, and overweight Middle Americans that was rarely seen on TV in any way, shape, or form. It was also continuing into the '90s the trend of successful stand-up comedians graduating to sitcom series that basically incorporated their stand-up character. Barr's unlikely rise through the stand-up world to TV was in fact a rather authentic expression of talent that went against the grain in that normally male-dominated world. In this way, *Roseanne* was much like *Cosby*, breaking down some systemic

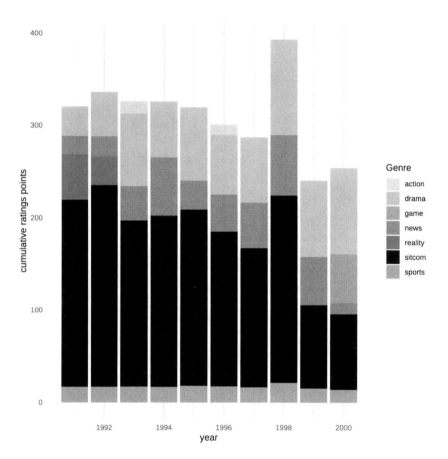

Figure 2.7. Ratings points earned by 1990s TV programs.

barriers but still with mass appeal, a sort of demented *I Love Lucy* return to having a female comedian at the top of the TV charts.

Roseanne's jokes were based on a family dynamic that was acerbic, caustic, and cutting but ultimately, because it was a sitcom, loving. The show was also a return to some progressive themes. There were gay characters in the show. Politically, *Roseanne* was working-class progressive (though later Roseanne Barr's personal politics would turn in the opposite direction). But authors such as McLeland (2016) have seen the show's main importance in how it framed sitcom motherhood:

> Tied in with the show's focus on family and memory is the way that it portrays the difficulty—the virtual impossibility—of parenting as well

Brief History of Situation Comedies

as one would like, especially given the cultural and material conditions of the working class in the Midwest during a recession. Roseanne is intimate enough with the experience of motherhood to acknowledge that it's possible to love and hate your kids simultaneously and that sometimes your past and your resources are a better determinant of your success as a parent than your knowledge or your intentions. The series undercuts romanticized representations of the work of mothering that leave children mostly off-screen or that focus only on the trials of parenting malleable babies and toddlers. Instead, *Roseanne* revels in the conflicts inherent in raising children to become independent adults with their own missteps, beliefs, feelings, and opinions and explores the ways that this can highlight or open up fault lines even in a normally unified co-parenting relationship like Dan and Roseanne Conner's. (p. 174)

While *Roseanne* was pursuing a "Mother knows least" strategy of comedy, two other shows were turning away from the nuclear family in their own ways and finding family-like structures in modern urban living. On *Friends*, the idea was to focus on how single twentysomething friends could function together as a surrogate family group. In this sitcom, three young men and three young women lived in New York City. They were quirky and not necessarily successful financially, though their surroundings seem to belie that. They had cool apartments and nice clothes. They spent a lot of time in a coffee shop. Ultimately, the show turned out to be about romances within the group, who might marry whom, and where this form of single-friend-family ultimately ended up. Was it just a stage? The series finale recognized that a group of six single friends was in fact a temporary solution to the family problem. Some of the characters moved to the suburbs (à la *I Love Lucy*), some were married, and the two main characters (Ross and Rachel) finally confessed their undying true love for each other. The series finale was a huge TV event, with 52.5 million viewers.

Friends was basically a sincere romantic comedy about guys getting girls, and girls getting guys, with an updated '90s progressive sensibility about issues of sex. It was traditional, though, in another sense. It recognized the demographic reality that people were getting married later in life and postponing the decision to have children and form nuclear families. But it still valorized that goal. The show's cute-guy-cute-girl romances were spiced up a little with progressive themes, maybe a nonwhite character here and there, some gay characters and comedic gay themes, and so forth. But the show was not transgressive comedically; as one of the most-viewed comedies of the decade, it was suitable for almost all audiences.

66　　　　　　　　　SITCOMS AND CULTURE

Friends felt updated for the '90s in the way that *The Dick Van Dyke Show* felt updated for the Camelot 1960s. Hairstyles, fashion, and lifestyle mattered a lot. Things looked clean. Programmers were addressing an upscale urban demographic as the fractionalization of television viewing started to pick up. Rather than having to address heterogeneous mass audiences, network programmers could afford to focus on the evolving Yuppie audience segment that emerged in the 1980s. This audience, in addition to being younger and whiter, was assumed to have more progressive and tolerant political and cultural tastes, though they were not particularly active politically. We presume that the *Friends* characters voted Democratic, if they indeed voted.[8] Being Republican would be a violation of good taste more than anything else.

A similar demographic segment was addressed in *Seinfeld*. We have an entire chapter devoted to this show (see chap. 5). *Seinfeld* was another example where a stand-up comedian was given a show that drew on his comedy and lifestyle. Starting out somewhat inauspiciously with only a four-episode agreement from the network, *Seinfeld* became arguably the last sitcom that could catalyze a national conversation about anything, in the way that *All in the Family* had done twenty-five years earlier. However, Seinfeld's takes on issues were much more distanced and ironic than what was seen in the relevance era. As opposed to *Friends*, which imagined marriage-delaying singles as still sincerely on the road toward something like that, *Seinfeld's* characters were extremely jaded about permanent relationships. Kramer told Jerry that marriage is a prison (S7E1):

JERRY: I had a very interesting lunch with George Costanza today.
KRAMER: Really?
JERRY: We were talking about our lives and we both kind of realized we're kids. We're not men.
KRAMER: So, then you asked yourselves, "Isn't there something more to life?"
JERRY: Yes. We did.
KRAMER: Yeah, well, let me clue you in on something. There isn't.
JERRY: There isn't?
KRAMER: Absolutely not. I mean, what are you thinking about, Jerry? Marriage? Family?
JERRY: Well . . .
KRAMER: They're prisons. Man-made prisons. You're doing time. You get up in the morning. She's there. You go to sleep at night. She's there. It's like you gotta ask permission to use the bathroom. Is it all right if I use the bathroom now?
JERRY: Really?

Brief History of Situation Comedies 67

KRAMER: Yeah, and you can forget about watching TV while you're eating.

JERRY: I can?

KRAMER: Oh, yeah. You know why? Because it's dinnertime. And you know what you do at dinner?

JERRY: What?

KRAMER: You "talk about your day." How was your day today? Did you have a good day today or a bad day today? Well, what kind of day was it? Well, I don't know. How about you? How was your day?

JERRY: Boy.

KRAMER: It's sad, Jerry. It's a sad state of affairs.

JERRY: I'm glad we had this talk.

KRAMER: Oh, you have no idea.

In other episodes, George was about to get married but ended up mistakenly killing his fiancée—and was quite happy about it. Jerry dated numerous women who became more gorgeous with each season, but he broke off relationships for a series of inconsequential character flaws (they talked too softly; they wouldn't try a piece of pie; with one, he never knew her name). Elaine had a steady boyfriend, but he was an idiot and that was seemingly the best she could do. In the end, not one of the characters was married, and no children were born or even discussed. It was as if, at the end of a fifty-year sitcom history that began around 1950, the nuclear family ideal had been fully rejected.

Seinfeld was one of the last ratings bonanzas of the network era. In 1998, it earned a 34 rating, pulling other NBC shows up with it and reversing the otherwise daunting downward trend of ratings declines. NBC's lineup of "must see" television comedies was a last spasm of network power; audiences' further moves toward cable and then other streaming services would partially destroy the ecosystem in the first decade of the 2000s and beyond.

Race in the '90s

We will see in chapters 3 and 4 that the dominant major-network sitcoms in the 1990s became less ethnically diverse than they were in the 1980s. Why? Newer broadcast networks were coming online to challenge the "Big Three" (ABC, CBS, and NBC) at the same time as cable channels were increasing in number. Channels such as TBS provided new outlets for sitcoms in reruns, but the new channels tended to fractionalize the audience more. Recognizing that Black and white television tastes could be very different, new broadcast networks such as the WB capitalized on catering to Black market segments with sitcoms featuring Black characters such as *The Wayans Brothers* (1995–99), *The*

Steve Harvey Show (1996–2002), and *The Jamie Foxx Show* (1996–2001). The Fox network had also been pursuing this strategy with shows such as *Living Single* (1993–98) and *Martin* (1992–97). These programs were more likely to feature cultural perspectives that seemed authentic to Black audiences; they were more likely to include references to hip-hop culture, with clothing and music styles that were more appealing: "While the major networks often presented sterile images of black households and characters that were meant to be relatable to mainstream audiences, only FOX had tapped into the energy and aesthetic surrounding hip-hop, which had become a driving force in pop culture at that point. The WB would help fill that void in a big way with programming that not only reflected the vibe of the streets, but embraced the art of the music and the artists that made it" (Brown, 2020).

The segmentation along racial lines was just a small part of what was to come. The idea that a single show could get something like a 30 share of households was fading with *Seinfeld*'s finale, which had over forty million viewers.

The 2000s and Beyond

Figure 2.8 shows that sitcoms were becoming a dwindling share of a dwindling overall network-TV pie. The internet had been burgeoning since the mid-'90s. Early in web history, video viewing was clunky and awkward, requiring some amount of technical expertise to download and view video streams. In the mid 2000s, the internet had started to achieve its real potential against broadcast and cable, with developments such as YouTube, Netflix streaming, and smartphones. Approaching 2020, with tech companies having moved in on both media production and distribution, network television had acquired the feel of being well off the vanguard of where media was going in terms of representing cultural advancement.

Yet networks still pursued the tried-and-true sitcom formats, and some were still influential. *Will & Grace* (1998–2006) became the first sitcom that was focused on gay lifestyles. Other sitcoms had approached the hurdle, including *Love, Sidney* (1981–83), which treated the homosexuality of its lead character in a very elliptical way, or *Ellen* (1984–98), starring Ellen DeGeneres, whose coming out as a lesbian is considered a milestone in gay representation on television. *Will & Grace* was sort of an *I Love Lucy* with a new family structure. Grace lived with her gay friend Will, but they often acted as husband and wife. Sometimes it was not clear who was the husband and who was the wife. Their friends Jack and Karen played the role of the kids, though their childish and irresponsible behavior was beset with sexual promiscuity

Brief History of Situation Comedies

and substance use. The show was consistently in the top twenty through the early 2000s.

Some of the other shows that featured through the 2000s were rolling dice to come up with new family configurations and situations. *King of Queens* (1988–2007) was something of a redo of *The Honeymooners* where an overweight delivery driver tried to keep up with a smart-mouth wife while his live-in father-in-law created issues between the couple. In *Everybody Loves Raymond* (1996–2005), the parents were again a problem, as Raymond and family lived too close to them for his wife's comfort. The "family" of *Two and a Half Men* (2003–15) was a newly single dad living with his degenerate brother in Malibu luxury. *2 Broke Girl$* (2011–17) focused on two waitresses struggling to make it economically in a Brooklyn hipster milieu. Other important shows such as *Parks and Recreation* (2009–15) and even the critically lauded *The Office* (2005–13) were not generally cracking the top thirty as far as ratings due to competition from reality programs and sports events such as NFL games.

Moving through the period, the number of influential sitcoms becomes even smaller. *Modern Family* (2009–20) consciously created an extended family out of all sorts of progressive combinations. The idea was to look at the inter-relationships of three families: nuclear, blended, and same-sex. There was a complicated family tree that interlocked all the characters. Meanwhile, *The Big Bang Theory* (2007–19) revisited the concept of *Friends*: three single men interacting with three single women, except they were science nerds. Worlds collided when sexually awkward men came up against attractive women. In the end, though, as with *Friends*, their general trajectory was toward establishing committed relationships that would possibly lead to nuclear families.

Sitcoms on Other Networks and Platforms

Starting in 2000, there was a renewal of the theme that sitcoms were dead. . . . The current generation of sitcoms has two fundamental problems. The situation, which is mind-numbingly familiar from one show to the next. And the comedy, which not only is a threat to national intelligence but often carries the unfortunate burden of not being funny. Network bosses don't like admitting any of this, but when they start pushing interchangeable sitcoms across the TV grid like checkers, schedule two *Drew Carey Shows* in a week, and renew the likes of *Veronica's Closet* and *Suddenly Susan*, it's clear that not only have the wheels come off the wagon, but they're traveling without a map.[9]

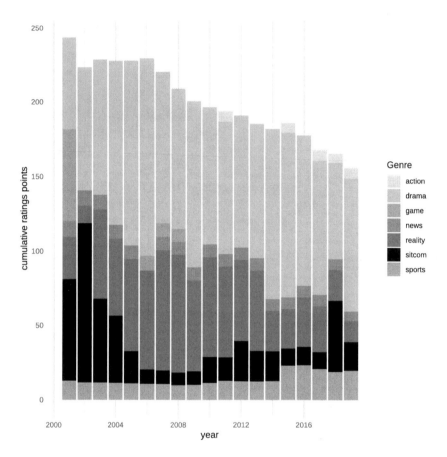

Figure 2.8. Ratings after 2000.

Yet, off the main networks, which were still hobbled by regulation and needed to address at least a somewhat heterogeneous audience, other sitcoms were being developed that pushed the envelope. These included shows such as Larry David's *Curb Your Enthusiasm* (2000–), a new, more improvised style of sitcom that extended the comic personality that had invented *Seinfeld*.

Other TV comedies developed or aired by premium cable services and streamers stretched the idea of the sitcom. For instance, *Schitt's Creek* (2015–20) had been developed in Canada and became extremely popular and award-winning in the US market. In the show, a rich family loses its wealth and must move far downward in social class, but they eventually learn to manage there.

Thanks to all the new scripted shows on various streaming services, viewers now have access to basically the entire sitcom oeuvre. Previously, viewers had been limited to shows that were currently running on the networks or in syndication. The economic model for producing sitcoms was oriented mainly toward syndication, where a show could become truly profitable, recouping the expensive investment that each episode required in its first run. Sitcoms that were very successful in syndication could engrain themselves in the American consciousness. *The Honeymooners*, produced for only one season in its original classic form, earned its legendary status through repeat viewing.

By the 2020s, though, a viewer could get a sense of the entire history of sitcoms if so desired and take any sort of stance whatsoever in their relationship to the American family structure. A sense of progress and change is almost inevitable when comparing early sitcoms to later, but this can also be accompanied by an ironic sense of distance from the whole thing and perhaps a more jaded take from producers on what can be done that is new in the sitcom genre.

Given that there are now more than five hundred scripted shows coming on in any television season,[10] we can find serial comedies all over the map, but they rarely feel like the typical multicamera sitcoms that started with *I Love Lucy*. In our final chapter, we will attempt to come to terms with the future of sitcoms and cultural representation, especially in a period where reckonings on cultural representation seem to have come to every corner of the television world.

The Narrative Arc of Network Sitcoms

Figure 2.9 shows ratings data for sitcoms and other genres on TV networks for the entire period under analysis (1950–2020). The chart helps us divide the trajectory of sitcoms into a few eras corresponding very roughly to decades, so we will speak of them in those terms.

In the 1950s, we see a period of *tradition*. From today's vantage point, we mostly remember this as a time when nuclear family values were being celebrated and TV programmers were assuming common denominators of family experience that would maximize audience. As we saw above, this is an overgeneralization, as many sitcoms did vary from the nuclear family mold. If we assume that *the mold* meant a white family—mom and dad, with about two kids—living in a suburban environment, sitcoms did not in fact fit this model exactly. Lucy was married to a Cuban. *The Honeymooners* lived in urban poverty with no kids. *Mama, Life with Luigi*, and *The Goldbergs* were ethnic families. But the overall energy moving toward middle-American values was palpable. While the shows themselves could have variant or novelty family structures, the mores portrayed within them generally could not stray from a conservative portrait of life that was ultimately much more sanitized than what most families would have been experiencing for real. Words like *pregnant* were not allowed. Husband and wife did not sleep in the same bed. While religious authority was not often mentioned or portrayed in sitcoms, a feeling of general comedic Puritanism was preserved so as not to offend those who would be the most offendable at that time. If Father did not always know best (because a lot of sitcoms featured the "dumb dad" character) then Mother certainly would.

The 1960s represent a rise in the popularity of sitcoms based on a trend toward *escapism*. Whether seeking retreat to the rural Southern settings that were so often featured or to the various magical scenarios that were developed, the vast of majority of sitcoms, especially in the first half of the 1960s, failed to confront cultural reality. Occasionally sitcoms would deal with counter-cultural characters such as hippies, often portraying them as threatening the fabric of community and family. Minority portrayals were extremely rare.

The latter half of the decade did see some very light loosening of cultural restrictions as shows tentatively pushed against cultural boundaries. *The Mon-kees* (1966–68) was a television version of the Beatles, with visual trappings of counterculture and some stilted hippie lingo, but ultimately it was as much a teenybopper phenomenon as its counterpart *The Partridge Family* (1970–74), which arrived in the early 1970s. Rock music in sitcoms was often actually bubblegum pop, and longer hairstyles were always introduced with very cute and clean characters who would be maximally acceptable across audience types. Protest culture was rarely seen in sitcoms except as a joke. During this period, critical energy understandably built up to see sitcoms merely as a bread-and-circus propaganda vehicle for continued consumption, so obvious was their studied refusal to recognize what was, in the words of the Marvin Gaye song, going on.

Most scholars recognize the 1970s as an important turning point in sitcom history—what has been called the *relevance* era. Some individual producers' genius can be credited; Norman Lear is the most salient example. A key fact seems to be that network economics was moving in the direction of focusing on a younger and more urban demographic, with less concern about offending vast swaths of the population. This shift came on the heels of a realization that audience segments were already in place for more adventurous and ultimately realistic situation comedy. The speed with which a show like *All in the Family* was accepted proved this point. While networks saw themselves as addressing America's concerns, America was getting demonstrably more urban, younger, and more ethnically diverse; sitcoms, though lagging behind the cultural

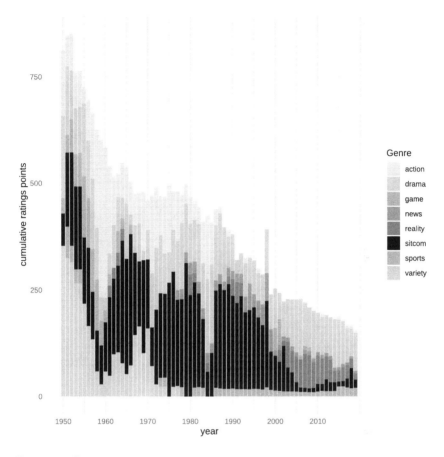

Figure 2.9. Sitcom ratings 1950–2020.

trends, were starting to serve those needs. The 1970s sitcoms were basically catching up with the Sixties, even given that many cultural observers define that era as extending well into years after 1970.

The period was in some ways a first glorious realization of sitcom possibilities, even though there were many features of this era that could also be criticized. While more liberal and progressive visions were being realized, they were still tightly bound within commercial constraints and most often were controlled by white male producers and writers. Many of the productions were redolent of a sense of white male guilt that had been developed in the '60s counterculture. Rock musician Frank Zappa had written (1966), in response to the Watts riots, "Hey, you know something people? I'm not black.

74 SITCOMS AND CULTURE

But there's a whole lotta times I wish I could say I'm not white." The character of Mike Stivic on *All in the Family* represented this view best, though his desire to show his inclusiveness and lack of bigotry would lead to awkward exchanges with Black or minority characters who didn't want their ethnicity to be their defining feature.

As the relevance shows became popular, they also couldn't escape the gravity of their own appeal. *Good Times* fell apart as the character of JJ became such a reminder of minstrel-show tropes that the other main cast members of the show, who wanted a soberer and more respectful portrayal, pulled out. *All in the Family* ran out of issues to address, and the follow-up to the show (*Archie Bunker's Place* [1979–83]) was widely considered to be a failure. The relevance shows that lasted the longest past the '70s were *The Jeffersons* and *M*A*S*H*, which appeared in the top twenty until 1984.

By the end of the relevance era, sitcoms seemed to be dying. But durable narrative forms are difficult to kill. With the success of shows like *Cosby* and *Family Ties*, we can see the 1980s as a decade of *neotraditionalism*. Yuppies were emerging, it was fine to be focused on material progress, and the social concerns of the '60s and '70s were starting to fade into an archaic nostalgia. The departure of *M*A*S*H* from the scene was the end of relevance; programs like *Happy Days* were more obvious indicators of preferences for entertainment that didn't offend or cause too much thought.

The '80s began a period of economic growth and lower inflation and an implied rejection of the idea that seeking wealth was a bad thing. Reverence for opulence appeared quite explicitly on television programs such as *Dallas* and *Dynasty*, which were seen as the defining shows of the era. The neotraditional programs also drew a bit from that well; it was seen as quite normal that most TV families (along with *Cosby* and *Family Ties*, *Growing Pains* [1985–92] is another popular example) were all doing quite well financially without much apparent effort.

As the '80s bled into the '90s, and as the era of network TV was starting to draw to a close, there was an *ironic* period that followed. The popular shows like *Friends* and *Seinfeld* were not traditionalist; they didn't focus on nuclear families. They were more purely focused on comedy and, in some senses, were developed with the idea that no "learning" should occur.[11] Ironic detachment was a much more commonly held cultural outlook by the '90s, perhaps an outcome or reflection of the fact that demonstrating sincere commitment through social institutions like marriage and childbirth was also becoming

Brief History of Situation Comedies

less common. *Cheers*, an '80s show that bled into the '90s, added to the roster of characters who were unlikely to admit sincere love or commitment, or to do so only grudgingly and very occasionally:

DIANE: Sam, if you'll admit that you are carrying a little torch for me, I'll admit that I'm carrying a little one for you.
SAM: [tentatively] Well, I am carrying a little torch for you.
DIANE: Well, I'm not carrying one for you.[12]

The '90s also saw sitcoms reaching maturity as a television form, perhaps not surprising after fifty years of development. Any successful individual sitcom will face the fact that ideas and situations start to dry up after some time. Most sitcoms were failures after one season or even a partial season. Those that managed to catch the whirlwind and last for multiple years would face an increasingly tough challenge to develop new story ideas without pushing the series into weird territory, sometimes described as "jumping the shark" (after the episode of *Happy Days* where Fonzie jumped over a shark in one of the more ridiculous story ideas). The genre as a whole now faced the challenge of individual shows. *Seinfeld*'s response was to have a show "about nothing," much as a modern artist would tire of the genre's conventions, break all the rules, and simply blow up the genre. The question is, what comes after that?

We deal more with the era after 2000 in our last chapter. Sitcoms, not to mention the idea of television itself, are changing greatly. Perhaps we can tentatively identify this as an *irrelevance* era. The idea of a sitcom is partially predicated on the idea of a network schedule that is rigid, that recurs every week, and to which people return comfortably as a matter of habit. As on-demand and binge viewing become more commonplace, the idea of binging/cycling through seasons of family-based sitcoms seems less enticing. While there are still work- and family-based comedies that are popular, they are seen by fewer people than was common in the network days, and they are made with production conventions that differ from those that were established in the 1950s and carried through for fifty-plus years.

Thus, while the death of the sitcom has been pronounced at various times, only for the genre to be revived, it is useful to see the years 1950 to 2000 as a sitcom life cycle that is worth looking at as complete, with a period of birth, growth, and senescence that is also relevant to the social trends we look at in the rest of this volume. As we prepare for these analyses, we next look at how other scholars have examined sitcoms' impacts.

NOTES

1. Episode descriptions from IMDB.

2. This Jack Benny episode from 1939 was accessed at Generic Radio Workshop (n.d.).

3. Newhart has said that he was not influenced by Benny, but at other times he did explicitly recognize the teaching: "He would give away the biggest and funniest lines to others. He would let other people have jokes. . . . Somehow that generosity ended up creating a show that's so much better and funnier than all other shows" (Rosenthal 2018).

4. "Cosby was a regular guest on Cavett's show in those days, but this night was special because he was on with Jack Benny. Jack Benny, whom he had first heard on the radio when he was a boy in the projects! Jack Benny, whom he had watched on TV as a teenager to learn the art of comic timing! He had so much respect for Benny that when Cavett brought him on, he didn't even try to needle the host the way he usually did, because he didn't want to compete with his hero. 'You haven't picked on me this time,' Cavett remarked. 'No, because Jack is here,' Cosby replied. 'He did you in pretty good.'" See Whitaker (2014).

5. Although, the NAACP did threaten a boycott of *Hazel* if a Black person was not added to the production staff.

6. An interesting sidenote: Smith also found that Americans' attitudes about crime became more *conservative* from 1945 to 1985. He saw this as a response to rising crime rates. Of course, television programs played their own role in perceptions of crime; this function became the main focus of the Cultural Indicators project. For sitcoms, though, crime is normally a secondary issue, if it is dealt with at all.

7. It had a 50+ rating, which was the highest ever at the time.

8. A joke from *Friends* (S5E12): "I strongly believe that we should support President Clinton . . . and her husband Bill."

9. Katz (1999).

10. Schneider (2022).

11. It was Larry David's intention that no "hugging" or "learning" should occur on *Seinfeld*. One gets the impression that any demonstration of sincerity would have been offensive to his tastes.

12. *Cheers*, S1E17.

Chapter 3 Frontis. Desi Arnaz and Lucille Ball invented techniques for modern TV production. *I Love Lucy* was the most popular sitcom of the '50s.

3

"Sitlit"

Sitcoms and Their Images, Content, and Effects

MOST SITCOMS ARE ABOUT families; that much is evident. Those that aren't are usually set in work situations in which the coworkers function as a secondary surrogate family, often seen as being more important than the characters' real families. The few sitcoms that are left over deal with miscellaneous fantastic situations (such as *Gilligan's Island* [1964–67]), and even in these, the characters end up relating to each other in quasi-family relationships. Thus, if a sitcom could be expected to tell us about anything, it would be the structure and function of the family.

Sociologists and others have been identifying trends in family structure since the beginnings of empirical social science; also, they have been frequently disagreeing. A major theme is that in the 1800s, the family developed into a sphere of life separate from the spheres of public life and work, meant to function as a haven for the male breadwinner, nurtured by a maternal figure who provides a space of respite and retreat (Lasch, 1977). Spigel (1992) identified the role of early television (1949–55) in shaping the introduction of TV technology to fit into this family structure, both technologically and in terms of its content. In this system, television is a companion for the woman who takes care of the house through the day and then a hearth around which the ever-closing family circle can gather. A nuclear family structure is assumed.

Research on television's impact on beliefs about the family and its depiction of families is prolific. Families can be portrayed in genres other than sitcoms, of course, but sitcoms often seem to get the lion's share of attention in research about televised families. If we cherry-pick a few contrastive data points (comparing, say, *Leave it to Beaver* [1957–63] to *Roseanne*) as a way to assess sitcom depictions and their role in social change, we might conclude that sitcoms have been a vital part of social progress, but empirical analyses often yield results that are more complex.

The metanarrative guiding most research and analysis about sitcoms starts with an assumed traditional structure of a nuclear family, with father as decision-maker, mother as homemaker, and two to three children born within that marriage. The structure is assumed to be largely affiliative, a setting within which individual problems are solved with parental guidance and adherence, in the end, to community norms. These families get along, they work within a fairly conservative set of "family values," and they move toward the same goals. The communities they represent are harmonious, and we can assume that other families within the same community look much the same. The metanarrative further assumes that this structure was dominant in the '50s and into the '60s, that it started to be challenged more in the '70s, and then it tends to collapse after that. This received narrative about sitcoms is true in some aspects, misleading in others.

At least two sociological conceptions of the nuclear family can be mentioned. A frequent take is on the dysfunction of the nuclear family, with its disconnection from larger support networks that could have been provided by an extended family (Sussman, 1958), its contribution to social isolation and anomie (Parsons, 1955; Yamane & Nonoyama, 1967), its subjection to capitalist modes of production (Engels, 2021), its contribution to environmental waste, and its links with suburban malaise: "Especially acute are some of the results of detaching people from the extended family of three generations or more, and throwing them together with strangers who come equally uprooted; for in many of these types of suburbs such extended families are completely non-existent" (Gruenberg, 1955, p. 133).

Sociologists such as Tönnies (1887) cemented in the academic imagination the idea that industrialization, specialization, and modernization led the Western world away from community-oriented forms of social organization (*gemeinschaft*) toward more corporative forms (*gesellschaft*). Those same three trends were emphasized by De Fleur in his classic textbook treatment of mass communication theory (Lowery & De Fleur, 1988), which sees mass society (and the communication patterns that come with it) as finalizing the transition from community experience, especially within the family, to more individualistic and nuclear experiences. A whole host of the supposed ills that spring from mass communication came out of this approach. Most of the time, when we hear about nuclear families in communication or media effects research, we are hearing critiques.

There is, however, a different take on the nuclear family that is a rejection or revision of the classical sociological idea that the nuclear family was created by industrialization. In the English-speaking world, nuclear forms of family pre-date industrialization, and references to these forms can be found as far back as the Bible. Some theorists have come to see the nuclear family as something like the preferred biological form, with the prevalence of extended families being due to other kinds of economic pressures. As Smith (1993) argues, "A strange mixture of Germanic customs and Christianity introduced a chance mutation into the course of human history. This individualistic mutant led to late marriage, low fertility and an age structure favorable to economic growth, capitalism, and eventually the first industrial revolution" (p. 346).

Possibly, the nuclear family created capitalism, not the other way around. Sociobiological conceptions, such as those offered by Wilson (1978), see the nuclear family form as one way of being evolutionarily adaptive, creating altruistic forms of social organization that are most likely to perpetuate genetic advantage across evolutionary timescales. Shorter (1975) synthesizes these two approaches to some degree:

> In earlier writings on the history of the family, sociologists acquired the bad habit of assuming that families before the Industrial Revolution were organized in clans or were at least highly "extended." Because any historian with even a passing familiarity with Europe's social history would realize at once the inaccuracy of that assumption, a revisionist reaction developed in the 1960s: the nuclear family was "unearthed" time and again in history, to the accompaniment of loud shouts of discovery. As often happens to revisionists, these writers fell over backwards attempting to overturn the conventional wisdom instead of merely correcting the sociologists' fantasies about clans and sprawling patriarchies, they tended to proclaim that at most times and places it was the conjugal family—mother, father, children, and servants—that had prevailed. The revisionists thus proceeded to create a little fantasy of their own: the nuclear family as a historical constant. (pp. 29–30)

History reveals that there have always been different ways of organizing family structure, a finding that anthropology would obviously confirm as well. Shorter does note, though, that nuclear structures were especially common in England and then in the United States. Yet the idea of an affiliative

Family Structure Realities

"extended" family, with Grandma and Grandpa and uncles and aunts living under the same roof, remains a romantic conception that was arguably encouraged by media portrayals, especially of "ethnic" families. As we will see below, a few sitcoms played an important part in the early romanticization of the extended family, even as they were preparing to pivot toward glamorization of the nuclear family in the 1950s.

Family Structure Realities

Working from US data, there are different ways to assess how many actual families were nuclear (or nuclear-ish) in the beginning years of sitcoms; two key figures are divorce rates and numbers of children living with two parents. In figure 3.1, we look at divorce and marriage choices. Around 1950, very small percentages of men and women were divorced (close to 2 percent, as shown in the figure). There were strong religious and cultural taboos against divorce that persisted into the immediate postwar period.

At any given time in the 1950s, about 20 percent of women had never been married; the number was 25 percent for men. Census data shown in the figure depict that both rates started moving upward in the 1960s. Among the population fifteen years of age and older, divorce rates were doubling quickly, plateauing eventually around 1990 at 10 percent for women. The rates of those who had never been married also started moving upward in 1960 and have never really leveled off at all. Marriage was becoming less of an option for people, meaning that, de facto, more families would exist in a nonmarried state.

Still, television's presumed early preference for nuclear families, apart from the idea, common in media criticism, that TV was serving an ideological purpose for industrial overlords, may have simply been gratifying majority desires in its audiences. Early surveys, predating television, show that ideals of nuclear family life were well entrenched. A 1936 Gallup survey found that people thought two to three children was the ideal family size.[1] A British survey in 1939, assuming the presence of a husband and wife in an "ideal" family, found clear preference for two children.[2] Even as late as 2012, families were still saying that 2 children were the best configuration.[3] Single-child families often encountered queries about when they would have more; the popular conception of the "only child" suggested certain pathologies that were likely to emerge for that child in adulthood (Falbo & Polit, 1986).

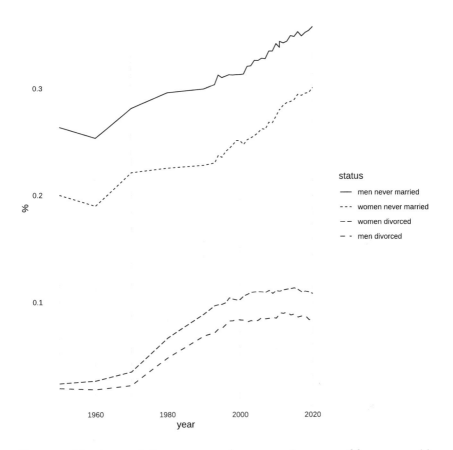

Figure 3.1. Marriage and divorce status of women and men over fifteen years old, 1950–2020.

Despite the public opinion preference for more than one child, sitcoms had no problem featuring only children. Often this was due simply to the fact that a sitcom can carry only so many characters, and sometimes there may be room for only one child. Well-known examples of only children in sitcoms included Little Ricky on *I Love Lucy*, Opie on *The Andy Griffith Show*, and Richie on *The Dick Van Dyke Show*. In these cases, the child was more of a flavoring to the adult-oriented plots. Other examples such as *Julia* or *The Courtship of Eddie's Father* (1969–72) were more interesting because the only-child theme was meant to add a certain sweetness/sadness to the comedy. In both of these

84 · SITCOMS AND CULTURE

latter cases, there was also commentary meant to approve of nontraditional, single-parent family structures: "We're OK too."[4] Even with these examples, it remains more common that sitcoms that explicitly identified as "family" shows usually had more than one child, but we will see below that sitcoms are less focused on children than one would think.

In the US, two measures of family size can give us some idea of realities that sitcoms were referring to. In the census, *family* refers to "a group of two people or more (one of whom is the householder) related by birth, marriage, or adoption and residing together; all such people (including related subfamily members) are considered as members of one family."[5] Comparatively, a *household* "includes all the persons who occupy a housing unit as their usual place of residence. A housing unit is a house, an apartment, a mobile home, a group of rooms, or a single room that is occupied (or if vacant, is intended for occupancy) as separate living quarters."[6] Obviously, then, households can include nonrelated individuals who are living together whereas families must be related in some way.

In the US, a consistent trend has been a decrease in the size of both families and households. Families living together decreased in size from an average of over 3.75 people in 1960 to under 3.25 now (see fig. 3.2). Households, which include people who live singly but also with nonrelated individuals, are now much under 3 people on average. These trends represent a variety of phenomena that we might expect to see represented in sitcoms, including a decline in fertility, an increase in age at first marriage, decreasing marriage rates, and so on. Also, it is more likely that children are living in households with only one parent or, sometimes, no parents at all. Figure 3.3 shows the percentage of children living in such arrangements, which has gone from under 15 percent in 1960 to around 30 percent in recent years.

Clearly, then, families and living arrangements have been changing in terms of structure. Much of this change happened from 1960 to 1990, but some of it still continues. From a nuclear norm of two parents and two-plus kids, it is the case empirically that other kinds of structures are becoming more common. Single-parent families are seen more; it is less common for people to be married, and families are having fewer children. Perhaps the most telling statistic for what families of the future will look like is that of the US fertility rate, which is at 1.78 births per woman in 2024. That is well below the theoretical "replacement rate" of 2 and well below the 1960 rate, which was 3.65.[7]

Yet, much television attention, even now, is still focused on the nuclear family. Even shows that are focused on nontraditional families are usually nuclear

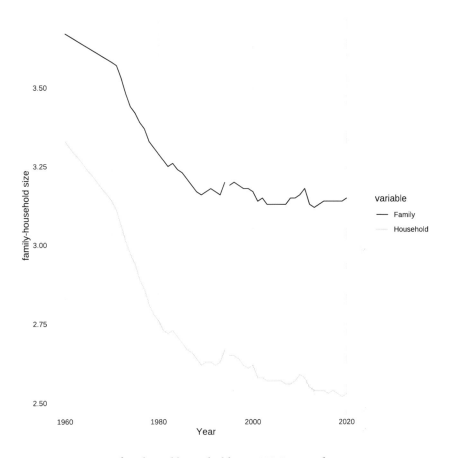

Figure 3.2. Average family and household size, US Census data.

in structure in the sense that they show how nontraditional families perform the same kinds of functions that 1950s families did. On television, we may be dealing more with *aspirational* notions of family structure that will appeal to viewers. Demographers recognize that desired family size does not always correspond to actual or achieved family size and that there may be differences between hoped-for ideals and what ends up being the reality. Also, there are tensions between what families hope to be and what economics permits them to be. Stresses on middle-class individuals since the 1980s have made it harder to sustain large families, even as immigration brings new populations that are likely to have higher birth rates.

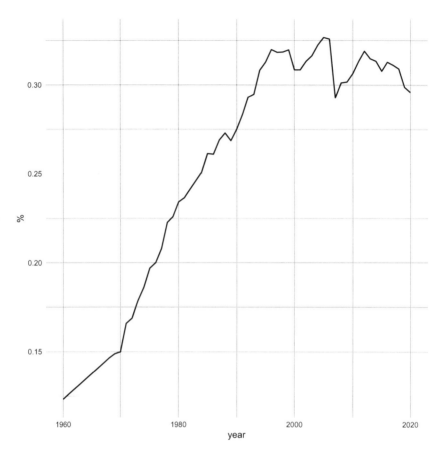

Figure 3.3. Percentage of children living in household with fewer than two parents.

1950s *Non*-nuclear Sitcom Families

Sitcoms are one place for all of this to play out culturally. While it is tempting to see sitcoms reflecting family change in a linear way, the real story is somewhat more complicated. Some of the most successful early sitcoms (pre-1960) showed that television was playing quite freely with family structure and that audiences were accepting family structure novelty as part of their entertainment package.

For the first part of the long run of *I Love Lucy*, the key family members were Lucy and Ricky, Fred and Ethel. Both couples were childless at the start. The series was one of the first with a classic four-character structure, which would become rather common in sitcoms. Because sitcoms often reflect an ideal nuclear family structure, even shows without the classic nuclear family *members* (Mom, Dad, kids) often have people fulfilling nuclear family *roles*. In *Lucy*, there is a child-role player (Lucy, also the protagonist) who needs guidance. The main character often has a best friend, in this case Ethel. Ricky plays the beleaguered father role, with Fred Mertz as an auxiliary parent (in a somewhat desexed aspect, if not as an actual mother figure).

Later, of course, anticipation around Lucy's pregnancy was an example of an early television blockbuster, and it became an example of how specific episodes could loosen taboos around something like pregnancy. After Lucy's child was born, a series of episodes did feature what was happening with Little Ricky (an actual child rather than someone simply acting childishly), but the integrity of the four-character structure was not really challenged or changed. As the show continued later into its run, the foursome had adventures as a quasi-family collective, including traveling to California and then moving to Connecticut, away from the closed quarters of the New York apartment. While the nuclear family structure was endorsed, it was not really the main message of the show. The two couples were the *real* family throughout. Two unrelated couples could be a family.

Within that show, the dramatic tension was focused on male-female conflict. Lucy's ambitions to leave the house and join Ricky's showbiz career were the constant theme, which were ever-thwarted by Ricky and Fred. Women schemed against men. These battles of the sexes were typical dramatic models for other sitcoms (the Burns and Allen show would be another example). In the *Lucy* template, the dad (husband) was all-knowing; he would eventually win every battle. His male friend always helped him. But viewer sympathy and affiliation went to the woman. She was the star; she did not play the straight man in the comedy duo. At the end of each battle, male dominance was reasserted, but it was a loving one in which the male assumed not just the privilege to rule but the responsibilities that went with it. With *Lucy*, as with many other sitcoms, the programs were primarily about feminine concerns, even when one sex was placed above the the other in terms of power dynamics.

A different four-character, male-female structure is found in *The Honeymooners*. Again, there are two childless couples. The hero (Ralph Kramden) is the childlike figure needing guidance; he has a best friend (Ed Norton) to assist with misadventures that lead to lessons. The most responsible parent figure is Ralph's wife, Alice, and she gets best-friend assistance from Ed's wife, Trixie. Ralph is nominally the father figure, but he is also one of the first of

88   SITCOMS AND CULTURE

many bumbling male sitcom figures. He pretended to act with male power, but he was ineffective and always gave up in the end. Alice played a more matriarchal role. A father-guide character was not present. Children were never needed in the show as Ralph and Norton both behaved like children needing correction. It is hard to imagine the portrayed Ralph Kramden as the father to anyone. The down-and-out characterization of the family fortune was also a comment on the fact that they could not afford children. In the battles between Ralph and Alice, the male misfortunes played to the domestic concern about what happens when the man is an ineffective provider. It was also an early example of how working-class males in sitcoms—unlike the talented Ricky in *Lucy*—were often portrayed as ineffective and of low intelligence (later examples such as *The King of Queens*, also about a childless couple in an urban setting, are quite parallel in structure to *The Honeymooners*, even to the point of the overweight male lead).

There was only one season of *The Honeymooners* in half-hour sitcom form, but it lived on seemingly immortally in reruns. In these episodes, the nuclear family of two childless couples struggling to survive in dingy apartments belies the notion that TV always glorified the suburban nuclear family. In some ways, it started out quite differently, perhaps exemplifying that working-class struggles could be both comedic but also soothing to those undergoing the same experiences. Also, the fact that sitcoms were often written by people coming out of New York urban backgrounds with vaudeville and nightclub sensibilities meant that writers would be likely to mine those experiences.

There was no doubt, though, that many real families were *aspiring* to move toward the suburban dream. Apart from the idea that the suburban ideal was somehow manufactured by media through an induction of false consciousness, suburbs offered materially better living conditions. Lucy and Ricky eventually left their urban apartment for greener Connecticut pastures. A sitcom such as *The Golbergs* began as a successful radio exploration of urban Jewish life and was one of the very first hit TV sitcoms. Here, the structure was originally an extended family emphasizing the ethnic form. As it moved into its later years, the matriarchally managed Goldbergs also moved to the suburbs, mimicking what many urban Jewish families were doing when they could. Maintaining an ethnic and religious identity became a theme of the show. It's worth pointing out that *The Goldbergs* was the brainchild of a woman producer/writer who continued the show from its radio origins well into the early television era, even surviving Red Scare attacks on some of its stars. Another popular early ethnic sitcom, *Mama*, focusing on a Norwegian family in San Francisco, was based on a book by a female author (Forbes, 1943). In an era in which broadcast entertainment was absolutely dominated by men, these women's successes marked sitcoms as a place where the concerns of women would be addressed and where perceptions of changes in family roles would be most noted across the development of television programming.

The abovementioned shows depicted family structures *from which* people were moving as they pursued economic opportunity and family stability away from the core urban areas. Families were identified in terms of their ability to provide interpersonal cohesion amid social dislocation, adhering more to the ethos that family structure can exist almost anywhere—and that it is often the challenge of the woman to provide that structure. Lucy's heroic comedic appeal was her boldness, and of course her comedic talent that carried the show. Ralph's appeal was that he was always faithful in the end, and the family would struggle on even under harsh conditions. *The Goldbergs'* extended-family values could persist anywhere, even in a move to the suburbs.

Nuclear Sitcom Families

As some of the earliest hits were setting a depicted family ground *from which* to move, other sitcoms were indicating *to where* families were going. They were also indicating that media producers, encouraging freer consumption in a booming postwar market, were sending families where they could do the most good as markets for consumer goods. These families were more likely to be nuclear in structure, but even in the classics that we remember as the archetype of the 1950s suburban ideal, there were differences.

Early family sitcoms have been well analyzed in terms of their relation to the political and social culture of the 1950s. No program was more orthodox in its conservative approach to a dad-dominated suburban nuclear family than *Father Knows Best*. This show had begun on radio; by the time it became popular on TV, it was solid propaganda for Middle America: "The sitcom relentlessly pursues social and political issues with a friendly, confident, authoritarian zeal that gives contemporary viewers of diverse political orientations much to think about. The Anderson Springfield America is so white, so Anglo-Saxon and so Protestant that even their seemingly Hispanic gardener goes by the name of Frank Smith!" (Marc, 1997, p. 46).

The Springfield of *Father Knows Best* was never specifically located, though the assumption was always that it was in the Midwest.[8] The show was well thought of in conservative political circles, so much so that an episode was produced with the Treasury Department called "24 Hours in Tyrant Land," depicting a Springfield under Communist rule. More typically, episodes solved minor kid problems, usually with a moralizing component. In "Close Decision" (S1E26) from 1955, "Margaret is upset that Bud is not doing his chores lately. Bud wants to go play in a baseball game, but Margaret puts her foot down and says he must rake the leaves first. When Jim finds out that the team is losing, he sneaks Bud out to go play. The team almost wins, but in the final play of the game there is a question of whether Bud tagged the player out at home. Admitting he didn't tag the player costs them the game, but he gains the respect of many for telling the truth."[9]

In the 1950s, other shows like *Leave It to Beaver* and *The Donna Reed Show* shared the same aesthetic, though perhaps not to the same degree. These types of family-friendly mini-dramas proved to be potent ratings gatherers for sitcoms, as would be seen in later examples such as *The Brady Bunch* in the '70s and *Cosby* in the '80s. Variants that might have been called *Mother Knows Best* also could have worked, such as in *The Partridge Family*, where a fatherless bunch of kids was guided by a wise mom.

The Four-Person Sitcom

A situation comedy, because it is intended to be repeated, must come up with a premise that defines (or is) the situation. Apart from the premise, the next-most important factor is: Who will be the main characters? Though every sitcom will have different characters who come in and out for each episode, a few of them recurring, there obviously needs to be a standard cast that reflects the reality of the premise, with whom viewers can identify over the course of the show. Most shows, as we have seen, are based on family structures. If sitcom families are, as we expect them to be, somewhat faithful to the family structures that one sees in reality, one would expect their sizes to be roughly comparable.

Many of the most important examples, and those that were often popular, were nontraditional families struggling to remain nuclear. In this sense, *nuclear* means serving as the protective haven as Lasch (1977) defined it. But especially from the '60s onward, family structure was being openly played with to create novelty and dramatic tension. Single fathers were the most common vehicle. The mother was often missing for some unspecified reason (divorce was usually not mentioned). In the *Andy Griffith Show*, the single father got help from a matronly aunt; together they raised an only child. Because Andy had a coworker who acted childishly (Barney), we essentially had the typical Dad-Mom-two-kid arrangement that was definitional of the nuclear family. Other single-dad show examples from the '60s include *My Three Sons* (1960–72) and *Gidget* (1965–66).

A lot of shows tend to group around four or five main characters.[10] Fast-forwarding a bit in our narrative, *Seinfeld* is one of the best examples of the common four-person structure. It depicts the adventures of four friends, each of whom plays a kind of role that is very common in sitcoms. The characters very much function as a family, though their resistance against traditional concepts of family (getting married, having children) is a major theme of the show. An important lesson of the series might be that when your real family is dysfunctional, a surrogate family will emerge. But that one might be dysfunctional too.

The show emerged from the stand-up comedy routines of Jerry Seinfeld. Though he played a professional comic on the show, Seinfeld was often the straight man to his three partners. Elaine was his female friend, though they once dated. George was his best friend, as he had been since high school. Kramer was the "wacky neighbor," always coming over unannounced and borrowing things from Jerry. The characters' interactions were daily, such that they formed a de facto family, with Jerry as the father-figure head of it.

How do the roles break down in terms of family structure? One of Jerry's functions was to be the centered, successful, and solid person around whom the foibles and travails of the other characters percolated. He was the surrogate father. We see this on many other sitcoms (*The Bob Newhart Show* would be an example, with an imperturbably deadpan Newhart doing slow takes to a cast of dysfunctional characters around him). Jerry tolerated the other characters out of friendship, but of course always with exasperation. Their success often depended on and rotated around him.

Elaine was a quasi-wife figure, though she honored it in the breach, always dating a new guy, not exhibiting too many maternal characteristics. She presented an interesting evolution in sitcom characterology by playing a female best friend to a male, much against the observation from the movie *When Harry Met Sally* that such friendships are impossible.[11] Elaine occasionally came near a sexual renewal with Jerry, and there was even some talk that they could be married someday, but it never happened. But she was the closest thing to a mother that the three guys would get in their surrogate family, perhaps an inevitability for the one female in the gang of four.

George, the best friend, also existed as a kind of wife figure for Jerry. In some ways, his crackpot ideas and schemes were similar to those in *I Love Lucy*, with Jerry playing the Ricky role, always needing to pull George back from the brink of disaster. George would always faithfully serve Jerry, though, and Jerry would remain true. Sitcoms are, of course, replete with these types of best-friend relationships, with roots and antecedents in comic characters who help heroes such as Sancho Panza in *Don Quixote*. Such a friend, servant, or helper will in some ways be the opposite of the hero character, and in male-male friendship relationships, there can be an extent to which the friend assumes a more feminine role.[12] Finally, Kramer was the (adult[13]) child, someone even George and Elaine, with all their problems, could play an advisor role to. To the extent that situation comedy is often a carnivalesque reversal of the normal order of things (Bakhtin, 1984), characters such as Kramer show what happens when all normal impulses (to have jobs, to have relationships) are dispensed with.

We might argue that the nuclear family, and the struggles to define what it is or should be, are common across the entire history of sitcoms, leading to many variants around the four-person structure. Other examples of the structure that have replicated nuclear families without actually being traditional nuclear families are:

All in the Family: Archie, dad; Edith, mom; Mike and Gloria the (adult) kids—or is it the reverse?

The Andy Griffith Show: Andy, the dad; Aunt Bee, the mom; Opie and Barney, the kids.

The Monkees: Mike, a phlegmatic dad; Mickey, a more nurturing mom figure; David and Peter, children.

The Bob Newhart Show: Bob, the dad; Emily, the mom; Howard, the (next-door neighbor) adult child; Jerry, Bob's colleague who refused to grow up and needed fatherly advice from Bob.

Sex and the City (1998–2004): Carrie was the most responsible—a parent figure. Miranda also took a more responsible parent role. Samantha and Charlotte featured as characters that seemed to need more guidance.

Two and a Half Men: Alan, the dad; Berta, the housekeeper/mother (but she wore the pants); Charlie and Jake were the kids who needed control.

The Golden Girls: Dorothy, the dad; Sophia, the mom; Rose and Blanche, the children.

Is the four-person structure inevitable or ideal? Of course not. Ensemble sitcoms with more than four or five main characters have worked well. *Friends* and *The Big Bang Theory* showed that six or seven equal characters could work well, especially when focused on younger-generation individuals pursuing new family structures. Workplace comedies such as *Mary Tyler Moore* or

Cheers also often need more than four main characters, as they become en-semble shows.

Family Structure Portrayals in the Media

There are numerous studies examining content patterns in media as a way to study American family structure over the years. Not all of it looks at sitcoms, but because family portrayal is the major theme of sitcoms, it is useful to review the research before we look at empirical patterns derived from data.

Much research centers around power distribution in families, along with family structures. Lantz et al. (1968) examined the power distribution of fam-ily portrayals in New England magazines during the colonial period. He found that males were accorded what he called "general" power in these portrayals, but females had considerable "subtle" forms of power that could be exerted in family domains such as courtship and finances. In the courtship area, most portrayals emphasized that women had "veto" power over men, who in turn could choose to make courtship advances. In regard to finances, once married, women often exerted control over resource allocation decisions in families. These themes are not uncommon in sitcoms, where women control household decisions, often against dads or other men who are seen to be making unwise or impetuous decisions.

Advertisements are like sitcoms in that they are a mass-produced media artifact with lots of attachment to and relevance for family imagery. Brown (1982) saw ads mostly as reflecting cultural values rather than influencing them toward change. His study of "intimacy" in magazine ads found that men and women in romantic or family relations were found to be gradually pictured closer to each in a study period extending from 1920 to 1977. He saw this as an increase in family intimacy, presumably connected with a more romantic notion of married life. It's also consistent with the idea of the family developing as a protected space away from public life. Other relationships, like father-daughter and mother-son, showed no consistent changes. Husband and wife intimacy was seen as being lowest during the family stages, during which the couple had children at home.

On television, as we have already seen, families initially were mostly shown in sitcoms, and they were often, though not always, traditional in nature. Butsch's work (Butsch, 2000; Glennon & Butsch, 1982) documents class portrayals in television, with sitcoms most often favoring middle-class fami-lies over working-class ones. In the fewer shows where working-class fami-lies are portrayed, male characters are shown as buffoonish and inept (*The*

Honeymooners, The Simpsons), needing their wives to get them out of scrapes. Conversely, in middle-class shows (*Father Knows Best*), fathers are competent and generally are equal partners with their wives. Middle-class status often seems to go with material status that seems *higher* than middle-class (lavish homes and apartments, ability to afford servants, etc.). Even in later shows such as *Friends*, where the characters were often working in jobs that were lower middle class at best, their material surroundings were much more luxurious than what they would have been able to afford in New York City. These portrayals are seen as derogating working-class lifestyles in the service of television's drive for middle-class acceptability and profit generation.

Scharrer (2001) tested some of these ideas empirically, with analyses of sitcoms from the '50s to the '90s. She found that sitcoms tended to increase their negative portrayals of fathers over the years. She surmised that this was due to the increasing role of women in the workforce, which was depriving males of some of their presumed superiority over women in the family situation, as men lost the breadwinner role. Scharrer also confirmed that men were portrayed more buffoonishly when the family in the sitcom was lower-class, supporting Butsch's analysis.

Moore (1992) looked at family portrayals on TV from 1947 to 1990, the majority of which were situation comedies. He found that 63 percent of the shows were "conventional" families (couples with or without children). The rest were single-parent families or "contrived." Almost 90 percent of the families were seen as being middle class or higher. Percentages of nonconventional families did increase greatly from the '50s to the '80s, such that by the '80s, there was an even split between conventional and nonconventional. Moore noted that male roles tended to be numerically exaggerated in the nonconventional families, ignoring the demographic reality of the situation, which was more often the case of a single mom.

Thomas and Callahan (1982) compared TV families from lower-class and middle-class backgrounds in terms of their "happiness." Again, the majority of family programs analyzed were in fact sitcoms. Programs were coded on how affiliative family members were with each other, how problems were resolved, and the qualities of characters in the portrayed families. They found that lower-class families were *happier* overall than middle-class families. They concluded that lower-class satisfaction could be seen as part of a general scheme in which television supports status quo political and economic arrangements, such that viewers would be happier with lower levels of attainment.

Larson (1991) studied sibling interactions in typical sitcoms from the '50s (such as *Leave It to Beaver*) and compared them to sibling interactions portrayed in 1980s sitcoms (such as *Cosby*). She hypothesized that interactions would be more conflictual in the '80s and that the '50s sitcoms would portray an overly idealized version of family life. She supported that hypothesis and also found that there were fewer examples of affiliative and identifying behavior directed between siblings in the 1950s (siblings did not perform "services" for each other). Siblings in 1950s sitcoms were seen as more positive but not really performing functions for the family. Siblings in the '80s were seen as less positive toward each other but also playing more of a role in the families that were depicted.

Douglas and Olson (1995; also see Olson & Douglas, 1997) examined the idea that families had become more conflictual from the 1950s to the 1980s. They were thinking about typical comparisons that people would make between a show such as *Father Knows Best* and *The Simpsons* or *Roseanne*. Their data—in which coders evaluated episodes selected from four TV sitcoms in generations roughly corresponding to the '50s, '60s, '70s, and '80s—yielded a more complex conclusion. The family did not become uniformly less functional across the years, as some were quite harmonious in the 1980s (*Cosby*, for instance), and there were dysfunctional ones in the 1950s (*The Honeymooners*). They did find change, though, particularly in husband-wife relations (becoming more "expressive" and "receptive" across time), and they also noted the more dysfunctional portrayal of the working-class family in all generations.

Women in Sitcoms

There is voluminous media research on the representation of women on TV. Not all of it focuses on sitcoms specifically, but even research that looks at TV in general is in fact focusing on sitcoms because sitcoms form so much of the body of content. As we will see in chapter 4, much of this research was conducted from a cultural indicators perspective. We will present our own detailed empirical analysis of the issue for sitcoms in that chapter. Here, we review a variety of other studies that have provided a critical take on the representation of women in sitcoms.

Most research examining portrayals of women in sitcoms starts from a critical perspective, assuming two things: (1) that TV marginalizes women's roles in a variety of ways, but (2) that there are individual sitcoms that buck these trends, even as the genre itself slowly moves in a more progressive direction.

96 SITCOMS AND CULTURE

As always, the true picture is muddied. A desire to focus on the well-known "liberating" sitcoms is the first tendency. Conclusions drawn from those salient sitcoms are sometimes overturned when we look at the larger data picture. Among sitcoms that were in the network top twenty from 1950 to 2019, 117 (25 percent) were female-led, meaning that a female was the main star or the show was named after her (see table 3.1). Of the rest, 219 were male-led (47.8 percent), reflecting typical male-female imbalances that have been seen in much TV programming over the years. The remaining 122 programs were mixed in terms of lead, such as in family-oriented programs where there was no clear star or where there was an ensemble cast. The table shows the female-led programs ordered by total ratings points that the program gathered over the years. There is a bias toward earlier programs because overall ratings were higher in those years.

The table shows that many of the portrayals can be considered traditional (in the judgment of this author), but they do not necessarily involve housewife portrayals. When women are singled out to lead shows, it is often *not* in housewife roles but in other contexts that are considered more novel. The widow character is seen frequently. Early on, situations where single women would not have been out of place (secretary, teacher, maid) were used to allow women to be leads while staying within a traditional framework. Later, it became acceptable to show divorced characters. No doubt there was some thought that audiences would be more interested in plot ideas that were not quotidian, given the obvious escapist entertainment angle that many sitcoms were taking.

Of the top fifteen shows portrayed, roughly half were nontraditional roles for women in some way. We've already reviewed what most critics see as the most important one, *Mary Tyler Moore*. Others such as *One Day at a Time*, *Maude*, and *Alice* were specifically political responses to the women's liberation movement.

Reactions to *Maude* provide an interesting example of media criticism on the topic of women's portrayals in sitcoms. The character of Maude was devised as a brassy, assertive, somewhat older woman; she was very different from the stereotypical sitcom mom. Perhaps most unusual was that she was a political activist supporting a variety of progressive/liberal causes. She was the anti–Archie Bunker—in fact, *Maude* was a Norman Lear spin-off of *All in the Family*. In the most noted episode, Maude found that she was unexpectedly pregnant at age forty-seven; she decided to have an abortion. The program was successful in the ratings, but later reruns were boycotted by the Catholic Church and some advertisers.

Table 3.1. Female-led sitcoms

Program	Total Ratings	Lead role	Role type
I Love Lucy	374.9	Housewife	Traditional
One Day at a Time	177.2	Single mom	Nontraditional
The Lucy Show	165.4	Widow	Traditional
Roseanne	162.9	Working mom	Nontraditional
Laverne & Shirley	140.4	Single women	Nontraditional
December Bride	137.6	Widow	Traditional
Bewitched	127.1	Housewife	Traditional
The Golden Girls	126.1	Retired	Traditional
Here's Lucy	119.4	Widow	Traditional
Alice	117.3	Working single mom	Nontraditional
The Mary Tyler Moore Show	116.3	Working single woman	Nontraditional
Maude	98.1	Retired, women's libber	Nontraditional
Murphy Brown	96.1	Career woman	Nontraditional
Mama	81	Housewife	Traditional
Our Miss Brooks	68.4	Teacher, single	Traditional
Private Secretary	64.6	Secretary	Traditional
Hazel	52.8	Maid	Traditional
Rhoda	50.7	Single	Nontraditional
Grace under Fire	49.5	Single mom	Nontraditional
The Doris Day Show	43.5	Widow	Traditional
Veronica's Closet	38.1	Single, business owner	Nontraditional
227	37.7	Housewife	Traditional
Designing Women	33.8	Women business owners	Nontraditional
The Gale Storm Show	28.8	Cruise director	Traditional
Angie	26.7	Waitress	Traditional
Jesse	25	Single mom	Nontraditional
Julia	24.6	Single mom	Nontraditional

(*Continued*)

98 SITCOMS AND CULTURE

Table 3.1. Female-led sitcoms (*Continued*)

Program	Total Ratings	Lead role	Role type
Phyllis	24.5	Widow	Traditional
The Donna Reed Show	24.5	Housewife	Traditional
Flo	24.4	Waitress, single	Traditional
Funny Face	23.9	Student	Traditional
The Patty Duke Show	23.9	Teen	Traditional
9 to 5	19.3	Working women	Nontraditional
Gloria	18.7	Divorced mom	Nontraditional
Caroline in the City	18	Cartoonist	Nontraditional
Suddenly Susan	17	Single	Nontraditional
Room for Two	16.7	TV producer and mom	Nontraditional
Fired Up	16.5	Business partners	Nontraditional
Ellen	14.8	Business owner	Nontraditional
Hope and Gloria	14.6	Neighbors	Nontraditional
The Nanny	12.5	Nanny with benefits	Nontraditional
Mom	6.7	Mother/daughter	Nontraditional

Kypker (2012) notes the irony that *Mary Tyler Moore* is seen as the leading women's rights program, even though *Maude* was much more explicitly a feminist and more of a success in the ratings. Relatively few women characters were as strongly identified with political feminism as Maude; Bea Arthur's own later characters (e.g., in *The Golden Girls*) were toned down in terms of stridency.

Yet even *Maude* could not live up to the expectations of all of the feminists who were hoping to see their issues show up in prime time. While intersectional ideas about feminism were not yet gaining currency at the time of *Maude*, some critics pointed out her basically privileged and still-traditional position: "Maude is a housewife living off her husband and a wannabe left-wing activist paying or exploiting a poorer woman to carry out the housework chores besides: she seems to adjust her right-on thinking as befits her lifestyle.... Maude is married and clearly prioritizing her husband and daughter over other relationships, and is thus committed to the nuclear family, the very institution that, in radical feminist thought, lays at the root of women's' oppression" (Kypker, 2012, p. 143).

Nevertheless, the show was noted for dealing with first-time-on-TV issues such as abortion and rape (Kypker, 2017). As with most of the shows that first attempted to address social issues head-on, there was a *damned if you do and damned if you don't* quality, perhaps due to the oppression of expectations, which simply means that shows that are newly focused on social issues cannot represent those issues in ways that all stakeholders desire.

In the next chapter, we have a detailed and updated analysis of the numbers of women characters shown in sitcoms across their entire history. Our results will confirm some observations seen frequently in the literature that women are put in second place in terms of their numbers relative to men. On the other hand, we will also see throughout the book that sitcoms are one of the places where women's concerns receive more attention on TV and that women gained increasing power over these issues across the years under study.

Prejudice and Black Characters in Sitcoms

In the '70s, *All in the Family*'s Edith Bunker observed (S1E8), "Well, you sure gotta hand it to 'em. I mean, two years ago they was nothin' but servants and janitors. Now they're teachers and doctors and lawyers. They've come a long way on TV." Edith herself was, of course, part of a sea change in how TV was dealing with Black characters, who had indeed been stigmatized or ignored in the early years of TV.

The roots of television situation comedy are found in radio, and as we have seen, radio's roots stretch back into the vaudeville and minstrel forms that preceded it. As much as these roots tapped into forms of entertainment that were highly racialized, this meant that radio situation comedy would also draw on racial themes, and inevitably this would reappear in television well past its early years.

As noted above, *Amos 'n' Andy* was one of the first radio hits and one of the most popular programs in the golden era of radio, remaining on the air into the 1950s. In the program, two white actors voiced stereotypical Black characters (Means Coleman [1998] calls this "blackvoice"), portraying an all-Black world for a largely white audience (though not all white, as the program's popularity did cut across racial boundaries). The show became a well-referenced cultural touchstone, with catchphrases readily entering the American lexicon. By and large, mass audiences accepted the idea that Black laziness, shiftlessness, and consistent misuse of grammatical vocabulary

100   SITCOMS AND CULTURE

were proper in a comedic context. There was opposition as well, though, with some sectors of the Black press calling for a boycott of the program's sponsors (Shankman, 1978). The boycott did not succeed, but members of the Black intelligentsia and middle class established the basis for future objections to the show. *Amos 'n' Andy* made the transition to television, though it was difficult. The white originators of the series were replaced by Black actors. With visuals added, the stereotypical nature of the program became even more apparent, and it offended a larger range of audience sensibility. The NAACP picked up the objections to the show, pressuring CBS to remove it. The pressure was finally successful in getting CBS to cancel the show, even though it was still fairly high in the ratings. Even after the cancellation, re-runs continued into the '60s.

Apart from *Amos 'n' Andy*, there were other shows that used racial stereotypes quite frequently or as the main situational premise. *Beulah* (1950–53) was about a Black maid for a white family; it exploited the long running "mammy" stereotype (Bogle, 2001). It also raised objections, but still it lasted about three years. Other ethnicities got into the game too, with *The Goldbergs* sending up Jewish immigrants. *Mama* was a popular version of a Scandinavian family, and *Life with Luigi* gave the treatment to Italian immigrants. Some of these shows were more successful than others, but as racial advocacy groups objected, TV also seemed to be learning the lesson that white families were the safest subject, and thus early sitcoms tended to stay within that boundary.

By the 1950s, the echoes of vaudevillian racial comedy were starting to fade, if only ever so slightly. Sitcoms were not new in ethnicizing entertainment. The American melting pot meant there were ethnic versions of theater and music productions that were making legitimate artifacts that would influence the course of American art. The Yiddish theater and "race" music record labels would be only two examples. Both comedy and music, in the radio years especially but certainly in TV times as well, were heavily influenced by the output of Jewish entertainers and businesspeople (Karp, 2018). Much of what America was consuming as its mainstream entertainment was performed by people outside of its racial mainstream. But this was much less so for Black-originated art, especially in television, which in the early sitcom era still had to be subordinated to economic dictates and conservative Hollywood sensibilities.

Whiteness and the 1950s–'60s

We reviewed above how notions of whiteness were developing historically in sitcoms alongside and in comparison to other ethnicities. This cultural construct owes a lot to how sitcom families were portrayed in 1950s and 1960s situation comedies. Many of the most popular sitcom vehicles focused on families whose race (or its constructed absence) was part and parcel of a vision of middle-class success that was unrealistic, even for many whites. Given that the main purpose of the shows was to sell appliances and soap, it is not surprising that producers and networks gravitated toward situations that would be economically aspirational and optimistic for many (creating demand) and objectionable to few. The popularity of the shows indicates that producers were not missing their mark. Nevertheless, the literature on this form of racial essentialism tends to be rather fugitive in nature, perhaps understandably focusing on the negative impacts on the depicted racial outgroups rather than the holistic view of what it might do to the cultural whole.

Situations that were quintessentially white exemplified Middle America. Critical ideas about Middle America have been codified in a variety of types of literature, such as Sinclair Lewis's *Babbitt* (1922) or Sherman Anderson's *Winesburg, Ohio* (1919). In these works, the ordered-ness and prosperity of small town-life masks loneliness, lack of meaning, and outright hypocrisy, suggesting that Middle America is a dysfunctional euphemism for a society more focused on social control than it wishes to admit. Sociological studies of Middletown (i.e., Muncie, Indiana) in the 1930s (Lynd & Lynd, 1929) found a society cleaved into two groups: the working class and the business class. Eighty-six percent of families were living in nuclear arrangements, in owned homes if possible, with the production of children considered the norm. Black families were not much considered in the study, again emphasizing that the Middle American norm was assumed to be white. Midwestern cities were considered better models for this norm compared to Southern ones because they did not feature as much obvious exclusion of Black people.

Cultural attacks on Middle America, though, are themselves also polemical. The argument for a society that wanted to supplant traditional Middle-American forms of social organization based on religion, community, free enterprise, Judeo-Christian morality, and so forth was most often focused at its root on the liberation of individual expression and behavior. Such liberalism could also overflow into libertinism. As well, the social problems that were considered to deserve the most attention in America—starting with concepts like juvenile delinquency and burgeoning into a whole host of ills such as divorce, teen pregnancy, urban violence, and political unrest—were most common in urban centers, not in the Middle America that was most frequently criticized by urban cultural elites. They were problems that were statistically more likely in cities, towns, and neighborhoods that were less white. Thus, while various countercultural developments such as the Beat movement were leaving Middle America aside in favor of the liberated individual, on the evening news America itself was developing into a nation fixated on the problems not of Middle America but of its opposite, the inner city. The keystone of difference between Middle America and the inner city was the racial variable.

Where did television sitcoms come down in this mix? The early ones normally attempted to avoid trouble. Clearly, especially early in their history, sitcoms and most television shows were not considered part of elite cultural production. Artists who attempted to make their way in TV—those who might have wished to take on social issues more directly—often complained that business overrode everything else. Even though the very earliest years of TV were considered by some to be an artistic garden simply due to the chaos and novelty of it all (referred to as the Golden Age of Television), business interests and sponsorship factors quickly destroyed that artistic freedom (Barnouw, 1978). The tendency to push toward mass programming for heterogeneous (i.e., mainly white) audiences emerged very quickly.

The Adventures of Ozzie and Harriet (1952–66), *Father Knows Best, Leave It to Beaver,* and *The Donna Reed Show*—all very successful programs—were forerunners in the equation of whiteness with happiness and success. But they also, for critics, came to stand in for the idea that suburban existence was plagued by malaise: a blandness and lack of meaning and, above all, a manufactured absence of definable cultural characteristics. Other ethnicities, when they existed, tended to provide spice against this assumed background (lack of) flavor. Even most white audiences knew that their family was probably not measuring up to Ozzie Nelson's, but the cultural mainstream was pretty clear about the vision of stability and success that was being sought.

Inevitably, the happy-family shows started to need to find ways to break out of the nuclear family situation for novelty, but ethnic families were still politically touchy. New solutions were needed. Shows like *My Three Sons* and *The Andy Griffith Show* did away with mothers, which worked because a single dad figuring out how to raise kids was a proven plot idea (going back to *Bachelor Father* [1957–62]). Only at the end of the '60s did any Black family situations get introduced, quite tentatively, with *Julia.*

Yet most real white families failed in some way to measure up to the standard seen in the early sitcoms by virtue of lack of income, the absence of one or more parent from the family, or the absence of children. These would be obvious markers. Harder to demonstrate but also easy to assume would be the fact that most white families did not live up to the *moral* standards seen in a show like *Father Knows Best*, either by choice or by the fact that the white sitcom families were impossibly perfect. Thus, while Black and other minority families were being stigmatized by their absence from TV, white families were stereotyped in a way that is something different from what is now called *reverse racism*. Rather, it was the imposition of a set of standards that some families might have lived up to some of the time but that few families could live up to all the time. If the cultural critique of Middle America was accurate, many sitcoms only heightened the absurdity of trying to live up to an impossible standard. But how many people saw these shows as something to emulate in any case? To the extent that audiences accepted the standards as real (there is no consistent evidence to support this hypothesis), it sets up the scene for later cultural wars over what whiteness really means.

All in the Family and Race

As the '60s came to a close, the disconnection of the '50s sitcom ideal from reality was becoming more and more apparent. At some point, the genie would break out of the bottle. Although it was not the first sitcom to deal with issues of prejudice, *All in the Family* (*AITF*) was certainly the most important and still the most recognized entrant in a field of sitcoms that tried to deal with social issues from a self-admittedly liberal and progressive standpoint.

All in the Family was an American version of a British show called *Till Death Us Do Part* (1965–75). In England, *Till Death* was created as a commentary on English working-class racism at a time when immigration issues were being hotly debated in the UK. While the show's creator intended it to be a comedic way to illuminate the absurdity of racism, many viewers found the main character, Alf Garnett, to be sympathetic. It was not at all clear that viewers of the show were getting the antiracist messages, leading to much controversy over the show (Schaffer, 2010).

A lot of this was recapitulated in the show's American incarnation. The working-class East Ender of *Till Death* became a loading dock worker in Queens, and other character types were directly imported but reformatted for American audience needs. The huge success of the English show was also achieved in America, as *AITF* became the number 1 show in the years 1972 to 1976.

An early review doubted whether the show could be successful, for an understandable reason: "The main problem with this show is that in order

104 SITCOMS AND CULTURE

to achieve laughs in a family satire, there must first be an underlying feeling of love among all parties. Without that foundation, all that comes out is just plain hate. CBS has said it put this show on the air hoping that audiences will laugh at all sides, realizing that all the hate in today's world is absurd. It doesn't work. It just adds to the problem" (Cameron, 2014).

As it turned out, many viewers *could* identify with a bigot. Vidmar and Rokeach (1974) tested whether the character of Archie Bunker would have the liberalizing effect assumed by his creators. They found that selective perception and selective exposure were powerful motivators in reactions to *All in the Family* and that those who started out with prejudicial views were likely to see the Bunker character supportively. Surlin and Bowden (1976) found that selective perception meant that those who perceived themselves as sociologically similar to Bunker tended to find him a sympathetic character, even though the intent was to show him as a villain. Lasch (1983) took seriously the idea that there could be real political roots for Archie's resentments, noting that his working-class values were casualties of the culture war or revolution being waged by liberals such as Norman Lear.

Yes, it can be very difficult to cast a villain as the main character in a sitcom. Archie Bunker, even early on but especially over the years, was allowed to demonstrate more human qualities, including Middle American values that could not be so easily cast aside. He was hard-working, and he supported his family—even the liberal son-in-law he so often fought with. In the episode "Games Bunkers Play" (S4E8), Edith tried to humanize Archie somewhat for his main nemesis:

EDITH: You want to hear why Archie yells at you?
MIKE: Ma . . . I know why he yells at me. He hates me.
EDITH: Oh, no, Mike. Archie yells at you 'cause he's jealous of you.
MIKE: Ma, I don't want to listen to this!
EDITH: Oh, now, wait a minute. You will listen to me! Archie is jealous of you.
MIKE: Oh, come on, Ma.
EDITH: Now, that ain't hard to understand. Mike, you're going to college and you got your whole life ahead of you. Archie had to quit school to support his family. He ain't never gonna be nothing more than he is right now. But you, you got a chance to be anything you want to be. That's why Archie's jealous of you. He sees in you all the things that he could never be. So the next time Archie yells at you, try to be a little more understanding.

With the emergence of a kinder portrayal of Archie, it was little surprise that the various sides of humanity that comprised the mass audience might also develop their own take on the racial and social issues that were the theme of the program.

All in the Family was an opening salvo in a move toward sitcoms claiming some territory in the field of social debate. Producers—the auteurs of sitcoms—were seeking vehicles to take positions on issues of social and cultural change. From the 1970s onward, opportunities began opening up as well for more Black characters in television, with sitcoms often leading the way. Mostly these shows were still under the control of white producers, but the feeling of advance past the '50s–'60s position was palpable. However, not all observers were satisfied with these increases. Gray (1986) observes that sitcom portrayals seemed oriented toward "assimilationist" ideologies and individualism, without recognition of social inequality. He asserts the basic objection that Black shows like *The Jeffersons*—or later *Cosby*—were hiding the fact that "television's idealization of racial harmony, affluence, and individual mobility is simply not within the reach of millions of Black Americans" (p. 239). In plainer terms, both shows were being "whitened" much along the lines of moral acceptability from the 1950s.

Three shows are worth noting in the '70s expansion of Black characters on network sitcoms; all three produced some critical attention in the literature. Arguably the most popular was *The Jeffersons*. The show spun off a character from *AITF*, George Jefferson, a successful Black businessman who sparred frequently with Archie Bunker. The show posited that George's family had economic success and moved to a luxury apartment on the East Side of New York, where they were "fish out of water." George was also about as racist as Archie, though of course "Whitey" was his main target. His wife Louise ("Weezie") took on the role-type of Edith in *AITF*. The Jeffersons also had friends who were an interracial couple, which was a first on network TV. For authors such as Acham (2004), the show represented the "integrating face" of Black sitcoms in the '70s. As a network show in the '70s–'80s, it still had to be able to attract a heterogenous racial audience, which meant it could not read as exclusively culturally Black. Notably, though, the show was also reacting to years of hesitancy, after the *Amos 'n' Andy* debacle, to show Black characters in any stereotyped way because of the likelihood of protest against such portrayals. The obvious move, then, was to show Blacks being successful, which itself became a point of contention for its failure to show the economic realities under which many Blacks lived. Despite misgivings from some critical quarters, the show was highly successful across a ten-year run.

An attempt to show Black families in more realistic economic conditions (but holding together as a family under such conditions) was found in *Good Times*. The show focused on an entire intact nuclear family, partly as a response to the crisis of fatherlessness in Black communities, without overly idealizing the economic realities of the family's situation, as would have been typical for white sitcom families in the 1950s. The show frequently took on issues of concern to Black communities, and there were a variety of nuanced characters who managed to show a broader palette of Black life. The show stayed in the top twenty for two years before it began to approach a form of Black comedy that was too reminiscent of the minstrel days. The exaggerated tropes were still popular, springing the JJ character to national prominence; it was hard for the producers to eschew continuing to mine the slapstick comedy in favor of the more nuanced and issue-oriented portrayals that the other actors wanted. Lead actress Esther Rolle's criticism of JJ was telling for the dilemma faced by Black shows in an era when any Black show was trying to meet a number of different expectations:

> He's [JJ] 18 and he doesn't work. He can't read and write. He doesn't think. The show didn't start out to be that. Michael's role of a bright, thinking child has been subtly reduced. Little by little—with the help of the artist [Jimmy Walker], I suppose, because they couldn't do that to me—they have made him more stupid and enlarged the role. [Negative images] have been quietly slipped in on us through the character of the oldest child. I resent the imagery that says to black kids that you can make it by standing on the corner saying "Dy-no-mite!" (Acham, 2004, citing an *Ebony* article by Louis Robinson)

A show that came under similar criticism, though in some different ways, was *Sanford and Son*. Acham's (2004) chapter on the show highlights the tensions involved with creating a program around a character, in this case Redd Foxx, who represented authentically Black comedy but who was not necessarily uplifting in the way that some parts of the Black audience had hoped their characters would be. Foxx's stand-up act was very obscene but also very funny. It was mainly attuned to the kind of Black audience he would have encountered on the "chitlin' circuit." At times, he horrified those with white sensibilities.

Sanford and Son portrayed a Black man and his son running a junkyard in Los Angeles. They were near the bottom of the economic ladder. They lived within a mostly Black world, with only a few whites for comic relief.

On *Sanford*, Foxx's jokes were toned down for network TV, and audiences loved it. *Sanford* was in the top twenty for five years. Yet its very popularity attracted criticism from the same Black intellectual circles that did in *Amos 'n' Andy*. Eugenia Collier characterizes the show as basically a white show because she did not see community-oriented Black values guiding it. Rather, she saw deplorable characters exhibiting the values of white humor. For Collier, "White American humor—at least as shown on TV—is frivolous, cruel, and often absolutely stupid. The result is egocentric women with more time and money than brains and compassion—Lucy, for instance, and Maude—and child-men who are constantly outwitted and outmaneuvered by wives and children, especially by young-adult daughters. No wonder the nation has taken to its heart that good old-fashioned snarling American bigot, Archie Bunker" (Collier, 1973, p. 101).

Comparatively, Foxx was exhibiting the same values: "The Sanfords themselves are great examples of sick American humor. Fred (Redd Foxx) is a selfish, immature old man who rules his adult son, Lamont (Demond Wilson), by wheeling, scheming, faking illness, and carrying on like a spoiled child—the same techniques perfected by Lucy and repeated on countless situation comedy shows."[14] Acham did not go as far as Collier. She asserts that the authentic Black roots of Foxx's comedy came out frequently. There are numerous assertions of Black power—and white inferiority—within the context that "the man" is still white. Foxx's own prowess as a businessman, being a club owner, and a pioneer for Blacks in network TV also counts on the positive side of the ledger.

Taken together, these three very popular network shows could never have achieved the multiple expectations that were being placed on them. They had to attract white audiences, meaning the entertainment had to be understood across a sometimes wide cultural divide. Yet they also had to stand for Black life in general, even though among Blacks there were widely varying hopes for what that should look like. Some Black audiences were fine with Black low comedy even if other Black class segments were appalled by it; such had been the case even with extreme examples like *Amos 'n' Andy*. The oppression of expectations for the Black sitcom became even stronger in the 1980s with *The Cosby Show*.

Cosby

Cosby is paradoxical. *The Cosby Show* was number 1 for five years, consistently garnering very high ratings. Moreover, the show was designed specifically *not* to embody stereotypes but to show a Black middle-class family that would be in many ways similar to the various white middle-class families that had been portrayed over the years. In these families, as we saw above, both parents are competent, and the focus is almost always on minor problems that can be solved within half an hour, leading to the messages of family cohesion that these sitcoms prefer. Apart from its Brooklyn setting, *Cosby* is very much a Middle American show. Viewers loved this format, as the show crossed racial boundaries quite successfully in terms of audience.

Not all critics were so enthused (Tucker, 1997). Jhally and Lewis (1992) focused on what these images did *not* show: a Black underclass still quite far from a position of social justice or equality: "In order to be successful and stay on the air, *The Cosby Show* had to meet certain viewer expectations. This, as we have seen, meant seducing viewers with the vision of a comparable affluence that the Huxtables epitomize. Once television has succumbed to the discourse of the American dream, in which a positive image is a prosperous one, it cannot afford the drop in ratings that would likely accompany a redefinition of viewers' expectations. TV series that depart from conventional viewer expectations are necessarily short lived" (p. 142).

Jhally and Lewis's study had actually been funded by Cosby himself. While they admitted the program had some good intentions, ultimately any situation comedy depicting a comfortable middle-class existence does not work in their vision of capitalism as grounded in systemic inequality. For Jhally and Lewis, the American dream itself, the subtext and the pretext of the majority of US sitcoms, was a false promise. Thus, even if many of their Black interviewees were relieved that *Cosby* did not partake of the worst Black stereotypes, they thought it was still too far divorced from what the majority of Black people were experiencing in real life. Ultimately, *Cosby* was propaganda for capitalism and a smoke-screen diversion from continuing racial inequality. They noted that programs in the UK were more likely to be based on working-class characters, but such characterizations would be impossible in the US (an opinion that ignores many of the early working-class portrayals such as *The Honeymooners* that we have already discussed). Later Black sitcoms such as *Roc* were in fact based on working-class portrayals, but it is unclear if these shows would have addressed Jhally and Lewis's critical points.

Jhally and Lewis's criticism echoed what Gerbner had defined earlier about television's portrayals of Blacks: the "bifurcated image" that tended to show Blacks in either a criminal or an underclass portrayal, or as living at the higher end of the socioeconomic spectrum.[15] Along with Jhally and Lewis, Means Coleman (1998) identified a similarly two-valence audience reaction. In her viewer reaction study, some participants were quite happy that a Black family was being portrayed as upper middle class and that blackness seemed to play a secondary role. Others saw it as unrealistic, not in tune with actual Black lived experience, or even a case of "whiteface," with a Black family aspiring to be something other than what they could really hope to be. There were also instances of viewers finding skin color biases in *Cosby*, favoring lighter-skinned or mixed-race characters, eliciting a form of prejudice that had long been present within African American communities. Innis and Feagin (2002) found something similar when they studied the reactions of their Black middle-class respondents. Frazer and Frazer (1993) went as far as to compare *Cosby* with *Father Knows Best*, basically arguing that it was a regressively idealistic portrait of male-female relations, without taking on the racial issues.

Yet Matabane and Merritt (2014) found that *Cosby* and similar shows like *A Different World* were effective in terms of promoting educational ideas to Black audiences. Many shows featured Bill Cosby's promotion of college attendance, especially at historically Black institutions such as Howard. Black viewers who watched *Cosby* were more likely to subscribe to values and to indicate needs that would promote college attendance whereas viewers who looked at more stereotypical Black media were less likely to endorse those attitudes. Rosenkoetter (1999) found that children could understand moral lessons embedded in *Cosby* (also in the program *Full House* [1987–85]). Moreover, children who watched prosocial sitcoms were more likely to engage in prosocial behaviors, as reported by their mothers. Bill Cosby himself had encouraged the view that television could be ennobling and educational, as seen in his academic work (1976) concerning his association with the *Fat Albert* cartoon program and its use in school curricula.[16]

Henry Louis Gates (1989) wrote an opinion column for the *New York Times* that summarized concerns from a Black perspective. He noted that Black viewers always eagerly anticipated the appearance of Black characters on TV, hoping that in some sense they would do well and contribute to positive racial representation. But Gates also echoed Lewis and Jhally's concern that the show was serving as a smoke screen for the still-existing realities of racial disadvantage and prejudice. For Gates, none of the "ghetto" sitcoms of the '70s had been realistic, and the pendulum swing of *Cosby* was going too far to the other side. He thought that a sitcom like *Frank's Place* (1987–88) showed a more realistic set of Black character types. The show was partly about how

110   SITCOMS AND CULTURE

a northern Black man dealt with a variety of people when he moved to New Orleans. However, the show was not successful with audiences and was ultimately pulled; many thought it was simply too realistic and sophisticated for network TV.

Ultimately, *Cosby* was being asked to do a lot. While it clearly provided positive images of a Black family, something that had been lacking even in the '70s' social-issue period, it was only one show and could not simultaneously address the needs of everyone. Cosby himself had been a critic of a Black culture that he saw as destructive and portrayed himself as a family values person (ironic, given what was later learned about him). Attacks on *Cosby* were often ideologically driven. For media criticism that must see every television development as bad, the fact that *Cosby* could be the number 1 show was a rejection of the idea that the white-controlled capitalist marketplace would never have allowed such a thing, and especially that the show could have been a product of a Black artist/producer. The reality was that mainstream white audiences, long assumed to be racially propagandized, cheerfully accepted *Cosby*. That meant something else had to be wrong with the show, and so ironically, but also perhaps inevitably, despite its attempt to avoid stereotypes, the critics found another way see its portrayals as damaging.

Cosby was unrealistic in the way that almost all sitcoms are, including the white ones. Fiction is a process through which individual stories are presented with an intent to stand for or represent something larger. As such, all fictional characters tend toward the stereotypical. But the stakes of such stereotyping are lesser for white audiences. With many more shows featuring white characters, a wider range of character types will be present, and they will be less likely to be racialized. For Black shows, as Gates (1989) put it, "It's not the representation itself (Cliff Huxtable, a child of college educated parents, is altogether believable), but the role it begins to play in our culture, the status it takes on as being, well, truly representative."

Whether sitcoms are or should be representative is ultimately the question we deal with in this book. In 2022, Marta Kauffman, a producer of *Friends*, created a professorship in Black Studies at Brandeis to atone for the much-noted lack of racial diversity on her show: "The series' failure to be more inclusive, Kauffman says, was a symptom of her internalization of the systemic racism that plagues our society, which she came to see more clearly in the aftermath of the 2020 murder of George Floyd by Minneapolis police and the worldwide protest movement that erupted around it. That reckoning was the catalyst for her decision to pledge $4 million to her alma mater, the Boston area's Brandeis

"Sitlit"   111

University, to establish an endowed professorship in the school's African and African American studies department" (Braxton, 2022).

In reality, though, it could be entirely plausible that the white twentysomethings of *Friends* would have few or no Black friends; such racial segregation is quite common even now. Clearly, both *Friends* and *Cosby* are being asked to do something other than be realistically representative; they are being asked to be *aspirationally* representative of a desired social structure. Casting strategies that are aspirational have become much more common in later years, as we review in our final chapter.

After *Cosby*

From a statistical standpoint, the *Cosby* years were a high point for Black representation and ratings success on network television (see chap. 4 for more analysis). Moving into the '90s and 2000s, the picture became more complicated. Although the three main networks continued to have the largest audiences, competitor networks came on the scene: Fox, and later the WB and UPN. Fox was the first to figure out that a narrowcasting strategy toward Black audiences could siphon viewers away from the Big Three. The strategy would have the same two-sided effect that we have seen throughout this chapter. While this strategy was positive in the sense that more Black characters could be on television, and also more Black producers and writers could work behind the scenes, there was also a continuing sense of ghetto-ization, especially given that popular sitcoms on the big networks became whiter.

Figure 3.4 shows ratings data for some of the important Black sitcoms that were developed during this era. Although not a sitcom, *In Living Color* (1990–94) was the first hit for Fox that turned its new audience's attention to Black-produced comedy with a hip-hop sensibility. Fox was not necessarily interested in racial uplift, and so the program had plenty of focus on low comedy that caused consternation among some critics. There were breakout stars from the show, most notably Jim Carrey, who went on to movie superstardom. Schulman (1992) is an example of a critic who worried that a Black comedy not focused on positive racial portrayals would be too damaging:

> At a time when one might claim with at least some degree of assurance that overt displays of racial prejudice are considered socially unacceptable on television, white and Black audiences alike are apt to wince at Fox's updated version of the old disreputable pantheon of demeaning images of African Americans, remarkably un-changed in substance from their historic antecedents: the nurturing Mammy figure, the sultry temptress,

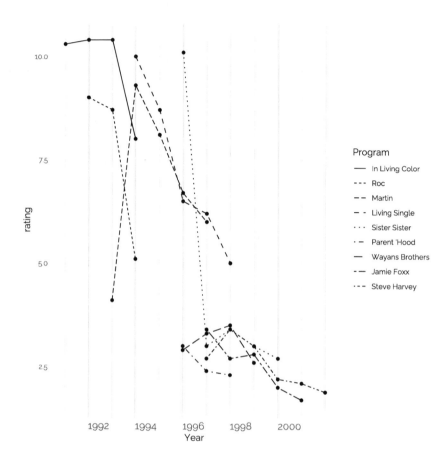

Figure 3.4. Black-led sitcoms on Fox, WB, CW.

the deferential Uncle Tom, the flashy con-artist operating just outside the law, the happy-go-lucky Negro whose banjo has been replaced by a "boom box." Along with these stereotypes are the accompanying marks of the underclass: mispronunciations, dialect, malapropisms, social backwardness, and extreme naïveté—all things that have historically helped to rationalize keeping Blacks in subordinate roles. (p. 2)

Cooks and Orbe (1993) suspect that *In Living Color* would suffer from the same dynamic that troubled *All in the Family*: audiences would not necessarily see the satire. They note that producer Keenen Ivory Wayans sought to show all aspects of Black life, not just the Black bourgeoise (an obvious reference to *Cosby*). Their study found that Blacks were more likely to watch the show than whites but also more likely to perceive some of the characters as stereotyped. Although Cooks and Orbe may have been applying a standard that few sitcoms measure up to, they did not think that *In Living Color* provided much of a vehicle for social learning.

The sitcoms that came out of the era were more varied than that. Shows like *Roc* (1991–94) and *Living Single* did not stray as much into stereotype territory. Shows that did test boundaries, often flagrantly crossing them, such as *Martin*, were more successful in the ratings. After the initial wave of programs appeared on Fox, in the second half of the 1990s a second wave appeared on upstart networks such as the WB and UPN. Zook (1999) analyzed all the programs. While noting the regressive aspects of programs such as *Martin*, where Martin Lawrence's turbulent personal life and attitude toward women seemed to be reflected in the show, she appreciated the overall opportunity to have more varied aspects of Black life being seen, sometimes realistically, through the TV lens. She also notes, though, that the period was short-lived, as proven by the ratings declines in figure 3.4. The new networks, Zook argues, used Black audiences as a stepping stone toward larger viewerships that would, perforce, have to include more white viewers. Few Black shows that emerged in the '90s could transcend that barrier; stronger ratings performers on Fox, for instance, were the low comedy *Married with Children* and the animated hit *The Simpsons*.

Sitcom attempts to deal with racial issues are always treading a fine line, facing the conflicting expectations of subgroups within various communities that hope for more than just entertainment but positive representation as well. White producers could have issues capturing culture accurately or sensitively, but few shows were entrusted solely to Black production teams. More serious shows like *Roc*, *The Sinbad Show* (1993–94), and *Frank's Place* were troubled with the perception that too many issues in a sitcom meant ratings trouble. Still, with all the criticism and concern about what the Fox, WB, and UPN shows were putting out in terms of images of Blacks, Zook sees it as in important interlude, a transition from the period when monolithic networks had *no* Black representation to a period when multichannel availability, along with still-greater sensitivity to racial issues among programmers, meant a more diverse set of views that could be seen from a comedic perspective.

Effects

It is reasonable to ask, what is the effect of all this? In the realm of sitcom research, for every study that attempts to quantitatively assess whether images matter to audiences, there are probably five studies that either look at content

114   SITCOMS AND CULTURE

qualitatively or just make idiosyncratic critical judgments about their effect. From this body of research, it is easy to reach conclusions about sitcom effects that are preformed ideologically. Sitcoms are programs that imprison women. They denigrate working classes. They enforce consumer enthusiasm. They encode racist stereotypes. Fewer critics seem willing to concede that sitcoms might play a role in social advance or that they even just offer a pleasant escape with its own rewards and value.

On representations of women, as we will see in the next chapter, Signorielli found over the years that women were consistently outnumbered by men on TV, and they still are, even on sitcoms. Does this have an effect on perceptions about women? Most early studies found a lot of sex stereotyping that seemed to be reflected by viewers. As the '80s wound up, though, after a wave of more progressive programming had made it onto TV, Signorielli (1989) found that:

> The cultivation analysis provides *mixed* support for the general hypothesis that those who watch more television will have more sexist views and the mainstreaming hypothesis that certain groups of respondents who espouse very different views as light viewers, will, as heavy viewers, have more similar outlooks in regard to woman's role in society. There has been an overall striking trend between the 1970s and 1980s for fewer respondents to agree with sexist statements, and in the analyses of more recent samples the implementation of simultaneous controls results in small but statistically significant negative coefficients, probably due to interrelations with education. (pp. 358–59)

Seemingly, TV had progressed (haltingly, perhaps) along with society; relationships between viewing and sexism were by no means crystal clear. Morgan et al. (1999) looked at the issue in relation to a specific sitcom example. *Murphy Brown* (1988–98) was one of the noted sitcoms where the idea was to portray a strong professional woman. On the show, it was decided that Murphy would have a baby out of wedlock. This created a storm when then–vice president Dan Quayle criticized the decision. In a 1992 speech, Quayle laid out a conservative response to progressive TV trends:

> Ultimately, however, marriage is a moral issue that requires cultural consensus and the use of social sanctions. Bearing babies irresponsibly is simply wrong. Failing to support children one has fathered is wrong and we must be unequivocal about this.
>
> It doesn't help matters when prime-time TV has Murphy Brown, a character who supposedly epitomizes today's intelligent, highly paid professional woman, mocking the importance of fathers by bearing a child alone

and calling it just another lifestyle choice. I know it's not fashionable to talk about moral values, but we need to do it. Even though our cultural leaders in Hollywood, network TV, and the national newspapers routinely jeer at them, I think most of us in this room know that some things are good and other things are wrong. And now, it's time to make the discussion public.[17]

Crotty (1995) thought that Quayle might have had a point, citing high rates of single motherhood and divorce. Spurred on by the controversy, Morgan et al. (1999) looked at whether TV viewership was related to less traditional outlooks about family conceptions. They concluded that indeed, there may be some evidence that television may cultivate less traditional sex-role conceptions for women. Heavy viewers were more likely to be accepting of such situations.

Buerkel-Rothfuss et al. (1982) found that children who watch family shows (again, many if not most of them are sitcoms) also believe that real-life families tend to show support and concern for other. They also investigated parental co-viewing and found that parental involvement with children's viewing could greatly mediate the effects of such programs. In this context, sitcoms seem to have something of a prosocial effect.

A similar prosocial effect was found by Collins et al. (2003) when they determined that exposure to a single episode of *Friends* resulted in more awareness of condom use as part of safe sex practice. In "The One Where Rachel Tells . . ." (S8E3), Rachel experienced an unplanned pregnancy. A discussion of condom efficacy (the rate was said to be 97 percent) was specifically part of the program's dialogue:

RACHEL: Ross, there is no pressure on you. Okay? I mean you can be as involved as you want.

ROSS: Yeah, I need uh . . . I'm just—I don't know—I don't understand, umm, how this happened? We—we used a condom.

RACHEL: I know. I know, but y'know condoms only work like 97 percent of the time.

ROSS: What? What? What?! Well they should put that on the box!

RACHEL: They do!

ROSS: No they don't!! Well they should put it in huge black letters!

RACHEL: Okay Ross, come on, let's just forget about the condoms.

ROSS: Oh well, I may as well have!

RACHEL: Listen, y'know what? I was really freaked out too when I found out. . . .

ROSS: Freaked out? Hey no, I'm not freaked out! I'm indignant! As a consumer!

RACHEL: Y'know what? Let's, let's talk later.

ROSS: No! No! I want to talk now! Okay? I—In fact, I am going to talk to the president of the condom company!

RACHEL: Okay, y'know maybe I should come back. (Crane & Kauffman, 2001)

In the tradition of entertainment-education research, Moyer-Gusé (2008) found the program effective in transmitting messages about caution with condoms to young viewers and changed perceptions for around 50 percent of young viewers.

Later on in the course of TV history and development, Holbert et al. (2003) conducted an examination of impacts of TV genres on support for women's rights. Across large samples in 1997, 1998, and 1999, they found small but *positive* relationships between exposure to sitcoms and support for women's rights, which were measured as support for legalized abortion and "women's liberation." Thus, empirical studies focusing on sitcoms have not conclusively shown that exposure to sitcoms is related to more sexist conceptions.

There seems to be some stronger evidence about racial stereotyping effects. As noted above, satires of racism are not guaranteed to be perceived as such, as in the case of the Archie Bunker studies and replicated with shows such as *In Living Color*. Mastro and Tropp (2004) found, experimentally, that white viewers exposed (in a single program) to stereotypical characters in a sitcom were more likely to express stereotypical views in response; these responses interacted with their previous exposure to Black people, but even people with personal experience with Blacks were still more likely to express stereotypical views after the exposure.

Shows that are the first to represent a social group tend to attract research attention. Though *Will & Grace* was not the first show to feature gay characters or even gay leads, it was seen as the first major success in the subgenre and was highly rated on the NBC schedule. Cooper (2003) tested audience reactions to the show and their preferences for the various characters. He found that the show could "be useful in making gays more familiar and less the Other to a heterosexual audience" (p. 531). However, Battles and Hilton-Morrow (2002) argued that "mere representation" was not enough; they criticized the show for being situated within a heterosexist cultural context. In their analyses, "to become visible is to enter into a dominant discourse that marks the boundaries of normalcy" (p. 101). Analyses and critiques of *Will & Grace* reflect some of the same patterns seen with *Cosby*: lack of representation or negative representation is seen as problematic for presenting problematic conditions of existence; normalized representation is also criticized for eliding those same conditions. As with *Maude*, shows that make progressive moves will still have critics situated to their left, and ideological positions do color research hypotheses and effects that can be found.

"Sitlit"   117

The literatures on both sex role stereotyping and racial/ethnic stereotyping are focused on phenomena that are still real, even if they do not look as they do when investigations into television portrayals began in the 1950s (see Mastro [2009] and Smith and Granados [2009] for reviews). Along with violence, these issues continue to be seen as two major foci worthy of research and policy attention. But little of the effects research is specifically about sitcoms.

Critical Studies and Sitcom Effects

What do critical theorists have to say about sitcoms? Scholars have found them to be marvelous sites in which to explore all sorts of enactments and maintenances of a variety of cultural perceptions. As we note at various points in this volume, sitcoms of the '50s and '60s are the easiest targets for the idea that sitcoms existed to propagandize a very specific traditional version of family life. Sitcoms strived to be in the middle, and as Gerbner argued, *the middle really meant conservative. Leave It to Beaver* and other shows are easy targets for this sort of criticism, but sitcom evolution meant that critics would also have to evolve. Although sitcoms unquestionably showed progress on representation of various groups, the critical bars have been moved up as the shows themselves have become more progressive. The show that seemed radical in the '70s seems archaic now, just as the comedy that seemed funny in the '70s also may not work now. Contemporary attacks on shows such as *Seinfeld* and *Friends* for whiteness are much different from the racial criticisms of the '50s. Active stereotyping and its discontents gave way to the softer prejudice of demographic distortions, which could be more easily ignored.

If all the considerations of the cultural critic could be met, what would the end product look like on television? Is there even room for the sitcom in such a world? Oftentimes specific shows seem to bedevil the critics—for example, there was the progressive *Roseanne*, which stood up comedically for working-class families, and then Rosanne Barr herself, who found later that her offensive tweeting tangled her show's reboot in a wave of twenty-first-century cancellations,[18] with some echoes of how early sitcom stars such as Lucille Ball also faced down political attacks.

Although sitcoms, as we have argued, receive less critical attention than other genres—especially as the idea of TV studies itself seems in danger (Gray & Lotz, 2019)—it seems worth singling out a few important readers and monographs, such as Morreale's edited volume (2003), Dalton and Linder's collection (2016), Marc's criticism (1997), and Acham's study (2004), which is not solely focused on sitcoms but has several good chapters focused on Black

118   SITCOMS AND CULTURE

shows. If a standard critical source on sitcoms has not yet emerged, these books and some others surely prove useful in holding comedies' feet to the fire of evolving cultural standards and practices.

What do critical theorists have to say about media effects?

> There is a major flaw in thinking that administrative research is focused on effect, while critical research is not. It is true that administrative research looks at the causal chain of "who says what to whom with what effect." But the effect is short run. But it is altogether wrong to overlook the giant effects [emphasis added] aimed for by the Frankfurt School—the production of consciousness, false and true, and ultimately on society. More than that, the ostensible reluctance of the Frankfurters to use the term effect is itself a giant statement that society continues at an uninterruptable standstill, and that the media serve to reinforce the status quo. In other words, "no change" is their major effect. (Katz & Katz, 2016, p. 9)

Although most cultural critics are long past the point at which the Frankfurt School started, with many different assumptions and methods, it is impossible to read them without holding in mind the idea that we would only pay attention to the distortions and unrealities of the sitcoms unless we thought they had some impact on social reality (ultimately the point of this book) and the ground on which social science and critical studies eventually meet. The archaic and outdated images we hold from early sitcoms can still be powerful in terms of how we think about the impact of modern sitcoms and can be played upon successfully for creative effects (see, for instance, *Wandavision* [2021]). The more limited empirical research that exists, though, also suggests that we might maintain an open mind about sitcoms. Are they a place only for bread-and-circus commercial exploitation? Can they be something more than a propaganda vehicle for Middle America, and maybe even occasionally a channel for social uplift and progress?

NOTES

1. Gallup Organization. (1936). Gallup Poll # 1936–0057: Power of the Government/Federal Budget/Family Size/1940 Presidential Election (Version 3) [Dataset]. Cornell University, Ithaca, NY: Roper Center for Public Opinion Research. https://doi.org/10.25940/ROPER-31087041.

2. British Institute of Public Opinion. (1939). BIPO Survey # 54, January, 1939 (Version 3) [Dataset]. Cornell University, Ithaca, NY: Roper Center for Public Opinion Research. https://doi.org/10.25940/ROPER-31082650.

"Sitlit" 119

3. 60Minutes/Vanity Fair. (2012). CBS News/New York Times/60 Minutes /Vanity Fair Poll: Taxes/Entertainment (Version 2) [Dataset]. Cornell University, Ithaca, NY: Roper Center for Public Opinion Research. doi:10.25940/ROPER -31091577.

4. Growing up as a child of divorce in the 1960s, I find it interesting to look back at the social movements designed to support and normalize single parenthood, seen in the development of groups such as Parents without Partners. The movement away from the notion of divorce as a social problem was memorialized in some of the sitcoms of the 1970s.

5. Statista (n.d.).

6. U.S. Census Bureau (n.d.).

7. World Bank (n.d.).

8. Springfield became a trope, later ironically mined in *The Simpsons*.

9. IMDB (n.d.).

10. Ensemble shows (with an early example like *M*A*S*H* and later examples like *Taxi* or *Cheers*) might have more, perhaps as many as seven. With fewer than four, it can be difficult to fulfill all of the quasi-family roles that are often seen as necessary to carry forward the dramatic purpose of a sitcom.

11. Other post-*Seinfeld* sitcoms did explore this kind of relationship more, such as *The Big Bang Theory*, where Sheldon and Penny had a meaningful friendship, given that any sexual aspect to it was ruled out from the start by Sheldon's personality.

12. This was seen quite obviously in *The Odd Couple* (1970–75), where Felix, the best friend, also had the characteristics typically assumed by a wife, with an interest in cooking, cleanliness, and home-keeping. This was compared to Oscar Madison's more stereotypically male features such as sloppiness, womanizing, and an interest in sports.

13. In *King of Queens*, Arthur lived with his adult daughter and her husband. They had no children, so of course Arthur played the role of the kid. He marked well the issue of everyone's return to childlike status as we age but also fulfilled the need for a quantum of youthful innocence and mischievousness that many sitcom structures seek out.

14. Collier (1973, p. 101).

15. Media Education Foundation (n.d.a).

16. "In order for schools to keep pace with our fast-moving society they will have to incorporate a diversified curriculum, a curriculum which will make use of the technology available to them in the form of educational hardware and software. Perhaps one of the most useful and least expensive innovations will be the widespread incorporation of the television set as a vehicle to promote learning. The impact of television on children has already been established through numerous [sic] research" (Cosby, 1976, p. 136).

17. Quayle (1992).

18. Koblin (2018).

Chapter 4 Frontis. John Amos and Esther Rolle were the stars of *Good Times*, Norman Lear's realistic portrayal of Black urban life.

4

Family, Life, Love, Good, House

The Universe and Demography of Sitcoms

FROM THE FOREGOING CHAPTERS, we can construct an interesting and informed take on sitcoms in relation to US society. But we still don't have the information we need to see if we can view them as true cultural indicators. To do that requires some forms of data collection that allow us not just to look at the salient and interesting examples of sitcoms that we and others have reviewed but also to look at all of them as a group, from a macro perspective.

The motivation for this data-gathering activity centers around how people have watched television, especially in past years. While viewing television in the 2020s may mean a rather selective process determined at least partially by viewer interests and proclivities, the patterns of viewing over the history of sitcoms tended much more toward viewing whatever was on offer, facilitated by Klein's system of "least objectionable programming" (Shales, 1977, p. B1). Gerbner incorporated this fact into his view that we should study the message "system," not just individually interesting programs. He also thought that effects from that system should be looked at on the macro level. On any given issue, an interesting or outlying program might portray one image while the bulk of programming viewed could display countervailing tendencies. *The Mary Tyler Moore Show* may have promoted female liberation, but did all programs tend to do that? *The Cosby Show* might have eschewed racial stereotyping, but would such patterns be in evidence across the body of shows? This section provides an empirical and critical analysis of the universe of sitcoms that appeared on US network television from its inception in the late 1940s to the 2020s.

A few printed sources have lists of all network television shows, and these sources provide key information about the shows, their stars, their producers, and typical show plots. An early example is Mitz (1980; see also Javna, 1988), which focuses only on sitcoms. Mitz does not include every show that was broadcast but rather gives a year-by-year summary of the sitcoms that were most popular and those that were also-rans. Brooks (e.g., Brooks & Marsh, 2009) produced a series that collects, encyclopedically, all network television programs since inception. This resource is essential for the history of US television; a random perusal can open up many interesting research avenues. These sources, and a few others, offer textual details about programs, plot summaries, character lists, names of producers, ratings, and so forth. However, these details are not readily analyzable quantitatively, since the data are not in machine-readable format.

Digital sources such as IMDB and Wikipedia also now present near-complete collections of information about sitcoms, and they are evolving in real time. It is rare that any sitcom that had at least one episode does not have a page on IMDB that offers the ability to mine data about the sitcom, its characters, its producers, and its episodes. The wealth of data available is such that it has been barely utilized in terms of analysis, but it is potentially very valuable as a cultural indicator. The same can be said for Wikipedia, though with some differences. IMDB has a database that is well structured for collecting certain kinds of information about shows and characters whereas Wikipedia proves to be very good for identifying as many sitcoms as possible to include in the database.

In this chapter, we use two sources of data. First, we use the complete Cultural Indicators message system data, a collection inaugurated by Gerbner beginning in 1967 and running until 2015. These are samples of network programs that were human-coded for issues such as violence, gender representation, and demographics of characters. We'll call these the CI Data. Second, we compiled information from IMDB about programs that could be identified as US situation comedies. We used web scraping and interaction with the IMDB API to compile a list of sitcoms that were broadcast on US television from its inception (1940s) until today. Our final result is a database of about one thousand programs, ending in the year 2021. We gathered information about each show including its main characters, their gender, and their ages. For each show, we extracted information into our database about seven main characters, so our character database is comprised of more than seven thousand individual entries. We'll call these the IMDB Data.

Before we look at some of the data in detail, we'll briefly peruse the list of sitcoms that comprise our universe. Our Wikipedia-derived list started with more than 1,500 programs. This included shows that would classically be

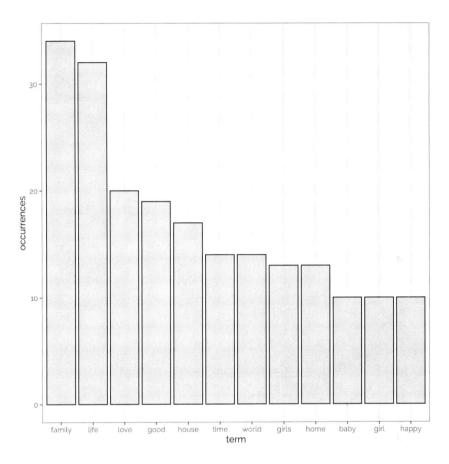

Figure 4.1. Top words appearing in sitcom titles.

counted as true sitcoms but also others that we don't spend as much time on in this book, such as animated shows (e.g., *The Simpsons, The Flintstones*), shows that were youth-oriented (such as various Disney comedies), or shows that were shown only on the internet and never on a true TV network. For that reason, it is difficult to give a true estimate of the number of situation comedies in existence, and of course this number is continually growing. When we use the Wikipedia data to seed our IMDB search, we get the final list of around one thousand programs. It includes long-running and successful programs such as *My Three Sons* (380 episodes), *Make Room for Daddy* (1953–1964, 343 episodes), and *The Big Bang Theory* (280 episodes). It includes short-running bombs (as rated by the IMDB audience) like *Homeboys in Outer Space* (1996–1997,

21 episodes, 3.5 rating), *Joanie Loves Chachi* (1982–1983, 17 episodes, 3.7 rating), and *Cavemen*[1] (2007, 15 episodes, 4.4 rating). There is much in between those two poles. The Wikipedia list that we used to seed our database is, of course, crowd-generated and therefore may not include each and every sitcom ever shown, however briefly, on a network. Programs that were one-off stinkers or lasted only a few episodes are less likely to appear in our data. IMDB often does have some information on these seldom-seem shows, but it can be difficult to exhaustively discover and classify what all of them are. Combining these two sources, though, gives an excellent approximation of a universe of sitcoms with a variety of key variables about them that can be analyzed.

To get started, figure 4.1 shows one interesting analysis of the data: a frequency analysis of words that appear in our sitcoms' titles. The top five terms, in order, are *family, life, love, good*, and *house*. The terms alone tell us a lot about the ideology and dramaturgy of sitcoms; they'd make a good sitcom title on their own, perhaps. They set the tone for the kinds of things we can look for in our data, and they confirm that when we want to know what our culture is saying about the family and life in general, sitcoms can be a good place to look.

The CI Data

Our proposition is that situation comedy can be a valuable cultural indicator. Our data for this section comes directly from the Cultural Indicators project (Gerbner, 1973) described above. Here, we focus on the second prong of Gerbner's research approach: message system analysis. This type of content analysis allows us to explore television's role as a cultural indicator, which means seeing its message system as both a repository of cultural meaning and a conduit for it. Thus, it is ultimately a crucial arena in which ideas about cultural reality are forged and maintained.

The point is not only to use television programs as a mirror for reality. As was quickly learned as the CI analyses began, television messages can distort the real world in a number of ways. While television is intended to be a representation of reality in many ways, it is not necessarily realistic. There is much more violence in the TV world, there are more men, there are more youngish people, and there are many more of certain kinds of occupations (doctors, police officers, lawyers). Given these disparities, a cultural indicator is primarily useful in comparison to other kinds of indicators, to serve as an empirical measure of what the culture privileges. What are its concerns, and what are the rewards and punishments for those within it?

In Gerbner's conception, one of the important roles of the cultural indicator is to let us know about types of people in terms of their casting and fate:

"Casting and fate are the building blocks of story-telling. Ours is a bird's-eye view of what large communities absorb over long periods of time. It attempts to answer questions about the television all viewers watch but none see: What is the cast of characters that animates the world of television? How are women and minorities (seniors, racial and ethnic groups, poor and disabled persons, etc.) represented? And, finally, how do they fare in that world— what is their share of heroes and villains, winners and losers, violents and victims?"[2]

Gerbner and his team's project would end up taking thousands of person-hours to watch and code prime-time television programs. Especially in the early days, resources for computer-assisted coding were slight; even in later years, just about everything had to be done by hand, with boxes of videotapes meticulously recorded and coded. The usefulness of the data would be to see how culture produced by large organizations rendered judgments about types of people in terms of the ways that such types were placed in dramatic situations. Any dramatic or comedic situation ultimately gives some type of appraisal, and so the positions of characters in relation to those judgments are of high interest, especially when they can be quantified, allowing us to recover that which we watch but do not see.

Thus, in this section, we use Gerbner's Cultural Indicators dataset to provide a look at how situation comedies can function as cultural indicators. The data here are a broad-brush portrait; later, we will get into finer-grained analyses. The CI dataset contains hundreds of sitcoms that were coded over the years as well as thousands of characters who appeared in those shows. From this dataset, we can provide one comprehensive picture of this television genre in terms of breadth and in terms of time, going back to the earlier days of network television.

Our broad research questions are focused on the demography of the television world, especially in comparison to the real world. Information about gender, age, race, and marital status in situation comedies can be compared to actual statistics to get a sense of possible distortions and, moreover, whether cultural change over time is related to social change. Compared to other critical analyses of sitcoms' social role, which tend to focus on individual programs, our analyses in this chapter can add to the picture at the thirty-thousand-foot level, benefiting from Gerbner's bird's-eye view.

Some Details[3]

The overall Cultural Indicators dataset is based on forty-seven weeklong annual samples of prime-time programs collected between 1967 and 2015.[4]

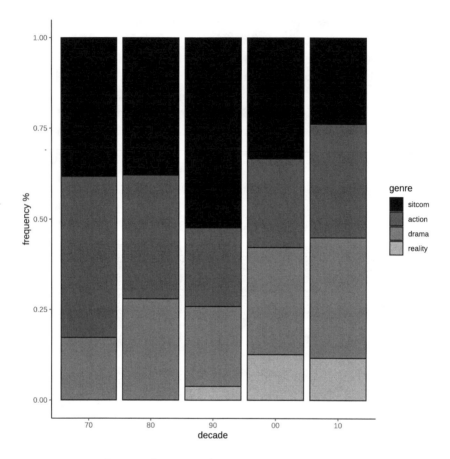

Figure 4.2. Distribution of programs by genre.

This represents data on 3,468 programs and 12,635 major or supporting characters. Only broadcast network programming (ABC, CBS, NBC, FOX, UPN, WB, and the CW[5]) was included. While the CI data analyze a number of kinds of programs, in the final analyses four major genres are included: action, drama, sitcom, and reality. The data are mainly about fictional programming, thus things like news and sports are not coded. The samples were coded at the Annenberg School for Communication (1967–1992) and then at the University of Delaware (1993–2015). The sample weeks were drawn around the same time each year, in late September and early October, avoiding special events such as sweeps periods or the World Series.

From these data, except for certain comparisons, we extract the portions that deal only with situation comedies. Out of the total of almost 3,500 programs coded, 1,338 (38%) were situation comedies. Normally, these were half-hour serial comedy programs, although there were some occasional deviations from this format. Of the 12,635 characters in the overall dataset, 4,326 (34%) were from situation comedies.

Figure 4.2 shows the distribution of types of programs across the years of the sample. Clearly, sitcoms were comprising a very important share of the total number of televised stories—a third or more—and characters that Americans were seeing on any given night, especially during years in which network television was the main source of entertainment.

Coding

At the Annenberg School, coders were hired to code the programs, while the data collected at the University of Delaware were gathered by junior and senior communication majors enrolled in a course on media message analysis. Throughout, all coders underwent extensive training, consisting of discussions to explain coding schemes as well as hands-on coding of programs that had been specifically selected and precoded for the training process. Although various measures were added to or removed from the recording instrument over the years, the core variables were coded every year, and the variables used in this study had identical coding schemes in all samples.

Coding reliability was measured at both the program and character levels. General reliability for the CI data is reported in a number of places. Signorielli et al. (2019) reported Krippendorf's alphas[6] averaging 0.79 for measures of violence. They also note that not every Violence Profile, the source of most of the data, reported reliability. Signorielli et al. (1982, p. 163) provide a good indication of the types of reliability that were obtained throughout the project. The George Gerbner Archive also contains information on how reliability was assessed.[7] Three-fourths or more of the programs in these nineteen samples, and roughly 80 percent of the characters, were coded by two independent coders to provide these reliability tests, but with the passage of time, it has not been possible to excavate exact analyses for all variables.

The study examines two units of analysis: the television program (situation comedy) as a whole and major/supporting characters. Minor characters are excluded. Major/supporting characters are those whose roles were essential to the storyline; coders were instructed to include the character if the character's omission would substantially change the plot.

128   SITCOMS AND CULTURE

Results

Program-Level Characteristics

Mostly we are interested in analyses at the character level. However, the CI data contain interesting observations at the program level as well; they provide good context for later judgments we can make about characters. The CI coders analyzed each program for major themes, focusing on things like crime, violence, family, health, and a few others. The data confirm what we would obviously expect: that sitcoms are primarily about family. Almost 85 percent of sitcoms were coded as reflecting family issues in some way; almost 40 percent of them were seen as being *primarily* about family. By comparison, 80 percent of sitcoms have nothing to do with crime, and only 2 percent of them are mainly about crime. Similarly, few sitcoms deal with law enforcement; only about 3 percent are focused mainly on that issue. Across all programs (not just sitcoms), the theme of family is negatively correlated with crime and law enforcement, meaning that family-oriented programs tend not to deal with violence and crime issues, and vice versa. Although these results are not unexpected, they confirm the idea that sitcoms are the place where television speaks about the haven of family, the personal, and social issues. Even in workplace sitcoms, issues of family are raised implicitly, if not explicitly as well.

The CI team coded extensively about violence portrayals in programs. In sitcoms, there is far less violence than in other programs. Of the four major types of programs, sitcoms have the least number of violent acts per episode (around 1.5). Action programs have the most—almost 9 per episode. The overall average for all types of programs is around 4.5. This does not mean that sitcoms do not have *any* elements that can be considered violent. Gerbner argued throughout his career that "happy" or slapstick violence should also be counted as such portrayals can also contribute to desensitization around the violence issue. To the extent that some of these portrayals occur in family-oriented sitcoms, they might be worth considering from the standpoint of the issue of domestic abuse. Threats to commit violence, such as Ralph Kramden's "to the moon, Alice!" could have been counted as violent, although this example occurred before CI coding began. In addition to outright violence, which is rarer in the sitcom, issues of power between men and women, and adults and children, are raised quite often.

A few other observations about programs: CI coders analyzed whether "offensive language" (the category also encompasses "explicit" language) was

Family, Life, Love, Good, House   129

used in programs. The coding showed that in the 1990s, about 40 percent of programs had such instances. In the 2000s and the 2010s, that number went up to around 60 percent. This confirms that the regulatory atmosphere became freer for sitcoms' use of language in the 1990s and thereafter, as coarse dialogue became more common.

Sex is shown in sitcoms at rates similar to action or drama shows. Almost 80 percent of the sitcoms coded by CI had some reference to or portrayal of sex. Usually it was considered "incidental" by the coders; smaller portions were significant or major aspects of the show. Also, a good chunk of it was coded as "comic"; fumbling scenes of sex gone wrong or sexual misadventures would likely account for many of those instances.

Character-Level Variables

In the CI data, there are many variables for each unit of analysis. We focus on two major types: demographics and other character features. In terms of demographics, in this section we analyze the following: gender, age, race, and marital status. Gender was measured simply as male or female, with the coder using his or her judgment.[8] Table 4.1 shows the results for this and other static demographic analyses. Almost 60 percent of characters in sitcoms were male, a percentage that matches closely what other studies have found of the overall network television universe (Signorielli, 1989).

Age is measured in the CI dataset through estimations that coders make. Since it is normally virtually impossible to estimate an exact age from what is seen in a television narrative, coders used broad categories that delineated "social age." These categories were "child/adolescent," "young adult," "settled adult," and "elderly, old." There was also a coding for "chronological age," which was an estimation of the actual age, but it should be considered rough. The average estimated age across the entire sitcom character data file was 32.5. Table 4.1 shows that the large majority of characters fell into the young adult (32.4%) or settled adult (53.8%) category. The table also shows the average estimated chronological ages for each of those categories.

Race was measured with the following categories: "white," "Black," "Asian," "Native American," and "other." As expected, the large majority of characters were white (81.2%) regardless of period (see table 4.1), followed by Black (16.9%), other (1.1%), and Asian (0.8%). There were only 28 Native Americans over the five decades, and the proportion was less than 0.1 percent. Only about 2.5 percent of characters were identified as Latino.[9]

130 SITCOMS AND CULTURE

Table 4.1. Frequencies and averages in sitcoms, by demographic categories

	Frequency	%	
Male	2523	58.3	
Female	1800	41.6	Chron. age
Child	410	9.4	13.06
Young adult	1402	32.4	25.27
Middle adult	2331	53.8	38.75
Older	142	3.2	60.97
Can't code	37	.8	16.02
White	3490	80.6	
Black	724	16.7	
Asian	34	0.7	
Native American	0	0	
Other	47	1.0	
Not married	1861	52.2	
Impending	101	2.8	
Married	1133	31.8	
Separated	39	1.0	
Formerly	306	8.5	
Remarried	10	.2	
Mixed	39	1.0	
Live with	53	1.4	
Same-sex marriage	19	.5	

Marital status was measured only if coders thought a character was fifteen years or older, which is consistent with the age qualification for the marital status survey of the US Census. The initial variable had multiple categories: "not married," "married," "marriage-impending," "separated," "formerly married," "remarried," "mixed," "live with," and "same-sex relationship." Throughout the whole dataset, not married comprised the largest proportion (52.3%), which was about two-thirds as high as married (31.8%). They were followed by formerly married (8.5%), marriage-impending (2.8%),

Family, Life, Love, Good, House   131

living with (1.1%), mixed (1%), separated (1%), same-sex relationship (0.5%), and remarried (0.2%).

Demographics over Time

Figure 4.3 shows how the ratio of the two genders varied within decades across the sample. In five-year periods, the female proportion was the highest in 2000–2004 (46.4%), followed by 1995–1999 (45.1%), 1985–1989 (43.8%), 1980–1984 (39.8%), 2005–2009 (39.1%), 1967–1975 (39.0%), 1990–1994 (39.0%), 2010–2015 (38.4%), and 1975–1979 (35.9%). The variance over the decades was statistically significant: $\chi2$ $(df, 8) = 22.37$, $p = 0.004$. However, via regression analysis, we see no significant *linear* relationship across the years ($p = 0.246$). Thus, in the CI sitcom data, gender ratios remained generally consistent, with males predominating.

Figure 4.4 shows the distribution of age categories across the periods of analysis. Young adult and settled adult (noted in the figure as "middle") comprised a dominant proportion across. Very young and very old characters were much rarer.

Figure 4.5 shows the distribution of race categories across the sample periods. The proportion of white characters was higher than 70 percent in every period. The highest was 1967–1975 (90.7%), followed by 2010–2015 (89.8%), 1980–1984 (88.2%), 1975–1979 (85.4%), 2005–2009 (80.7%), 1990–1994 (79.1%), 1985–1989 (77.8%), 1995–1999 (77.1%), and 2000–2004 (73.7%). Via regression analysis, we see a slight but significant decline in the proportion of white characters across the years ($b = -0.002$, $t = -2.21$, $p = 0.033$). Numbers of Black characters increased in each decade but decreased again the 2010s. Asian and Native American characters appear very infrequently.

For marital status, to display the comparison more simply, we combined "married" and "remarried" into "married," and other categories were merged into "nonmarried." After the recoding, the frequency of nonmarried characters (2,838) was about 2.5 times more than married characters (1,145) over the decades. Figure 4.6 shows the changes in marital status across the five-year periods of analysis. Nonmarried characters were shown most frequently in the period of 1995–1999 (77.7%) and in the period of 1990–1994 (77.7%). The variance over the decades was statistically significant: $\chi2$ $(df, 8) = 152.15$, $p < 0.001$. Via regression analysis, we see a significant increase in the proportion of nonmarried characters across the years ($b = 0.004$, $t = 3.19$, $p = 0.003$). Marriage became slightly less common.

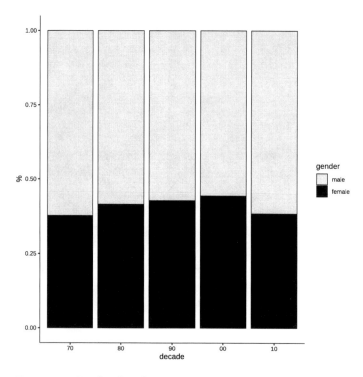

Figure 4.3. Gender distribution in sitcoms by decade.

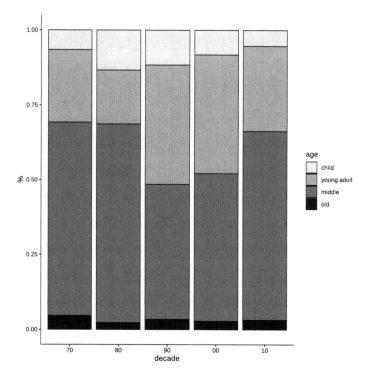

Figure 4.4. Age distribution in CI data.

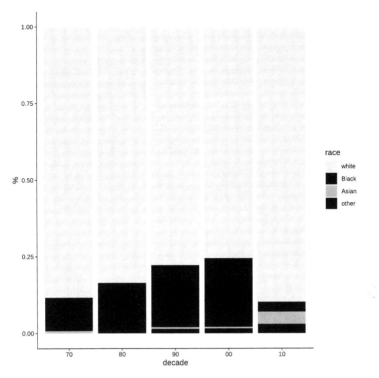

Figure 4.5. Character race in sitcoms by decade.

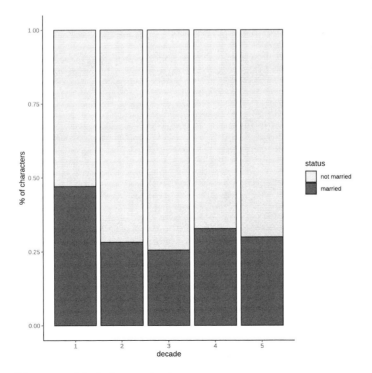

Figure 4.6. Marital status in sitcoms.

134 SITCOMS AND CULTURE

Multivariate Comparisons

GENDER BY AGE

Across all sitcoms in the CI dataset, the average estimated age of women was 31.25 whereas men averaged 33.37. The average age by gender in each decade was consistently about two years higher for males than females, with slight but not very significant variation across the decades, as seen in figure 4.7.

AGE BY GENDER AND MARITAL STATUS

The gender-age difference was much heightened when considering marital status. Married characters were on average 39 years old whereas unmarried or those who couldn't be characterized were younger at 31.9. Married men were oldest of all at 40.5 years; youngest were unmarried females at 30.43. The pattern within decades (table 4.2) shows that unmarried characters tend to age similarly by gender, but married females are usually younger than the men, usually by around 3 to 5 years.

RACE BY AGE, GENDER, AND MARITAL STATUS

About 17 percent of characters in sitcoms were Black. In the overall dataset (all programs, not just sitcoms), the number was closer to 12 percent. The difference is not surprising, given that comedy has historically been a more likely place for Black-led shows or Black actors on white-led shows. Among shows that were not sitcoms, the figure was around 9 percent. Racial breakdowns did not show much variance by gender; each race measured was roughly 42 percent female. Black characters tended to be younger (30.3 versus 33.1 years of age for white characters).

The most interesting comparison is for marital status of different racial groups. Table 4.3 shows that 33 percent of white characters could be coded as married while the number was only about 27 percent for Blacks and Asians. The number for Latinos, who could be coded as either Black or white within the data, was higher than for whites.

Comparisons to Demographic Statistics

As we might have expected, some of the results from sitcom demography were distorted when compared to the real world. The gender results were most obvious: There was almost always a rough fifty-fifty male/female split in the US population, but the sitcom tendency, when looking across all the characters in the database, was 60 male / 40 female. Figure 4.3 shows that

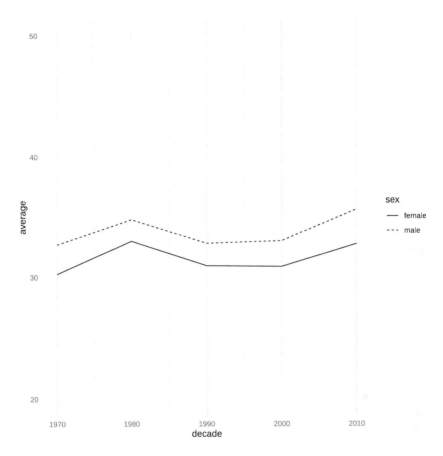

Figure 4.7. Female and male average age by decade.

percentages of women were inching up but also declined somewhat in the last decade. Below, we will look at the gender representation issue with our IMDB dataset, but the male predominance in number of characters seems to be durable, even given the developing importance of women's issues after the 1970s "relevance" period, and also given the importance of female-led sitcoms at various points in sitcom history.

Within the gender disparity, we see another reversal of reality in that sitcoms tend to show younger females while the average age of females in the population is at any time older, given longer lifespans for females. This is again an example of the fact that although women's issues did progress across the decades of sitcoms, some of the structural distortions remained quite persistent.

136   SITCOMS AND CULTURE

Table 4.2. Average age of sitcom characters, by gender and marital status

Decade	Marital status	Male	Female
1970s	Not married	28.60	29.37
	Married	37.92	33.45
1980s	Not married	35.93	32.66
	Married	44.82	40.69
1990s	Not married	33.10	24.6
	Married	39.38	36.89
2000s	Not married	33.04	29.60
	Married	34.38	36.89
2010s	Not married	35.00	31.68
	Married	42.61	38.34

Table 4.3. Percentages of married characters, by race

	White	Black	Asian	Latino
Not Married	66.6	72.7	72.6	61.7
Married	33.3	27.3	27.3	38.2

With race, Blacks have achieved proportional or even greater representation in sitcoms compared to demographic reality. The current population percentage for Blacks is around 13 percent; in the sitcom world, the numbers have sometimes been closer to 16–17 percent. Other races have had a harder time achieving this goal. Native Americans appear not at all in the sitcom CI database. They are about 2 percent of the US population, so we should expect to see them occasionally. Asians show up at 0.8 percent in the sitcom database; they are closer to 6 percent of the US population. Most glaring is the discrepancy between the real world and sitcoms for Latinos. They are 19 percent in the real world but only 1.4 percent in the sitcom database. While the CI coding methods may have undercounted Latinos who would otherwise simply have been coded as Black or white, the difference appears to be real in a world where Latino-oriented shows are much rarer than Black ones.

Character Features

Next, we look at some subjective features of characters, breaking those down by the major demographic categories analyzed in the previous section. The

CI dataset coded each character as "good" or "bad" or something in between. Table 4.4 shows the breakdown of good and bad characters by each of the demographic categories.

In general, most sitcom characters were categorized as good or mixed. Relatively few characters, especially in sitcoms, played a villain role. There were comic nemeses, such as Newman in *Seinfeld*, but even those characters were rarely seen as bad or evil. Thus, small differences in how character types were categorized as bad were informative. The table shows that males were more likely to be seen as bad than females (4.7% vs. 2.6%; χ_2 $[df, 4]$ = 24.64, $p < 0.001$). As characters aged, they were also more likely to be seen as bad (children, 1.7%; younger adults, 3.4%; adults, 4.5%; older, 3.5%; χ_2 $[df, 16]$ = 49.54, $p < 0.001$). With race, we see that white characters are slightly more likely to be bad than those from any other race (4% vs. 3.2%, χ_2 $[df, 4]$ = 20.87, $p < 0.001$). Finally, nonmarried characters were more likely to be seen as bad than married ones (4.1% vs. 2.4%, χ_2 $[df, 4]$ = 41.39, $p < 0.001$).

In addition to whether a character is seen as good or bad, other character attributes are coded in the CI dataset. These attributes were not coded every year, and in some years it was difficult to establish good reliability in assessing them. Nevertheless, they still provide a helpful window into how character types were portrayed. The attributes, judged on a five-point scale, were "attractive," "powerful," and "smart." Table 4.5 shows mean values of these attributes by the four demographic categories that we are analyzing. Regarding gender, female characters' average attractiveness score ($M = 3.89$) was 1.15 times higher than that for male characters ($M = 3.38$). This difference is statistically significant, $t(2718.7) = -16.93$, $p < 0.001$. There was no significant difference on the other variables, powerful and smart, within gender.

As the table shows, all three of the character attributes were significantly different by social age. Concerning attractiveness, the young adult group ($M = 3.9$) was seen to be the most attractive, followed by child/adolescent ($M = 3.51$), settled adult ($M = 3.48$), and older ($M = 2.98$). The variance across social age was statistically significant, $F(4, 3115) = 50.59$, $p < 0.001$. Interestingly, when it comes to the powerful variable, the rank exactly followed the age order; the older the social age class was, the higher its power was. Thus, the older group was the highest ($M = 3.41$) followed by settled adult ($M = 3.27$), young adult ($M = 3.23$), and child/adolescent ($M = 3.05$). The variance was statistically significant, $F(4, 1639) = 5.01$, $p < 0.001$. While the age order was also found on the smart variable as well, the result was not statistically significant, $p < .07$.

Race was significantly associated with the attractive and smart variables. The bivariate comparison showed that nonwhite characters were seen as less

Table 4.4. Percentages of "good," "mixed," and "bad" characters, by demographic category

	Good	Mixed	Bad
Male	54.1	35.2	4.7
Female	60.0	32.6	2.6
Child/adolescent	52.5	38.2	1.7
Young adult	57.2	31.8	3.4
Settled adult	56.4	34.4	4.5
Older	50.7	36.6	3.5
White	56.1	34.2	4.0
Other	4.0	33.4	3.2
Married	63.6	27.9	2.4
Not married	54.7	34.9	4.1

Table 4.5. Character attributes by demographic category[1]

	Attractive	Powerful	Smart
Male	3.38[a]	3.22	3.65
Female	3.89[a]	3.29	3.64
Child/Adolescent	3.51[a]	3.05[a]	3.51
Young adult	3.90[a]	3.23[a]	3.62
Settled adult	3.48[a]	3.27[a]	3.67
Older	2.98[a]	3.41[a]	3.96
White	3.67[c]	3.26	3.57[c]
Nonwhite	3.58[c]	3.24	3.67[c]
Married	3.67[b]	3.23	3.43[b]
Not married	3.58[b]	3.30	3.51[b]

[1] *a* denotes statistically different, $p < 0.001$, b - $p < 0.01$, c - $p < 0.05$

attractive but smarter than white characters. Regarding attractiveness, white characters' average score was 1.03 times higher than nonwhite characters'. While the gap was not substantial, the difference was statistically significant, $t(858.5) = -2.32, p = 0.020$. With that being said, nonwhite characters' average smartness score ($M = 3.67$) was higher than that for white characters ($M = 3.57$). The difference was also statistically significant, $t(1107.3) = 2.01, p = 0.045$.

Marital status was significantly associated with being more attractive and smarter. Regarding power, characters not married ($M = 3.23$) showed a higher score than married characters ($M = 3.20$), but the difference was not statistically significant, $t(931) = 1.63, p = 0.10$. Unmarried characters ($M = 3.51$) also displayed a higher smartness score than married ones ($M = 3.43$). The variance was significant, $t(1783.9) = 3.10, p = 0.01$.

The IMDB Data

Unlike the CI Data, the IMDB data are gathered with a minimum of human coding effort. Programs are identified through crowdsourced lists on Wikipedia. Data about the programs are harvested from the IMDB programmer interface (the API). Data are then cleaned to eliminate errors, such as programs that are incorrectly classified, and for other minor discrepancies.

We ended our data collection period in the year 2021. The earliest sitcoms we gathered were from the late 1940s, so we have a dataset of eighty-plus years' worth of programming. The dataset includes 1,001 programs. The earliest included is *The Aldrich Family*, dating back to its radio origins in 1939 and appearing on television from 1949 to 1953. The latest to appear in the database is *Wandavision* (2021), a Marvel comic book character miniseries that pays homage to sitcom history.

Figure 4.8 shows the growth in the production of sitcoms over the years. Early years of network sitcom production started to burgeon in the 1960s, then ramped up in the later '80s and '90s as new networks came on the scene. Eventually, production reached a height in the early 2000s with the advent of various streaming services and other platform availabilities for series to be produced. The decade of the 2010s showed a slight drop-off, but there was still an enormous number of sitcoms and sitcom-adjacent programs in the era of "peak TV." The total number of episodes represented in this database is 62,866—about three and half years of continuous viewing if one were to binge all the episodes without sleep.

The IMDB database allows us to examine two demographic variables: age and gender. These are drawn from actor profiles contained within the IMDB

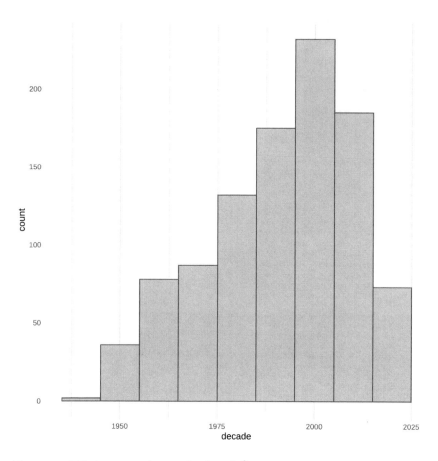

Figure 4.8. US sitcom production by decade.[2]

[2] Programs are classified by the year they started production.

API; other characteristics such as race are not recorded. The IMDB data permits a look at fewer variables than those coded in the CI data; because they were human-coded, the CI data have room for more subjective characteristics to be included. But the IMDB data are much more complete chronologically, containing as they do many more programs (versus the yearly sample of CI). There are trade-offs to using either dataset singly. Using them both, we can improve both the breadth and the resolution of our data picture. An additional feature of the IMDB data is that it contains audience ratings, which allows some perspective on how audience preferences are related to age and gender composition of programs.

Family, Life, Love, Good, House 141

Gender and Age

Across sitcoms in the IMDB data, 1940–2021, males comprised 59.4 percent of the characters that appeared. Compare this number to our finding from the CI dataset: 58.3 percent. The estimates accord very well. Figure 4.9 shows the proportion of males in each decade. The data show that ratios of males tended to be higher in the earlier decades and generally that the fraction declined incrementally through the years. However, even in the last decade the proportion was still around 57 percent male. A linear regression model based on the IMDB data (fig. 4.9a) shows when, at the current rate of change, an equal gender distribution might be expected: perhaps around 2040. This differs somewhat from the CI data, which showed some gradual decrease in frequency of male characters, but recall that the IMDB data have an earlier starting point. In simple terms, then, things are equalizing, but there is a way to go.

We computed character age from IMDB information about the actor's birthdate. From this we know their actual age when they appeared on the program. This is more accurate than the estimation methods used with the CI data. Although older actors sometimes play younger characters and vice versa, this calculation gives us an accurate sense of the ages of American sitcom casts. The average age across the entire dataset was almost exactly thirty-five years old. Figure 4.10 shows the trend in average age across the decades.

The data are roughly comparable to the CI data, summarized in figure 4.7. Both show a trend toward younger characters across the decades, though the IMDB data comprise an earlier starting point. Both also show an interesting trend back *upward* in age in the 2010s. Again, the concordance between the two datasets provides confidence in their reliability and validity. When we break down the change in age by gender and decade (fig. 4.11), we see that men have consistently been about three years older than women; the differences track very well across each decade.

"Youth" in Sitcoms

American TV has typically compressed the age categories that are seen in its programs. Those most shown are in the middle of the age distribution, more specifically the younger middle. CI research over the years has noted television's preference for this population stratum, which is explained most obviously by the quest for advertising dollars targeted at higher consumer spenders. Gerbner et al. (1980) wrote, "In contrast to the distribution of age groups

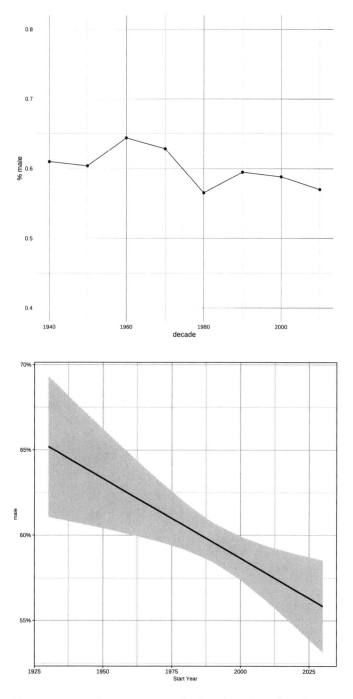

Figure 4.9. Gender composition by decade and predicted change in gender and composition.

Family, Life, Love, Good, House 143

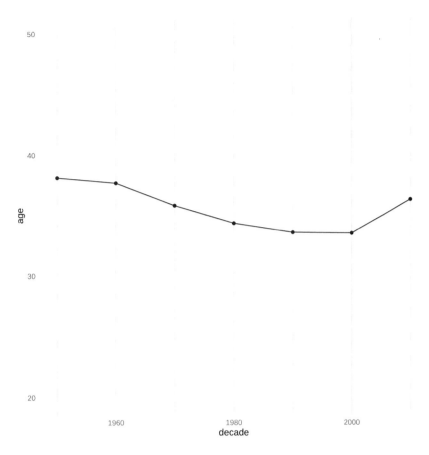

Figure 4.10. Average age by decade.

in the American population, the television curve demonstrates a pronounced central tendency: it bulges in the middle years and grossly underrepresents both young and old people. More than half of TV's dramatic population is between 25 and 45" (p. 380).

Figure 4.12 shows the tendency very clearly in our sitcom database. Sitcoms, along with most of the rest of television, are focused on young adult to middle-aged categories of viewers. That tendency has become even more pronounced throughout the years, especially for women. The female differences are especially interesting due to the well-known preference for Hollywood actresses to have more youthful appearances. The special sitcom version of this is the very attractive woman who is married to the less attractive or older

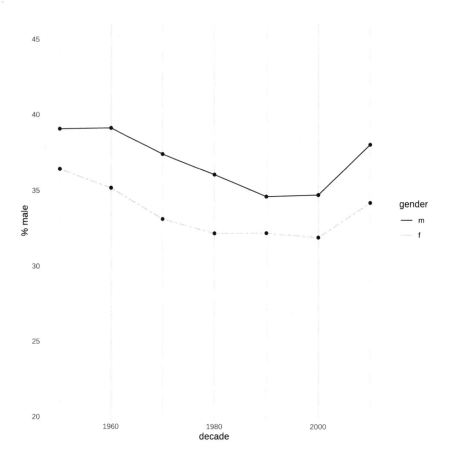

Figure 4.11. Male and female average age by decade.

man. Examples would include Ralph Kramden's wife, Alice (Audrey Meadows), who made herself plainer to win the role. Kevin James played an overweight man of dubious intelligence in *King of Queens*, with wife Leah Remini as his notably fitter and hotter wife, Carrie. Jerry Seinfeld, a man of average appearance, dated an increasingly beautiful set of supermodels throughout his show's reign. On *Modern Family*, lead character Ed O'Neill was sixty-three; his wife, played by Sofia Vergara, was thirty-seven and considered to be a sex bomb.

The sitcom preference for younger audiences developed most obviously when CBS abandoned its older-skewing rural sitcoms for the relevance movement of the '70s. The trend toward youth was long-lasting, changing

Family, Life, Love, Good, House 145

direction only in the 2010s. Why did sitcoms trend somewhat older in the 2010s? At that time, sitcoms were more likely to be produced on networks. As the number of alternative options to network TV increased in the streaming and on-demand world, the networks themselves started to skew older again. Networks that were still paying attention to sitcoms were thus again tending toward a more conservative programming strategy. Some of the sitcoms that were greenlit in the 2010s show this tendency, with much older leading characters. Some of them had leading roles over sixty, such as *$#*! My Dad Says* (2010–11), with seventy-nine-year-old William Shatner. *Retired at 35* (2011–12) starred George Segal at age seventy-seven. Older comedians like Robin Williams were getting vehicles again. *Roseanne* was rebooted as *The Conners*, with sixty-six-year-old John Goodman in the lead. Sixty-nine-year-old Kathy Bates took the helm in *Disjointed* (2017–18), about a marijuana dispensary.

The other factor to note is that the US population was itself aging. Figure 4.13 shows that the average sitcom character's age was actually higher than the US population from the '60s through the '90s. In the final two decades, the two demographics tracked very closely, indicating that sitcoms were at best a lagging cultural indicator for age, at least until recently. Whether sitcoms continue to age will be an interesting open question, as it is indeterminate whether the younger audiences that emerge in the age of social media will attend to the sitcom genre much or at all.

Main Characters

In IMDB, the first character listed is generally the main or lead character of the series. When considering representation issues, we should give more weight to the lead character. In this subsection, we look at the age/gender analyses only for characters who are listed as leads. It turns out, perhaps not unexpectedly, that the gender disparity is larger for gender when considering only main characters. Series leads are 65 percent male versus the 59 percent average that we saw when considering all characters. Figure 4.14 shows how this varied over the decades.

Apart from the starker gender disparities, what is interesting is the absolute male supremacy in the '60s, '70s, and '80s, especially given that the '70s are considered to be the decade when women's issues were being taken up more consciously. This reminds us that prominent shows don't always reflect accurately what is going on in the body of programs—in all of the different shows to which people will be exposed.

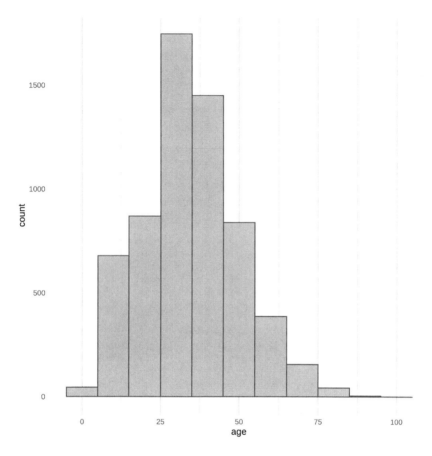

Figure 4.12. Histogram of age distribution in IMDB data.

There were 115 shows in our dataset that started sometime in the '70s. Shows that did well that were female-led included *Mary Tyler Moore, Maude, Good Times, Rhoda* (1974–78), *Phyllis* (1975–77), *Laverne and Shirley* (1976–83), and *Alice*. There were fewer that turned out to be audience duds, such as *The Girl with Something Extra* (1973–74), in which Sally Field had ESP, and *Karen* (1975), a vehicle for Karen Valentine, who had been on the more successful *Room 222*. Many more of the unsuccessful shows were male-led, such as *The New Bill Cosby Show* (1972–73) or *The Bob Crane Show* (1975). Shows that were being greenlit, as always, often were vehicles for stars who had some sort of proven potential, and these continued to be mostly male, even though TV was catching up somewhat with the social change that had been occurring

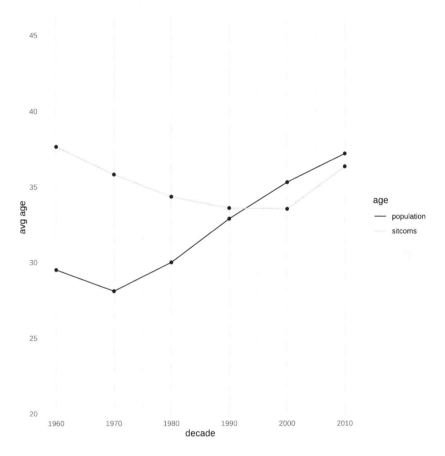

Figure 4.13. Sitcom character age compared to US population by decade.

throughout the '60s. The successful female shows also had some proven stars, at least in the case of *MTM*, but they also often had Norman Lear on their side, and so creatively the female-led shows were more innovative. In any case, audiences, while flocking to the new women's shows, were still seeing mostly a diet of male comedians. The sitcoms of the '70s were thus still a lagging indicator for gender.

Audience Ratings

The IMDB data include a cumulative rating score, which is crowdsourced from IMDB users. These ratings should not be confused with Nielsen ratings, which are actual measures of frequency of viewing the program (recall that

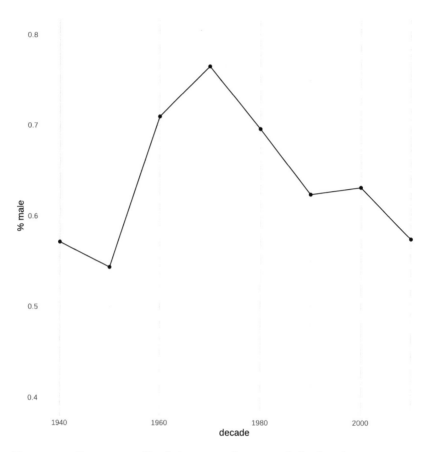

Figure 4.14. Percentage of lead characters that are male by decade.

we analyzed this type of data in chap. 3). The IMDB ratings data are interesting as they reflect the cumulative opinions of people interested enough to use IMDB, whom we can assume are more actively TV-oriented than the average viewer.

Figure 4.15 shows the distribution of how IMDB users rate sitcoms. The mean IMDB rating, out of 10, is 6.87. The lowest-rated program was *Kirk* (1995–97), which was a failed vehicle for Kirk Cameron, who had been on the very popular *Growing Pains*. Its IMDB rating is 2.7. The highest-rated program is *The Office* at 9. This is the US version of the popular British sitcom.

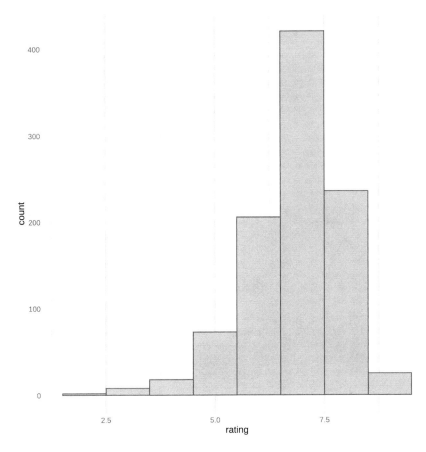

Figure 4.15. Distribution of IMDB ratings.

IMDB ratings are neither a perfect correlate nor a predictor of a program's success. Some programs are highly rated by IMDB users as cult classics, even though they did not succeed in the marketplace as measured by number of episodes. *My World and Welcome to It* (1969–70) has a very high IMDB rating (8.8). Its humor was more sophisticated than the average sitcom, based on the literary approach of James Thurber. But it achieved only moderate ratings and was canceled after one season.

At the other end of the spectrum, programs that had very long successful runs, such as some of Tyler Perry's shows, have very low IMDB ratings. Those divergences likely reflect the racial segregation of the audience components

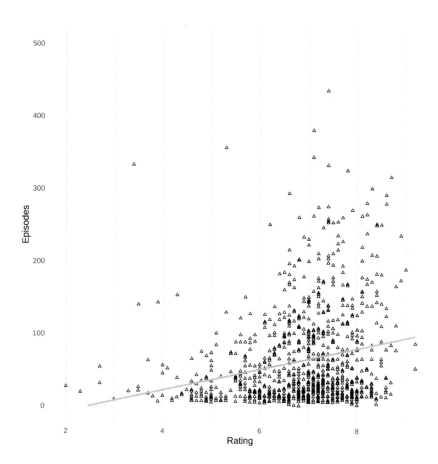

Figure 4.16. IMDB ratings and episodes, their relationship.

for those programs. Overall, though, there is modest and significant correlation between IMDB ratings and number of episodes ($r = 0.23$), as seen in figure 4.16's trend line.

There are two interesting predictors of audience perception of sitcoms. First, older shows are rated more highly. Several reasons would explain this, since it is not necessarily the case that older sitcoms were better. IMDB's inclusion of older programs may exclude some that were very short-run and would have been rated lower, whereas more recent shows of lesser popularity are simply more likely to have been included. Second, IMDB ratings come from audiences that are judging from today's perspective. There may be some nostalgia effect as audiences look back at sitcoms versus what they see today.

Third, as the years progress, there are many more sitcoms in the marketplace, so one might simply expect average quality to decrease with the number of shows produced.

Nevertheless, shows tended to have more episodes in the earlier days. In our data, sitcoms from the '50s averaged more than one hundred episodes. The number declined almost monotonically through the decades, such that by the 2000s the average was about fifty-two, almost half of what it was when TV began. Clearly, competitive forces were making it harder for sitcoms to sustain long runs.

Concerning gender and age, males are more likely to be in shows that are highly rated by the IMDB users. This is partially connected to the chronological effect discussed above: sitcoms from early years were more popular, and their stars were more likely to be male. In fact, when controlling for chronology, the effect of male characters on audience preference disappears. Also, it may be that IMDB users themselves are more male and so may show some bias in their ratings.

IMDB audiences' highly rated programs also tend to have somewhat older characters (again measuring the actor's age at the time the character was on the show). This may also be due somewhat to the chronological effect described above, as average age did decrease across most of the decades, but the effect does persist when controlling for the start year of the program.[10]

Overall, then, the IMDB data tend to counter at least some myths about audience preferences—namely that they will always prefer younger-skewing shows. However, male characters were more likely to be in shows that were more popular, and males were simply more likely to be in shows in the first place.

Discussion

This section provides a very broad look at the demography of television sitcoms from 1967 to 2015. The findings' value lies in their scope across fifty years of TV history; they provide many initial avenues into inquiry for other researchers interested in this period. First, we see that sitcoms were always a main portion of the TV diet. With many viewers watching three to four hours of television a night and sitcoms comprising 35 to 40 percent of that total, we know that many individuals watched thousands of hours of sitcoms in their lifetimes. That alone suggests the importance of sitcoms' influence. They were particularly prevalent for a period in the 1970s in terms of quality and then again in the 1990s, as cycles and trends

152 SITCOMS AND CULTURE

in television entertainment (the "must-see TV" phenomenon) drove producers to that genre. Across the years, though, it is the stability of sitcoms that is most interesting.

Over time, demographics remained relatively stable within the genre. Sitcoms were basically male-dominated (by a sixty-to-forty ratio); that proportion fluctuated in nonsignificant ways. Age groups also remained relatively stable; sitcoms were the domain of the young adult, with middle-aged adults coming in second. It was not much of a place for older people. Children, though of course common in the family sitcom, were also less frequent. Race shows perhaps the most interesting pattern. The frequency of Black characters did increase across the periods examined, until about 2004. Indeed, at one point some of the most popular sitcoms starred Black characters, such as in *The Cosby Show* when it was number 1. Later in the 2000s, as Black viewership (along with other viewership) fractioned among cable and internet outlets, and as the TV network audiences aged into an older demographic, percentages of Black characters on networks declined. Finally, we see that nonmarriage was relatively more common than marriage among all characters. This variable needs to be explored in greater detail, but it does implicate the frequency with which sitcoms now deal with those who are premarriage (again, the younger adult category) and eventually ending up there (*Friends*) or in family situations postmarriage that create interesting narrative opportunities (*One Day at a Time, Alice*). Even in earlier years, sitcoms were always struggling to find narrative alternatives to the traditional, and perhaps somewhat boring, nuclear family.

Characteristics of these demographic types were also suggestive. Males and whites were more likely to be "bad." Married people were most likely to be "good." Young, female, and white people were judged to be more attractive. On the other hand, not-married and older people were judged to be smarter. Nonwhite characters were also judged to be smarter, perhaps counter to some ideas about stereotyping across the years of TV history.

Here we only touch on the analyses that are possible with these datasets, which are to our knowledge the only ones that consistently code TV programs over such a long period. From that perspective, even a relatively straightforward descriptive analysis is a useful place to start. From this place we can make some conjectures for further investigation. A cursory examination of sitcoms over the years would suggest that much changed: women's roles changed, there were more roles for minority characters, sexual attitudes freed up, and a much coarser humor was also possible. In some ways, change seems to be the rule as we traverse the decades from the late '60s to where we are today.

And yet, our data also show an underlying conservatism, perhaps not surprising given what we know about television as an institution. Even in periods of secular social change, television still needs to create mass audiences, especially in the sphere of network television that this study examines. As new channels for video entertainment opened up, especially in the latter half of the period covered by this dataset, the flagship network TV stations found themselves dealing with an aging and whiter audience. Some sitcoms in later years have sought to break out of this mold, but networks that still pursued the sitcom genre, such as CBS, found that their most popular vehicles had white casts. An example would be *Two and a Half Men*, a program with no minority main characters and a star who was seen by many as a poster child for toxic masculinity. The show *Big Bang Theory* had one main character who was not white, but again the show seemed to mainly address itself to majority audience sensibilities.

None of this is surprising from an economic standpoint; one can expect the networks to maximize audience and profit. But given that the networks still usually attract the largest (though diminishing) audience, it speaks to the potential power to cultivate tendencies toward social conservatism while other sectors of society push in the opposite direction.

NOTES

1. *Cavemen* is worthy of special note. Considered by some to be one of the worst shows of all time, it used popular advertising figures, made up as apelike cavemen, as the focus of the sitcom. The characters were supposed to send up modern racial prejudices, but too many viewers thought they were actually racist, and the show was pulled.

2. Gerbner (n.d.)

3. These methodological details are presented elsewhere, often in more detail—most recently in Signorielli, Morgan, & Shanahan (2019).

4. No data were collected in 2007 or 2014. Prime-time programs were those broadcast between 8:00 p.m. and 11:00 p.m. on Mondays through Saturdays and between 7:00 p.m. and 11:00 p.m. on Sundays.

5. UPN and WB were part of the project between 1995 and 2006; they merged into the CW in 2006.

6. A statistic measuring intercoder reliability.

7. George Gerbner Archive (n.d.).

8. No provision was made for other codings; a very small number of cases (only three for the entire dataset) could not be coded.

9. The race measure did not include *Hispanic* or *Latino*, which is an ethnicity. Only 1.5 percent of characters in the dataset were coded as Hispanic.

10. Regression coefficients for this analysis: male ($b = 0.027, p = 0.288$), age ($0.0032, p < 0.001$), year = $-0.013, p < 0.001$).

5

Textual Analysis

THUS FAR, OUR DATA analyses have been focused at the macro level. In this chapter, we focus at a more micro level on one particular show: *Seinfeld*. Here, we use textual and critical analyses to examine features of this sitcom that are interesting from a cultural indicators perspective, in a way that complements the usual cultural criticism approach. We use the textual data to measure and test certain assumptions about how dialogue is distributed in a sitcom, how words are used, and ultimately how gender, class, sexuality, and other issues are worked out through the words characters are given to say. We use textual analysis as an exploratory tool to reveal things that might be interesting for students of sitcoms.

Seinfeld as Data

Seinfeld was on network television from 1989 to 1998, across 173 episodes. As we have been arguing in this book, all sitcoms are to some extent about society, but *Seinfeld* was very particular and intentional in its desire to point out social conventions, oddities, and hypocrisies to comedic effect. Jerry Seinfeld's status as the ultimate observational comic positioned him well to create a show that was ostensibly "about nothing"—and therefore actually about everything.

In our analysis, we use a database of all dialogue (a corpus) from *Seinfeld* that allows us to show how words are used by different characters at a micro level and whether and how those micro usages cumulate into meaningful patterns. As well, we can get a sense of the demography of *Seinfeld*, one of the few shows with enough episodes and enough viewership to create its own world, and give a sense of its importance as a cultural indicator, even though it is only one program.

156   SITCOMS AND CULTURE

A linguistic corpus is simply a body of text or speech that is compiled for analysis (Kennedy, 2014). Examples of corpora include the *American English* corpus from Google N-grams (155 billion words), the Corpus of Historical American English (475 million words), and the *Wikipedia Corpus* (1.9 billion words). There are various media-based corpora, including the *TV Corpus* (325 million words; we use it elsewhere a bit in this volume), and news-based corpora that come from newspapers and online sites. Clearly, many corpora are very large. They represent bodies of data that are machine-gathered and often require intensive computing power for analysis.

In the case of *Seinfeld*, we have data that are transcripts from each show. These data were compiled by scraping scripts from online sources, then arranging lines of dialogue and stage direction in sequential order across every episode of every season.[1] Not only is the dialogue text available, but it is connected to metadata such as which character speaks a line. For this analysis, we added some other metadata, such as the race of the character speaking and the gender.

Words in *Seinfeld*

A sitcom is ultimately the words that characters say to each other. Jerry Seinfeld himself has become known as a word-focused comedian, honing his bits across multiple performances with very exacting attention to word choice. He doesn't improvise. So, word style, frequency, and choice can tell us a lot about the sitcom.

To get started, we look at word frequencies in *Seinfeld*. In this kind of analysis, words can be counted in two different ways. A *word type* is a recognition that a certain word has occurred in a text. Once a word like *the* occurs, we count that as one word type. The previous sentence has thirteen words that make up the sentence but only twelve word types (*once, a, word, like, the, occurs, we, count, that, as, one, type*). Because *word* occurs twice in the sentence, there are more words than word types. After a word is counted, future occurrences of the word don't add to the type count. A *word token* counts the frequency of the word use. Thus, in the sentence analyzed above, *word* is one type, but there are two tokens for that word. So, our example sentence has thirteen tokens but only twelve types. Any corpus will have more tokens than types.

For basic statistical analysis of a corpus, we can first look at the ratio of word types (showing the *vocabulary* of that corpus) to tokens, showing how lexically diverse the corpus is. The *type-token ratio* (TTR) can be as high as 1,

Textual Analysis

where every word used is never repeated. The lower it goes, the more words are repeated, and the discourse is considered less lexically diverse.

In the *Seinfeld* corpus, there are 502,256 words (tokens). These tokens are drawn from a vocabulary of 18,999 word types. Thus, the type-token ratio (Richards, 1987) is 0.037, which seems pretty low. Words are repeated a lot. However, any TTR measure tends to go down quickly as corpora get larger, so there needs to be some way to standardize the statistic. One way is by measuring TTR in segments and then averaging those segments together. Using this procedure, we see that the mean segmental type-token ratio (MSTTR; Johnson, 1944) for *Seinfeld* is 0.69. In other words, for every 100 word tokens spoken in the show dialogue, there are about 70 word types that contribute to the discourse.

With this result, we can use some benchmarks to understand how lexically diverse *Seinfeld* is. Since it is a sitcom, the genre frequently criticized for its mass production and low standards, we might expect it to be less sophisticated verbally than other quality media texts. On the other hand, *Seinfeld* is a depiction of people living in an upscale and urban(e) environment. Seinfeld himself is a word craftsman, so on that basis we might expect a more lexically diverse text. As figure 5.1 shows, however, many media texts hover closely around an MSTTR of 0.70. To see real variance in lexical diversity, we need to look at texts that are purposely created with lower word diversity for children (e.g., *The Cat in the Hat*, 0.55) or that are created with poetic and rhythmic considerations in mind for creating effect with audiences (e.g., Martin Luther King's "I Have a Dream" speech, 0.62). The King James book of Job, another poetic text, is also relatively low at 0.64. The modern texts shown in figure 5.1 are remarkably close; *Seinfeld* sits next to George Orwell, Arthur Conan Doyle, and Charles Darwin. Only James Joyce, master language manipulator and inventor, pushes his diversity statistic above 0.75 (*Ulysses* at 0.77). Even *Finnegans Wake*, with its freestyle invention of words that seem to purposefully defy understanding, sits in the lower 70s.[2]

Another way to assess a text via its word choice and use is by measuring its *readability*. There are many measures that can be used for this task; the most commonly used is the Flesch readability index (Flesch, 1948).[3] Readability scores are commonly used when assessing grade levels for reading. Words with fewer syllables and shorter sentence lengths are hallmarks of the readable text. We can get some idea of readability by selecting two texts cherry-picked for difference on these two dimensions. Jacques Derrida and other authors in the genre of critical theory are frequently criticized for dense

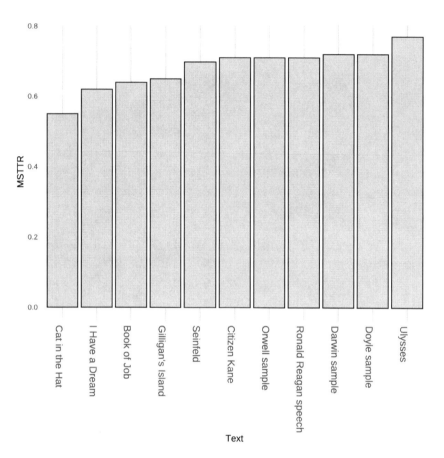

Figure 5.1. Lexical diversity in selected texts.

language. A sample from *Of Grammatology* (Derrida, 1998), chosen at random, illustrates:

> After having explained why "a dead language with a perfect ideography," that is to say a communication effective through the system of a generalized script, "could not have any real autonomy," and why nevertheless, "such a system would be something so particular that one can well understand why linguists want to exclude it from the domain of their science," Martinet criticizes those who, following a certain trend in Saussure, question the essentially phonic character of the linguistic sign: "Much will be attempted to prove that Saussure is right when he announces that 'the thing that constitutes language [*l'essentiel de la langue*] is ... unrelated to the phonic character of the linguistic sign,' and, going beyond the teaching

Textual Analysis

of the master, to declare that the linguistic sign does not necessarily have that phonic character." (p. 19)

This passage scores 45.2 on reading ease, which is considered "very difficult to read."[4] For contrast, we can look at the following passage from *The Old Man and the Sea* (Hemingway, 1952), a work celebrated for its spare prose and direct literary effectiveness:

> They picked up the gear from the boat. The old man carried the mast on his shoulder and the boy carried the wooden box with the coiled, hard-braided brown lines, the gaff and the harpoon with its shaft. The box with the baits was under the stern of the skiff along with the club that was used to subdue the big fish when they were brought alongside. No one would steal from the old man but it was better to take the sail and the heavy lines home as the dew was bad for them and, though he was quite sure no local people would steal from him, the old man thought that a gaff and a harpoon were needless temptations to leave in a boat. (p. 16)

This passage scores 79.8 on readability. It is "easy to read."

The measure of readability for the *Seinfeld* corpus is 92.9, or "very easy to read." It is around a third-grade reading level, if compared to texts that are scored for scholastic use. Several facts are worth pointing out. First, of course, *Seinfeld* is not meant to be read; it is meant to be heard and seen. Any television or film script is therefore likely to score higher on readability than printed texts. Even so, some texts such as Shakespeare that were also meant to be seen and heard come in at much higher grade levels. But with modern TV, we are not surprised to note that dialogue is short and to the point; indeed, it has often been punched up for comedic effect, to make sure that jokes hit quickly and that the number of viewers doesn't dwindle. The main reason for the high readability of *Seinfeld* is short words and very short sentences. Many lines of dialogue are only word long: "oh," "yeah," "okay," and so forth. *Seinfeld* may be an extreme example, though. Comparing it to some other sitcoms is instructive because in some ways it seems to reside at the apex of sit-comedic textual simplicity. Table 5.1 shows three readability scores for *Seinfeld* compared to five other sitcoms. The comparators were chosen more or less arbitrarily, and in each case, about twenty scripts were gathered for analysis.

It's clear that any of the sitcoms would be considered very easy to understand, which we already know from having seen any of them. They are meant to be like candy to consume. But does *Seinfeld* show us something interesting by being the *most* parsimonious in its use of language to achieve comedic

160 SITCOMS AND CULTURE

Table 5.1. Readability of six sitcoms

	Readability	Mean sentence length	Mean word syllables
Seinfeld	92.9	5.84	1.27
Barney Miller	86.98	6.14	1.34
Bewitched	87.12	6.89	1.33
Friends	89.59	6.94	1.30
Will & Grace	89.97	7.57	1.29
Father Knows Best	89.54	7.7	1.29

effect? It has the shortest sentence length and shortest words of any of the comparison programs.

A scene from the famous "Soup Nazi" episode (David, 1995) shows how dialogue tightens, following an inverted funnel shape toward the comedic climax, as the final sentences are three words, two words, and then one word only, followed by the punch line. Everything is monosyllabic.

BANIA: This guy makes the best soup in the city, Jerry. The best. You know what they call him? Soup Nazi.
JERRY: Shhhhh! All right, Bania, I—I'm not letting you cut in line.
BANIA: Why not?
JERRY: Because if he catches us, we'll never be able to get soup again.
BANIA: Okay. Okay.
GEORGE (ordering): Medium turkey chili.
JERRY: Medium crab bisque.
GEORGE: I didn't get any bread.
JERRY: Just forget it. Let it go.
GEORGE: Um, excuse me, I—I think you forgot my bread.
SOUP NAZI: Bread—$2 extra.
GEORGE: $2? But everyone in front of me got free bread.
SOUP NAZI: You want bread?
GEORGE: Yes, please.
SOUP NAZI: $3!
GEORGE: What?
SOUP NAZI: No soup for you! [snaps fingers]

Clearly, easy readability (watchability) does not distract from the effect of the show and, obviously, is in fact a component of it. Part of the artistry in a

Textual Analysis

161

sitcom that transcends its genre is that it does so in a way that it still remains sellable at a mass level, even while going above and beyond banality in some manner. Using hypersimplified primary-color language, *Seinfeld* still built complex narratives that had to be completed within twenty-four minutes. Later years of the show created very intricate structures where three or four separate storylines would converge at the end, somewhat like a Bach fugue, while still maintaining textual parsimony. Simplicity and readability of word choice did not mean lack of sophistication.[5]

The Upper West Side culture of *Seinfeld* may also be partly explanatory. There is some evidence that urban and northern people speak English at a faster rate than others (Jacewicz et al., 2009). This is consistent with *Seinfeld*'s parsimony. Moreover, the program shows a fascination with word usage and style, with episodes focused on "close talkers," "low talkers," and others who violate Grice's conversational maxims (Grice, 1975). Grice noted that generally, a conversation assumes an agreement about quantity, where one provides only the information needed to move the conversation along and no more. When *Seinfeld* characters violate this and other conversational maxims, it is for comedic effect (King, 2017).

Most-Used Words

Admittedly, examining *Seinfeld* from the standpoint of readability and lexical diversity can only be an introduction to understanding it from a cultural indicators perspective. It tells us something about the structure of the language used, but it doesn't help us gain much additional perspective on cultural meanings embedded in the program. The idea that it is parsimonious in its use of language would be interesting mainly to comedy writers and to linguists. A way to start to make more progress on meaning through text analysis is by looking at word frequency. We can start with an analysis of the most frequently used words.

In any English corpus, the most used words are always going to be common words like *the* and *a*. These are called *stopwords* when they are removed from analysis, allowing us to analyze words that carry more meaning and are frequent in the text. When these stopwords are removed, we can see the words in *Seinfeld* that are most commonly used and their frequency (fig. 5.2). Figure 5.2 shows the most commonly used words in the popular *wordcloud* format.

It would be beyond the scope of our work to look at every one of these words in detail, but here we choose three. *Know*, of course, is a very common word. It is considered to be the fifty-ninth most common word in the Oxford

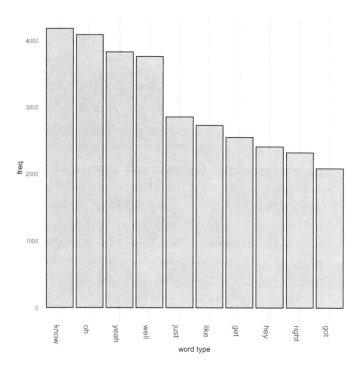

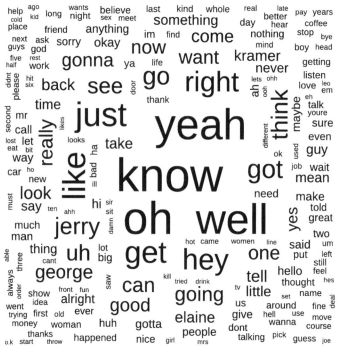

Figure 5.2. Most used words in *Seinfeld*.

Textual Analysis   163

English Corpus (OEC;[6] *the*, *be*, and *to* are ranked one, two, and three), so it is not surprising that it would occur frequently in a show that uses simple language. The tenth most common word in *Seinfeld* is *go*; it is forty-ninth in OEC. Finally, *want*, or its variant *wanna*, occurs 1,774 times in *Seinfeld* (it's ninety-three in OEC).

These words pop up frequently in the monologue that Jerry delivers before the very first (pilot) episode, which quizzes the audience about what they know, what Jerry knows, what we want, and whether we know where we want to go:

> JERRY: [Doing stand-up in a nightclub] Do you **know** what this is all about? Do you **know**, why we're here? To be out, this is out ... and out is one of the single most enjoyable experiences of life. People ... did you ever hear people talking about "We should **go** out?" This is what they're talking about ... this whole thing, we're all out now, no one is home. Not one person here is home, were all out! There are people tryin' to find us; they don't **know** where we are. Did you ring? I can't find him. Where did he **go**? He didn't tell me where he was **going**. He must have **gone** out. You **wanna go** out, you get ready, you pick out the clothes, right? You take the shower, you get all ready, get the cash, get your friends, the car, the spot, the reservation. Then you're standing around, whatta you do? You **go**. We gotta be getting back. Once you're out, you **wanna** get back! You **wanna** go to sleep, you **wanna** get up, you **wanna go** out again tomorrow, right? Where ever you are in life, it's my feeling, you've gotta **go**. (Seinfeld, 1989)

The monologue is built from the simplest and most common concepts; through juxtaposition and repetition, it achieves a comic effect. Its keywords are a cornerstone for understanding what the forthcoming episodes will be about. In *Seinfeld*, *going somewhere* is always a key theme, even given the context that no one is actually going anywhere. Going often seems to replace doing or simply being. *What we want* is another key theme, especially *not* knowing what we want, as *Seinfeld* is especially about people who can't decide with whom to have relationships. The show cannot avoid the fact (because it is a sitcom) that it is about people who create a quasi-family and whether this structure can survive the pressure for them to create a more traditional family. *Wanting, going, knowing* (and their negations) are three streams leading to a river that pushes the characters through a variety of adventures that, although they come to stable conclusions at the end of each episode, never seem to finally resolve.

Another reason that *know* appears so frequently is that it occurs quite a lot in the phrase *you know*. Words that occur together are called *collocates*. *You know* is the most frequent collocate in *Seinfeld*, occurring 2,157 times (there are more, counting the times that it is transcribed as *y'know*). One reason for its frequency is that it is simply a common speech pattern, used for musical reasons and as a kind of linguistic adaptor that we all . . . like, you know . . . use too much. Its appearance in the show conveys a realistic sense of how people talk, plus a little more. Look at how often it occurs, again in a segment from the pilot episode (Seinfeld, 1989):

JERRY: Wouldn't it be great if you could ask a woman what she's thinking?
GEORGE: What a world that would be, if you just could ask a woman what she's thinkin'. . . .
JERRY: **You know**, instead, I'm like a detective. I gotta pick up clues, the whole thing is a murder investigation.
GEORGE: Listen, listen, don't get worked up, 'cause **you're gonna know** the whole story the minute she steps off the plane.
JERRY: Really? How?
GEORGE: 'Cause it's all in the greeting.
JERRY: Uh-huh.
GEORGE: All right, if she puts the bags down before she greets you, that's a good sign.
JERRY: Right.
GEORGE: **You know**, anything in the, in the lip area is good.
JERRY: Lip area.
GEORGE: **You know**, a hug, definitely good.
JERRY: Hug is definitely good.
GEORGE: Sure.
JERRY: Although what if it's one of those hugs where the shoulders are touching, the hips are eight feet apart?
GEORGE: That's so brutal, I hate that.
JERRY: **You know** how they do that?
GEORGE: That's why, **you know**, a shake is bad.
JERRY: Shake is bad, but what if it's the two-hander? The hand on the bottom, the hand on the top, the warm look in the eyes?
GEORGE: Hand sandwich.

In *Seinfeld*, *you know* is also often used to tell another person that he's doing something or saying something wrong:

GEORGE: **You know**, I can't believe you're bringin' in an extra bed for a woman that wants to sleep with you. Why don't you bring in an extra guy too?

What is also interesting about *you know* in Seinfeld is that there is no sort of catchphrase that Jerry uses in every episode. Ralph Kramden would say, "To the moon!" JJ on *Good Times* would say, "Dyn-o-mite!" Henry Winkler as the

Textual Analysis 165

Fonz in *Happy Days* would simply say, "Heyyyyy!"[7] Seinfeld's catchphrases were found more in diction, with his way of saying "you know . . ." (with a slight pause and musical inflection) often being a way for him to begin an instruction to other members of the family in his quasi-father figure role.

Catchphrases can sometimes be a sign of the sitcom devolving into its "jump the shark" phase, as writers rely on reliable if cheap laughs for beloved lines that audiences come to expect. *Seinfeld* did that less. Some would say that Jerry's greeting of his archenemy with "Hello, Newman" would be an example of a catchphrase, but it appears in only eight episodes, mostly toward the end of the show when the Newman character gets more developed. The same is true for perceived catchphrases from other characters like Kramer, who says, "Giddyup" or "Hey buddy" in relatively few episodes. What can often seem like a catchphrase comes from the fact that a phrase is musically memorable, and we see it often in reruns. That *Seinfeld* avoided cheap lexical and comedic repetition that comes from stock phrases is notable. Speech *patterns* are the catch-themes in the show, along with nonverbal tropes (Kramer entering a room or doing certain things with his hands while speaking) that are notable.

This is not to say that repetition is not used to effect in *Seinfeld*. Repetition has classically been understood as an effective rhetorical device. Rhyme, alliteration, anaphora (repetition of phrases in succeeding sentences or clauses, as in Martin Luther King's "I Have a Dream" speech) and epistrophe (repetition at the end of the clause: "of the people, by the people, for the people" [Abraham Lincoln]) are a few of the many tools of repetition rhetoricians have identified that help speakers gain persuasive effectiveness. Undoubtedly, our preference for repetition in pleasing speech is related to our liking of similar devices in music and song. As verbal hooks, they help aid memory, and we evolve to find that which we remember to be pleasing as well.

It is always dangerous to try to theorize or explain comedy, but we should also note that philosopher Henri Bergson thought that repetition was very important to the comic. Bergson offered the metaphor of the jack-in-the-box for his idea of why repetition is funny. A mechanically repetitive simulation of a living being, the jack-in-the-box is continually repressed by another force:

> Let us scrutinize more closely the image of the spring which is bent, released, and bent again. Let us disentangle its central element, and we shall hit upon one of the usual processes of classic comedy, repetition.
>
> Why is it there is something comic in the repetition of a word on the stage? No theory of the ludicrous seems to offer a satisfactory answer to this very simple question. Nor can an answer be found so long as we look

166 SITCOMS AND CULTURE

for the explanation of an amusing word or phrase in the phrase or word itself, apart from all it suggests to us.... The repetition of a word is never laughable in itself. It makes us laugh only because it symbolizes a special play of moral elements, this play itself being the symbol of an altogether material diversion. It is the diversion of the cat with the mouse, the diversion of the child pushing back the Jack-in-the-box, time after time, to the bottom of his box, but in a refined and spiritualized form, transferred to the realm of feelings and ideas. Let us then state the law which, we think, defines the main comic varieties of word-repetition on the stage: In a comic repetition of words we generally find two terms: a repressed feeling which goes off like a spring, and an idea that delights in repressing the feeling anew. (Bergson, 1914, pp. 72–73)

Obviously, it is an overreach to explain all comedy with a single conceptual mechanism, as interesting as it might be. Still, using text analysis to locate word repetition, especially repeated collocates, can turn up some interesting examples of Bergson's thesis. In the episode "The Hot Tub" (S7E5), George is having a phone call with Texan baseball colleagues who continually, though congenially, sprinkle their speech with *bastard* and *son of a bitch*. George's boss overhears the conversation, wrongly of course (another comedic device, the misunderstanding bystander), which lands George in hot water at work:

GEORGE: Hello?

CLAYTON: Uh ... is that you, George?

GEORGE: Yeah, it's me. Is this Clayton?

CLAYTON: Well listen, you **son of a bitch**! You know where we are? 30,000 feet above your head, you **bastard**!

GEORGE: What are they doin' lettin' you **bastards** on an airplane? Don't they know that's against FAA regulation?

CLAYTON: Hey, hush up, now! I can't hear him!

GEORGE: Listen. I want you guys to send along those agreements the minute you land. Our boys can't wait to kick your butts!

ZEKE: When's that **bastard** comin' to Houston?

CLAYTON: Hey, Zeke wants to know when you Yankee **bastards** are comin' to Houston!

GEORGE: You tell that **son of a bitch** no Yankee is ever comin' to Houston. Not as long as you **bastards** are running things.

CLAYTON: Hey, uh, speak up, George, I can't hear ya!

GEORGE [Mr. Wilhelm comes in and hears George yelling louder]: You tell that **son of a bitch** no Yankee is ever comin' to Houston! Not as long as you **bastards** are running things!

MR. WILHELM: George! George, get a hold of yourself!!!

GEORGE: Mr. Wilhelm . . .
MR. WILHELM [shocked]: What's the matter with you?!
GEORGE: Well I—I . . . (Seinfeld, 1995)

Not only are *bastard* and *son of a bitch* repeated multiple times in the colloquy, but George is even given an opportunity to repeat a full sentence with both phrases, tightening up the jack-in-the-box spring even further until its release, which Mr. Wilhelm eventually tamps down on. The word *bitch* occurs eleven times in the episode, and *bastard* fourteen times. They are also comic leitmotifs that tie together an A and B story within the episode, all centered around instances where people misunderstand profane words when they are used in nonprofane contexts.

Some of these textual examples show us that *Seinfeld* is a comedy about conversation. Although Michael Richards as Kramer had memorable physical bits, much of the show is focused around things that happen at a coffee shop table. They are characters who analyze every word, to the point of overanalysis. They are gifted anthropologists and linguists, parsing the difference between kinds of handshakes, tones of speech, and minute variations in situations and what they ultimately mean socially. Complicated social comedic effects are achieved with word parsimony, magnifying their effectiveness.

Profanity

Seinfeld was a show that was, at the time of its popularity, pushing a few standards-and-practices limits. One of the most popular episodes ("The Contest," S4E11) was about who could refrain from masturbation the longest. To comply with network censorship, it seemed necessary to avoid the actual word, so the writers skillfully substituted *master of one's domain* (with winks and nods) to let the audience know what the real topic was. The word *masturbate* never occurred in this or any *Seinfeld* episode.

We noted above (fig. 2.1) that sitcoms have displayed a gradual "coarsening" of language. They were starting from a place of prudishness, where a word like *pregnant* was considered too dangerous (replaced with terms like *expecting* or *condition*). *I Love Lucy* successfully removed some of those barriers. Levine (2006) notes the surge in titillating programming that began in the '70s, and with the advent of cable TV in the '80s, which was not subject to the same language restrictions as over-the-air networks, audiences could see shows with ever-rougher or sexier language.

Shows like *Seinfeld* that were on networks still had to deal with the language issue, but they were also itching to deal with titillating topics, partly

168   SITCOMS AND CULTURE

to be able to compete with cable. Some word choices show how things were freeing up even on the networks. The word *ass* (not the donkey) is an example. Some early sitcoms had no problem emphasizing the ass itself; *I Dream of Jeannie* would be an example. Later "jiggle" sitcoms such as *Three's Company* were even more explicit. But the word itself would not have appeared, along with other words like *suck* (as in *this sucks*). These terms fell into a gray area where they were not explicitly prohibited—like George Carlin's "seven dirty words"—but there was near-universal self-censorship.

By season 3, though, *Seinfeld* deployed *ass* with some regularity. Elaine objected to a store-window mannequin that bore an uncanny resemblance to her person: "You think you can pose me however you want? That's my **ass** in your window!" Kramer's friend Mickey (a little person) worried about losing his job to a competitor: "The kid I stand in for, he's growing. He was four feet last month, now he's like four-two and a half. He shot up two and a half inches. I can do four-two, four-three is a stretch, any higher than that and I'm gonna be out on my **ass** doing that para-legal crap." Kramer instructs a flunky to get Bette Midler a sandwich: "Yeah, white meat. And if I see one piece of dark meat on there, it's your **ass** buster." By season 6, apparently the writers were getting so comfortable with *ass* that they created an entire episode around the Assman character ("The Fusilli Jerry," S6E20), a proctological joke at Kramer's expense. The word *assman* occurs in one episode as many times as *ass* does across the entire series.

From a text-analysis perspective, though, *Seinfeld* is a clean show, which matches Jerry Seinfeld's own comic personality. Word searches using pregiven dictionaries of profane terms are possible using text analysis software. Ironically, the term such software turns up most frequently in *Seinfeld* is *Jerry*, which is considered a racist term from the World War II era for German people, but obviously that usage is now archaic. After that, *hell* is the word that comes up most frequently. It was a term that never would have been heard in a damning or swearing context in '50s sitcoms, but it became gradually acceptable with the secularization of American society that occurred in the '70s and beyond.

Although Jerry Seinfeld deals with most issues freely, he did not delve very much into the blue genre of comedy. Among sitcoms that were based on stand-up personae, it was not unusual for comedians to clean up their act for television. Such was certainly the case with Redd Foxx, whose appearances on *Sanford and Son* were much less raunchy than his famous albums from the race record market. Other bluer comedians who appeared on network TV included Sam Kinison in *Charlie Hoover* (which had an

Textual Analysis

unsuccessful stint on Fox [1991]), Chris Rock (*Everybody Hates Chris* [2005–09]), George Carlin (*The George Carlin Show* [1994–95]), Andrew Dice Clay (*Bless This House* [1995–96]), and Richard Pryor (*The Richard Pryor Show* was a variety show, not a sitcom; it absolutely tested standards-and-practices boundaries and did not last long[8]). Comedians with a hard edge, such as Don Rickles, had a famously difficult time transitioning formats from stand-up to sitcom. A few of the raunchier comedians did make the transition. Roseanne Barr would be a good example; in *Roseanne*, she made it her business to offend sensibilities as much as possible—and did so quite successfully.

With *Seinfeld*, nothing had to be cleaned up. One of the hallmarks of the show was its ability to deal with topics that were on the margin of social acceptability through the use of knowing references and analogies to get the issue across without using the actual offensive word. The technique itself is funny. In a show dealing with whether men like to perform oral sex on women ("The Rye," S7E11), there is this exchange:

ELAINE: I can't believe I'm going out with this guy. Wow! He's so cool. Maybe he'll write a song about me. That would be amazing. "Oh, Elaine, you are so beautiful. So, so beautiful. Not to mention your personality which is so, so, interesting. If you want, you can quit your job and never work again." Jerry, you have got to come see him. He is so terrific.

JERRY: Maybe he'll write a song about you.

ELAINE: Yeah. Right. Like that really matters.

JERRY: So, I take it he's spongeworthy?[9]

ELAINE: Oh, yeah.

JERRY: Well, he's a musician. I guess they're supposed to be very, you know, uninhibited and free.

ELAINE: Well, actually, he's—he's not that way at all.

JERRY: Oh, no?

ELAINE: Yeah. In fact, he. . . .

JERRY: Come on. Come on.

ELAINE: I don't wanna!

JERRY: Elaine, you're among friends.

ELAINE: Well, actually, he, um, doesn't really like to do . . . everything.

JERRY: Oh.

ELAINE: Yeah. It's surprising.

JERRY: Yes, it is. It is surprising. Does that bother you?

ELAINE: No. No, it doesn't bother me. I mean, it would be nice. I'm not gonna lie to you and say it wouldn't be nice.

JERRY: Sure. Why not? You're there. (Seinfeld, 1996)

170   SITCOMS AND CULTURE

In an unprecedented way for a network sitcom, we hear a discussion about oral sex, and we learn that it is actually something of an expectation, since Elaine is surprised and Jerry confirms that it would be a normal behavior. The words *oral* and *sex* are never used. A similar technique is seen in the episode "The Mango" (S5E1), where George and Jerry discuss a sexual technique that Jerry developed and George can't master.

These comic strategies—pushing the boundaries of what is culturally acceptable in a group communication context, making sure everybody knows what the issue is without using the actual words—were actually not new with *Seinfeld*. As mentioned above, Lucy and Ricky did it with the issue of pregnancy by softening the imagery of it to a point that the lingering Puritan reservations could be removed. Still, they could not use the word *pregnancy* itself. Sitcom couples sleeping in the same bed took a while; Mike and Carol Brady were still in separate beds in the 1970s. Clearly, on these kinds of cultural issues, at least until the '70s, sitcoms were lagging social reality. Incremental reform and liberalization in the '60s meant that the '70s could be more direct: Mike and Gloria Stivic were clearly having sex a lot on *All in the Family*; also, one heard the toilet flushing frequently in the house. Bob and Emily Newhart were in the same bed, and there were frequent insinuations that they had an active sex life. By *Seinfeld*'s time, some sitcoms had become so raunchy (such as *Three's Company* in the '70s with its stupidly executed double entendres and physical comedy and *Married with Children* in the '80s with profane comic antiheroes in every role) that *Seinfeld* was something of a refreshing take on sensitive issues without clubbing people over the head in a lowbrow way.

The actual profane words that we hear in *Seinfeld*, then, are nothing like Carlin's seven dirty words (still basically verboten on today's network television) but second-tier coarse words that became so common by the '90s that they were not really considered profane. Examples include the word *sex*, which appears 142 times in *Seinfeld*. Frank Costanza wonders baldly about fowl copulation: "Let me understand, you got the hen, the chicken and the rooster. The rooster goes with the chicken. So, who's having sex with the hen?" Kramer advises Elaine on how sex is tied to money: "Now, see the two of you need to work on trust . . . and then and only then will there be a free exchange of sex and discounts. . . . Cornerstones of a healthy relationship." George boasts about his ability to go without sex: "I can do six weeks standin' on my head. I'm a sexual camel." Sex as an act still has numerous comic possibilities; the word itself is less shocking. Other words that appear in Seinfeld with some frequency that are coarse but not really profane include *whore*, *scrotum*, *poop*, *penis*, *hell*, *damn*, and *crap*.

Textual Analysis 171

An interesting example of reference to profanity is in the episode "The Keys" (S3E23), where characters mumble obscenities that can't quite be heard, or the articulation of the obscenity is cut off but everyone still knows what it means.

JERRY: I never should have taken his keys away. But he drove me to it! I had no choice! He wouldn't take 'em back. Elaine, you saw it, remember? I said, "Take the keys back." He wouldn't do anything. You saw it, didn't you see it?
ELAINE: Yeah, yeah, I saw it. (mutters under her breath) I mean, it's complete bullshit. (Seinfeld, 1992)

And in "The Non-fat Yogurt" (S5E7), Jerry, who has explained to a young boy that all comedians don't swear, reacts as follows when the boy destroys one of his audiotapes: "What the *beep* [fuck] are you doing? You little piece of *beep* [shit]!" Again, pursuing the strategy of comic repetition, the word *fuck* is bleeped out several times in the course of the episode.

All in all, *Seinfeld* is a world of characters who deal quite often in prurient matters, but they are polite enough to soften the blow for wider audience appeal. There is no insistence that the audience receive the comic on his own rough and raw terms. Comic integrity is not predicated on offense but on the audience surprise of being mildly shocked, only to realize that everyone else was a little shocked as well, and nothing bad happened. *Seinfeld* is your safe guide, should you choose it, to transitioning toward a more relaxed Upper West Side morality.

Gender

As we have seen, the tradition of cultural indicators research on American television has been quite clear that there are imbalances between portrayals of men and women. Nancy Signorielli conducted numerous studies over the years based on the CI dataset, which showed both that there were more men than women on TV and that representations were skewed toward less "respect" for women than men (Signorielli, 1989). In later years of the CI dataset, the man-woman imbalance is around sixty to forty. Even given progress through the years, it has been hard to approach the fifty/fifty level that might reflect demographic reality better. Yan et al. (forthcoming), using the entire CI dataset, found that the imbalances did improve over the years and that the lessening distortions were correlated to changes in real-world data such as marriage rates and women's employment. They summarized the entire fifty-year history of cultural indicators data on women's portrayals:

Positively correlated changes do not mean that women have been represented "correctly" on TV in the period. First, of course, it is entirely subjective as to what correct representation would be. It would be hard

172   SITCOMS AND CULTURE

to imagine media effects research of our genre ever reaching a conclusion that such a state had been reached. Still, the current study confirms some findings from previous studies about women's underrepresentation. As Signorielli found 35 years ago (1984), the average female proportion of all TV characters since the new century began (40.15%) is still lower than the average female proportion in the U.S. population (50.64%). In the same period, they are consistently whiter (CI: 83.19%, US: 79.69%) and more unmarried (CI: 63.22%, US: 26.63%) than women in the real world. . . . Taken together, while the present study finds that there is overall a positive correlation between the TV world and the real world in terms of change over time, female underrepresentation on TV still exists, although less than it was when the CI project began. (p. 12)

In cultural indicators research, representation has always been measured by the appearance of a character. There is less research on the details of how that character functions within the show, apart from some subjective coding judgments that are made about character qualities. With our dataset of *Seinfeld* scripts, we can do some more to parse differences between how females and males are used in the show, with text analysis to help generate and even possibly confirm hypotheses.

With *Seinfeld*, we have a show that is putatively progressive, liberal, or even libertine in its outlook. Marriage is not a pressing concern. While the characters' parents seem weighted down with dysfunctional traditionalisms, Jerry and his friends studiously avoid that sort of burden. Given the show's ethos, it is interesting to look at whether the distribution of comedic duties is at all equitable as far as gender in concerned. Spoiler alert: In some important ways, it is *not* equitable. Because three out of the show's four main characters are male, it is difficult to achieve quantitative gender equity, assuming that such is a desirable goal.

We begin with an analysis of who gets lines of dialogue in the show. Figure 5.3 shows the number of lines for the most frequently appearing characters. Jerry, of course, gets the most, and the four lead characters obviously also get the lion's share of lines, since they, by definition, appear in every episode. Sixteen characters are shown in the figure; these are the top line-getters. Four of them are women.

The distribution of lines over time among the four leads is also interesting from a gender perspective. Figure 5.4 shows how many lines were allotted to each of the four main characters in each season. Jerry, as the focal point, always gets the most lines, which is again obvious. However, there was a diminishment of his dominance as the series matured, particularly because episodes evolved toward more multiline plots that did not always involve Jerry. Elaine's early lines were normally fewer than George's, particularly in

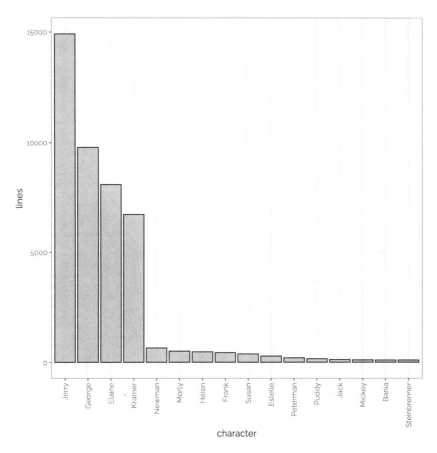

Figure 5.3. Frequency of characters' lines in *Seinfeld*.

season four due to a maternity leave. After that period, her lines were much more similar in quantity to George's. Jason Alexander had threatened to leave the show after he was left out of an episode ("The Pen," S3E3), fearing that Elaine's role was going to overtake his. But Julia Louis-Dreyfus also felt that she had to compete for storylines.

The similarity in line quantity for Elaine and George makes it interesting to consider who was Jerry's real sidekick. Most viewers would probably answer George, but there are arguments to be made that he and Elaine played at least equal roles. As we argued above with relation to the four-character structure, usually a male lead will have a wife or wife equivalent. Even though Jerry and Elaine had dated, and they did have a brush with sexuality, Elaine was framed much more as "one of the guys." Originally the show had been intended to have four male leads; the Elaine character was a revision. She was

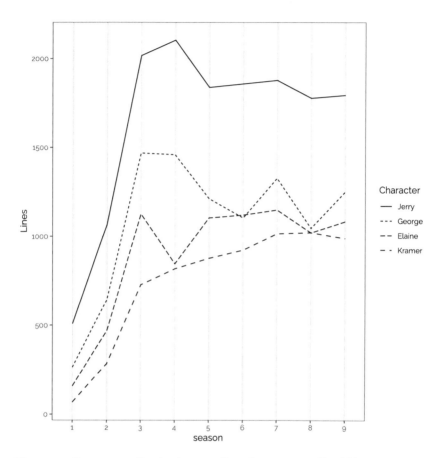

Figure 5.4. Frequency of main character lines by season on *Seinfeld*.

stronger than George and pushed him around often, and there were times when George's character was quite feminized. Did George function more as a wife to Jerry (who never acquired one and rarely thought about it)? Ultimately, Elaine and George probably played some shifting (and competitive) roles in relation to Jerry, which would also explain the rough equivalence of their line quantity and their equal importance in the show.

Kramer's line quantity gradually increased. He had also been left out of one early episode ("The Chinese Restaurant," S2E11), but the four-person model, so strong in many other sitcoms, was attractive. The runaway success of Kramer's character drew more storylines, as he could be involved with some of his concerns and his own sidekicks (such as Mickey the Little Person).

Textual Analysis

Table 5.2. Lines in *Seinfeld*, by gender

	Main character	Not a main character
Male	79.5%	60.2%
Female	20.5%	37.0%
Other/can't code		2.8%

As we saw in chapter 4, numbers of women on TV have been equalizing over the decades but still not reaching parity. The highest sitcom percentage we saw in our CI data was about 46 percent. In *Seinfeld*, the dominance of men is more than that. As noted, three out of the four main characters are men. Of all lines delivered in the show by any character, 75 percent were said by men. When breaking down line quantity across main characters versus all others, there was still an imbalance (79 percent of the main-character lines were male, versus 60 percent of the non-main-character lines; see table 5.2).

Seinfeld was basically a man's world. The appeal of the Elaine character was that she was quite feminine but could hang with the guys on an equal basis. She was more assertive and powerful than George and could put up at least an equal claim to friendship with Jerry, which was the main currency of the show.

Seinfeld is obviously not alone in the comedy world in focusing mainly on the concerns and perspectives of men. Jerry Lewis had famously ranted at various times that he thought women should not be funny because stooping to the comic diminishes their idealization as "miracles" that produce babies. Author Christopher Hitchens (2007) allowed that there were some funny women, but most of them were "hefty, dykey, or Jewish or some combo of the three." Empirically, most comedians over the years have been men, though it is impossible to prove whether it is something biological or simply a result of sexism. The magnitude of growth in women's comedy after, say, 2000 suggests that the latter argument might hold more weight.

Jerry Seinfeld himself completely discounts whether there should be any concern whatsoever with identity or equity in comedy: "People think it's the census or something," Seinfeld said of the assertion that all pop culture should accurately reflect society. "This has gotta represent the actual pie chart of America? Who cares? Funny is the world that I live in. You're funny, I'm interested. You're not funny, I'm not interested. I have no interest in gender or race or anything like that" (Wieselman, 2014).[10]

176 SITCOMS AND CULTURE

Many episodes of *Seinfeld*, though, prove that Jerry Seinfeld is *quite* interested in gender and race; it would be difficult to imagine any kind of social commentary comedy *not* being aware of these issues. He is disclaiming responsibility for the idea that his particular show should be a form of affirmative action for race and gender. He implies that had he paid attention to those issues, the show would have been less funny, as if made by a committee of DEI bureaucrats rather than comedians.

Still, it is difficult, based on an analysis of distribution of dialogue alone, to assert any sort of sexist motive in *Seinfeld*. The character of Elaine will remain one of the more finely drawn female portrayals in American sitcoms. It is hard to note any particular traditionally feminine quality in Elaine without coming across other qualities that are traditionally masculine. Actress Julia Louis-Dreyfus was able to convert her success in the role into other ground-breaking female-led sitcoms—something that only a few female American actresses have achieved. Nevertheless, the numerical disparity in female and male presence in *Seinfeld* is important to consider from a cultural indicators perspective. Could it be the case that this particular Upper West Side culture was simply less inhabited by females, making it in fact an accurate portrayal of the context that it was representing? It seems unlikely, but in a world of mostly male bachelors seeking to avoid commitment, maybe the issue should not be completely set aside.

Perhaps the best explanation is that just that the *sensibility* of the show was male. Pew Research did a survey at the end of *Seinfeld*'s run that is instructive. Males were more likely to have reported watching the show. Other factors that were related to *Seinfeld* viewership were youth, higher education, higher income, and being single. This, of course, was exactly the demographic that the network hoped to attract, so it was unlikely that executives would press too much on a show that was delivering the desired audience segments. For the well-off, young, single male, a sitcom about lack of commitment, about total acceptance of irony and detachment as a lifestyle, with a never-ending supply of beautiful-but-flawed models as girlfriends who could be dumped from episode to episode, that was a major aspect of the ethos of *Seinfeld*.

So, *Seinfeld* distorts gender parity, which means it is not accurate in that sense as a cultural indicator. In another way, though, it may be spectacularly accurate. Insofar as it privileges the concerns of men, who seek to absent themselves from various social contracts that might bind them to women, it is in fact a far cry from the '50s sitcoms that attached men to families. In the '50s, while Dad had the sitcom power, he also had the responsibility. As we noted

Textual Analysis

above, American family life to some degree has been moving away from that nuclear model. Less marriage, fewer children, more women in the workplace, and more abortions are among the variety of social trends that have moved in a more or less linear direction since the 1950s. And opinion has also moved in same the direction, even if haltingly, toward approving these trends.

These moves were part and parcel of the various women's liberations that sitcoms tried to keep up with over the years. Whether the liberations turned out to be advantageous for women as a group is an open question, but in *Seinfeld*'s portrayal of the situation, it's hard to see how women do better. Elaine's jobs were for a series of incompetent men, and they were dead-end. When she got the chance to run the J. Peterman catalog, she flopped. At the end of her mega-story arc, she was nowhere near ahead of where she had been when she'd started. George had accidentally murdered his fiancée but was not that upset about it. His job incompetence was a main part of his character profile. Kramer never had any ambition and seemed happiest of all of the characters. Jerry, of course, controlled his own destiny, parlaying detached irony into commercial success and a swinging bachelor lifestyle, both of which promised to go on forever. If we are looking for the comic antithesis of *Father Knows Best*, it may have been *Seinfeld*.

Race

Seinfeld was attacked for its failure to have very many Black characters. More than 98 percent of lines in *Seinfeld* were delivered by white actors. The measure is biased from the start, of course, by the fact that the main characters were all white, and they delivered about 75 percent of the lines on their own. Of lines delivered by others who were not main characters, 93 percent were given to white characters. If we go by the demographics of the Upper West Side of New York, the main location of *Seinfeld*, at the time of Seinfeld's popularity, Black characters would have been about 8 percent of the total. Interestingly, that percentage has declined more recently to about 5 percent,[11] presumably as a result of the gentrification of Upper West Side neighborhoods.

Again, as noted above, Jerry Seinfeld himself doesn't subscribe to the idea that programs should be representative. As we will see below with *Friends*, there is an argument to be made that the picture of a segregated, gentrified yuppie New York circle of acquaintances that emerges could be entirely accurate. Sitcom writers write what they know.

The list of Black characters that got lines in Seinfeld is about two dozen people. Some were celebrities who appeared as themselves (Bryant Gumbel,

178   SITCOMS AND CULTURE

Al Roker, Danny Tartabull). They were individuals whom white Upper West Siders might know from television or sports, not necessarily from their neighborhood. The Black character who got the most lines was Jackie Childs, a takeoff on Johnnie Cochran, who gained fame during the OJ Simpson trial. Other characters tended to appear in fairly subservient roles, such as Carl the Exterminator, Sid (who parked cars in the neighborhood), or Rebecca DeMornay (not the famous actress; she works at the homeless shelter).

Seinfeld did from time to time use race as basis for humor. Often it involved clueless white people trying to figure out the right thing to do in the presence of racial sensitivities. In "Cigar Store Indian" (S5E10), Jerry kept doing things that offended an attractive Native American woman, someone he would have liked to date. In "Diplomat's Club" (S6E21), George was trying to flatter his Black boss, so he did racially inappropriate things such as artificially finding a Black friend. In one episode (S6E4), Jerry stated that he liked Chinese women. Elaine said, "Isn't that a little racist?" Jerry replied, "If I like their race, how can that be racist?" Perhaps most tellingly, in S9E15 Elaine tried to figure out her new boyfriend's race, as he did with her. When they both figured out that they were white, they were disappointed, having hoped perhaps for something a bit more exotic or cooler from each other. They decided to visit the Gap.

In some ways, these were refreshing portrayals of white characters saying they wanted to be progressive, but they were just not very good at it. Other episodes were clumsier. The character of Babu Bhatt (S3E7) was very much a cartoon of a Pakistani immigrant. The episode based around the Puerto Rican Day parade in New York (S9E20) was pulled from syndication due to objections about the use of the Puerto Rican flag.

In a show that ran as long as *Seinfeld*, it's not surprising that every character became a type, if not an outright stereotype. Yet there were few pernicious attempts in *Seinfeld* to stereotype people based on race. Satires of Jewish American characteristics were perhaps the most common, with cartoonish portrayals of rabbis, Florida retirement-home types, and Borscht Belt comic tropes. Even the character of George seemed Jewish, though it wasn't clear that he was. *Seinfeld* obliquely attacked antisemitism in its episode about "antidentites" (S8E19)—people who hate dentists.

KRAMER: You're a rabid anti-dentite! Oh, it starts with a few jokes and some slurs. "Hey, denty!" Next thing you know you're saying they should have their own schools.

JERRY: They *do* have their own schools!

Textual Analysis

179

The absolute dominance of white people in *Seinfeld* shows that the characters practiced self-segregation not dissimilar to what happens in reality. The trajectory of the Upper West Side toward gentrification after the *Seinfeld* years may show that the process was already underway in the *Seinfeld* depictions, as seen in its lifestyle of characters that extracted an upper-middle-class living without marriage or fancy suburban homesteads. They could afford it, as all their income was devoted to one person and one person only.

Gayness and Tolerance in *Seinfeld*

Fear and anxiety about being gay occurred occasionally in *Seinfeld*. There were twenty-four lines of dialogue in which the word stem *gay* appeared in episodes where a basic idea of *Seinfeld* was depicted: that main characters were quite pleased with the idea that they tolerated difference, even though it sometimes frightened and horrified them. Most actual uses of the word *gay* occurred in S4E17 ("The Outing"), in which a reporter from a college newspaper who overheard a conversation between Jerry and George mistakenly assumed they were gay. Jerry was actually romantically interested in the reporter, so he was horrified when he realized that she thought they were gay. This led to emphatic denunciations from George and Jerry to deny that they were gay, though they were also quick to add, "Not that there's anything wrong with that!" (a statement accompanied by vigorous head shaking and nonverbal indicators of progressive tolerance of gay people).

The episode aired in 1993, early on in sitcoms' more open attitude toward gay characters, as was seen in *Will & Grace*. At the time, the episode won an award from GLAAD for outstanding comedy episode, presumably for the inclusion of the line "not that there's anything wrong with that." Other episodes, though, showed *Seinfeld* characters manifesting worry that they might be gay as a sort of comic panic. For example, in "The Note," S3E1, George got a massage from a handsome man and was afraid when "it" moved in response.

JERRY: What's with you?
GEORGE: A . . . ah . . .
JERRY: Yes, a . . .?
GEORGE: A man gave me . . .
JERRY: Yes, a man gave you . . .?
GEORGE: A man gave me . . . a massage, uh, uh
JERRY: So?
GEORGE: So he . . . had his hands and, uh, he was uh . . .
JERRY: He was what?!

GEORGE: He—he was uh touching and rubbing.

JERRY: That's a massage.

GEORGE: And then I took my pants off.

JERRY: You took your pants off?

GEORGE: For my hamstring.

JERRY: Oh.

GEORGE: He got about uh, two inches from . . . there.

JERRY: Really?

GEORGE: I think it moved.

JERRY: Moved?

GEORGE: It may have moved, I don't know.

JERRY: I'm sure it didn't move.

GEORGE: It moved! It was imperceptible but I—I felt it.

JERRY: Maybe it just wanted to change positions? You know, shift to the other side.

GEORGE: No, no. It wasn't a shift, I've shifted, this was a move.

JERRY: Okay, so what if it moved?

GEORGE: That's the sign! The test; if a—if a man makes it move.

JERRY: That's not the test. Contact is the test, if it moves as a result of contact.

GEORGE: You think it's contact? It has to be touched?

JERRY: That's what a gym teacher once told me.

In another episode, Elaine was conscripted to act as a date for a handsome man who was posing as straight. She fell for him and then hoped to convert him to "our team" ("The Beard," S6E15). She found out that was not possible, although much comic attention was given to the conversion attempt.

ELAINE: Oh it was such a great night.

JERRY: And did they suspect anything?

ELAINE: No, I was a fantastic beard. I held hands, I called him honey.

JERRY: And we discover yet another talent. Posing as a girlfriend for homosexuals.

ELAINE: Oh it was such a great night. Oh.

JERRY: You said that already.

ELAINE: Oh I did?

JERRY: Yeah.

ELAINE: Oh.

JERRY: Oh no. Don't tell me. You like him?

ELAINE: He's incredible.

JERRY: Yeah, but?

ELAINE: Yeah, I know.

JERRY: So?

ELAINE: What?

JERRY: Not conversion. You're thinking conversion?

ELAINE: Well it did occur to me.

JERRY: You think you can get him to just change teams? He's not going to suddenly switch sides. Forget about it.

ELAINE: Why? Is it irrevocable?

JERRY: Because when you join that team it's not a whim. He likes his team. He's set with that team.

ELAINE: We've got a good team.

JERRY: Yeah, we do. We do have a good team.

ELAINE: Why can't he play for us?

JERRY: They're only comfortable with *their* equipment.

ELAINE: We just got along *so* great.

JERRY: Of course you did. Everyone gets along great when there's no possibility of sex.

It was a characteristic of *Seinfeld* that serious issues, as with the implications here of conversion therapy, were dealt with humorously and didn't seem that threatening. It was simply assumed that Elaine's mission was a fool's errand, as were many other of her romantic misadventures.

Kramer's friend Mickey was one more example of *Seinfeld*'s ethos of liberal tolerance. Mickey was a little person. He palled around with Kramer on various capers. His height was sometimes used comically, as when he was a stand-in for an eight-year-old soap opera actor. Kramer and Mickey got into physical fights that were funny because of the height difference. On *Seinfeld*, the strategy of dealing with difference was to recognize it and make it part of the comic outcome. But much of the time, the height difference was *not* part of the narrative. Mickey and Kramer went on double dates. He was a funny character on his own terms. But he didn't take any crap. When George called him a "midget" (because George often represented clueless people), Mickey let him know, threateningly, that it's "little people."

Topic Modeling

The characters on *Seinfeld* talked a lot. What did they talk about? In this section, we use topic modeling to analyze *Seinfeld* dialogue. Topic modeling uses software that analyzes speech and attempts to capture its topic with pregiven dictionaries. Thus, a dictionary composed of the words *love, like, happy,* and *joy* (among others) might be seen as capturing "positive emotion." A dictionary composed of the words *hate, jealous, envy,* and *spite* might be seen as capturing "negative emotion." The program we use is called EMPATH (Fast et

182   SITCOMS AND CULTURE

al., 2016).[12] In reality, the dictionaries are more complex, and there are almost two hundred different categories that can be analyzed. We used EMPATH to analyze a few of the most frequently encountered speech types in *Seinfeld*, with a special focus on how speech differed among the four main characters.

Our dataset starts with almost forty thousand lines of dialogue. These are, out of almost fifty-five thousand total lines in the show, the ones spoken only by Jerry, Elaine, George, or Kramer. They alone offer sample sizes large enough to make some potentially interesting conclusions. In these lines of dialogue, most actually cannot be characterized by EMPATH. Many short lines and one-word responses like "yeah" or "OK" simply fail to generate enough information for EMPATH to know what the line is about.

The most encountered category (topic) in Seinfeld is "speaking." They talked about talk. This is not surprising, given what we have argued above: that *Seinfeld* is very much a comedy about communication and word usage. An example of a Jerry line that is coded as being about speaking is:

JERRY: Oh, she's really great. I mean, she's got like a real warmth about her and she's really bright and really pretty and uh . . . the *conversation* though, I mean, it was . . . *talking* with her is like *talking* with you, but, you know, obviously much better.

Words that contribute to the speaking category are italicized.

When we compare this across the four main characters, we find that George was most likely to use words that were about speaking. This was consistent with the comedy style of the neurotic, talks-too-much George. Kramer, the physical comedian, was least likely to use this type of speech. See table 5.3 for a summary of this and the other comparisons in this section.

Next most encountered is "violence." It might seem odd to encounter violent speech in a sitcom, where levels of actual violence are much lower than in action programs. However, we should recall that comedy is often based in conflict, and so the opposition of interest that can create comic outcomes often requires oppositional or even violent speech. An example of dialogue that is tagged as violent is from Kramer (S9E16), when he was serving as a fake patient for medical students. He had to portray a certain disease:

KRAMER: Yes, yes, I will! I'm gonna make people feel my gonorrhea, and feel the gonorrhea themselves.

Comedy is about sparring. Here, the *make people feel* comes off as violent. Imperative statements and commands can be tagged as violent. In our data,

Textual Analysis   183

though, there is little difference in the frequency with which characters use violence in speech; all were equally likely to engage in it some degree, though at about half the frequency with which they used dialogue about speaking.

After violence comes types of speech that reflect "positive emotion." An example of text coded as positive emotion is from Kramer:

KRAMER: Well, Elaine Benes! Well, it's great to have you! Boy, is it possible that you're even more beautiful than the last time I saw you?

The line, though, was delivered somewhat ironically, pointing out an example of where text analysis would miss a nuance. Again, though, as with violence, all characters used speech coded as positive emotion at about the same rate. Kramer was slightly higher than the others, but the difference is not statistically significant.

Finally, we look at "negative emotion." An example of speech that involves negative emotion is from "The Pony Remark" (S2E2):

JERRY: I know, I hated those kids. In fact, I hate anyone that ever had a pony when they were growing up.

Jerry got in a lot of trouble for this line when he found out that his aunt, sitting at the table with him, actually had a pony while she was growing up in Poland.

It is not hard to see why negative emotional speech is important in comedy. All the characters in *Seinfeld* did it to an extent, but Jerry and George did it the most. Their ironic, cynical take on just about everything led to acerbic negative generalizations about all kinds of people, situations, and outcomes. Right from the start of the series (S1E2), Jerry let Elaine know what their dominant tone would be, as he invited her to a wedding:

ELAINE (skeptically): A wedding?
JERRY: There's a lot of people to mock.

Across the entire show, Kramer was *least* likely to use this sort of language. His child role in the show may have predisposed him more to optimism, and generally his philosophy about other people was more accepting than Jerry's and George's.

As a comparison, we can look at similar data from the program *Friends*. We find that *Friends* also had speaking, violence, and negative or positive emotion as the main topics embodied in its dialogue. Mostly these categories appeared with equal frequency for the six main characters, with one exception. Monica was much less likely to use negative emotional speech than the

184   SITCOMS AND CULTURE

Table 5.3. EMPATH categories in *Seinfeld*

	Jerry	George	Elaine	Kramer	ANOVA
Speaking	0.0055[b]	0.0069[abc]	0.0051[a]	0.0047[c]	10.45***
Violence	0.0023	0.0024	0.0018	0.0022	2.258
Positive emotion	0.0026	0.0027	0.0026	0.0032	1.70
Negative emotion	0.0054[a]	0.0053[b]	0.0048	0.0041[ab]	4.28***

Superscripts indicate which characters differ from each other significantly.

others, by a large margin. This may have to do with her mother-like role in the series. However, the topics modeled in *Friends* are quite similar to *Seinfeld*'s, suggesting some structural verbal qualities that we might look for across all sitcoms, or at least across all sitcoms of a similar era, as these both aired in the '90s. One other difference of note is that *Friends* had a fair amount of "wedding" talk whereas *Seinfeld* had very little. The plot of *Friends* was oriented toward people finally settling down whereas *Seinfeld*'s was not, so this is not surprising. The character that engaged in wedding talk the least was Joey, the confirmed womanizing bachelor.

*

Ultimately, what can we learn from the types of data analysis in this chapter? With textual analysis, we must recognize that the various forms of doing this type of work, while growing in complexity and power, are still limited. Computers, based on dictionaries alone, are not smart enough to always know what the true meaning of a sentence is. Often they will get it wrong. Meaning is especially difficult to catch with irony or comedy, where the tone of voice or the context of what is uttered can make all the difference. However, as long as we are not too hung up on deriving laws of comedy from our analysis, looking in detail at text and being able to quantify aspects of it can be useful. In context with our macro-level data on the universe of sitcoms, looking at how lines break down by character gender, race, age, and type adds some brushstroke detail to our picture. These types of data will increasingly become more available—and can be analyzed more efficiently—such that different sitcoms could easily be compared to each other on textual choices, allowing an entirely new kind of cultural indicator to enter the scene.

Textual Analysis

Seinfeld's Progressive Bubble: "Not That There's Anything Wrong with That"

Seinfeld has a legitimate claim to being the best sitcom ever made. The writing is terrific. Oftentimes the complexity of interweaving storylines is itself funny, confirming Mark Twain's observation that the most difficult story to create is the humorous one. Like any successful artistic product, *Seinfeld* captures something real; the people shown, though they are exaggerations, do exist. Its audience reach across the '90s was the last major explosion of mass media effectiveness for the sitcom in the legacy media era. For these and other reasons, we should be interested in the cultural picture that these characters portray.

Our data tend to confirm that this culture is male dominated but female obsessed. It's a white culture, but it is convinced that it is open to and tolerant of just about anything. Tolerance is in a progressive direction. When Elaine found out that a potential date was pro-life, that ended the relationship for her. She defaced her boyfriend's "Jesus fish" on the back of his car. Religion is usually a topic of scorn, as when George joined a Latvian Orthodox church so as to make it with a girl. Jerry's Judaism was mainly cultural, and of course it was quite often a source of humorous send-ups targeted at his own people. When Jerry criticized his dentist for converting to Judaism so he could tell Jewish jokes, we understand that Jerry and others believed they had a pretty mature sense of self-deprecation, which allowed them to apply this form of humor to other groups.

At the same time, *Seinfeld* wanted you to know that it tolerated values of expression. When Kramer refused to wear an "AIDS ribbon" in a march and was attacked by menacing gay activists, his only explanation for why he didn't need the ribbon was that "this is America." There is still an individualism in this culture that matches *Seinfeld's* own personal yardstick of worth: Is it funny?

Still, some audiences found it hard to relate. *Seinfeld* was lower rated among Black viewers. Comedy is very culture specific. There have been plenty of Black-led shows that white people weren't watching, so this was not unique to *Seinfeld*.

It is worth pointing out, though, that the phenomenon of *Seinfeld's* progressivism occurs precisely in communities like the Upper West Side, where the social impacts of that tolerance, throughout the '90s, were *least* likely to be felt. In some of these most progressive of communities, racial diversity is lower, abortions are fewer, and crime is lower. It is easier to be tolerant.

186 SITCOMS AND CULTURE

Pew identified the "progressive" left as the least racially diverse of Democrat-leaning groups.[13] *Seinfeld* in some ways hearkened back to the idea of "limousine liberalism," where people preach views that won't really affect them. They have "luxury beliefs." The show's "bystander" ethic was made quite explicit in the final episode. *Seinfeld* frequently noted social inequalities (because it was a keen observer of social reality), and it may even have given warrant to grievances that followed from them. But it generally moved on with nothing to say. An exception might have been when Elaine left a restaurant because she disagreed with the owner's views on abortion (S6E5), but Jerry stayed and quite happily continued his meal. The producers clearly highlighted the bystander ethos when the main characters were sentenced in the final episode to prison for failing to intervene in the commission of a crime that they found actually a bit funny. They were guilty of violating a Good Samaritan law, something that had never applied to them in their irony-soaked existence.

Seinfeld's liberal bubble predated the full emergence of tensions that had been simmering for quite a while, when the realities of a riotously and unstable set of divisions within culture were becoming much more evident. The culture wars of the 2020s make *Seinfeld* seem as much of a golden-era utopia as *Father Knows Best* must have seemed to people in the '60s. Whatever happens around them, *Seinfeld*'s characters will still be who they are, relatively untested by the issues of social difference that are implicated in their weekly scripts. This is the privilege of comedy. If there's a problem related to an issue of difference, *Seinfeld* can mock it but offer a final "not that there's anything wrong with that" to send a virtuous signal.

NOTES

1. The dataset was obtained from https://data.world/rickyhennessy/seinfeld-scripts; additional metadata were added by the author.

2. Other than for Seinfeld, all figures were estimated using the Measures of Lexical Diversity website: https://www.reuneker.nl/files/ld/#.

3. The formula used is RE = 206.835 − (1.015 × ASL) − (84.6 × ASW). RE = readability ease; ASL = average sentence length; ASW = average number of syllables per word.

4. In fairness to Derrida, he is possibly outdone by Proust, whose very long sentences earn him quite low readability scores, as in the opening of *Swann's Way* (1928), where the first two paragraphs score 27.5, a very, very, very low readability score. Readers of Proust who have marked their own text with guiding punctuation will agree. Yet the low readability does not detract from the perception of artistic greatness; perhaps it enhances it.

Textual Analysis

5. In an interview with Howard Stern, Jerry Seinfeld talked about choosing whether to use Greek or Roman slave ships as a punch line to a joke. He chose Greek because it was only one syllable.

6. Oxford English Dictionary (n.d).

7. Other catchphrases include Ricky Ricardo: "Lucy, you got some 'splainin' to do!" Fred Sanford: "You big dummy!" Homer Simpson: "D'oh!" It is interesting, though, that these catchphrases are often revealed as misrememberings or mashups of lines that were actually said in the show. Not only do viewers overestimate the number of times that such phrases are said, but they also often get the actual words wrong.

8. The show lasted two months. It had poor ratings, and network executives did not like the hard-edged humor (Watkins, 1994).

9. This is a knowing reference to another episode ("The Sponge," S7E20), in which Elaine tried to corner the market on birth control sponges.

10. In S1E8 of *All in the Family*, Lionel and Archie had an exchange that is reminiscent of the pie-chart approach to representation:

> ARCHIE: Jim Bowman, our neighbor down the way, just sold his home to a family of coloreds.
>
> LIONEL: No! Two doors away. Can you believe it? Does Mike know about this?
>
> ARCHIE: Yeah, he knows about it. All he can say is 12% of the neighborhood ought to be black.
>
> LIONEL: Twelve percent? Aw, no. If you followed that kind of thinkin', 88% of the Harlem Globetrotters oughta be white.
>
> ARCHIE: I never thought of that.

11. NYU Furman Center (n.d.).

12. EMPATH is one example of the fast-growing suite of tools available to text analysts. The method uses "unsupervised" classifications that look for the presence of words and their closeness to each other to determine whether a "topic" is addressed in the text. Chen et al. (2023) reviewed a variety of problems with how topic modeling is used in the literature. Mostly they found that topic modeling was used in conjunction with other approaches, as we do here. There are continued concerns about its reliability and validity. Evolutions in large language models seem likely to overtake it as a research tool.

13. Pew Research Center (2021).

Chapter 6 Frontis. Elizabeth Montgomery, Dick York, and Agnes Moorehead of *Bewitched*, an example of the escapist sitcoms of the 1960s.

6

Sitcoms, Cultural Indicators, and Social Change

AT THE BEGINNING OF this book, we posed several questions. We asked (1) whether sitcoms act as a mirror on the culture, as some have claimed; (2) whether they might act as a causal force in making or producing social change; (3) whether they can hold back social change that might be occurring for other reasons; and (4) whether they are simply entertainment, without much impact on or relation to social and cultural reality. Our response is that all four questions can be answered affirmatively, though with different weights, contexts, and emphases placed on each answer. After answering these questions, we take a broader perspective on how sitcoms contribute to cultural indicators theory.

Funhouse Mirroring

Mirrors reflect things, though they don't always do so accurately. Depending on the angle and placement of the mirror, the type of glass used, the lighting, and so forth, things may appear to be different from how they would appear in reality. Some mirrors, such as the funhouse mirror at a carnival, derive their entertainment effect quite consciously from warping the vision that we expect to see.

It seems quite clear that if television sitcoms were absolutely accurate depictions of real family life, no one would watch them. Even with the advent of so-called reality programs and their rise to popularity—in some ways at the expense of sitcoms—we understand that each show is a conscious production that selects and frames certain things over others. No television program will perfectly represent reality, which is ultimately too boring to be worth our viewing time.

190 SITCOMS AND CULTURE

The potential danger of confusing fiction with reality has been studied since the time of Plato. Sitcoms will inevitably fall victim to stereotyping and other distortions. While dramatic portrayals can be more or less nuanced, in a repetitive environment such as a sitcom, various characteristics are going to be exaggerated for comedic effect. Any character who doesn't start out as a type is likely to become one. Nevertheless, most sitcoms are hoping that audiences will perceive the program as realistic—something that *could* happen—with a plot and character types that lend narrative plausibility to the proceedings. In developing cultural indicator concepts, Gerbner thought carefully about the narrative style of television, along with its potential effects:

> The dominant stylistic convention of Western narrative art—novels, plays, films, TV dramas—is that of representational realism. However contrived television plots are, viewers assume that they take place against a backdrop of the real world. Nothing impeaches the basic "reality" of the world of television drama. It is also highly informative. That is, it offers to the unsuspecting viewer a continuous stream of "facts" and impressions about the way of the world, about the constancies and vagaries of human nature, and about the consequences of actions. The premise of realism is a Trojan horse which carries within it a highly selective, synthetic, and purposeful image of the facts of life. (Gerbner & Gross, 1976, p. 178)

When examining sitcom TV as a mirror, then, we start from the assumption that there is a desire to be realistic enough to gain audience acceptance for the material, along with a simultaneous recognition that production and institutional practice are likely to encode differences from reality. Moreover, from our vantage point with over fifty years of data about sitcoms, we can focus especially on how TV images have tracked actual social change. We will look at this for images of gender, race, and family structure.

Gender

Comparing gender representation in sitcoms to reality starts out as a relatively easy task. Absolute proportions of males and females in the real world don't change over time: Women always comprise close to 51 percent of the population. In our various datasets, remarkably, the numerical advantage is always switched. Even when taking statistical margins of error into account, we see that men usually comprise about 60 percent of the characters who appear in sitcoms, even though sitcoms are often focused on domestic environments where the concerns of women as well as men, not to mention children of

Sitcoms, Cultural Indicators, and Social Change

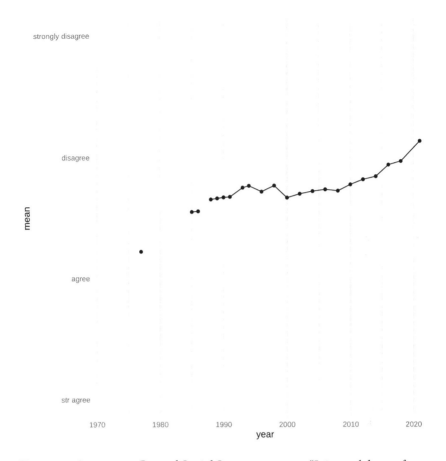

Figure 6.1. Answers to General Social Survey statement "It is much better for everyone involved if the man is the achiever outside the home and the woman takes care of the home and family."

both sexes, mean that we would be likely to see them more equally. So there is clearly still a simple basic distortion in this particular mirror, one that begs an explanation.

The numerical demographic distortion of sitcoms did not change that much with regard to gender over the years, in spite of the enormous changes in *attitudes* about women. For instance, figure 6.1 shows how US survey respondents changed their attitude in the real world on whether it is better for women to stay home while men work. After the mid-1980s, majorities always disagreed with this idea, but lately, *vast* majorities disagree with it. Other measures of attitudes about women show similar patterns. People are quite generally comfortable with the idea of equality for women. In this context, the resilience of numerical inequalities between men and women in sitcoms is puzzling because it seems that audiences would obviously not object to more equalized portrayals; they would appreciate seeing more women.

What about *roles* for women? Do sitcoms encourage the idea that women should be homemakers? Obviously at the very beginning they did, but what about later? The CI dataset includes data on occupations for characters from 1986 to 2012. In the overall dataset (not just sitcoms), coders could assign an occupation to characters 85 percent of the time. In the sitcom data, it was somewhat harder to assign occupations, which could be done only 75 percent of the time. Sitcoms do have a bit more of a marked tendency to have characters where we don't know what their occupation is, such as in *The Adventures of Ozzie and Harriet*, where it was never quite clear what Dad did for a living. In other less domestic shows, it is usually more obvious what a character does for a living.

In sitcoms, the code for "housewife" is used only about 4 percent of the time for all characters (see table 6.1). Not surprisingly, women fill this role 95 percent of the time. That in itself is likely a distortion. It still is a reality that, among stay-at-home parents, the frequency of women is much higher: One estimate suggests that 27 percent of mothers stay at home versus 7 percent of fathers.[1] But the rate of women versus men in the role is still far higher on TV than in reality. Stay-at-home dads in sitcoms are not unheard of for comic novelty, obviously, and the motherless family has also been a frequently seen plot. But if sitcoms are accurately portraying gender and family structure, we'd expect to see a few more men in stay-at-home roles.

There is no single answer as to why these distortions persist. One likely explanation is that production and writing staffs still tend to be predominantly male, and they write what they know. The *Hollywood Diversity Report* in 2022 found that male/female disparities were equalizing in terms of number of actors shown, but wider gaps still existed for producers, directors, and writers (Hunt & Ramon, 2022). Yet the male/female character disparity persists in sitcoms, perhaps reflecting historical male dominance in the writers' rooms and production venues within network TV. Comedies in particular have been associated with maleness on writing staffs.

Another idea could be that the *public* environments portrayed in sitcoms (offices, work, hospitals, etc.) might simply have more men in them in reality, and so perhaps there is some accuracy to the portrayal. This is a very speculative argument, especially given the fact that so many sitcoms are domestically

Sitcoms, Cultural Indicators, and Social Change

Table 6.1. Male and female occupations in sitcoms, N and (row %)

	Male	**Female**
Unknown	370 (51.3)	351 (48.7)
Not working	77 (67.5)	37 (32.5)
Housewife	6 (4.6)	124 (95.4)
Student	247 (54.3)	208 (45.7)
Professional	533 (66.1)	273 (33.9)
White collar	213 (59.8)	142 (39.9)
Blue collar	110 (60.1)	73 (39.9)
Military	11 (73.3)	4 (26.7)
Police	28 (90.3)	3 (9.7)
Criminal	7 (58.3)	5 (41.7)
Other	68 (66.7)	34 (33.3)
TOTAL	1670 (57)	1254 (43)

based, so we might even expect to see *more* women than men if accuracy were the issue. Future research can examine shows by their settings to track gender portrayals and see how things are being shown in the work and home environments, as well as how such portrayals track real-world change.

Hermann et al. (2022) reviewed the entirety of cultivation literature on sexism and gender roles. They found a continuing tendency of television viewing to be associated with relatively more sexist outlooks, even persisting into the twenty-first century. Of particular interest for the study of sitcoms, though, they found that television viewing was essentially *unrelated* to attitudes about women in the public sphere (such as in business or in politics), but there continued to be cultivation of sexism about roles for women in the private (domestic) sphere. "This public/private distinction fits closely with the rise of 'ambivalents' who endorse equity in the public sphere/workplace, but maintain traditional views about the domestic/private sphere. It also fits the notion of a growing 'egalitarian essentialism,' which insists on equality for women and men while also believing there are fundamental differences between them" (p. 17).

Signorelli has also documented gender disparity across programs in terms of occupations portrayed. Working with these same CI data (all programs, not just sitcoms), she found:

194 SITCOMS AND CULTURE

> The types and prestige of occupations found in network prime-time broadcast programs differ by both sex and the level of character diversity.... The women in the programs with mostly minority characters or all White characters are often not seen as having an occupation—their occupation is not made known to viewers or these characters are depicted as not working outside the home. This image is particularly telling for the Black women in the mostly minority programs where 6 of 10 are not seen working outside the home.... Overall, this analysis found that the women, particularly Black women in the mostly minority programs, have the least diversity and prestige in terms of the jobs in which they are cast. Similarly, White women in the all-White programs are the least diverse in terms of the types of jobs in which they are found. Men's occupations are equally diverse in all types of programs except for the lack of law enforcement jobs in the mostly minority programs. (Signorielli, 2009, pp. 15–16)

Apart from the housewife comparison, there are significant differences in other categories. Figure 6.2 shows the percentages of women and men who are shown as "professional," meaning in occupations such as doctor, lawyer, and so forth. Although there is considerable variance in the data from year to year (depending on which sitcoms were being programmed in that year and relatively small sample sizes in each year), the percentages of men who are professional are virtually always higher than women. The overall difference, across all years, is 32 percent males, 22 percent females. What is most interesting is that there is no observable trend up or down across the years depicted.[2]

The preponderance of professional males can mean different things from a cultural indicators standpoint. It could reflect reality. For instance, although numbers of female medical students and doctors are rising, doctors are still about two-thirds male.[3] The same is true for lawyers, who are also two-thirds men. In the world of sitcoms, there any number of professional women over the years have served as counterexamples to these demographic facts (e.g., lawyer Claire Huxtable on *Cosby*), but the macro-perspective of cultural indicators provides a different angle on the issue. In sitcoms, women tend to be less professional.

Also worth noting, though, is that the proportion of women receiving higher education has come to outweigh men (Reeves, 2022). Depending on the field, the disparities can be quite noticeable. In media and communication schools, the proportion can sometimes be close to seventy to thirty in favor of women.[4] Assuming these disparities persist, sitcoms of the future, while again acting mostly as a lagging indicator, might eventually catch up with the

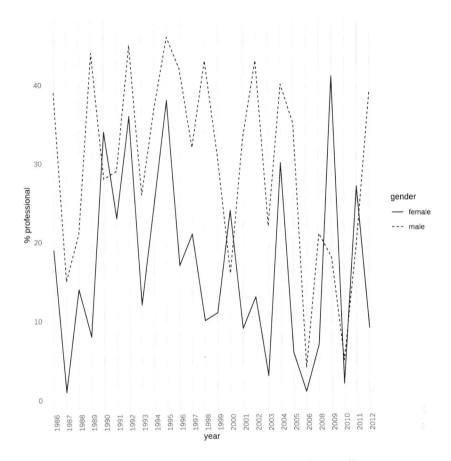

Figure 6.2. Percentages of men and women seen as "professional" in sitcoms, 1986–2012.

reality of more women across all professions and the presence of more women among production elites.

It is interesting that the difference in professional men versus women is *not* seen when programs other than sitcoms are analyzed. These are action, drama, and reality programs, in which professional women are more likely to be seen. Medical shows have been including women as doctors for quite a while. In fact, in the nonsitcoms, the rate of professionalism among men and women is about equal at around 33 percent. Given the findings of Hermann et al. cited above, it seems reasonable to conclude that, despite the well-known relevance examples of women's liberation in sitcoms, sitcoms are actually still one of the more conservative places for women's roles on TV, perhaps sustaining the idea of egalitarian essentialism discussed above.

Even given that we still see more males than females, we should recall that no clear-cut evidence exists that sitcoms *specifically* cultivate prejudice against women (see chap. 4), and we even have some evidence that sitcom viewers are likely to support *more open* attitudes about women. On the question of sexism, then, our answers to the four questions posed at the outset of this chapter are:

1) Do media messages act as a mirror on the culture? They are at best a funhouse mirror, with significant numerical and qualitative distortions.

2) Are sitcoms a causal force in making or producing social change? Certainly, some specific sitcoms can be lauded for developing more progressive tendencies. At the same time, many sitcoms still harbor stereotyped or even dysfunctional portraits of women, or of men in relation to women.

3) Do sitcoms hold back social change that might be occurring for other reasons? No one argues that sitcoms are a primary driver of social change. The reluctance of sitcoms to show variety in women's roles before 1970 certainly shows that sitcoms were a *lagging* indicator of social change through the 1950s and 1960s. Even after that period, there have been significant swings back and forth in relation to the presentation of women. It is notable that the turn to traditional programming in the '80s was the pendulum backlash to the relevance period. Compared to other programs, sitcoms still seem somewhat more conservative when we look at them across their entire history.

4) Are sitcoms simply entertainment, without much impact on or relation to social and cultural reality? Entertainment, even in a more "woke" and progressive era (see below), still comes first. Many sitcoms with regressive social ideas and portrayals that would now be considered completely archaic were greenlit in the past because of misguided ideas (from our presentist perspective of today) that they would be funny or entertaining. For women's issues, despite the best intentions of many producers, it seems likely that we are still producing images today of women and family life that will be considered outmoded and unwatchable in a few decades.

Certainly, the days of *Donna Reed* types of portrayals are past us. At the same time, more recent programs such as *Everybody Loves Raymond* were quite popular with large audiences with a mom in a stay-at-home role. The same was true of *Home Improvement* (1991–99), also with a stay-at-home mom. Sitcoms such as these developed a "not that there's anything wrong with that" attitude toward housewives. Interestingly, both shows had stars (Patricia Heaton and Tim Allen, respectively) who express more conservative political profiles than the average Hollywood figure. While LaLaLand programming tendencies may move ever more progressively, if slowly, toward nontraditional family structures, these and other shows demonstrate that the culture wars are in fact still quite oppositional, with large audience segments that still might like to see things "the way they were."

Race and Minority

Sitcoms did not start out well on the issue of race. As discussed previously at various points in our narrative, after disasters such as *Amos 'n' Andy*, network programmers simply chose to avoid Black characters, let alone Black-cast programs. After this period of absolute absence of Black characters in sitcoms, the relevance era of the '70s ushered in a period when numerical representation was roughly equal to Black population percentages (though emphatically *not* so for Asians and Native Americans). Interestingly, sitcoms turned out to offer, after the '70s, the *most* opportunity for Black shows on national TV. Across the total sitcom dataset, almost 17 percent of the characters are Black. Note that the Black population percentage in reality is about 12.5 percent, so in some sense Blacks are *over*represented in sitcoms. On nonsitcoms, the percentage is only 9 percent across all years.

This comedic Black presence is itself an issue. The relative confinement of Black people to comedy roles is not limited to the '50s, with most of the major Black television hits coming from the sitcom world across all years of TV. As we have seen, this trend created issues for Black social critics (see discussions, e.g., in Bogle, 2001a) who did not favor lower-brow Black comedy for being too reflective of the mugging and jiving of the minstrel era. We see this even in later programs such as *In Living Color* and the youth-oriented hip-hop-influenced programs on Fox, UPN, and the WB. But for programs that attempted to avoid this trap, there was the accusation that the "true" Black experience was not being portrayed (*Cosby* being the archetypical example). Relatively few programs seemed to find a reasonable middle ground (*Frank's Place* was one example), but audience popularity was an issue for them.

198 SITCOMS AND CULTURE

From a cultural indicators standpoint, it is hard to translate quantifiable demographic racial characteristics into specific stereotypes. Our CI dataset shows that nonwhite characters score about the same as others on dimensions such attractiveness, power, and intelligence. After the 1960s, when programmers started to tentatively include more Black characters, there was sometimes even a tendency to avoid portraying them as villains or in stereotyped criminal roles, specifically to avoid social and critical backlash. Yet Gerbner argued that television mostly saw Blacks in a bifurcated way: either as criminals or as doing very well economically, not suffering from any sort of systemic racism. Michael Morgan commented on Gerbner's view:

> With the vast middle of the African American experience erased from the airwaves, the result is that Black criminals become the face of urban issues like poverty and inequality, in the process creating an often-unspoken climate of fear and anger and resentment that makes it virtually impossible to solve our inner-city problems, including crime, by any other means than policing and punishment. If, on the one hand, there's this glowing image of African Americans that can make it seem to some that we've overcome issues of inequality, then when Blacks do step out of line, it's almost as if they're ungrateful, and therefore deserving the harshest punishment.[5]

For Gerbner, the comparison was a result of comparing news to fiction. In the civil rights crises of the 1960s, progressive thinkers were worried that the absolute frequency with which viewers would see Black criminality on the news, without any other context, would support very hard-line law-and-order policies. Even if crime rates were higher in Black communities, as was the case, Gerbner and others thought that the overemphasis on it would obscure the fact that vast majorities of Black people were working as hard as anyone, obeying the same social rules, but overly suffering from stereotypical conceptions nurtured by news programs. Such a conception rings true again in the 2020s, with frequent debates on policing reform.

The counterpart image of Blacks as succeeding above and beyond any sort of racism that Gerbner had in mind came from sitcoms and other dramatic programs. As we have seen, though, the oppression of expectations on these programs—that the relatively small number of Black-led scripted shows must show the entire range of Black experience—often led to controversy and even failure.

For other minorities portrayed in sitcoms, our data allow us to say less. Asians in sitcoms were few and far between and continue to be so. Some

Sitcoms, Cultural Indicators, and Social Change 199

examples show how they were, by virtue of their rarer appearance, almost always stereotyped. There is the case of Mrs. Livingston from *The Courtship of Eddie's Father*, a Japanese housekeeper played by Mitoshi Umeki. She very quietly advised the single dad on romantic affairs; she herself was desexed in the role. On *Happy Days*, Pat Morita played Arnold, the Japanese owner of the drive-in where the kids hung out. He played it with a very exaggerated accent, not his own. One of the more delightful Asian characterizations was Yemana from *Barney Miller* (1975–82). Jack Soo's take was not exclusively Asian. His slow deadpan jokes gave him an equal role to other detectives on the multi-ethnic show. The actor, Soo, had spent time in an internment camp. In our CI data, though, fewer than 1 percent of characters were coded as Asian. It is very much a case of "symbolic annihilation" (Gerbner & Gross, 1976), at least until recently. Low rates of Asian appearance may have been somewhat understandable in the early years of sitcoms because the Asian population in the US was also relatively low. Now, however, Asian citizens represent more than 6 percent of the US population, a number that is growing.[6] Recent shows such as *Fresh off the Boat* (2015–20) are attempting to broaden comedic portrayals of Asians, but the enterprise is still in a nascent stage.

Focusing on Native Americans, tellingly, we have no characters that were coded in the CI database. Recall that the CI database is a yearly sample. So while there certainly are some individual characterizations from TV history that we can remember, they were so infrequent in sitcoms that the CI sampling missed them (in nonsitcoms, the rate was a tiny 0.33 percent). Some portrayals are worth remembering, though, perhaps as negative examples. The cowboy-and-Indians series *F Troop* (1965–67) featured entire tribes of Native Americans, most if not all of whom were played by white Hollywood comedy actors. As we noted above, *Seinfeld* delved briefly into the issue of prejudice against Native Americans, in a comedic way, with a portrayal by actress Kimberly Norris Guerrero. Media scholars have noted the general categories of stereotype that have been applied to Native American in media over the years: noble savage, environmentally conscious steward, and so forth (Tan, Fujioka & Lucht, 1997). Few of these stereotypes seemed applicable in the world of sitcoms. Most recently, *Rutherford Falls* (2021–22) was a sitcom with a Native American showrunner; it was canceled after two seasons.

Finally, there is the issue of the portrayal of homosexuality. We are again somewhat limited by the data available. The CI database contains some information about same-sex relationships in programs only, not at the character level. These data were gathered only after 1999, which presumably reflects the fact that programs started to address gay themes semiseriously only in the '90s (Gross, 2001). In the sitcoms coded from 1999 to 2015, 82 percent had no reference in any way to homosexuality or gay characters. About 4 percent of the programs had some characters that were known to be gay. Fewer than 1 percent of programs depicted an active gay relationship.

More data is available from other sources. The gay activist organization GLAAD found in 2021 that 11.9 percent of characters on scripted series (not just sitcoms) were gay.[7] If we look at their report from 2015, the last year of our CI data collection, the number was similar to our CI data: 4 percent. So, it is clear that there has been significant growth in gay representation on television in recent years.

Concerning whether exposure to television is related to negative attitudes about gay people, Nisbet and Myers (2012) actually found a reversal or a tipping point. Reasoning that gay images on TV had changed their nature in the 1990s, moving from absence to positivity, they thought that exposure to TV would cultivate *more* acceptance of homosexuality. They collected data on visibility on TV from a variety of sources. Figure 6.3 is reproduced from their work, showing the concurrence of the rise in gay characters and attitudinal acceptability. Their work includes more than just sitcoms, but the patterns of parallel increase are instructive. From a media effects or cultivation perspective, they did in fact find the expected shift across the years.

> As our findings demonstrate, social or cultural shifts can eventually enter the mainstream of television content, in this case, as public acceptability of homosexuality increases. In turn, shifts in television content toward more representations of gays and lesbians are reflected in the views of heavy television users that reinforce the newly established cultural order. Furthermore, television's tendency to hypostatize and stereotype everything and the politics of political correctness may push television toward ever more positive portrayals of newly emerging minority groups such as homosexuals, a path previously followed by African Americans, and may explain the rapid explosion in the visibility of homosexual characters in recent years. (p. 75)

Patterns of parallel increase do not necessarily prove causality, but they may be the best form of evidence that the cultural indicators researcher has available. Relatively few studies in the history of media effects research can avail themselves of a natural field experiment type of design that would be required to show whether, for example, people exposed to images of gay

Sitcoms, Cultural Indicators, and Social Change

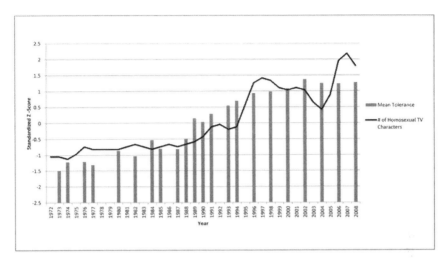

Figure 6.3. Increase in gay TV characters and tolerance of homosexuality (Nisbet & Myers, 2012).

characters across long swaths of time would show identical or different attitudes compared to those who were not. Trends in content data compared to trends in survey attitudes can thus finally be only instructive, not conclusive. With this in mind, we will explore below whether the phenomenon posited by Nisbet and Myers can be substantiated more specifically with sitcoms and see how durable the idea is across different issues of representation.

We return again to our four research questions, now applied to minority groups:

1) Do media messages act as a mirror on the culture? On issues of race and minority portrayal, the long period up to 2015 has examples of fits and starts. Distortions of minority groups are often extreme, usually tilted toward underrepresentation of groups. Yet social activism and change within the Hollywood production institutions are also manifest and turn up on TV in interesting ways. Black people specifically were the minority group that was too large to ignore. Moreover, programmers eventually found that tapping Black audiences and markets could be a profitable enterprise. The period of absence from the '50s and '60s led to the '70s where Black shows had a significant presence on the three main networks. After the '80s and the dominance of *Cosby*, the development of new TV networks

meant new places for Black representation but also segmentation, with whiter shows on the three legacy networks. None of the advance was without controversy, but sitcoms now move toward the near future with Black casts and audiences always assumed to have a place at the table. That is a shift from sitcoms' beginnings.

2) Are sitcoms a causal force in making or producing social change? Typically, sitcoms have been a lagging indicator. The entire American Civil Rights Movement of the '60s occurred without sitcoms taking much notice. But neither were sitcoms completely irrelevant. Sitcoms have often been a site within which larger discussions can take place. Successful minority-led sitcoms showed that underrepresented groups *desired* representation. Even if sitcoms were seen as silly or inconsequential, to have one's own group represented in that world still meant something. Overall, though, the kind of progress on social issues that can be measured in changes in public attitudes as surveyed in polls almost always precedes the serious appearance of that viewpoint in sitcoms. There are relatively few that are cutting edge.

3) Do sitcoms hold back social change that might be occurring for other reasons? On issues of race, the period of the '50s and '60s was clearly one of sticking our collective heads in the sand. Certainly, the symbolic annihilation of various minority groups could have been something that made its own contribution to slowing down the pace of change that might have been quicker. Had there been more humanized portraits of Black people on sitcoms and other shows, we can only speculate whether Gerbner's ideas about the bifurcated image would have had continued validity.

4) Are sitcoms simply entertainment, without much impact on or relation to social and cultural reality? As we have seen in almost every chapter of this book, Americans have had no problems with images of minority groups in entertainment. Early vaudeville comedy was mostly based on the idea of ethnic comedy, which was then baked into early sitcoms. It's hard to take it out even in a more progressive era. If ethnic comedy in all of its forms had been contexted within a variety of portrayals of the different groups, the overall sense of ethnicity as entertainment might have been different across the years we studied. As happened more often, though, underrepresented

Sitcoms, Cultural Indicators, and Social Change   203

groups were sometimes relegated to comedy, where minority groups can only be jesters or buffoons. This has changed greatly in more recent years, but images that recall this history can be a very sensitive topic. Also, the reality was that the segregated world of entertainment that existed for many years (and can still be seen in the audience segmentation that occurs quite frequently) meant that majority groups simply might not understand comedy that was created for someone other than themselves. Whether sitcoms can forge a more integrated or even multicultural approach to comedy that can be both authentic and successful in the mass market is an ongoing project.

Family Structure—Marital Status

Sitcoms appear to be purpose-built to tell us how family life should be structured. Yet they distort many aspects of the way that we live. As we saw in figure 4.6, sitcoms (and television in general) tend to favor unmarried individuals. A Pew study in 2019 showed that the share of people ages twenty-five to fifty-two who were married was around 53 percent.[8] In our overall sitcom dataset, the percentage is 32 percent. In the US, that percentage has been shrinking, as we noted in figure 3.1. Divorce rates are going up, and the percentages of people who never get married are going up, but TV still underrepresents married people. We see a relatively realistic portrayal of marriage rates in our data from the '60s and '70s, around 50 percent. After that, though, rates of married characters drop to about 33 percent and generally stay there across the decades.

In reality, sitcoms had been distorting family portrayals almost from the beginning across a variety of dimensions (for instance, with age, as we have seen). The "regular" sitcom families of the 1950s (the white nuclear ones that became the stereotype) were themselves only part of the picture that was giving way to other options when CI data collection began. In the quest for narrative novelty, sitcoms gradually have gone through almost every family configuration possible. A single dad was most common early on (*Andy Griffith, My Three Sons*), with sainted mothers absent from the picture for no reason. Single moms were considered more shameful and almost taboo, more so if it was by reason of divorce. However, by the 1970s, even sitcoms recognized that reality (*One Day at a Time, Alice*), at least partially. Sitcoms could have one dad, two dads, or even three dads (*Full House*). This type of multiplicity was less available with moms. Sitcoms could have no kids, one or two, or sometimes six (*The Brady Bunch*). Sitcoms could have multiracial families, as when white families adopted cute Black children (*Diff'rent Strokes* [1978–85]). More recently, even gay families are possible (*Modern Family*). The endless permutations of how one can arrange a family have been a boon to sitcom producers.

Examples of traditional nuclear families have become slightly less common in sitcoms. When we see them, they are sometimes fodder for negative commentary, as in the 1980s, when a traditional family in a sitcom was seen as a failure to reflect cultural reality, returning to a much-loathed earlier era that propagandized "family values." That in itself is also problematic because many families still are organized in a nuclear fashion. In 2020, almost 75 percent of US children lived with two parents. It is true that this number has been declining as the ethnic composition of the US changes, but if sitcoms were accurately representing family structure, most of the families would still be nuclear. Yet it seems fair to say that attack and devalorization is the dominant tone in critical evaluations of sitcoms' portrayal of the traditional family.

If we are holding sitcoms to a strict standard defined by progressive political values, we should remember that American society itself changed rather slowly on some of these issues, such as gay marriage. The *Obergefell* decision of the Supreme Court codifying gay marriage came only in 2015, at the very end of our period of CI data collection. Prior to this, there had been very, very few instances of committed gay unions on sitcoms, although *Roc* did actually have a storyline as far back as 1991 ("Can't Help Lovin' That Man," S1E8). *Modern Family* dealt with the issue as Proposition 8 (banning gay marriage) was defeated in California in 2014. Whether legal change on gay marriage would have come faster had television programs dealt with the issue more frequently is something we'll never know, but it seems like television programming that had been advancing progressively on some other issues was getting around to themes of gay marriage rather late.

The other way that sitcoms present diverse family structures is by focusing on something other than the family, usually the workplace. With these types of shows, the message usually is that you can find family in other places. Shows that bring dysfunctional and quirky individuals to places where they find and support each other are very common (*Taxi*, for instance). As we discussed previously, these shows often develop roles for characters not unlike those found in a nuclear family. In a world less focused on marriage and home, post-'90s characters needed at least "a place where everyone knows your name" (*Cheers*). Particularly in the '90s and thereafter, and even before, sitcoms were becoming aware that childbirth was also inevitably becoming less common

Sitcoms, Cultural Indicators, and Social Change   205

(*Friends, Living Single, Seinfeld*). Sitcoms recognized this demographic transition, and their quest to develop younger audiences was matched by the fact that writers and producers were coming from a world that had also changed demographically.

We return to our four research questions one last time:

1) Do media messages act as a mirror on the culture? In terms of how sitcoms represent families, the mirror is again a distorted one. Across the great body of sitcoms, response to social change on family structure was often lagging.

2) Are sitcoms a causal force in making or producing social change? When sitcoms begin to intervene on social issues, it can be notable. Such a period of sitcom activism occurred in the 1970s. We may also be seeing some new forms of television in activism in sitcoms of the 2020s, but it is too early to evaluate their impact.

3) Do sitcoms hold back social change that might be occurring for other reasons? This is still a very difficult question to answer empirically. Family change is happening, along with various demographic transitions that are taking place in the US. Sometimes it is in a direction that sitcoms seem to like, with more novelty of family structure and less focus on nuclear forms. The hypothetical question of whether this change might have occurred faster without the generally conservative influence of entertainment television programming is still an open one. Shanahan and Jones addressed the idea in 1999:

One hypothesis is that television's messages may impede or retard social change that is due to social activism and other forces, though Gerbner feels that "positive" social change is generally achieved despite television, which seeks to maintain the status quo in favor of social elites. With respect to specific social issues, social change generated from other social sectors is as important as or sometimes more important than television's messages. For instance, the gradual liberalization of attitudes about proper social roles for women is undeniable. Yet television throughout those years clearly portrayed women in less-powerful social positions, and fewer women have always been depicted. Did television tend to retard the liberalization process? Or did television speed the process by virtue of some specific messages that may have been more salient to social perception? Or, alternately,

206 SITCOMS AND CULTURE

was television out of the loop on this social movement? In general, these remain interesting and basically unaddressed questions for cultivation researchers. (Shanahan & Jones, 1999, p. 47)

For sitcoms specifically, the retardation argument applies well to many programs. But the idea of television as a conservative force working to maintain the status quo is also at odds with many people's vision of Hollywood production as favoring a very liberal perspective and becoming ever less traditional, even coarse. This is a paradox we attempt to untangle in our final sections.

4) Are sitcoms simply entertainment, without much impact on or relation to social and cultural reality? When someone set out to produce a very silly sitcom like *Gilligan's Island*, it's hard to imagine that any social or cultural impacts were considered. Yet producer Sherwood Schwartz indicated that his idea behind the show was to depict diversity and difference, addressing what he called "the most important idea in the world today": the need to see how people of different classes would live together (on the desert island that served as his sociological laboratory, "where I could put them that they couldn't get away from each other").[9] His island's "family" diversity was in fact rather limited by today's standards, but if even *Gilligan's Island* can be considered to have had some relevance to social issues, then the vast body of shows that are often derided for being nothing more than television candy, devoid of any nutritional content, might be worth our attention as more than just entertainment.

Sitcoms, TV, and Social Change

Gerbner developed his theories first in the late 1950s and then more fully in the '60s. He was responding to a television system that was very much a servant of dominant political and economic institutions. At its outset, program content on TV was literally controlled by advertisers. The producers of a sitcom like *Father Knows Best* actually collaborated with the government on propaganda. Red-baiting tactics in Hollywood affected a variety of sitcoms, many of which self-censored for fear of running afoul of the McCarthy machinery. The ideological guardrails and self-imposed proclivities of the television institution were obvious.

Gerbner's most noted theoretical achievements were in the area of cultural indicators (measuring and analyzing television content) and cultivation (assessing relationships between exposure to content and beliefs about the world). Less discussed was the theoretical foundation on which he premised the whole enterprise, which he called "institutional process analysis." In this work, Gerbner (1973) outlined what he believed were the critical observations about how the media system worked (fig. 6.4). He posited a variety of actors and roles, enumerating the leverages they could produce within the system to achieve desired outcomes. At the foundation of his institutional system was political authority, which wielded the leverage of law and the threat of force on the activities of the system. Next, above political actors, were "patrons," who wielded the leverage that controlled the economic resources that flowed into the system. Gerbner's view was basically materialist, which implies that capitalist control over resources determines the "superstructure" of messages that will be produced, which ultimately must serve the needs of that capital. Toward the very end of Gerbner's long list of actors, we find the creative personnel ("experts") who actually create the messages that can exist within the system and, finally, audiences, who may attend to those messages (Morgan, 2012). Their leverages come only after and are predicated on those found in the "base" of the system.

Controversies over the influence of the base versus the superstructure are common in critical communication theory (e.g., Williams, 1973). Gerbner did not avail himself much of the jargon of critical theory. Neither did he believe in linear propagandistic effects of media messages, where people just imitate what they see. Nevertheless, although he did not espouse the most simplistic critical theories, he did have a view of television as tightly woven within the political and economic systems. He did not shy away from a view of what the media systems were in service to: "Television is the central cultural arm of the business and industrial or the political establishment. Its direct clients are not consumers of specific programs but business and industrial sponsors or public corporations or governments. Therefore, it is relatively insulated from direct public involvement (although keenly aware of the importance of public relations)" (Gerbner, 1980, p. 8).

Gerbner and Gross (1976) articulated the view further: "Once the industrial order has legitimized its rule, the primary function of its cultural arm becomes the reiteration of that legitimacy and the maintenance of established power and authority. The rules of the games and the morality of its goals can best be demonstrated by dramatic stories of their symbolic violations. The intended lessons are generally effective and the social order is only rarely and peripherally threatened" (p. 177).

The view was a very accurate one for TV of the 1960s. In the "vast wasteland" era of television, programs' intent was either bland escapism (such as

FIGURE 1
Major power roles, sources, and functions affecting mass communicator decisions

Power roles Internal to media	Typical sources of power	Typical functions
1. CLIENTS	Resources for investment, subsidy	Specify conditions for supply of capital, facilities, operating funds
2. SUPERVISORS	Organisational hierarchy	Formulate policies and supervise implementation
3. COLLEAGUES	Solidarity	Set standards; protection
4. COMPETITORS	Scarcity	Set standards; vigilance
5. AUXILIARIES	Services	Supply, distribution, access
External to media		
6. AUTHORITIES	Legislation and enforcement	Regulate the social order, including communications
7. ORGANISATIONS	Appeal to authorities, interests, and publics for support or protection	Demand favourable attention
8. EXPERTS	Specialised knowledge	Impart information, skills, set standards
9. PATRONS	Attend to media messages	Form publics that patronise media

Figure 6.4. Reproduced from Morgan (2012), Gerbner's scheme for assigning media functions and roles.

most of what we looked at in our review of 1960s sitcoms) or more baldly pro-US messages supporting police power, military prowess, and glorification of strong individuals solving social problems with decisive and authoritarian action.

Gerbner et al.'s findings on TV violence make good sense within this framework. Conservative political authorities seemed fairly happy with an action-soaked TV diet with programs, such as *The FBI*, that created strong support for law-and-order policies. Some of the more liberal or progressive elements of the political establishment showed concern over TV violence, but the issue was also used to distract attention from a variety of other social ills that could explain the problem. Most of the political attempts to rein in

Sitcoms, Cultural Indicators, and Social Change 209

TV violence did not go very far. While sitcoms were not affected much by the violence debates, sitcom-based sexism issues found strong corroboration in Gerbner's institutional view. Prior to the 1960s, both political and economic authority had always been male. Incursions of women into leadership roles in politics or business were very minor at the time Gerbner was writing. The sexism of sitcoms in the 1960s, then, and the preference for traditional families were entirely of a piece with political and economic power at that time. Thus, Gerbner's focus on issues of both violence and gender made quite a bit of sense from the perspective of the 1960s television system; he and his colleagues found much evidence that television viewing was cultivating conceptions in directions that were preferred by dominant political and economic actors.

Gerbner and colleagues began assessing the *effects* of television's message system in the mid-'70s (e.g., Gerbner & Gross, 1976). Much of their early work and the work that it spawned—which has become hundreds of studies (see Hermann et al., 2021 for a summary)—has been quite consistent with this theoretical outlook. Heavy viewers were in fact more fearful of the world (Gerbner, 1998), and they did tend to be more traditional in their gender outlooks (Signorielli, 1989). Politically, Gerbner identified what he saw as television's tendency to "blur" and "blend" issues (Gerbner, 1987), homogenizing social differences into a cultural "mainstream" of great power (Gerbner et al., 1982). He also thought that this blurred and bended cultural center of gravity tended to be "bent" toward the conservative right on social issues. Television was seen not as a mechanism of social change but much more as maintaining a social status quo in the face of other forces that might augur for more disruptive social change (Shanahan & Jones, 1999). Clearly, though, social change was occurring in spite of the fact that television may have been a mainly conservative force. In the face of television's resistance to social change, might change have occurred faster if television had not acted as a governor on it? It's a difficult hypothesis to test; there are few empirical data that can support this idea at the macro level, but notions of television's retardation of the pace of change and progress have appeared from time to time in the literature.

With respect to sitcoms, we've seen here that harbingers of change were occurring even before Gerbner's first cultivation tests were occurring in the mid-'70s. The relevance sitcom wave began in the early '70s, responding to social and demographic change that had already occurred in spite of television's patent conservatism in the '50s and '60s. It raises the question: If television was so intertwined with the desires and goals of political and economic power, why would it have even been willing to green-light the

210   SITCOMS AND CULTURE

programs of the relevance era, which were clearly a progressive move *against* conservative social authority carried out for the most part by self-identified progressives?

Many explanations are possible. One is that Gerbner's picture of influence as mainly flowing upward from a materialist base should be reconsidered. Gerbner's theory was an entirely accurate depiction of how television worked in the '50s and '60s—primarily as a servant to conservative advertising interests. But did the force of influence start to reverse downward through the system, with cultural actors (writers, creators, producers) gaining power as the decades wore on? This possibility hinges on whether *cultural* capital can be as important as economic capital.

"New State Religion"?

Gerbner often analogized television to religion (1977). In the days before widely available mass media, institutions that could control narratives wielded important influence, with the church being the most obvious example. Gerbner often also cited Andrew Fletcher, who said that "if a man were permitted to make all the ballads, he need not care who should make the laws of a nation" (Morgan & Shanahan, 1996). These views imply media's cultural power, basically a form of cultural capital, that authorizes Gerbner's entire enterprise toward being cognizant of and assessing what the culture is up to. But this recognition can create a tension against the idea that cultural institutions are always lapdogs of economic power. Even in the days of "old state religion," the church was never wholly subservient to political or economic power; it was always a contest among the various estates.

In looking at TV of the '50s and '60s—the TV that Gerbner was initially responding to—it is understandable why he would tend to draw the line of influence mostly upward from economic capital. But trends in the '70s made it obvious that programming institutions and creatives could, even if only gradually at first, wield their own forms of capital. As the new state religion (TV) tended to develop its own priesthood, those skilled in the creative and technical arts were increasingly needed to generate the profits desired by the old-line holders of economic capital. The values and aesthetics of elites that seemed to permeate the safe sitcoms of the '50s were not necessarily held by those with expertise to create programs. We do see even in sitcoms, which are still a basically conservative form of TV, that access to technical and creative skill could grant—albeit slowly—new freedoms to a rising class of media producers who could shake off the bonds that limited their predecessors.

Sitcoms, Cultural Indicators, and Social Change 211

In the new state religion, as in the old one, the idea is to get everyone basically on the same page. It creates support for those using power to pursue interests. Gerbner's idea of "mainstreaming" captured the essence of TV as a quasi-religious enterprise. As his results started to cumulate through the '80s, findings emerged in which groups that would normally diverge on some social or cultural perception were found to be more similar as heavy viewers of TV. This was commonly seen when comparing liberals and conservatives, who obviously tend to have different views on issues like race, sex, abortion rights, and so forth. In many cases, heavy viewers who self-identified as liberals or conservatives were more similar in their outlook than light viewers who identified as such. For cultivation theorists, this simply meant that heavy viewers, since they shared more of the same narrative environment and were on the same page, were thus also more similar in outlook. "By 'mainstreaming' we mean the sharing of that commonality among heavy viewers in those demographic groups whose light viewers tend to hold divergent views. In other words, differences deriving from other factors and social forces may be diminished or even absent among heavy viewers" (Gerbner et al., 1980, p. 15). There are many examples of these mainstreaming findings in the literature, and they continue to pop up frequently. The implications for social control are clear: Homeostasis helps a society have majorities that agree with each on other on what the state of the world is. The idea of a mainstream mass-communicated central cultural outlook, serving as a kind of social thermostat, is quite appealing and consonant with the many examples of mainstreaming findings that have been observed.

In a religious metaphor, TV programs are the liturgy. We consume them frequently, much more often than in the days when church attendance was weekly. The intent of liturgy is to induce acceptance of a creed, something like the Catholic Baltimore Catechism. In sitcoms, the liturgy became a weekly representation of how families are structured and how men and women relate to each other, to children, and to work. The early creed to be accepted was the oft-criticized stereotype of the white nuclear family and the Middle-American family-values belief system that has popped up so often throughout this book.

But the history of sitcoms does also strain the mainstreaming metaphor. Why do various schisms appear in how gender roles, or racial roles, or family structures are portrayed across their history? We should be clear that Gerbner never argued that television viewing was the only thing that influenced cultural perceptions. His data made it clear that it wasn't even necessarily the strongest thing. Many other social forces shaped how culture was moving, independently of what was seen on TV. Even so, the idea of television as a mainstreaming force is coming to be questioned more and more often, particularly as the institution of television itself changes toward a greater fractionalizing of the audience and the choices it can make.

Cultural Elites: The "New Class"?

It is worth noting that the classes of people who make television—writers, programmers, actors, award-giving institutions, and even studios—were (1) always more liberal in outlook than the business interests that controlled them and (2) have tended to gain more influence in terms of how they can use cultural capital in their own favor. It is fitting to conclude this work with the notion that the cultural products that Gerbner would mainly have seen as an index of something wider and more powerful can also have causal impacts, on their own, in terms of how society evolves and develops.

Many theorists have noted how technological and cultural elites can compete with the classes that once exclusively held power/capital. Sociologist Alvin Gouldner coined the term "New Class" to represent this group, whose power comes from expertise and which exploits its capital within institutions such as education, science, culture, and the media (Gouldner, 1979). Gouldner argued that these emerging elites held a type of capital just as important as the control of the base economy as it became the case that economic productivity could not be achieved without the compliance of this technocratic new class. This new class is trained in certain forms of discourse; it engages in credentialling activities that admit certain members and over time develops ideological stances that come to be required for membership in it. In some ways, the new class begins to function as a priestly class, raising again Gerbner's old questions about culture as the new state religion. Gouldner emphasizes that the class acts like any other: It seeks to maximize its profits from the capital it controls.

Christopher Lasch (1995) was not in full agreement with Gouldner's idea that the new elites represent a class, but he also saw many connections developing between cultural and political elites, rather than dependencies:

> One might add the more jaundiced observation that the circles of power—finance, government, art, entertainment—overlap and become increasingly interchangeable. It is significant that Reich (1992) turns to Hollywood for a particularly compelling example of the "wondrously resilient" communities that spring up wherever there is a concentration

Sitcoms, Cultural Indicators, and Social Change 213

of "creative" people. Washington becomes a parody of Tinseltown; executives take to the airwaves, creating overnight the semblance of political movements; movie stars become political pundits, even presidents; reality and the simulation of reality become more and more difficult to distinguish. Ross Perot launches his presidential campaign from the "Larry King Show." Hollywood stars take a prominent part in the Clinton campaign and flock to Clinton's inaugural, investing it with the glamour of a Hollywood opening. TV anchors and interviewers become celebrities; celebrities in the world of entertainment take on the role of social critics. (p. 38)

This diverges from Gerbner's early view of the culture industry more as simply the handmaiden of old-line capital, the cultural arm. By contrast, more and more we hear references to Hollywood elites who are out of touch with Middle America, whose programming is seen more and more as inscribing a "woke" agenda onto its viewers. Mainstream news media are also known to be quite liberal in outlook and composition, working in concert with Hollywood to promote liberal and now even progressive cultural approaches. These observations are very much at odds with how the media worked in the 1950s.

None of these debates conclusively reject Gerbner's formulations about TV and its relation to power, but they do prompt us to examine the multiple ways and directions in which influence can flow in his system. If Hollywood is now mainly a progressive institution, however the term *progressive* is defined, and if cultural capital can compete with economic capital, we should expect to see a more muddled and confusing contest for how images are transmitted to Americans through television.

In the world of sitcoms after 2000, we do see this, in terms of both what is present and what is missing. Of sitcoms that appeared on the over-the-air networks after 2000 and made the top twenty, only one (*Everybody Loves Raymond*) focused on a nuclear family situation, defined as mom, dad, and some kids. Meanwhile, two out of that group of shows were portraying more progressive family situations (*Will & Grace, Modern Family*). The remainder were mostly nonfamily setups (*Becker* [1998–2004], *Just Shoot Me* [1997–2003], *Big Bang Theory, Friends*) or alternate non-nuclear family arrangements (*Frasier, Two and a Half Men, Mom* [2013–21]). For fans of the nuclear family, the argument for its "symbolic annihilation" is tempting. The period after 2000 in sitcoms is in some ways the opposite of what had been seen with the 1950s nuclear-coms.

This is not to say that sitcoms somehow became raving propaganda sites for the most outrageously different lifestyles. There are still groups within

214   SITCOMS AND CULTURE

American society that have yet to see *their* sitcom. In some ways, the sitcoms of the 2000s are changing, moving, but still relatively conservative, probing neither the artistic nor the representational grounds that we see more commonly in films. There is still a least-common-denominator mentality attached to the sitcom, even if the numbers of the denominator are much smaller than they were in the network era.

But if we compare sitcoms to other TV genres, such as action programming, they may seem more progressive. Network schedules are still littered with action-oriented police dramas where Gerbner's critiques are still entirely relevant. Programs like *Law & Order* and its multitude of spin-offs seemed tailor-made for Gerbner's ideas about social control that were formulated fifty years ago. The cultural atmosphere of the 2020s is in some ways very similar to that of the late 1960s, with fear about urban violence, racial distrust, and rising levels of violence in society accompanied by always exaggerated levels of violence in the media. What is different, arguably, is the level of political polarization around the issues.

Is There a Cultural Mainstream Anymore?

Worry about cultural and political polarization has been percolating since the 1990s. Gerbner's notion of a cultural mainstream, which was offered mainly as a critique of cultural and political homogenization, can be a nostalgically pleasant memory when we confront the fractionalization that seems so prevalent now. The time when we watched the same programs, watched the same news, and talked about it all around the watercooler also seemed to be a time when we agreed on at least a few basic cultural realities as being truthful. Even if that tendency is a reference to a false golden age, cultural and political polarizations do now seem much different from each other. Theorists refer to *affective polarization*, which means that groups don't like each other based more on emotion and identity than on specific policy positions. Iyengar et al. (2019) argued that increased "sorting" of individuals in terms of political identity, along with the new "high-choice" media environment, explains polarization, which has been increasing since the early '90s. They noted that these polarizations spill over into the social world, with people expressing much less likelihood of marrying someone from the other political party, for instance. Now, you can learn a lot about groups by knowing which party they vote for: the TV networks they watch, the cars they drive, the foods they eat, and many other things.

Sitcoms, Cultural Indicators, and Social Change   215

The high-choice media environment is now much different from what Gerbner was trying to explain. Over-the-air television is less dominant. Sitcoms on cable networks and streaming services show an incredibly multivalent picture. All kinds of constituencies find their own shows, though relatively few can gain the kind of mass audience that was possible even as late as the 1990s. Red-state viewers can watch *The Ranch* (2016–20) or *Last Man Standing* (2011–21) with their unreconstructed "toxic" male heads of household. Blue-staters have *Schitt's Creek*, where downfallen wealthy elites are forced to live among a rural "basket of deplorables," a sort of *Green Acres* for the post-postmodern age.

Thus, as the new classes were discovering their cultural power, polarizing factors were threatening it and breaking it up. No single sitcom can now command a mass audience anywhere near the size that *Seinfeld* got in the 1990s, when the trend toward affective polarization began. After 2000, network sitcoms were getting ratings one-half to one-third of what *Seinfeld* drew. A successful and long-running cable sitcom like *It's Always Sunny in Philadelphia* (2005–) routinely draws fewer than 1.5 million viewers per episode. The decline of mass audiences for television especially affects sitcoms. The world of network television seemed purpose-built for a kind of series that viewers could come back to week after week—but no more often than that—for an easy visit with some friends. With so many new options available to viewers, it seems less necessary to have a few sitcoms that tell everyone how families should live. The networks' racial fractionalization of sitcoms that went on during the 1990s can now occur at a much narrower level, even to the point that sitcoms now seem less relevant or interesting because they apply to only small groups of people.

The death of sitcoms has been pronounced at various times throughout their history, but they have always bounced back. Now one wonders, though. It seems likely that there will always be a place for domestic comedy in some form, but the expensive network-led mass-oriented form is suffering. Much of the oxygen is taken from the room by reality programs. They are less expensive to produce, and they can do an efficient job of showing novelty-family situations, as had been the province of the sitcom. Programs such as *Here Comes Honey Boo Boo* or *Duck Dynasty* trade in the same rural-family comedy that was sitcom-popular in the 1960s, with little need for writers or expensive actors. Younger folks still interested in marriage can check out *The Bachelor* or *The Bachelorette*, even though the arranged marriages rarely successfully take, which is itself interesting from a cultural indicators standpoint. In the creative golden age of TV that emerged after the '90s, the flagship programs were not sitcoms; they were serious dramas like *The Sopranos* or *Mad Men* or *Breaking Bad*. The influence of those shows aimed to turn producers and creators with serious artistic vision toward cinematic television, with sitcoms perhaps reeking too much of videotape and canned laughs to garner much attention. *Curb Your Enthusiasm*, perhaps the best example of a successful sitcom in the quality TV era, derives its energy from polarized culture wars but has little to say about maintaining or keeping a family, or being in the workplace for that matter. It is very much a story of the atomized misanthropy of one person.

At the same time, let's remember that every era of sitcom continues to live on, especially on cable channels that simply eat up sitcom content. Cable channels like TBS took the place of the old independent over-the-air TV stations, where sitcom reruns for shows like *I Love Lucy* were always on. Newer free streaming services also gobble up sitcom deals, so shows like *Seinfeld* are assured runs for as long as a few viewers tune in. Not only can viewers get some sense of how the culture regards (or disregards) current family structures but they can also see an entire history of that evolution and binge on it if they so choose. The extent to which newer sitcoms can reference the older—and also the extent to which narrative avenues are opened up or closed off by an awareness of that history—is something relatively new, but its power grows from day to day.

Age, Period, Cohort

This leads to some final observations about sitcoms and their cultural and social influence. It seems fair to say that sitcoms have mostly—with a fair number of interesting exceptions—been *lagging* indicators with respect to social change. TV, when it does change, is often catching up. At the same, it also seems fair to ask whether the cultural capital of the new media class is such that TV forms like sitcoms could become *leading* indicators of social change. American discussions around identity—not only in the family—are changing so rapidly that one imagines that future sitcom producers, if there are many, will want to be riding those waves.

Studios are undergoing a variety of reckonings, especially after the George Floyd protests of 2020. Building on the #metoo protests that had started in 2017—a specifically Hollywood-oriented phenomenon—casting and programming strategies have changed radically to focus more on diversity. Many studios and stars rushed to admit to complicity in white supremacy. Although

Sitcoms, Cultural Indicators, and Social Change   217

there is still little peer-reviewed data on the topic, casting is visibly more diverse after 2020, with some observers claiming—perhaps hyperbolically—that it was almost impossible for white people to be hired in Hollywood. In the world of feature film, the *Hollywood Diversity Report* (Hunt & Ramon, 2022) found that the composition of feature film actors was proportional to the population percentages in the 2020–21 season. This was a real jump from 2019. In the TV version of the report, the category of "people of color" among broadcast leads is considered not proportionate but showing gains. Women are considered to be proportionate across acting categories, not proportionate among production categories, and showing gains since 2019. It seems to many that a real reversal in Hollywood has occurred. Will it be possible that Hollywood *leads* social change? The world of sitcoms is perhaps less touched by this phenomenon, and there are fewer data about recent sitcoms, but it leads to the question of how social change occurs at a mechanical level and how sitcoms could expect to fit into that. Especially because sitcoms have normally been somewhat more diverse than other shows, the question of how sitcoms will deal with future social change is particularly interesting.

Theorists who explain social change look at a variety of factors. One model posits three concepts: *age, period,* and *cohort* (Lu, Amory & Shi, 2021). *Age* explains what happens in the processes of growing older, such as whether people become more conservative as they age. *Period* refers to events that happen in a specific time frame that produce change, such as recent cultural reckonings. Finally, *cohort* refers to generational changes that can propagate throughout a system, for instance when Boomer children of the '50 and '60s came of age and spread around their cultural influence. These concepts can help us a get a grip on how sitcoms have played a role in social change and whether they will in the future. To these three concepts we should add the notion of population demographic composition, whose changes can be related to age, period, and cohort.

Across the years that we look at in our data, the US population has been getting older. Birth rates have been decreasing, and there is about a ten-year difference in the average age of a US person now compared to 1970.[10] For sitcoms, the 1970s to 1990s move toward addressing youthful white spenders (à la *Friends*) starts to lose some vitality as groups age into a phase of life where they are empirically more focused on marriage and children yet also still likely to be watching over-the-air sitcoms. When a star like Matt LeBlanc moves from *Friends* to the family-oriented *Man with a Plan* (2016–20), that seems to be targeting the aging of the audience.

At the same time, things are not the same across all demographic groups. Median ages are lower among Blacks, Hispanics, and Asians (table 6.2), and immigration patterns suggest that this trend will continue or strengthen. Family structure also differs, with lower marriage rates across the board, but especially for Black people. There are differences in family size and structure too. Family size is decreasing across the board, but less so for Blacks and Hispanics. From a cohort perspective, though, it is unclear whether these new contributors to the coming American "majority-minority" (Craig, Rucker & Richeson, 2018) will be sitcom viewers. They have so many other choices. Nevertheless, an increasing diversification of the portrayal of sitcom families and workplaces would be expected to take place under a new demographic regime.

If we see sitcoms themselves as social actors (they are born at a certain period, and they continue to exist and exert influence through reruns), the 1970s cohort seems most noteworthy. This revolutionary golden period for sitcoms established the idea that the genre can be more than a filler, instead building strong writing and social awareness with entertainment and actual comedy. Later sitcom producers still refer back to *All in the Family* and *Mary Tyler Moore*, which are becoming urtexts for how to do progressive comedy, especially in terms of making sure that comedy and progressiveness are both there in equal amounts. *One Day at a Time*, the initial single-mom sitcom of the '70s, was rebooted successfully with a Hispanic cast. Episodes of *All in the Family* and *The Jeffersons* have been redone live, with new actors, to great effect. Sitcom viewers who grew up with these shows in the '70s not only developed nostalgic memories of them but also expected future sitcoms to be able to live up to that standard. These standards were often not met, though, as the sitcom started to wheeze through the later periods of its life cycle.

In terms of period effects, we need look no further back than the present to see what cultural effects can be wrought in an extraordinarily short time frame. From 2016 to 2022, we saw that the Trump presidency and its polarizations, the #metoo and George Floyd reckonings, and the global effects of the pandemic meant some startling changes in how we consume culture. Almost all cultural artifacts, especially in the media, are now understood through red-blue political dichotomies, racial fractionalizations, and rural-urban sensibility divides. Not only that, but media consumption shot up in this period, as people were COVID-confined to their homes and work was occurring only in a mediated way for many. There were thus stresses on concepts of both family and workplace, the bread-and-butter topics of the sitcom. For most of their history, sitcoms were the vehicle that was supposed to put something of

Sitcoms, Cultural Indicators, and Social Change 219

Table 6.2. Family and demographic differences, by race and ethnicity

	Median age[1]	Marriage rate, % of women *not* married by age 35[2]	Family size, average number of children per mother[3]	Family structure, % of children living with two married parents[4]
White	43.7	31.5	2.3	75.5
Black	34.6	61.6	2.5	37.9
Hispanic	29.8	37.4	2.6	61.9
Asian	37.5	25.9	2.2	—

1. https://www.brookings.edu/research/new-census-data-shows-the-nation-is-diversifying-even-faster-than-predicted.
2. https://www.census.gov/content/dam/Census/library/publications/2021/demo/p70-167.pdf.
3. https://www.pewresearch.org/social-trends/2015/05/07/family-size-among-mothers.
4. https://files.eric.ed.gov/fulltext/ED615659.pdf.

a bridge across these types of chasms. We have yet to see whether sitcoms can achieve another rebirth in the context of how all these aspects of the American patchwork are changing. Previous predictions of the sitcom's demise were always wrong, so it seems unwise to make that bet again. Yet it also seems prudent to look at the long-view span of our data—1950 to 2020—with the idea in mind that genres can themselves wear out, as both social conditions that made the genres seem natural and worthwhile change and as ideas for new creative directions seem to run out at the same time.

Examining sitcoms through an empirical lens can continue to offer many avenues for understanding culture. Still, though we are armed with data, we must return to critical viewings to reach tentative conclusions. Williams (1954) offered that works of art are the best way to assess the "structure of feeling" of a given era, the totalized sense of what anything might mean at any given time in human interaction. When we look numerically at aspects of sitcoms, such as their populations, we are looking at what Williams called "precipitates," or aspects of the culture that we have distilled out for closer examination. He notes that when we have measured the work against its "separable parts," as we have done in this book, there is an element that is still found only in its totality. To understand these totalities, there is no alternative but to view and critique the programs.

220 SITCOMS AND CULTURE

But structures of feeling can also be deceiving, as when we assume that dominant cultural tendencies, or stereotypes about those tendencies, hold across an entire body of work. Not all sitcoms in the '50s were about white nuclear families. Even the '60s, with its bland escapism, had programs that were trying to break the mold. The revolutionarily relevant '70s offered much silliness as well. And so on through the decades, the panoply of programming that was offered frequently defied its own cultural milieu. Thus, there is still much to discover through a variety of ways of looking at sitcoms: through micro-level viewing of single episodes, through tracking of significant series, and through macro-level examinations of their totalized demography.

*

Will the sitcom survive? Cultural forms can die. Rock and roll and jazz both seem to be on life support, even though they both have been mainstays of the American cultural history. Digital technology was not kind to certain types of popular music, and arguably it also has not been kind to sitcoms, which have a certain analog comfort to them when produced in the *live in front of a studio audience* context. These were forms that thrived in the era of gatekeepers, with magazines and radio to tell us what records to buy and TV networks to select our shows for us. Although the new freedoms of cultural production and reception are here to stay, with much to recommend them, we can also be mindful of what is lost. It may not be too much to say that Gerbner's mainstream, along with its troubling notions of political homogenization and social control, also provided a comforting cultural center of gravity. That question is for another book. It could not be resolved in twenty-four minutes.

NOTES

1. Livingston (2018).
2. The CI data do not contain occupation codes after 2012, so any change in that last decade is unobservable.
3. Association of American Medical Colleges (2021).
4. This was the author's observation during a term as the dean of a media school.
5. Media Education Foundation (n.d.b).
6. U.S. Census Bureau (2022).
7. GLAAD (2021).
8. Pew Research Center (2021).
9. Youtube (n.d.).
10. U.S. Census Bureau (2016).

Afterword Frontis. Joey Bishop, one of the many stand-up comics whose acts were translated into sitcoms.

AFTERWORD

As the reader and editor reviews for this book rolled in, I had the opportunity to use the material in the book in several ways. One setting was a class at Indiana University, where I taught the history of sitcoms as a way to understand social change. Two things worried me about the class. First, I didn't know how students would respond to material from the very early days of sitcoms, where one can expect to encounter many archaic images and a fair number that are objectively offensive. Also, I worried that students would simply not like to too many old programs, such as those in black and white. But, in order to really grasp the impact of the programs across long courses of social change, I felt it was necessary to start from the beginning.

It turned out that these concerns were generally unfounded. Students were quite happy to see the older sitcoms, even when they needed significant context to aid their understanding. Sitcoms work well in a classroom setting; they can be viewed in twenty-four minutes, leaving lots of time for lecturing about them and the social conditions they portrayed and for discussion. Concerning offensive imagery, there certainly were cases where it could be uncomfortable, but the students generally accepted that we were viewing them for a reason, not for any sort of approval of specific images or concepts.

I thought it might be a good idea to use the course as a way to gather some additional data. In each class, we watched a sitcom episode, then had a lecture and discussion about it. Students were then asked, via an online survey, to assess the sitcom in terms of its funniness, and they also rated how much they thought the various social groups portrayed in the episode were stereotyped. My intentions were quasi-scientific at best; I assumed I would use the data to help plan future iterations of the course. I realized, though, that even if the sample was small and not representative, and even if students were in fact not naïve viewers of these programs but had been given lots of information that could bias their view in one way or another, I might still see some interesting patterns in these data.

I had a sneaking suspicion that stereotypes remain funny at some level, even for students in a class specifically devoted to examining them—and exposing them—in the sitcom context. Every period seems to be dealing with guilt about the use of stereotypes in its humor while believing that it is doing a better job of getting rid of such images. Yet the issue never goes away. Some stereotypes that were once believed to be eradicated pop up in new guises. At other times, as one group is successful in tamping down stereotypes against themselves, stereotypes are then targeted against other groups. It led me to consider whether stereotypes can ever be truly eliminated from humor.

Negative group characterization undisputedly has been a feature of American humor from its outset. Mark Twain was considered a progressive forerunner of an American humor that prized tolerance and gentleness of spirit. Yet his work partook liberally of stereotypes that were common at the time against groups such as Blacks and Native Americans (Harris, 1975). With forms of humor that deal with the human condition, it can be difficult to be funny without offending someone, because aggression itself is part of the human experience. As more recent examples, Richard Pryor often lampooned "Whitey"; Don Rickles attacked every ethnic group including his own; comedians all the way up to the '70s and beyond were making jokes at the expense of women; Lenny Bruce and George Carlin were attacking "establishment types"; and there are many other examples.

In the psychological literature, there are theories that focus on humor as a form of aggression, sometimes termed *disparagement humor*. Freud (1905), for instance, considered that disparagement provides a cathartic outlet for impulses that might otherwise lead to violence. A joke teller relates a joke to a hearer, both of whom derive satisfaction from the cathartic release of aggressive tendencies against a third-party target. Other theories consider aggressive humor a form of establishing a feeling of superiority over a target (e. g., Gruner, 1997). Social identity theory (Tajfel & Turner, 2004) offers an explanation similar to superiority theory, arguing that social group (in group) status is maximized against the social group that is targeted in the humor (Ferguson & Ford, 2008).

Afterword

While some theories suggest that aggressive humor will minimize real aggression, others suggest that it might give warrant to or increase real aggression. Zillmann (1983), for instance, investigated how exposure to aggressive humor can prime aggressive cognitions, making individuals more likely to engage in aggressive behaviors or to perceive aggression as acceptable or normal. Also, Zillmann's work suggested that prolonged exposure to aggressive humor may lead to a diminished emotional response to aggression and a higher tolerance for aggressive behavior in real-life situations.

My "study" obliquely took on this issue of how to deal with stereotyping in humor in a media-oriented classroom. These data were gathered from the class in spring 2023. The class was focused on the role of situation comedies in social change. Various programs were screened from across the history of US sitcoms, from as early as the 1950s to very recent ones. In total, thirty-four episodes were viewed in their entirety by all fifty students in the class. Each time the students viewed a sitcom, they were asked to fill out a short survey about the episode that they had seen. The surveys were not part of the students' grade in the class. Names were recorded to create coder IDs and then later discarded.

The surveys asked two basic questions. Students were asked to rate the shows on dimensions of being *funny, entertaining, realistic, thoughtful,* and *sad,* using a scale from 0 to 100. Then, students rated how much they thought that certain groups were stereotyped in the episode. Any group that formed an important narrative part of the show was included for them to rate. Not all shows included each group. Men, women, and white people were included in every show. Other categories that were frequently included, depending on the show, were Blacks, older people, and children, among others. Some groups, such as Asians and Jews, appeared relatively infrequently.

In brief, I found a small but positive and significant correlation between perceptions of funniness and stereotyping ($0.14, p < 0.001$). Overall, students thought that shows were funnier when they also perceived more stereotyping. When controlling for the date of the episode, the relation remained significant ($0.16, p < 0.001$). Thus, the pattern of finding that stereotypes are funny does not depend on the date of the episode. I also looked at stereotyping for five groups that appear frequently in many episodes: men, women, white and Black people, and older people. Table A1 shows the relationships for each variable, along with a control for episode date as well.

In each case but one, there is a positive relationship between funniness and stereotyping for the specific groups. The only group that does not show

Table A1. Relationship between stereotyping and funniness for subgroups

		β	sig	N	β, episode date
Men		0.238	0.001	1111	.209
Women		0.163	0.001	1092	.197
White		0.177	0.001	824	.145
Older		0.154	0.002	387	.203
Black		-0.054	ns	404	.345
	before 1970	-0.66	0.001	83	
	after 1970	0.083	ns	320	

a positive association is Black characters. Here, the students yielded a small negative nonsignificant association, along with a very positive association for episode date. In this case, early representations of Black characters (before 1970) were seen to be highly stereotyped and *not* funny (such as in the program *Amos 'n' Andy*) compared to programs that started to appear after the '70s. After 1970, there is a smaller positive association, which is not significant due to the sample size. There were mixed associations for other groups that were shown less often (e.g., Asians, gay characters, Jewish and characters) and are less compelling due to the smaller sample size.

The associations can be better understood by looking at some of the shows that instantiate these stereotypes and their perceived funniness. Students do not necessarily consciously think or believe that stereotypes are funny. Mostly their comments reflect an understanding that stereotyping should be avoided in humor. Yet they also show a tolerance for stereotypes, within certain limits. In an *I Love Lucy* episode, rated by the students as the funniest of all of the episodes they watched, one student wrote, "I think the depiction of Ricky as the Latin Lover trope is a stereotype, and the relationship of Ricky and Lucy sometimes feels almost parent and childlike." But the same student then added, "Lucy is a comedy genius, the writing is impeccable and hilarious even today, and the loving and compassionate relationship between Ricky and Lucy makes it all work."

The student could be doing various things in making these judgments. He or she might be excusing the stereotype, simply tolerating it, or even potentially fooling himself or herself into believing that it is acceptable to enjoy the stereotype if it is named and recognized within its context.

Another highly rated episode was from the series *Curb Your Enthusiasm*. A rater critiqued the show for "Portrayal of Jewish people, stereotyping of

Afterword 227

Japanese people, portrayal of women." But this rater then offered comments on positive aspects of the show: "Critique of normalized social conventions, representing Jewish voices, portraying older people in a non-stereotypical way." Many commenters thought this particular episode was highly stereotyped *and* quite hilarious.

Students were quicker to note stereotypes against groups where such stereotyping has received public attention within the span of their upbringing. The program *All-American Girl* (1994–95) was one of the first to star an Asian American character (played by Margaret Cho), but it quickly foundered on accusations of stereotyping, as mentioned by one student who noted, "The overall portrayal of Asian characters was very stereotyped and Americanized to create better traditional family roles, such as over exaggerated accent lisps, following of family traditions, and creation of relation tensions. The show revolves around traditional man-hungry women and a culture barrier in marriages, which shows how much it relies on creating traditionalist views of elderly—down to the show's resolution of following tradition over your own mind or apologizing."

The strongest correlation between stereotyping and funniness applied to men (0.238). The survey indicated that the respondents were least likely to see disparaging images of men as being problematic (not funny). In viewing a *Honeymooners* episode, the following comment was indicative of students' tendency to respond: "I was pleasantly surprised by how funny *The Honeymooners* was. There are definitely some aspects that haven't aged well, like the gender dynamics. However, there are also some admirable qualities. Audrey Meadows' character is portrayed as very strong, and considerably smarter than her husband. The depiction of the working class is also a very important aspect of the show. While some of it is played for laughs, some of it is very revealing." The student responded positively to how the show broke the stereotype that the man is more powerful than the woman but also downplayed the stereotype that the working-class man is less intelligent than others.

A tentative conclusion is that even if stereotypes themselves are morally problematic, their presence does not preclude the perception of a show's funniness by audiences who consider themselves to be progressive in their avoidance of stereotyping. Clearly, though, not all stereotypes are created equal. Viewers consume them within social, cultural, and political contexts that send messages about which groups can be stereotyped more safely than others. Our data showed that men were the safest group to lampoon; undoubtedly, older white men seem to currently present a legitimate focus for disparagement humor.

*

After teaching the class, I needed to update myself on sitcoms that the students were watching. It has become an ongoing enterprise. A thorough and complete viewing of *Schitt's Creek* was revelatory in regard to the issues discussed above. The program is replete with stereotyped images (gay, rural people, older men) and was initially off-putting to me. Several episodes in, though, and especially by the end, I felt that the show could take its place alongside other quietly evolutionary sitcoms. Even the clownish "basket of deplorables" characters in small-town Canada had been given dimension, and the redemption for the shallow yet well off seemed to send a healthy message. A better remake of *Green Acres* could not have been envisioned. It yielded some hope that the ever-endangered sitcom could continue to thrive and flourish in new culturally relevant variants while remaining, ultimately, still funny.

—James Shanahan

February 8, 2024

Bloomington, IN

Appendix A Frontis. Bea Arthur in *Maude*, a 1970s women's liberation sitcom.

APPENDIX A

Situation Comedies Referenced

$#! My Dad Says* (2010–11). A son moves in with his aging father.

2 Broke Girl$ (2011–17). Two waitresses struggle to advance themselves in Brooklyn.

Addams Family, The (1964–66). TV adaptation of the well-known Charles Addams comics focusing on a ghoulish nuclear family.

Adventures of Ozzie and Harriet, The (1952–66). A family sitcom that eventually transitioned to TV in the 1950s and became a major hit.

AfterMASH (1983–85). Characters from *M*A*S*H* find themselves together again after the Korean War.

Aldrich Family, The (1949–53). The television continuation of the radio sitcom adventures of American teen Henry Aldrich.

ALF (1986–90). An alien puppet.

Alice (1976–85). A single woman making her way with a son, based on the Scorsese movie.

All in the Family (1971–79). Bigot Archie Bunker faces off against his more liberal family members. The top sitcom of the 1970s.

Amen (1986–91). A deacon in a Black church has comedic adventures. One of very few church-based sitcoms.

Amos 'n' Andy (1951–53). Extremely popular radio send-up of Black life in its television version. Caused a civil rights controversy and was eventually removed from the TV air.

Andy Griffith Show, The (1960–68). Part of the '60s wave of rural sitcoms. Andy Taylor is the sheriff of a small North Carolina town. With a cool demeanor, he solves minor problems experienced by local residents.

Archie Bunker's Place (1979–83). The continuation of *AITF*.

232 APPENDIX A

Bachelor Father (1957–62). A wealthy bachelor raises his niece.

Barney Miller (1975–82). A multiethnic police precinct in lower Manhattan.

Beulah (1950–53). A Black maid serves a white family, with many comic misadventures.

Beverly Hillbillies, The (1962–71). The sitcom hit of the 1960s. Rural mountaineers strike it rich and move to LA.

Bewitched (1964–72). A woman with magic powers attempts to live as a regular housewife.

Big Bang Theory, The (2007–19). Four science nerds live together and look for love.

Black-ish (2014–22). An upper-middle-class Black family and their issues.

Bless This House (1995–96). Family vehicle for raunchy comedian Andrew Dice Clay.

Bob Crane Show, The (1975). A man quits his job to return to med school.

Bob Newhart Show, The (1972–78). Stand-up comedian Newhart plays a psychologist whose patients have a variety of wacky problems.

Brady Bunch, The (1969–74). A blended family in the 1970s.

Cavemen (2007). Paleolithic pitchmen get their own sitcom (failed).

Charlie Hoover (1991). A middle-aged man has a miniature alter ego.

Cheers (1982–93). Fun with friends in a bar "where everybody knows your name."

Cosby Show, The (1984–92). Popular stand-up comedian as father and professional. Number 1 show of the 1980s.

Courtship of Eddie's Father, The (1969–72). Single dad raises a son with the aid of a Japanese housekeeper. Eddie schemes to get his father remarried.

Curb Your Enthusiasm (2000–). Larry David, cocreator of *Seinfeld*, flouts all social conventions, annoying everyone around him.

Danny Thomas Show, The (aka *Make Room for Daddy*) (1953–64). Showbiz dad and his family in 1950s–'60s America. Many family permutations reflecting the departure of various female stars.

December Bride (1954–59). Older ladies looking for companionship.

Delta House (1979). TV version of the hit movie *Animal House*, about a fraternity.

Dennis the Menace (1959–63). A television version of the popular comic strip. A mischievous boy troubles his neighbor.

Dick Van Dyke Show, The (1961–66). Rob Petrie writes for a comedy TV show in New York. He lives in the suburbs with his wife (Mary Tyler Moore) and son. The experiences of Jewish producer Carl Reiner, somewhat ethnically sanitized for network viewing.

Diff'rent Strokes (1978–85). Two young Black children are adopted by a white man.

Different World, A (1987–93). Life at an historically Black college.

Disjointed (2017–18). Fun in a marijuana dispensary.

Donna Reed Show, The (1958–66). Archetypical nuclear family sitcom.

Situation Comedies Referenced

Ellen (1994–98). Stand-up comedian Ellen DeGeneres's show, with the first gay coming out on network TV.

Everybody Hates Chris (2005–09). Chris Rock's childhood, as narrated by himself.

Everybody Loves Raymond (1996–2005). Ray and Deborah live too close to Ray's parents.

F Troop (1965–67). An inept squad of cavalry in the American West.

Family Ties (1982–89). Formerly hippie parents raise children in the 1980s.

Family Matters (1989–98). Working-class Black family with their annoyingly nerdish neighbor.

Father Knows Best (1954–60). Quintessential 1950s sitcom portraying Midwestern nuclear family ruled by benevolent and omniscient dad.

Fibber McGee and Molly (1935–56). A working-class husband and wife.

Flintstones, The (1960–66). Animated couple living in the Stone Age with their best friends.

Flo (1980–81). A spin-off of *Alice*.

Frank's Place (1987–88). A Black professor from New England inherits a restaurant in New Orleans.

Frasier (1993–2004). Spun off from *Cheers*; a radio psychologist lives with his dad in Seattle.

Fresh off the Boat (2015–20). An Asian family making it in America.

Fresh Prince of Bel-Air, The (1990–96). A young man is sent from the inner city to live with his wealthy relatives.

Friends (1994–2004). Six single friends have romantic adventures in New York City.

Full House (1987–95). Three guys raise kids.

Gale Storm Show, The (1956–60). Show centered around a cruise director.

George Burns and Gracie Allen Show, The (1950–58). Comedian George Burns and his wife, Gracie, in a Hollywood setting. Gracie typically seeks to get over on George with schemes.

George Carlin Show, The (1994–95). Sitcom vehicle for the stand-up comic. Carlin is a cabbie.

George Lopez Show, The (2002–07). Mexican American family in LA.

Get a Life (1990–92). A man in his thirties is a loser and lives with his parents.

Gidget (1965–66). Teen beach adventures bring the surf craze to sitcoms.

Gilligan's Island (1964–67). A variety of characters are thrown together and marooned on an island.

Girl with Something Extra, The (1973–74). Man and wife, but she has ESP.

Goldbergs, The (1949–56). The first real sitcom hit. A Jewish extended family stays together and assimilates into American culture.

Goldbergs, The (2013–). A Jewish family in the 80s.

Golden Girls, The (1985–92). Four women share life in retirement.

234   APPENDIX A

Gomer Pyle, USMC (1964–69). A bumpkin in the marines is a source of endless frustration to his sergeant.

Good Times (1974–79). Struggles of a working-class Black family in the inner city.

Green Acres (1965–71). A city man moves to the country, where he does not fit in.

Growing Pains (1985–92). Alan Thicke is a 1980s dad.

Happy Days (1974–84). A nostalgic response to relevance sitcoms and the harbinger of the end of the relevance era.

Hazel (1961–66). A pushy maid rules a 1960s nuclear family.

Here's Lucy (1968–74). Lucille Ball's third network sitcom.

Hogan's Heroes (1965–71). Audacious show concept to explore the comedic aspects of life in a Nazi POW camp.

Home Improvement (1991–99). Tim Taylor has a TV show about tools and a nuclear family at home.

Homeboys in Outer Space (1996–97). Hip-hop themed astronauts have adventures in a space car.

Honeymooners, The (1955–56). A brief but important early sitcom. Bus driver Ralph Kramden, his wife, Alice, and upstairs neighbors deal with working-class concerns in urban squalor.

I Dream of Jeannie (1965–70). A magical genie creates problems for her "Master" in Space Age Florida.

I Love Lucy (1951–57). The most popular of the early sitcoms. Lucy is a New York housewife who hopes to get into her husband Ricky's nightclub act. Landlords Fred and Ethel share adventures.

In Living Color (1990–94). Black-led sketch comedy.

It's Always Sunny in Philadelphia (2005–). Four friends, sociopaths, and an odd millionaire run a bar.

Jack Benny Program, The (1950–65). An extension of the comedian's popular radio variety show that was one of the originals to advance toward the sitcom. A show within a show about Benny's radio program; he is the butt of all jokes.

Jamie Foxx Show, The (1996–2001). Jamie Foxx is pursuing dreams of stardom in LA.

Jeffersons, The (1975–85). A Black family does well economically and moves into a luxury apartment building.

Joanie Loves Chachi (1982–83). Unsuccessful spin-off of two loved characters from *Happy Days*.

Joey Bishop Show, The (1961–64). Vehicle for the Rat Pack stand-up comic persona. Joey has a talk show and a new wife.

Julia (1968–71). A single Black mother raising her son. One of the first sitcoms to break the racial barrier after the *Amos 'n' Andy* years.

Just Shoot Me (1997–2003). Wacky characters at a fashion magazine.

Karen (1975). Unsuccessful sitcom vehicle for Karen Valentine.

Situation Comedies Referenced 235

King of Queens, The (1998–2007). Delivery van driver Doug lives in Queens, NY. He generally is dominated by his smarter wife and frustrated by his live-in father-in-law.

Kirk (1995–97). A young illustrator is in charge of his brothers and sisters.

Larry Sanders Show, The (1992–98). Garry Shandling is the host of a network talk show.

Last Man Standing (2011–21). Tim Allen is a non-woke guy living among women.

Laverne and Shirley (1976–83). Working girls in 1950s Milwaukee.

Leave It to Beaver (1957–63). A 1950s family-oriented sitcom about the misadventures of a young boy in a Midwestern town.

Life with Luigi (1952). Italian-focused ethnic comedy. Canceled due to protests from Italian Americans.

Living Single (1993–98). Six Black single roommates/friends figuring out their lives and future paths.

Love, Sidney (1981–83). An older gay man shares his home with a single mom and her daughter.

M*A*S*H (1972–83). Army surgeons in the Korean War explore antiwar themes comedically.

Mama (1949–57). Successful early sitcom focusing on a Scandinavian family integrating in America.

Man with a Plan (2016–20). A dad needs to help with kids more when his wife returns to work.

Married with Children (1987–97). A dysfunctional, rude, loud, obnoxious family with no redeeming social value.

Martin (1992–97). Detroit DJ Martin is a difficult personality.

Mary Tyler Moore Show, The (1970–77). A single woman makes it on her own in the big city.

Maude (1972–78). A liberated woman dominates her family and friends.

Mike and Molly (2010–16). Two overweight people in a relationship.

Modern Family (2009–20). Multiple different family configurations coexist within the same show.

Mom (2013–21). A single mom returns to live with her own mom. They are recovering alcoholics.

Monkees, The (1966–68). Four cute guys live together and have a rock band.

Mork and Mindy (1978–82). A funny, cute alien in a relationship with a human.

Munsters, The (1964–66). An unusually scary, monstrous, and funny nuclear family lives among the rest of us.

Murphy Brown (1988–98). Newsroom comedy led by a strong female character.

My Three Sons (1960–72). An early entry in the motherless family genre. A dad raises three sons with the help of a cantankerous "uncle."

My World and Welcome to It (1969–70). Series based on the humor of James Thurber.

236 APPENDIX A

Nanny, The (1993–1999). Working-class woman becomes a nanny for a rich man and then marries him.

New Adventures of Old Christine, The (2006–10). A divorced woman deals with her ex-husband and his new wife.

New Bill Cosby Show, The (1972–73). Cosby-led variety show.

Newhart (1982–90). Comedian Bob Newhart reprises sitcom success as the proprietor of an inn in Vermont.

Odd Couple, The (1970–75). Two divorced men live together and drive each other crazy.

Office, The (2005–13). Life in the office at Dunder Mifflin paper company. Based on a UK sitcom of the same name.

One Day at a Time (1975–84). A Lear show about a single woman making her own way with two daughters.

Our Miss Brooks (1948–57). A radio sitcom about a teacher seeking love and dealing with fractious students and colleagues. It eventually transitioned to TV and even film.

Partridge Family, The (1970–74). A single mom has a traveling rock band with her five kids. She is assisted by their avuncular manager.

Patty Duke Show, The (1963–66). Identical cousins, both played by the star. Capitalized on the teen trends in media production.

Phyllis (1975–77). A spin-off from *Mary Tyler Moore*, featuring Mary's kooky landlord.

Private Secretary (1953–57). A secretary attempts to assist her boss, a talent agent.

Ranch, The (2016–20). A wayward son returns to run a ranch with his dyspeptic father.

Real McCoys, The (1957–63). A rural sitcom about an Appalachian family relocated to California.

Retired at 35 (2011–12). A grown son decides to join his parents in retirement in Florida.

Rhoda (1974–78). Mary Tyler Moore's saucy friend Rhoda gets her own sitcom.

Richard Pryor Show, The (1977). Short-lived sketch comedy show.

Roc (1991–94). Baltimore garbage collector and his family.

Roseanne (1988–97). Sitcom vehicle for comedienne Roseanne Barr. A warts-and-all view of a working-class family.

Rutherford Falls (2021–22). Whites and Native Americans clash comedically in a small town.

Sanford and Son (1972–77). Comedian Redd Foxx runs a junkyard in South Central LA. Based on a British show; part of the Lear relevance era.

Schitt's Creek (2015–20). Canadian series that was also very popular in the US. A riches-to-rags family winds up in a backward town and tries to integrate.

Situation Comedies Referenced

Seinfeld (1989–98). Adventures in the Upper West Side of New York with comedian Jerry Seinfeld and his friends George, Elaine, and Kramer.

Sex and the City (1998–2004). Four friends wear nice clothes and have sexual adventures in Manhattan.

Simpsons, The (1989–). Animated family sitcom.

Sinbad Show, The (1993–94). A bachelor adopts children.

Steptoe and Son (1970–74). British sitcom that formed the basis for *Sanford and Son*.

Steve Harvey Show, The (1996–2002). Comedian Steve Harvey as a high school teacher.

Still Standing (2002–06). Average everyday couple and their kids. Most everyone has a few problems.

Taxi (1978–83). A sitcom from the producer of *MTM*. The work milieu moves from newsroom to taxi garage.

That Girl (1966–70). A single girl moves to New York to live independently.

Three's Company (1977–84). A male roommate lives with two attractive women. He often pretends he's gay to avoid the prying landlord. When aired, it was TV's most risqué sitcom.

Till Death Us Do Part (1965–75). The English predecessor to *All in the Family*.

Two and a Half Men (2003–15). Dissipated Malibu songwriter Charlie lives with his sad-sack brother Alan, Alan's kid, and a mean housekeeper.

Veep (2012–19). An inside look at a vice president who has real human qualities and troubles.

Wandavision (2021). Comic book characters in a miniseries pay homage to a variety of types of sitcoms.

Wayans Brothers, The (1995–99). Younger members of the popular Wayans family with their own sitcom.

Will & Grace (1998–2006). A straight woman lives with a gay guy.

Young Sheldon (2017–2024). The origin story of Sheldon Cooper, the socially awkward genius of *Big Bang Theory*.

APPENDIX B

Sitcom Syllabus

This is a year-by-year sampling of sitcoms, selected to explore how family configurations, gender relationships, workplace settings, and social issues are pictured. Some are selected based on viewership, popularity, or historical importance. Others are selected simply to show sitcom variety and quality. Readings and interpretations are suggested for each program.

January 6, 1950 *Mama* (aka *I Remember Mama*), "Mama's Bad Day"
A domestic light comedy-drama focused on a Norwegian family living in San Francisco. Mama is having problems with all three children. Feeling unloved, she nevertheless prepares a wonderful new dish for supper. The family doesn't notice because Papa's boss took him to a fancy lunch, and that's all they talk about. Mama storms out. She quickly regrets it, though. She comes back to find that the family loved the dinner, and her strategies with all three children had been successful.

The show is based on the novel *Mama's Bank Account* by Katherine Forbes. It also became a film. Lipsitz (2003) has written a critical chapter on *Mama*. He is not thrilled with the assimilationist narrative: "The Hansens changed from a family deeply enmeshed in family, class and ethnic associations to a modern nuclear family confronting consumption decisions as the key to group and individual identity" (p. 17). Typical episodes show the more Americanized children presenting problems and challenges to the traditional old-country parents.

240   APPENDIX B

Lipsitz, G. (2003). The changing face of a woman's narrative. In J. Morreale (Ed.), *Critiquing the sitcom* (pp. 7–24). Syracuse University Press.

December 27, 1951 *Amos 'n' Andy*, "Andy Gets a Telegram"
   Andy gets a job opportunity in Brazil. Kingfish seeks to steal it from Andy but is foiled when it is discovered that the opportunity was fake, designed by Sapphire to keep Kingfish away from Andy's "bad influence." A long sequence shows Kingfish mangling the English language with sophisticated white service people.
   Hilmes (1993) reviews the radio roots of the program. The construction of blackness as an "other" to facilitate the assimilation of a variety of white immigrants to the US is seen as the main cultural function of the show, with its heavy blackvoice dialect and misuses of language.

Hilmes, M. (1993). Invisible men: *Amos ' n' Andy* and the roots of broadcast discourse. *Critical Studies in Media Communication, 10*(4), 301–21.

May 5, 1952 *I Love Lucy*, "Lucy Does a TV Commercial"
   Lucy gets drunk while filming a TV ad for cough syrup. Considered among the top two to three *Lucy* episodes, along with the pregnancy episodes.

September 15, 1952 *I Love Lucy*, "Job Switching"
   Ricky and Fred tell Lucy and Ethel that women could not do the man's work of bringing home the bacon. All agree to switch jobs for a week. Lucy and Ethel are dismal failures at a candy factory. Meanwhile, Ricky and Fred destroy the kitchen with their ineptitude. All agree after one day that they should go back to their proper places.
   Producer Jess Oppenheimer's book (1996) is a helpful look at the inside workings of the show. It is less about the Hollywood aspects of the Desilu phenomenon; it gives an excellent picture of the technical and creative hurdles faced in literally creating a new genre and the business acumen of both Lucy and Desi in relation to it.

Oppenheimer, J. (1996). *Laughs, luck—and Lucy: How I came to create the most popular sitcom of all time*. Syracuse University Press.

Sitcom Syllabus 241

September 13, 1953 *The Jack Benny Program*, "Honolulu Trip"

Jack is returning from his Hawaiian vacation with Rochester on a cruise ship. Falling asleep, he dreams that he is having an affair with Marilyn Monroe, who makes her first TV appearance. The sexual high jinks are pushed close to the edge for 1950s television, as Jack also encounters Dr. Kinsey doing interviews on board. The episode was later remade with Jayne Mansfield as the sex kitten.

Fuller-Seeley, K. H. (2015). Becoming Benny: The evolution of Jack Benny's character comedy from vaudeville to radio. *Studies in American Humor, 1*(2), 163–91.

March 15, 1954 *The George Burns and Gracie Allen Show*, "Gracie's Old Boyfriend, Dan Conroy, Comes to Town"

Burns has to deal with Gracie's he-man boyfriend, who comes back to town. He never really was a threat because Gracie loves George, but it doesn't seem that way for a while.

Gracie's misunderstanding of situations and simple English sentences is the root of all the jokes. Burns's reactions are of unflappable imperturbability. Along with Jack Benny, he establishes that cool comedy works on TV, where his monologues and fourth-wall-breaking comments go down smoothly across hundreds of episodes. Burns's autobiography (1955) is equally easy to consume. He gives all the credit for the success of his routine to Gracie in both their vaudeville and radio days as well as on TV.

Burns, G. (1955). *I love her, that's why!* Simon and Schuster.

October 22, 1955 *The Honeymooners*, "A Woman's Work Is Never Done"

Similar to *Lucy*'s job-switching episode, Ralph accuses Alice of sitting around all day. They agree to change jobs. Ralph is a tremendous failure and in the end agrees that what Alice does is as important as what he does.

December 24, 1955 *The Honeymooners*, "'Twas the Night before Christmas"

A version of the classic O. Henry story "The Gift of the Magi." Ralph hocks his bowling ball to buy a Christmas present for Alice. Her present for him: a bowling ball bag. At the end of the show, the cast greets the live audience.

Gleason's persona offers red meat for commentary (such as Sheehan, 2010) on how sitcoms portray the working-class male. The thirty-nine "classic" episodes of *The Honeymooners* are the urtext for the oft-encountered notion that sitcom males, when they are working class, are ineffective and often controlled by their wives.

Sheehan, S. T. (2010). "Pow! Right in the Kisser": Ralph Kramden, Jackie Gleason, and the Emergence of the Frustrated Working-Class Man. *The Journal of Popular Culture, 43*(3), 564–82.

January 7, 1956 *The Honeymooners*, "A Matter of Record"
Ralph drives Alice out of the house by calling his mother-in-law a "blabbermouth" over and over again, to great comedic effect. Norton brings a recording device so that Ralph can record a sweet message to get Alice to come back. He delivers a truly sentimental thought, which eventually works after some misunderstandings.
Sterritt's book *The Honeymooners* (2009) is an entry in the excellent *TV Milestones* series. The program is one of the riper sites for serious criticism and analysis, as it veers from comic to tragic, sometimes on a dime. Sterritt notes the many parallels between the show and Gleason's own upbringing, with the irony that *The Honeymooners* was portraying an urban lifestyle that people were attempting to move away from, along with the rest of the TV sitcom world that was turning toward the suburbs.

Sterritt, D. (2009). *The Honeymooners*. Wayne State University Press.

February 20, 1956 *December Bride* (1954–59), "Sunken Den"
Lily finds herself in trouble with next-door neighbor Desi Arnaz (as himself), who feels that work at Lily's son's house has caused damage to his den. Lily and Ruth find a way to get to talk to Desi by sneaking into his fan club. There is some physical comedy as the aging girls mix it up with Desi's teenybopper fans and some admirable physical stunts from these women of a certain age. *December Bride* did very well in the ratings by virtue of its association with Desilu and a favorable time slot next to *I Love Lucy*. Shapiro and Jicha (2015) say that even a test pattern could have achieved a good rating in their time slot.

Shapiro, M., & Jicha, T. (2015). *The Top 100 American Situation Comedies: An Objective Ranking*. McFarland.

Sitcom Syllabus

243

February 13, 1957 *Father Knows Best*, "Betty and the Jet Pilot"

Betty falls in love with a jet pilot from the local air base. It's her first true love. It's looking like he will propose, leading to heartfelt discussions about love from Father, who knows best. But the pilot is transferred to Alaska, and Betty's hopes are dashed. Early parts of the episode read like product placement for the Air Force, with Bud returning the pilot's missing helmet. When he returns it, he is praised by Father as a "good citizen," always a major theme for the series. There is an extended sequence of Bud being flown around by the pilot.

Marc's book *Comic Visions* (1997) contains an excellent section on *Father Knows Best*, including a good summary and discussion of the episode "Margaret Wins a Medal." Marc notes that this series, above all others, is the one where the wife never contests the husband's superiority. Worth decoding: Marc's observation that *Father* is "boldly precubist in its narrative structure" (p. 46).

Marc, D. (1997). *Comic visions.* Blackwell.

October 15, 1958 *The Danny Thomas Show*, "Rusty the Ward Heeler"

Rusty is nominated for class president. He convinces Dad, a big-time show-biz entertainer, to host a rally for his election. It's a big success, but Kathy (Mom) is upset that Rusty is learning the wrong lesson: She thinks that ice cream and cake and song and dance should not buy the kids' votes. Thomas's show is a hipper and sometimes more swinging version of *Father Knows Best*, except often Father is wrong and has to learn lessons himself. Eventually he is convinced that he was ill advised to perform at the rally and gives Rusty a lecture about winning elections on "privilege rather than merit."

Thomas's autobiography (1991) gives useful perspective on the show, which incorporated his unique storytelling style into the various episodes. Being a father who is absent a lot is an important theme. His skillful mix of various ethnic forms of humor—deployed against his own semidisguised origins (Lebanese)—steers the show toward a more modern Hollywood/New York esthetic of midcentury "gracious living" that still maintains roots in the ethnic comedy mixes of vaudeville and nightclubs, without the preachiness of the more didactic shows.

Thomas, D. (1991). *Make room for Danny.* Putnam.

March 26, 1959 *Leave It to Beaver*, "The Price of Fame"

Beaver gets locked in the high school principal's office overnight. After the fire department comes to get him out, Ward (Dad) lectures him for being

244   APPENDIX B

"conspicuous." Then, the next day, Beaver gets his head stuck in an iron fence. He's afraid to tell Dad, for fear of being lectured again. After all is over, Ward learns that he needs to moderate his strategy with Beaver because a child should always feel that he can come to his parents. The episode has a Tom Sawyer feel to it, although Beaver is not crafty; he sits in "the dumb row" at class. June Cleaver (Mom) calls him "the" Beaver, which strangely seems to have aided in conferring a semi-mythic status on him as a representative of 1950s boyhood.

Woods's (1995) article is one of several where the *Beaver*-type sitcoms are used to point out the unrealism of the traditional nuclear family. It's unclear, though, just how many people bought into these shows as anything more than bland escapism; there is little data about the effect of the shows on audiences. Some later studies found that sitcom viewers were more likely to accept *non*traditional family structures. At the same time, the value of a two-parent family, with one parent working and one staying at home, was apparent to many, if they were in an economic position to afford it. Woods points out that such a "traditional" arrangement was very dependent on class status.

Woods, J. (1995). *Leave It to Beaver* was not a documentary: What educators need to know about the American family. *American Secondary Education, 24*(1), 2–8.

February 24, 1960 *The Adventures of Ozzie and Harriet*, "A Trap for Ricky"
Ricky and Dave (the Nelson sons) seem to be interested in the same girl. The girls at their school seem to be mainly interested in "trapping" cute guys. Mom and Dad invite the girl over for dinner to see which brother she is more interested in. It seems an odd thing for Mom and Dad to do, but it happens. Dad keeps score, literally, about which brother she shows more affinity for. Eventually Ricky wins, but it turns out brother Dave was simply scheming all along on behalf of his brother. There is lots of good anthropological info about early '60s dating culture. Teen idol Ricky gets to sing two songs; at this point, he is the main star and attraction of the show.

Ozzie and Harriet is most often recalled as an absurdity, something to be criticized, a state of existence that was never real. But for polemicists on the right (such as Polsby, 1994), there still was enough of a glow around the '50s nuclear family to resuscitate the Nelsons: "In the face of the discouraging

Sitcom Syllabus

results of modernism for the community and the family, let me offer an example of a domestimorph[1] that is optimal for both community and family—*Ozzie and Harriet*—the very icon of the ridicule that has often been directed against traditional families. *Ozzie and Harriet* are an ostensive definition of what I mean when I say 'family'" (p. 533).

Indeed, from a statistical perspective, the Ozzie and Harriet–style family was the rule in 1960 and continues to be so today. Even so, the idea that *Ozzie and Harriet* and its ilk specifically were the root of liberal discontent with nuclear families is also something of straw man, easily lampooned but probably of little influence in establishing people's family preference patterns.

Polsby, D. D. (1994). Ozzie and Harriet had it right. *Harvard Journal of Law & Public Policy, 18*, 531.

January 5, 1961 *The Donna Reed Show*, "Character Building"

Donna writes a letter to the editor about being "firm" with raising children. The letter backfires when she discovers that she herself is responsible for some of the mistakes that her own kids are making. She tries to find the balance between being "firm" and "rigid." The outcome is that parents are not infallible, but they generally move in the right direction. Aspects of 1950s teen culture are still relevant in the early 1960s. Kids are not refractory, but they are sometimes just "hard to manage." Parents will wield authority but never abusively.

Donna Reed, due to its long and successful run, now stands in for concepts of home confinement for mothers that feminism objected to.

Morreale, J. (2012). *The Donna Reed Show*. Wayne State University Press.

November 3, 1962 *The Joey Bishop Show* (1961–64), "A Woman's Place"

Joey makes jokes on his TV show about women in politics. Ellie finds out, and her friends convince her to demand equal time on Joey's show. Joey refuses. In a sitcom version of *Lysistrata*, Joey is banned from the master bedroom. "There'll be no clinches," says Ellie. He finally relents but sets a trap for her: a Constitutional test. She finds out about the trap and defeats his plan, showing encyclopedic knowledge of the document. Women may or may not belong in the House, but they rule the house.

Joey shows the pitfalls of adapting stand-up personae to sitcoms. On the air for four years, it went through variations intended to increase its appeal

246 APPENDIX B

on NBC, then CBS (Brooks & Marsh, 2009). It never had the juice of *Make Room for Daddy*, from which it sprang. But repeated viewings show its Rat Pack charms.

Brooks, T., & Marsh, E. F. (2009). *The complete directory to prime-time network and cable TV shows, 1946-present*. Ballantine.

September 25, 1963 *The Dick Van Dyke Show*, "That's My Boy?"

Rob and Laura bring home their new baby. Because of a series of mix-ups at the hospital, Rob becomes convinced that they have been given the wrong baby. He does a variety of tests, such as comparing actual footprints to the birth record to convince himself that he's got the right one. But he still thinks he has the wrong one. He gets more and more worried and finally calls the other family to arrange a switch. They come over, and everyone hilariously realizes that both couples have the right baby. The other family is Black.

Austerlitz (2014) noted that *The Dick Van Dyke* show "exudes a vague liberal uplift" (p. 77). The series is moving into a modern sensibility, with a star who works in a creative profession, then zips home to his comfortable suburban house. His wife has every right to claim to be the most beautiful sitcom wife that has yet been on television. Yet he has friends who specifically *don't* reek of Middle America; they are carrying some of their ethnic roots forward into a somewhat more sanitized Camelot style of television. Austerlitz says that Van Dyke embodied the "casual grace" that John F. Kennedy had, and the same comparison could undoubtedly be made between Mary Tyler Moore and Jackie Kennedy.

When Carl Reiner developed the series, it didn't work with him as the star, even though it had come directly out of his experiences on *Your Show of Shows*, with its ties to variety and even vaudeville. Dick Van Dyke provided a less "ethnic" take on the character that fit well with the direction that television was moving, toward a suburb of greater cultural homogeneity yet still rooted in the funny, ethnically heterogeneous city.

Austerlitz, S. (2014). *Sitcom: A history in 24 episodes*. Chicago Review Press.

April 15, 1963 *The Andy Griffith Show*, "A Wife for Andy"

Barney decides that it's time for Andy to get a wife. He arranges various cattle calls of eligible local women to be inspected by Andy, to which Andy objects. Then Barney arranges a dinner with Helen, who is Opie's schoolteacher.

Although it's an awkward setup, it works, as Andy likes Helen, who then becomes his steady girlfriend on the show. Barney does not approve because it appears that Helen won't be a traditional wife who cooks for Andy; she's a "professional." Andy points out that this is how things are done in the twentieth century.

Railey's (2022) book on Griffith reveals that the star's concept of Mayberry did not come from his North Carolina hometown, which he hated. Rather, it was based more on the island community of Manteo, which Griffith adopted after doing summer theater there.

Railey, J. (2022). *Andy Griffith's Manteo*. History Press.

January 8, 1964 *The Beverly Hillbillies*, "The Giant Jackrabbit"
A kangaroo gets loose in Granny's yard. She thinks it is a "giant jackrabbit." Uncle Jed thinks that maybe Granny has been drinking. Ellie's "critters" are getting into everything. Jed calls Beverly Caterers (he thinks it's a person) to come fix them some supper. When they come, they are horrified and run away. The kangaroo escapes safely.

This is one of the most highly viewed episodes in American TV history; the program was in the midst of a very successful ratings run. Why? With this episode as their exemplar, McIntosh et al. (2000) postulated that people avoid "meaningful, serious stimuli" when the nation is under threat. This episode came a mere two months after the assassination of JFK. Putatively, these and almost all of the '60s sitcoms could be seen as a steam-release valve for the pent-up neuroses and crises of the decade. Nevertheless, their data showed that people chose *more* meaningful programs, not sillier ones, during times of stress. It doesn't do a lot to explain why so many people watched *Hillbillies*—one of the greater mysteries of American TV history.

Others have used *Hillbillies* to raise concerns about stereotyping. After a decade in which TV's rude stereotypes of Blacks, Jews, Italians, and other groups had all raised hackles societally, poor whites seemed perhaps the safest target. Writers on this topic find their original source in this quote: "Networks which have long since discontinued *Amos 'n' Andy* and other racist programs and which have shown some signs recently of reassessing their sexist images of women, continue to run shows such as *Hee Haw* and *Green Acres* and *The Beverly Hillbillies*. Al Capp's 'L'il Abner' appears in virtually every hometown newspaper. In their gross insensitivity to the feelings of Appalachian people, to their spiritual and material needs, and to the richness and variety of their

248 APPENDIX B

culture, the media have been agents of a broader pattern of cultural imperialism" (Whisnant, 1973, p. 129).

Newcomb (1979) reviews the entire genre of hillbilly TV, pointing out that hillbillies are always contrasted with slick urban hucksters, over whom they win in spite of their gullibility. They are children, with simple childlike goodness. Cooke-Jackson and Hansen (2008) report the case of CBS proposing a new *Beverly Hillbillies* series that would bring an actual family from Kentucky to California for televised high jinks. Public outrage quickly killed the idea.

Cooke-Jackson, A., & Hansen, E. K. (2008). Appalachian culture and reality TV: The ethical dilemma of stereotyping others. *Journal of Mass Media Ethics, 23*(3), 183–200.

McIntosh, W. D., Schwegler, A. F., & Terry-Murray, R. M. (2000). Threat and television viewing in the United States, 1960–1990. *Media Psychology, 2*(1), 35–46.

Newcomb, H. (1979). Appalachia on television: Region as symbol in American popular culture. *Appalachian Journal, 7*(1/2), 155–64.

Whisnant, D. E. (1973). Ethnicity and the recovery of regional identity in Appalachia: Thoughts upon entering the zone of occult instability. *Soundings, 56*(2), 124–38.

October 28, 1965 *Bewitched,* "Trick or Treat"

Darrin is hosting a Halloween party at home. This enrages Samantha, who feels that this is "discriminatory" to witches. Endora turns Darrin into a werewolf, which creates problems at the party. Eventually, though, Sam convinces Endora that Darrin is the only person who has agreed to take her on her own terms, by actually marrying into a witch family. Endora has to agree and removes the curse on Darrin. An interesting take on prejudice and stereotyping where Halloween is seen (jokingly, of course) as an insensitive anti-occult holiday.

Bewitched is a field day for feminist criticism, where witch tropes are always welcome (McCann, 2020). Samantha has powers that allow her to escape from household drudgery, yet she promises Darrin, her mortal husband, that she hopes for nothing more than to be a "normal" housewife. McCann sees Samantha as showing women some possibilities of how to escape servitude to men while staying within the bounds of prime-time sensibilities and mass network appeal. In the end, despite the fact that her great powers place her above Darrin, household peace and male dominance are maintained. But in *Bewitched,* as in many preceding sitcoms, the male dominance is sometimes

Sitcom Syllabus 249

only in appearance. At any time, the wife may choose to use facts that are on her side, which may be sexual (strongly implied to be in Samantha's toolkit). Or, they may reside just in a general charm over their husbands, who are, in the end, also in service to their wives, often on the losing end.

McCann, A. (2020). "Bewitched:" Between housewifery and emancipation. *Studia Universitatis Babeș-Bolyai-Dramatica, 65*(1), 245–59.

December 12, 1966 *The Monkees*, "Dance, Monkee, Dance"

The boys get sucked into signing lifetime contracts for dance lessons. In order to get out of the deal, they wreak havoc at the dance studio.

Faced with television's low-gear approach to cultural progress in the mid-'60s, it's a wonder that *The Monkees* got on the air. Hippies were still actively discriminated against in many parts of the country. Yet the commercial success of the Beatles was hard to ignore. *The Monkees* demonstrates what happens when narrative comes last in a sitcom. Weak storylines and cobbled together Marx Brothers routines could make for slow viewing, not to mention a very odd sense of psychedelic unreality. Terrific songwriting saved the show, though, and many of the songs did well commercially, fostering a Monkee-mania that eventually outdid the success of the show. Its unusual qualities helped it to stand out and be remembered by some as a "complex text that is part and parcel of the oppositional youth culture of the 60s" (Goostree, 1988, p. 58).

Goostree, L. (1988). *The Monkees* and the deconstruction of television realism. *Journal of Popular Film and Television, 16*(2), 50–58.

December 26, 1967 *I Dream of Jeannie*, "Jeannie Goes to Honolulu"

Major Nelson (Tony) goes to Honolulu, deceiving Jeannie about his destination. While there, he begins seeing the admiral's daughter. Jeannie, when she finds out, is jealous. Tony tells her a lie about a spy and a prince to throw her off the trail. When she catches on, she ruins Tony's dates with magical tricks. Hawaiian singer Don Ho is given a major role in the episode, with a significant middle chunk devoted essentially to a Hawaiian-themed music video. It's oddly disconnected from everything else in the episode. Dr. Bellows, Tony's boss and nemesis, is also on hand. As usual, Bellows does not figure out that Jeannie is a magical figure.

Jeannie is a gold mine for stereotype-focused criticism. Its star is always scantily clad, she calls her love interest Master, and he is basically a swinging

250   APPENDIX B

bachelor whose interest in Jeannie is fleeting or conflicted (though they eventually get married). In early episodes, Jeannie is confined to her bottle. Apart from criticisms for sexism, Bullock highlights the "Orientalism" of Jeannie, whose costume is a Hollywood harem-girl takeoff. Bullock tries to square the sexy-and-available image with more recent stereotypes of Muslim veiled women: "Both systems of representation envisage the woman as trapped and oppressed" (Bullock, 2018, p. 9). Interestingly, though, Bullock's audience research (2015) found that many viewers (perhaps most) simply did not see Jeannie as Muslim. She was a very secular genie.

Bullock, K. (2015). Visible and invisible: An audience study of Muslim and non-Muslim reactions to orientalist representations in *I Dream of Jeannie*. *Journal of Arab & Muslim Media Research, 8*(2), 83–97.

Bullock, K. (2018). Orientalism on television: A case study of *I Dream of Jeannie*. *ReOrient, 4*(1), 4–23.

March 20, 1968 *Green Acres*, "The Rutabaga Story"
   Oliver can't figure out what to plant. The extension agent gives him some research reports, suggesting that rutabagas might work. The townsfolk take the idea too far, calling in CBS to film a "Rutabaga Bowl." Sofia Loren is asked to be the Rutabaga Queen. They send Lisa up in a balloon so she can bomb rutabagas across the country to advertise. The Air Force has to get involved.
   White (1985) nails it, although he may not be fully aware of the strength of the absurdist strain in sitcomery:

> Unconsciously evoking the absurdist dramatists Beckett and Ionesco, the creators of *Green Acres* questioned the stability of the world and its comprehensibility (unthinkable in series TV), but in unpretentious terms that did not alarm the American public. Plainly put: The wonder of the series is that craziness always makes sense. There's true if faint logic at the core of every episode: When Oliver takes Lisa on a picnic, it becomes necessary to include most of the townspeople. Each uninvited guest brings something extraneous—another person or an accordion. When Oliver finally complains that even a bum has brought along a tuba, the response is the picnic could use a tuba. (p. 76)

Since the success of the show, the phrase *Green Acres* has been used to signify social and economic impacts from urbanites moving to the country. For example, Doye and Brorsen (2011) suggested that urban affinity for pastureland investment could be used to explain changes in land value.

Doye, D., & Brorsen, B. W. (2011). Pasture land values: A "Green Acres" effect? *Choices, 26*(2). https://www.choicesmagazine.org/UserFiles/file/cmsarticle _25.pdf.

White, A. (1985). How green were our acres. *Film Comment, 21*(3), 76–77, 80.

February 6, 1969 *That Girl*, "My Sister's Keeper"

Anne Marie is always looking for her big break as a New York actor. She finally gets one that she's just perfect for. There's only problem: Anne can't sing. Eventually the producer figures out that Anne can lip-synch the role. They bring in a professional singer. Anne meets her and befriends her. She tries to set the singer up with her agent to get more opportunities in showbiz. No one realizes, though, that the singer is actually a nun, so she's not that interested in doing well in showbiz. When Anne finally finds out, she's appropriately abashed and reverential. The singer is played by Marlo Thomas's real-life sister, Terre Thomas. Her brother appears in a short role as well. At the end, she bumps into her real-life father, Danny Thomas, playing a priest. "Excuse me, Father," she says.

Modern viewers of *That Girl* would see a show with its feet firmly planted in the sexual culture of the 1950s yet lurching toward the '70s as politely and demurely as possible. She is the first young female TV character to live on her own, but her independent lifestyle is sexually policed. Her father is constantly popping in to check up on her, invariably finding her in compromising positions that can be innocently explained away. Her boyfriend, Don, is handsome and willing. They kiss passionately, but it's always made obvious that he never stays over. Other women are constantly at Don's door, and some of them clearly don't have the integrity of Anne. Still, Don stays true. Eventually they get engaged, but the series does not end with a marriage. Producer Thomas wanted to emphasize that there could be other happy endings for newly liberated women (Newman, 2016).

Newman, E. L. (2016). From *That Girl* to *Girls*: Rethinking Anne Marie/ Marlo Thomas as a feminist icon. *The Journal of American Culture, 39*(3), 285–97.

252 APPENDIX B

September 15, 1970 *Julia*, "Ready, Aim, Fired"

Julia might lose her job as a nurse because the company is downsizing. And the HR guy is a racist. Julia's boss, the grumpy doctor, likes her and can't bring himself to tell her that she's fired. Julia gets called up to HR. She thinks that it is her boss who will get fired, but she offers herself instead. The HR director accepts the offer. Luckily, though, it turns out that Julia's colleague is getting married, so apparently she won't need the job anymore, and Julia is saved. The doctor finds out what Julia did, and there is a happy ending for everyone.

Julia, being the first sitcom entry with a Black lead in a long time, was bound to cause a ruckus. As many Black-led sitcoms would discover over the next twenty years, none of them could be all things to all people. *Julia* was hit for showing unrealistic images of a "white Negro," meaning that the character played by Diahann Carroll had a job, spoke well, and lived in a nice apartment. Yet she also was a single mom, so the show could be criticized for emphasizing Black fatherlessness. She was smarter than her white neighbor, which some white viewers didn't like. Given that there was immense civil unrest at the time and that *Julia* was the only show with a Black star, some read it as propaganda to show that if Blacks worked hard and acted right, they'd be OK too. As Bodroghkozy (2003) shows, the list of ways that people could disagree with what Julia was doing was long, depending much on the perspective and race of the viewer.

Bodroghkozy, A. (2003). Is this what you mean by color TV?. In J. Morreale (Ed.), *Critiquing the sitcom* (pp. 129–49). Syracuse University Press.

February 9, 1971 *All in the Family*, "Judging Books by Covers"

Archie is offended by Mike's effeminate friend, even though the friend is straight. Archie escapes down to the local pub to hang out with his own friends. One of the gang is an ex-football player whom Archie reveres as the most masculine of men. Archie is shocked when the friend tells him that he himself is gay. Arche is nonplussed: "Nowadays you can't bet on nothin'."

March 2, 1971 *All in the Family*, "Lionel Moves into the Neighborhood"

Archie is upset when a Black family buys the house next door. He concocts a plan to buy the house back and sell it to someone he approves of. He asks Lionel, his Black friend, to propose the purchase to the new owners. But Archie learns that in fact it is Lionel and his family who have purchased the house.

Sitcom Syllabus

March 23, 1971 *All in the Family,* "Gloria Discovers Women's Lib"

Gloria has gotten political. She is urging her mom that she needs to stop being so subservient and "do her own thing." Naturally, Archie disagrees. He is the "king" of the house. Normally, Mike is on Gloria's side in arguments with Archie, but this time he takes the male perspective. That's too much for Gloria, and she leaves the house. After a few days, Mike and Gloria come to an understanding that they are equal (although Mike indicates that, in the outside world, he is still the man, but they are equal in their bedroom).

Early 1971 was a Krakatoa for sitcoms. Although it took audiences some time to catch on, *All in the Family* dealt with more issues in the spring season than sitcoms had done throughout the entirety of the '60s. Gray (2021) points out that *Variety* had two opposing reviews of the program: One loved its audacity; the other was offended by its racial bigotry. Both turned out to be accurate, as the show was divisive for many. In order for TV to exorcise its sitcom demons, it seemed necessary for a total purge: "*All in the Family* represents an actual inversion of minstrelsy: where the general thrust of blackface was to mock the pretensions and toiles of black people. *All in the Family* instead satirized that of a white one, Archie Bunker—and his not inconsiderable ilk" (Cullen, 2020, p. 21).

With the passage of time, the program takes on the quality of an urtext: If any sitcom could be nominated for a Pulitzer in literature, this might be the one. ABC redid episodes with a live cast as part of TV special in 2019 (*Live in Front of a Studio Audience*). *All in the Family* did much to cement the idea that a sitcom could be both good and popular, inaugurating the "relevance" period of sitcoms that would last through the decade.

Cullen, J. (2020). *Those were the days.* Rutgers University Press.

Gray, T. (2021, January 12). Looking back on the legacy of *All in the Family* 50 years later. *Variety.* https://variety.com/2021/tv/spotlight/all-in-the -family-50-year-anniversary-1234878168.

McCrohan, D. (1987). *Archie & Edith & Mike & Gloria.* Workman.

January 28, 1972 *The Partridge Family,* "I Am Curious, Partridge"

Danny places racy articles about Keith and Mom in the local paper. Keith is then embarrassed at school because girls think he likes black garters and that he has a rose tattooed on an intimate area. Meanwhile, Mom is embarrassed at the local PTA because the other moms think she likes men in trench coats

254 APPENDIX B

and beards. This is an oddly sexual episode for 1972, building on the success of David Cassidy as a teen idol phenomenon. Keith has about as close to a nude scene as you can get in prime time, and Mom does a semi-striptease in hot pants at the PTA fashion show.

The show's success in prime time was as much a function of Cassidy's stardom as the show itself. Cassidy's memoir is hair-raising: "To tell you the truth, a lot of times the sex with strangers had become boring."

Cassidy, D. (1994). *C'mon get happy: Fear and loathing on the Partridge Family bus.* Warner Media.

October 13, 1973 *The Mary Tyler Moore Show,* "Hi There, Sports Fans"

Mary has been working at WJM for three years, and she wants more responsibility. So, Mr. Grant lets her hire the new sportscaster. But she must also fire the old one. The sports guy hits on her, '70s style, when they go out to lunch for the HR meeting. Mr. Grant puts pressure on Mary to hire his friend, but she goes with her own choice. When her choice is successful, she experiences a letdown that she spent two weeks agonizing over someone to simply read scores: "5–1, 3–2, 7–4." Mr. Grant lets her know that life is meaningless anyway. Mary gets a date with the new guy.

Armstrong's (2013) book on *MTM* is an engaging look at the program, especially the female writers who helped the male producers bring an authentic woman's perspective to the show.

Armstrong, J. (2013). *Mary and Lou and Rhoda and Ted.* Simon and Schuster.

February 16, 1974 *M*A*S*H,* "George"

A soldier turns up for treatment with strange bruises. Hawkeye figures out that he's being beaten up for being gay. Frank Burns wants him discharged. Hawkeye and Trapper find out a way to get Burns to admit to an ethical lapse on a medical exam. Frank drops the plan.

Although sitcoms were not creating many gay leads in the '70s, gay people and their issues were appearing a bit on the more progressive shows. Gross (2001) provides an excellent summary of the emergence of gay characters across all media, with television notably lagging in many ways.

Gross, L. (2001). *Up from invisibility: Lesbians, gay men, and the media in America.* Columbia University Press.

Sitcom Syllabus

November 8, 1975 *The Bob Newhart Show*, "Who Is Mr. X?"

Bob goes on a TV news show. He flirts with the seemingly nice female reporter, but she suddenly turns on him, unleashing an attack on the psychology profession. He mistakenly admits that one of his patients is an elected official. He refuses to say who it is, but it turns into a citywide hoopla. Everyone, even Bob's friends and family, wants to know who Mr. X is. Finally, the real Mr. X outs himself, and the situation is solved. Bob learns a lesson about seeking media attention and that women can "chew your legs off."

The '70s was a time of growth in psychology. People were being told that it was no shame to visit a psychologist. Group therapy, the main comedic vehicle for Newhart, is practically a '70s cliché. Nevertheless, Newhart's patients are a cast of neurotics who never get "cured." Every patient who was with him at the start of the show is there at the end. They function quite similarly to Newhart's children, which is important since this show is about a married couple who remain childless.

Many of the texts on sitcoms pay only brief attention to *Newhart*, which went under the radar in the '70s relevance wave. Thompson (quoted in Andrews, 2018) notes the unfairness, calling the show "quietly revolutionary." In some ways, *Newhart* was updating the Middle-America sitcom aesthetic, with a setting in Chicago rather than the coastal cities and a scaled-down nuclear family. Although it was less political than some of the other shows against which it ran, it could sometimes stray into issues, as when Bob suggested to his therapy group that being gay did not represent a problem.

Andrews. T. (2018, May). Bob Newhart's 'quietly revolutionary' sitcom ended 40 years ago. But it changed TV. *Washington Post*. https://www.washingtonpost.com/news/arts-and-entertainment/wp/2018/05/01/bob-newharts-quietly-revolutionary-sitcom-ended-40-years-ago-but-it-changed-tv.

December 30, 1976 *Barney Miller*, "Hash"

Wojo brings some brownies to the precinct, not knowing that they are "laced with hashish." All the detectives partake liberally. Confusion results. A Polish actor and a drama critic are locked up because they had been sword fighting with one another over a lousy review. They observe the maddening chaos in the precinct, describing it as "Chekovian."

Is *Barney Miller* TV's most Chekovian sitcom? Konstan (1988) makes a direct comparison of workplace TV sitcoms to Chekhov's "parlor plays," with *Barney Miller* as an outstanding example, arguing that its "mediate structure is

256 APPENDIX B

modelled on the family, with Barney Miller as father and the other detectives as sons" (p. 186). Konstan sees a transition in the sitcom, away from the public locations of ancient comedies to more private spaces:

> The location of ancient comedy in the public street, as against the interior scene of the sitcoms, seems a significant fact and not merely a matter of convention or a reflection of the difference between life in a Mediterranean town on the one hand and in a northern climate on the other. For all their staying power, conventions are generated and sustained by a relation to social life. Where public space was in antiquity perceived as a primary arena of social life, it has, in the comedies of television, come to seem impersonal and dangerous, the place where worship of money and the commodification of everything else reigns supreme. In such a world, the spaces that are cherished are havens of personal and sympathetic relations, even if they simultaneously serve the needs of the wider economy. (p. 189)

Konstan, D. (1988). The premises of comedy: Function of dramatic space in an ancient and modern form. *Journal of Popular Film and Television, 15*(4), 180–90.

September 13, 1977 *Happy Days*, "Hollywood, Part 3"

The *Happy Days* teens are starting to get older. They cannot stay in high school forever. As story ideas run out, they make a trip to Hollywood, as other sitcoms did before them. Fonzie thinks he might get cast as a James Dean type in a picture, but the producers end up liking Richie instead. Meanwhile, down at the beach, Fonzie is engaged in a battle with a nemesis known as the California Kid. He ties him in a race, so they decide to break the tie by seeing who can jump over a shark on water skis. The Kid backs out, then Fonzie does it. All is resolved when Richie decides he wants to go to school for journalism and he will turn down the movie contract, and Fonzie realizes it's OK to be a good mechanic, which is what he's best at.

Radio producer Jon Hein (2003) came up with the idea that "jumping the shark" represents the point at which a sitcom has run out of stories and just doesn't feel right anymore. Undeniably, this particular episode has an odd feel to it, with Fonzie wearing swimming shorts and his leather jacket, and generally the whole family looks really out of place in beachwear. There is a bit of sadness to it as we realize that adolescence ends in sitcoms as everywhere else. Even though they are making decisions about the rest of their lives (à la *American Graffiti*, which was a big component of the *Happy Days* nostalgia boom), there is to be no endless summer. In spite of all this, *Happy Days* went on, in variations, for another five years. Jumped sharks could not stop the sitcom that ended the relevance era.

Hein, J. (2003). *Jump the shark*. Plume.

November 1, 1977 *One Day at a Time*, "Bob Loves Barbara"

Sitcoms in the '70s had to begin dealing with the implications of the sexual revolution. Bob is stuck in the "friend zone" with teenage Barbara. He's very shy. He gets advice on women from Schneider, which is completely focused on how to "score." Bob gets a date with Wendy, the "student body," to put a notch in his belt and gain experience. Meanwhile, Mom has convinced Barbara that Bob is a nice boy and they should go out. When Bob shows up for the date, his personality is transformed to a smooth-talking ladies' man, but this turns Barbara off. Eventually, Bob breaks down and admits that his date with Wendy amounted to nothing. He did it just to impress Barbara. They have a heart-to-heart about sex, and they both agree that they should wait until they get married.

> BARBARA: You know, this whole thing is insane. When Mom was going to school, they had to keep it quiet if they did. Now you have to keep it quiet if you don't.
> BOB: Think we're the only two left?
> BARBARA: I doubt it. (Baser et al., 1977)

One Day at a Time was a feminist show that could get good male viewership as well, given the teenage idol status that was gained by Valerie Bertinelli as Barbara. Still, the show was a fairly realistic portrayal, as Dow (1996) notes in her chapter on the show. The newly single Ann Romano puts off suitors, urges her daughters not to make the same mistakes she did in relation to men, and deals with a variety of personal and social problems out of a small apartment in Indianapolis. Eventually, as she accumulates small successes, she develops into a feminist Horatio Alger story.

Baser, M. S., Weiskopf, K., & Wiser, B. (Writers), & Kenwith, H. (Director). (1977, November 29). Barbara's friend (Part 1) [TV series episode]. In N. Lear (Executive Producer), *One day at a time*. Los Angeles: TAT Communications Company.

Dow, B. (1996). *Prime-time feminism*. University of Pennsylvania Press.

February 21, 1978 *Three's Company*, "Days of Beer and Weeds"

Jack and Chrissie think they have found marijuana in Mr. Roper's garden. Also, Jack has been drinking Mr. Roper's homemade beer. They go to the police to find out what to do about the pot, but they just get themselves in trouble. Meanwhile, Mrs. Roper has put the pot plants in her arrangement for the flower show. Jack and Chrissie can't get there in time to save her from embarrassment. It turns out that the plants aren't grass after all, just a looka-like. Janet would have known this, since she runs a flower shop.

The emptiness of California culture finds its way into sitcoms in a myriad of ways. Jack is pretending to be gay to share an apartment with two attractive girls (this is based on an English show, *Man about the House*). He is hetero-sexually supercharged, though, and thus always quite frustrated by living in such proximity to the girls. A Santa Monica condo offers many enticements to the young Jack, who also seems to have inherited the physical comic timing of Lucille Ball. The show is straight farce, as raunchy as would be permitted on TV, leading to the emerging genre of "T & A" or "jiggle" programming (Levine, 2006), exemplified in other late '70s shows like *Charlie's Angels*.

Levine, E. (2006). *Wallowing in sex: The new sexual culture of 1970s American television*. Duke University Press.

January 27, 1979 *Delta House* (1979), "The Shortest Yard"
Dean Wormer discovers that Blotto has a talent for football. Blotto goes to a practice. He's very good, but he injures all the players on the practice team. He refuses to play in the game because of his pacifist principles, but the dean will punish Delta House if Blotto doesn't play. The Delta boys convince Floun-der to suit up instead, but he has no football skill. In the end, the gang pulls a variety of stunts and tricks on the opposition, and Faber wins the big game.

Animal House was a movie blockbuster that did not make the transition to sitcom successfully. Some of the characters from the movie appeared in the show and some did not, such as the main star, John Belushi. The movie's raunchy hu-mor could not work on prime-time TV in 1979. The show lasted only thirteen epi-sodes, despite decent ratings. Wasylkiw and Currie (2012) found that exposure to the movie was associated with more positive attitudes toward drug abuse and negative attitudes about academics, although undoubtedly this was a very short-term effect that may not have meant much in the longer term. Unquestionably, though, the movie fueled a rise in the prominence of Greek life on campus in the early 1980s. Mara et al. (2018) document some effects of fraternity membership, including negative effects on GPA, but *positive* effects on future income.

Mara, J., Davis, L., & Schmidt, S. (2018). Social animal house: The economic and academic consequences of fraternity membership. *Contemporary Economic Policy, 36*(2), 263–76.

Wasylkiw, L., & Currie, M. (2012). The *Animal House* effect: How university-themed comedy films affect students' attitudes. *Social Psychology of Education, 15*(1), 25–40.

November 30, 1980 *The Jeffersons*, "Put It On"

Louise's friends want her to go down to Bumpers to see some male strippers, all in good fun. She doesn't want to go, but she feels compelled when George won't let her. Once she's there, everyone enjoys some soft-core dancing, but she still feels uneasy. Meanwhile, George and Tom have come down to the bar, and they want to get the wives to leave. A husky female bouncer prevents that. So, George and Tom decide that if they strut their stuff (it being amateur night), Louise and Helen will rip them off the stage and everyone can leave. Things go further than intended, though, and George and Tom deliver a comic dance that falls somewhat short of Chippendale standards.

Rhym (1998) sees George Jefferson, intended to be the Black Archie Bunker, as exhibit A of Norman Lear's "New Minstrelsy." Bill Cosby of *The Cosby Show* is interpreted in a somewhat more appreciative light. *The Jeffersons* is the longest lasting of the Lear shows, extending an echo of the relevance era into the mid-'80s.

Rhym, D. (1998). An analysis of George Jefferson and Heathcliff Huxtable. *Journal of African American Men, 3*(3): 57–67.

November 5, 1981 *Mork and Mindy* (1978–82), "Mama Mork, Papa Mindy"

Due to the laws of extraterrestrial biology, Mindy is the father while Mork is the mother of a huge baby boy, birthed from an egg and played by Jonathan Winters. Mindy is dismayed by her very hairy baby. There are numerous opportunities for Robin Williams and Winters to engage in comedic mugging. Eventually, Mindy realizes that she will have to develop a parental feeling for the boy, named Mearth. She teaches him to play catch. After developing a closer bond, the child loves both parents equally and even agrees to call Mindy Mommy.

260 APPENDIX B

This is an opening sentence that you don't expect in a review of *Mork and Mindy*: "A central concern in critical Marxist accounts of mass culture has been the explication of the shape and operation of dominant ideologies in advanced capitalist society" (Goldman, 1982, p. 363). Goldman sees the character of Mork as an alien sociologist who "makes visible the normally hidden, socially constructed conventions that are the foundations for intersubjectivity" (p. 366). Mork from Ork sees problems with middle class society: "An episode typically begins by placing in question established forms of hegemonic values and practices; or conversely, alternative forms are introduced. In this fashion, problems are posed as matters of discrepancies between values and individual behaviors, and not as the manifestations of internal contradictions within social formations" (p. 368).

The contradictions exposed by Mork are always politely resolved; there is never a questioning of the class tensions or social structural conflicts that underlie the contradictions. Goldman notes that in the show's better moments, with Mork's reports back to the home planet, it could have been like Twain's *Letters from Earth*. But for a *Happy Days* spin-off with a huge youth audience, any tendencies toward knowing social satire were usually repressed.

Goldman, R. (1982). Hegemony and managed critique in prime-time television: A critical reading of *Mork and Mindy*. *Theory and Society, 11*(3), 363–88.

October 7, 1982 *Cheers*, "Sam's Women"
Sam dates beautiful but stupid women. Diane makes him feel uncomfortable about that, apparently for the first time in his life. They get into a big fight about it. He calls her a snob. She says that an intelligent woman would always be able to see through the kinds of pickup lines that Sam uses. Later Sam apologizes. But then he uses one of his typical stories on her, and it's clear that she's buying it. It's the beginning of a series-long bout of sexual tension between the two.

Cheers is dumb men and one smart woman. For Acland (1990), it's all about the use of language to naturalize a bar as a male space for refuge from women. It raises an interesting point for sitcoms in general, where depictions of traditional nuclear families were becoming less common. Can men find families apart from women? Meanwhile, anything in a sitcom can be seen from a critical perspective—just ask Hundley (1995), who sees beer as the sign through which male unity is encoded.

Acland, C. (1990). The "space" behind the dialogue: The gender-coding of space on *Cheers. Women and Language, 13*(1), 39.

Hundley, H. L. (1995). The naturalization of beer in *Cheers. Journal of Broadcasting & Electronic Media, 39*(3), 350–59.

February 28, 1983 *M*A*S*H*, "Goodbye, Farewell, and Amen"

The TV show has gone on much longer than the Korean War. Hawkeye has been put in a psychiatric hospital. Sidney forces Hawkeye to remember a traumatic battle incident before he can be released back to the unit. Peace finally comes. Major Winchester discovers Chinese traveling musicians. They surrender, and he mentors them. BJ goes back to his family, finally. All the characters receive satisfying though wistful conclusions to their narrative arcs. They say goodbye fondly and sadly. When families break up, no other emotion is possible.

The ending of *M*A*S*H* draws to a close the period of relevance sitcoms. Nighttime soap operas are taking over. When sitcoms come back, they will be watered down. The final episode of *M*A*S*H* is one of the most watched and most successful television events of all time. "From the vantage point of the later seventies and eighties, even many Americans who during the sixties had felt no particular affinity with the oppositional currents of the time could, via *M*A*S*H*, look back to the Age of Aquarius with warm affection. The nationwide upsurge of mourning—no weaker term is adequate—which accompanied the end of the series in 1983 registered the degree to which it had attracted the nostalgic investments of an anxious and bewildered America" (Freedman, 1990, p. 106).

Freedman, C. (1990). History, fiction, film, television, myth: The ideology of *M*A*S*H. The Southern Review, 26*(1), 89.

September 20, 1984 *The Cosby Show*, "Pilot"

Claire (Mom) is having some problems with the Huxtable kids. There are four of them. Most importantly, Theo just came home with four D's on his report card. Meanwhile, Cliff (Dad) is at work, where, as an obstetrician, he is convincing a reluctant father to get back in the delivery room. When Cliff gets home, he has to deal with the four D's. Theo says he doesn't need good grades because he doesn't plan to go to college. Cliff uses a Monopoly-money scenario to convince Theo that he'll need a college degree to make it in the world. The other kids present typical problems, such as Denise's pants for her date, which are too tight. Cliff gets a handle on everything, and finally Claire gives him dinner.

262   APPENDIX B

The year 1984 was a low point for sitcoms; very few were in the top twenty. But a new tidal wave was coming with the release of *The Cosby Show*. By 1985, it was the number 3 show and shot to number 1 after that. Along with *All in the Family*, it was the most written about American sitcom. For those who expected critical hosannas for a Black-produced show at number 1, there was anything but. Jhally and Lewis (1992) led the way. With a study financed by Bill Cosby, they highlighted the unrealism—the "enlightened racism"—of the situation. *Cosby* was a new *Father Knows Best*, though undoubtedly a much funnier version of the original.

Jhally, S. & Lewis, J. (1992). *Enlightened racism: The Cosby Show, audiences, and the myth of the American dream*. Westview.

March 7, 1985 *Family Ties*, "Cold Storage"
The Keatons are traveling to their Lamaze reunion. Alex and Jennifer go along to visit Grandma. Mallory has to stay behind to work on a paper. Annoying Skippy comes over to pursue his crush on Mallory. She wants him to leave but first asks him to help get a trunk out of the basement. They get locked down there overnight. Over the course of the night, Mallory realizes that Skippy is not quite so annoying and even gives him a platonic kiss to seal their friendship. They both feel a little less like outsiders.
Family Ties put teenage Reaganism (Alex) into contact with hippie parents. Raine (2011) found an explosion of sitcoms in the '80s that were dealing with middle- and upper-class families while those focused on the working class remained relatively stagnant.

Raine, A. J. (2011). Lifestyles of the not so rich and famous: Ideological shifts in popular culture, Reagan-era sitcoms and portrayals of the working class. *McNair Scholars Research Journal, 7*(1), 13.

January 17, 1986 *Webster*, "That's Rich"
Webster becomes obsessed with winning the lottery. George finally relents and allows Webster to get one lottery ticket. Everyone chooses their lucky numbers, including their ages. Before the drawing, Webster dreams about being rich, but Katherine (whom Webster calls *ma'am*) concludes the dream by saying that if you have love, you can be rich without money. In the drawing, they hit on the first five numbers. The last one comes down to Katherine's age. But she has lied on the ticket, making herself look younger. If she had said her

Sitcom Syllabus 263

true age, they'd have won a million. But they all recover by realizing they have love, so they are already rich.

TV's quest for family structure novelty led to a few shows with interracial adoption. Webster was taken in by a former NFL player and his socialite wife. Webster was tiny and just impossibly cute. They were a family of three. Many critics don't like the implications of the white couple "saving" the child, a scenario also seen in *Diff'rent Strokes*. But interracial adoption is a reality. A 2002 study by Dave Thomas Foundation for Adoption asked, "Suppose you were thinking of adopting a child out of foster care. You might be introduced to a child who is a Black/African American infant or toddler. Suppose you were thinking of adopting this child. For each one of the following, please tell me whether it would be a major concern, minor concern, or no concern at all for you in thinking about whether to adopt this child. The race of the child. Would that be a major concern, minor concern, or no concern at all for you?" Almost 55 percent of respondents said that race would not be an issue, but the rest expressed that there would be some degree of concern.

Dave Thomas Foundation for Adoption. (2002). Dave Thomas Foundation for Adoption Poll: January 2002, Question 78 [USHARRIS.02ADOPT. R705CF]. Harris Interactive. Cornell University, Ithaca, NY: Roper Center for Public Opinion Research.

October 15, 1987 *A Different World*, "Porky de Bergerac"
Denise is trying to get to know a cute guy. At the dorm, Jaleesa is running against Whitley for dorm monitor. Jaleesa proposes a campaign for dorm cleanliness in which anyone leaving garbage around is forced to wear a pig nose for a day. Denise violates the rule and then has to wear the pig nose on her date with the guy. The date turns out to have a certain amount of gallantry, and it all works out.

A Different World depicted life at an historically Black college. The first season was seen as a fairly bland spin-off of *The Cosby Show*. Production changes in later seasons led to a successful run, with a variety of social types figuring themselves out romantically. Some thought it was a fairly realistic portrayal;[2] Matabane and Merritt (2014) documented the positive effects among viewers.

Matabane, P. W., & Merritt, B. D. (2014). Media use, gender, and African American college attendance: The *Cosby* effect. *Howard Journal of Communications, 25*(4), 452–71.

264 APPENDIX B

October 25, 1988 *Roseanne*, "We're in the Money"

Dan gets some extra money. The family hopes they can all get something nice. It doesn't work out that way, but Dan and Roseanne get something for themselves without telling the kids. "Unlike the bourgeois feminism of a *Murphy Brown*, Roseanne Conner's 'proletarian' feminism expresses itself as a series of assertive responses to the daily personal injuries experienced by women who hold jobs with little power and prestige. Roseanne is rude, insubordinate, and rarely a passive victim, on either class or gender grounds. The show routinely provides a fantasy response to working-class women's attempts to sustain self-esteem in a world where they have little control" (Bettie, 1995, p. 132).

Bettie, J. (1995). Class dismissed? *Roseanne* and the changing face of working-class iconography. *Social Text, 45*, 125–49.

September 23, 1989 *The Golden Girls*, "Sick and Tired"

Dorothy has been feeling tired and flu-like for months. Every doctor says she's fine; all of their tests come back negative. She goes to New York to see a specialist. He says she's fine too. Sophia worries that her daughter might die. It's a cliff-hanger episode. In part two, Dorothy learns that she has chronic fatigue syndrome.

The Golden Girls goes against every fact of sitcom demography. The cast was all-women. They were old. Scholarly authors love to explore the show, most often for feminist themes. It is a cultural phenomenon. In San Francisco, *Golden Girls* Christmas episodes are done live by drag actors. "Like drag culture itself, these live performances of *The Golden Girls* occupy an in-betweenness, a marginal borderland between television text and audience participation, between male and female gender constructs, between normative and non-normative sexualities, and between the past and the present" (Patterson, 2016, p. 849).

Patterson, E. (2016). The *Golden Girls* Live: Residual television texts, participatory culture, and queering TV heritage through drag. *Feminist Media Studies, 16*(5), 838–51.

February 3, 1990 *Get a Life* (1990–92), "Counterfeit Watch"

Chris wants an underwater watch. He buys one at a local pawnshop, but it's a fake. Local cops enlist him to run a sting at the shop so as to catch the

Sitcom Syllabus   265

supplier of the fake goods. Chris botches the sting in every way, but they still manage to nab the crooks. A cop seemingly shoots Chris in the head as the last scene blacks out, but Chris just says, "Ow."

Chris was an adult paperboy living in his parents' garage. The series was a foreboding of the "failure to launch" phenomenon (Kins & Beyers, 2010), which is part and parcel of delayed moves toward adulthood in millennial generations, such as later age of marriage.

Kins, E., & Beyers, W. (2010). Failure to launch, failure to achieve criteria for adulthood? *Journal of Adolescent Research, 25*(5), 743–77.

May 2, 1991 *Seinfeld*, "The Deal"
Jerry and Elaine figure out how to have sex while remaining friends. George is doubtful, but he's willing to see if it works. One rule is that they don't have to stay over after having sex. But when Jerry tries to invoke the rule, Elaine is upset. They return to being just friends. Casual sex has its costs.

A national survey in 2018 asked, "Do you generally disapprove of people who pursue casual sex, hookups, or one-night-stands?" Only about a third expressed disapproval. Years of casual sex on TV must have played some role, as found by van Oosten and Vandenbosch (2017).

Cards against Humanity (2018). Cards against Humanity's Pulse of the Nation Poll: Public Issues Survey Wave 7, Question 11 [31115222.00010]. Survey Sampling International. Cornell University, Ithaca, NY: Roper Center for Public Opinion Research.

van Oosten, J. M., Peter, J., & Vandenbosch, L. (2017). Adolescents' sexual media use and willingness to engage in casual sex: Differential relations and underlying processes. *Human Communication Research, 43*(1), 127–47.

October 23, 1992 *Family Matters* (1989–98), "Number One with a Bullet"
Steve Urkel must go to the hospital because he has appendicitis. Carl is pleased because he will have three days without Urkel, who is his nemesis. However, when Carl is shot in the butt while on the job as a policeman, he is put in the same room with Urkel. Steve wants to be as much help to Carl as possible, but of course he just annoys him. But when Steve saves the day from a criminal who comes into the room to shoot Carl, all is forgiven. Urkel and Carl cement their friendship.

266   APPENDIX B

Urkel is the anti-Fonzie. He's Black; he's not cool. Fonzie is white and cool. It's a reversal of the normal stereotype. Urkel's nasal voice is more white than Black. He does well at math. He dresses poorly. The rest of the *Family Matters* cast are stylish and up to date. They tolerate Urkel at best. But Urkel becomes a major cultural sensation, with his tag line "Did I do that?" reflecting his lack of social awareness. For Quail (2011), a Black nerd character such as Urkel serves as a symbolic foil to define how Black males are usually supposed to be: hip, athletic, smooth with women, and not smart—all of the traits *not* possessed by Urkel.

Quail, C. (2011). Nerds, geeks, and the hip/square dialectic in contemporary television. *Television & New Media, 12*(5), 460–82.

December 9, 1993 *Seinfeld,* "The Cigar Store Indian"
Jerry buys a cigar-store Indian for Elaine, leading to accusations of racism. He would like to date Elaine's Native American friend, but he keeps tripping up on phrases (e.g., *Indian giver*) that make him seem even more racist.
Seinfeld is honest about his take on Native Americans. He's relatively clueless about them and expects them to give him some slack because he's only joking. Tahmahkera (2008) catalogs many of the appearances of Indian characters and imagery in sitcoms, which is almost always as an embarrassing stereotype.

Tahmahkera, D. (2008). Custer's last sitcom: Decolonized viewing of the sitcom's "Indian." *American Indian Quarterly, 32*(3), 324–51.

May 9, 1994 *The Fresh Prince of Bel-Air* (1990–96), "Papa's Got a Brand New Excuse"
Will's father shows up after fourteen years. He says he wants to make up for lost time. Uncle Phil sees through it, knowing that Will's "father" will leave as fast as he came. Uncle Phil is the *real* father.
Fatherlessness is considered to be a huge social problem (Blankenhorn, 1995). In sitcoms, usually the reverse situation is considered, where the mother has disappeared for some reason. In *Fresh Prince*, the Black child was rescued/adopted within his own race, which was also unusual at the time.

Blankenhorn, D. (1995). *Fatherless America: Confronting our most urgent social problem.* HarperCollins.

Sitcom Syllabus

September 2, 1995 *Seinfeld*, "The Soup Nazi"

Jerry and friends learn about a soup stand that it is out of this world. But the owner is an authoritarian. One must order in a specific way. Jerry snubs his girlfriend to get the soup. George and Elaine fail in the ordering process, and they are banned. "No soup for you!" Kramer, though, is friends with the Soup Nazi. The Nazi gives Kramer an armoire, having learned that Kramer's armoire had been stolen on the street. But when the Soup Nazi learns that the armoire was for Elaine, he complains bitterly. Later, Elaine finds old soup recipes in the armoire, destroying the Soup Nazi's business. He will move to Argentina, where all ruined Nazis go.

Nazis, when they are not systematically murdering people, are funny and very mockable. *Hogan's Heroes* did it for many seasons. Mel Brooks mined the theme reliably. In another episode, Seinfeld made out with his girlfriend during *Schindler's List*. Comparing Seinfeld to Kafka, Brooks (not Mel, 2020) observes, "While the scene of reading or viewing within *Seinfeld* is one of apparent indifference, a closer reading reveals something about Jewish humor, respect, and the tragic. *Schindler's List* is not the Holocaust, but a Hollywood mask for the horror. It generates a faux sentimentalism" (p. 7).

Brooks, L. (2020). Kafka's Seinfeldian Humor. *Comparative Literature: East & West*, 4(1), 1–14.

November 20, 1996 *The Wayans Brothers*, "Goin' to the Net"

Shawn meets an older woman in the newsstand. Marlon uses the brothers' new computer to search out "cyber-hoochies." Shawn thinks something special will develop with the older woman, but she just wants to play the field. Marlon has hooked up with a girl from the "risk takers" room on the internet. She wants him to do dangerous things like skydive out of a balloon, but eventually Marlon says that she should get a white boy from the Mountain Dew commercials.

The Wayans Brothers opens cold with a spoof of a 1970s Black sitcom, then abruptly cuts to signify that this will be an authentic '90s show depicting real Black experiences, not filtered through the lens of white producers. As it turns out, all the tropes from the white shows are present. The show is not out to uplift anyone. Many critics find it a return to minstrel stereotypes. Yang and Riser (2008) disagree: "It is our position that the Wayans brothers enact, and indeed exaggerate various stereotypical forms of black behavior in order to interrogate the white imaginary" (p. 731).

268 APPENDIX B

Yang, G., & Ryser, T. A. (2008). Whiting up and Blacking out: White privilege, race, and *White Chicks*. *African American Review, 42*(3/4), 731–46.

May 15, 1997 *Friends*, "The One at the Beach"

All the friends are going to a beach house for the weekend. Phoebe has a contact that might help her find her long-last dad. Chandler is trying to convince Monica that he could be boyfriend material. Everyone plays strip poker, except there are no cards, so they use a *Happy Days* board game. Ross and Rachel are having moments that remind them of their discontinued love affair; it seems like it might be leading somewhere. But Ross's current girlfriend, Bonnie, shows up, throwing a wrench into the situation. Rachel convinces Bonnie that she should shave her hair again, because she knows Ross hates this. Then Ross and Rachel have a passionate kiss. Phoebe finds her mother instead of her father! At the end of the episode, Ross must decide which bedroom to enter for the night: Rachel's or Bonnie's. Cliff-hanger . . .

Not many studies have used, as this book does, a corpus of sitcom dialogue for any purpose. But Tagliamonte and Roberts (2005) did. They studied "intensifiers," like when someone says, "That's *so* cool." One of their findings: "The highest popularity ratings for *Friends* correspond to the times when the characters use the most *so*" (p. 297).

Todd, A. M. (2011). Saying goodbye to Friends: Situation comedy as lived experience. *The Journal of Popular Culture, 44*(4), 855.

Tagliamonte, S., & Roberts, C. (2005). So weird; so cool; so innovative: The use of intensifiers in the television series *Friends*. *American Speech, 80*(3), 280–300.

February 2, 1998 *Everybody Loves Raymond*, "The Checkbook"

Ray annoys Deborah while she is doing the bills. She makes Ray take over the family checkbook. Naturally, he is no good at it; he bounces checks, gets the electricity turned off, and so forth. To hide it from Deborah, he creates a fake checkbook. He needs to borrow money from Robert, telling him that Deborah has a "problem" that is affecting their finances. The whole family gets involved. Everything finally crashes down when Deborah tries to cash a check at the bank.

In the sitcom world, the wife manages the finances, even if the husband putatively controls the money. Redbook (1994) conducted a survey about family checkbooks. They asked, "Who's more likely to have trouble balancing

Sitcom Syllabus

a checkbook—a man, a woman or are they equally likely to have trouble balancing a checkbook?" Results showed that 44 percent thought men would, whereas only 14 percent said a woman. The remainder (40 percent) said it would be equally likely for a man or a woman to have trouble.

Redbook (1994). Redbook Poll: August 1994, Question 3 [USEDK.94AUG. R03]. EDK Associates. Cornell University, Ithaca, NY: Roper Center for Public Opinion Research.

October 14, 1998 *The Nanny* (1993–99), "Once a Secretary, Always a Secretary"

Maxwell calls Fran his nanny on a TV interview, even though she has recently become his wife. She hates the "n-word." Still, she realizes that she now has become a woman of leisure. She tries to fit in at the country club, but that doesn't work. She is able to make up with Maxwell, as she determines that she wants to be involved with the kids and in fact, even though she is now a wife, remain also as the nanny.

This particular Cinderella has a horrifying Queens accent and sleeps her way to social improvement. She is, on the surface, shallow. There is also much to love about her, though. The show is lowbrow funny and quite popular with gay audiences.[3] Drescher's fantastic wardrobe and campy, over-the-top persona make for much success in reruns.

December 10, 2000 *Curb Your Enthusiasm*, "Affirmative Action"

Larry makes a bad joke about affirmative action when he meets Richard's Black doctor. "I tend to say stupid things in front of Black people," he says. It's an honest admission from a white guy who wants to maintain his liberal credentials in Hollywood. Later, at a restaurant, he runs into a Black woman he had passed over for a job. She accuses him of racist hiring in his *Seinfeld* days. Later, Larry needs to call the doctor to get a prescription for his wife. It's after hours, so he has to go to the house to pick it up. There is a party going on there, filled with distinguished Black professionals. They make Larry repeat his joke. He issues mea culpas, and it looks like he is about to get the prescription when the woman turns up again and attacks him for biased hiring.

Jews and Blacks have had their issues over the years. For Gillotta (2010), David's character—which is himself—is a modern manifestation of the *schlemiel* tradition in Jewish literature. Jews have a "middle" position in regard to race: aware of discrimination against themselves historically but also in a position to assimilate ethnically as white. They are "off white."

Gillota, D. (2010). Negotiating Jewishness: *Curb Your Enthusiasm* and the *schlemiel* tradition. *Journal of Popular Film & Television, 38*(4), 152–61.

February 26, 2001 *King of Queens,* "Inner Tube"

Doug lies to Carrie so that he can go play football instead of going to a work event with her. He gets sick playing football, but Carrie believes his lie that he had to work late. In a feverish dream sequence, he becomes characters from classic TV as he works through his guilt about lying to Carrie. Most prominently, he is Ralph Kramden. Eventually, his lying is too much for him, and he tells Carrie/Alice, "I'm a mope. But I love you, baby." When he wakes up, he rushes to be with Carrie to explain what he did. He utters the same exact words as Kramden. Rather than giving him a hug the way Alice hugged Ralph, Carrie throws a drink in his face.

"A number of recent situation comedies on U.S. television depict smart, witty, and attractive women who are married to inept, overweight, and immature men" (Walsh et al., 2008, p. 123). It's hard to ignore in the world of sitcoms. While Walsh focuses on the more recent phenomenon, it is, of course, as old as sitcoms themselves and, as their *Beauty and the Beast* reference implies, maybe as old as domestic storytelling. "The beauty (e.g., Jane) commonly 'liberates' the beast (e.g., Tarzan) by finally accepting him 'as is'" (p. 132).

Walsh, K. R., Fürsich, E., & Jefferson, B. S. (2008). Beauty and the patriarchal beast: Gender role portrayals in sitcoms featuring mismatched couples. *Journal of Popular Film and Television, 36*(3), 123–32.

October 29, 2002 *Just Shoot Me* (1997–2003), "'Halloween? Halloween!'"

A hot new model has come to the magazine office. Dennis and Jack fight over her. At the Halloween party, the model makes a play for Dennis, who is dressed as Robin Hood. But she thinks he looks like Peter Pan. She also thinks he is a woman; the model is a lesbian. Dennis plays along because he is so attracted to the model. Eventually, of course, she discovers that he is a man. Office romances have come a long way since 2002.

Just Shoot Me is one of the texts examined by Kim et al. (2007) in their look at heterosexual scripts. The program is an experimental lab for both masculine and feminine toxicity, starting from its premise as a place (a fashion magazine) where vapid models are pursued by shallow and predatory men: "Taken together, results suggest that via the Heterosexual Script, television offers mutually impoverished constructs of male and female sexuality, which may ultimately preclude boys' ability to say no to sex and girls' ability to say yes" (p. 156).

Kim, J. L., Lynn Sorsoli, C., Collins, K., Zylbergold, B. A., Schooler, D., & Tolman, D. L. (2007). From sex to sexuality: Exposing the heterosexual script on primetime network television. *Journal of Sex Research, 44*(2), 145–57.

April 3, 2003 *Will & Grace*, "Sex, Losers, and Videotape"

Will is dumped by his boyfriend. He forms a "losers' club" with his nutty boss, Mr. Stein, but it's quickly broken up when he meets the sex-crazed Karen. Meanwhile, Grace is trying to make a sexy tape for her boyfriend, but her best efforts merely make her seem like a raunchy Lucille Ball. Jack agrees to help her with acting lessons. It works; she finally makes a sexy tape. Mr. Stein and Karen decide to break up because the losers' club is more important than love. Platonic relationships are long-lasting; sexual romance is always short-lived.

Will & Grace was a show with gay characters; there weren't too many others at the time. Can such a show make a difference in attitudes? Schiappa et al. (2006) say yes in their study of college students who were exposed to the program. Prejudicial attitudes were lessened after viewing. Whether the attitudes remain changed is unknown, but the study is reminiscent of some of the earliest studies from the days of film that found exposure to a film like *Birth of a Nation* had an effect on prejudicial attitudes.

Schiappa, E., Gregg, P. B., & Hewes, D. E. (2006). Can one TV show make a difference? *Will & Grace* and the parasocial contact hypothesis. *Journal of Homosexuality, 51*(4), 15–37.

February 23, 2004 *Two and a Half Men*, "Ate the Hamburgers, Wearing the Hats"

Alan selects remote cousins to be Jake's guardian in the case of his death, which angers Charlie. Charlie takes Jake out for the afternoon, and Jake gets injured playing basketball. At the emergency room, Charlie learns what is required to take care of a ten-year-old. Upon returning, Alan realizes that Charlie can be responsible enough to take care of Jake and decides to change his will.

Charlie is a single, irresponsible, boozing bachelor. He has lots of money and a Malibu beach house. He sleeps with new women every night. Alan is divorced and forced to bring Jake to live with Charlie. He is softer and weaker, but he is responsible. They provide two different role models for Jake, a

272 APPENDIX B

not-very-bright kid. Normally, Charlie's irresponsibility is rewarded, and Jake gravitates toward him as the fun uncle, which Alan must always rein in. "Repetitive storylines over many years of *Two and a Half Men* stick to a plotline dependent on identifying Charlie as a real man, while Alan's alternative masculinity does not achieve true cultural articulation" (Hatfield, 2010, p. 546).

Hatfield, E. F. (2010). "What it means to be a man": Examining hegemonic masculinity in Two and a Half Men. *Communication, Culture & Critique, 3*(4), 526–48.

January 3, 2005 *Still Standing* (2002–06), "Still Bonding"
Judy wants Bill to spend more time with daughter Lauren. But like many fathers and daughters, they have a difficult time relating. They decide that they will lie to Judy, making up activities that they did together. They nearly get caught, but they also finally realize that maybe they could spend a little more time together. Bill will never be sensitive, but he is a good dad.
Still Standing is what standard family sitcoms became by the 2000s. Parents are marginally functional. Kids are wiseacres. Dad is overweight, but Mom looks good. It all supports Scharrer's (2001) thesis that working-class dads are buffoons.

Scharrer, E. (2001). From wise to foolish: The portrayal of the sitcom father, 1950s–1990s. *Journal of Broadcasting & Electronic Media, 45*(1), 23–40.

February 2, 2006 *Everybody Hates Chris*, "Everybody Hates Picture Day"
Chris would like to find a cool outfit for picture day at school. He's the only Black kid there, and a good picture would go a long way toward establishing his popularity. Although money is an issue, he gets mom to get him a suitable outfit. White bullies steal the outfit, though. Clueless white school admins don't help. His nerdy white friend is an ally, but Chris does not succeed in getting a good set of clothes for the picture. Mom forgives him in any case.
Henderson (2011) reflects on issues of race and gender in sitcom writing rooms, including her own experience on *Everybody Hates Chris*: "Othering becomes a method of silencing points of view, the ideas of those who are othered effectively die on the vine. If the other wishes to survive, she or he quickly learns to present ideas that are acceptable to the more powerful writers in the room. It is this process that leads to the homogenization of ideas. This is nearly always the process for half-hour comedies" (p. 50).

Henderson, F. D. (2011). The culture behind closed doors: Issues of gender and race in the writers' room. *Cinema Journal, 50*(2), 145–52.

April 4, 2007 *The George Lopez Show* (2002–07), "George Is Lie-able for Benny's Unhappiness"

One of Benny's (George's mom) old boyfriends comes back to visit. To protect her, George says that she has died. It turns out that George has been lying a long time to protect Benny from the repeated visits of this toxic boyfriend. But this time he seems different, more sincere. After some flashbacks to childhood, with weird large-head special effects, George is forced to admit all his lies. Benny gets to hook up again with the boyfriend, although it's still doubtful whether anything good can come of it.

After a long run of network shows with no Hispanic leads, *The George Lopez Show* does a reasonable job of translating Hispanic culture (specifically, Mexican in LA) to a larger audience. By and large, it succeeds without delving too much into negative stereotyping (Markert, 2004). It is a return to the loving ethnic send-ups of the 1950s, seen in shows like the original *The Goldbergs*.

Markert, J. (2004). "The George Lopez Show": The same old Hispano? *Bilingual Review/La Revista Bilingüe, 28*(2): 148–65.

April 21, 2008 *The Big Bang Theory*, "The Bat Jar Conjecture"

All the gang (Leonard, Howard, Raj) would like to enter the Physics Bowl, so they ask Sheldon to be on the team. But then, he is annoying, so they kick him off. Sheldon gets his own team, comprising him and other nonphysicists. Only Sheldon will give the answers. Meanwhile, the guys get Sheldon's nemesis Leslie to be on their team. It all comes down to solving one final very complicated equation. Neither the guys nor Sheldon can get it. Out of nowhere, the janitor on Sheldon's team gives the right answer. It turns out he was a physicist back in Russia. But Sheldon refuses to offer that answer, so the gang's team wins.

Bednarek (2012) examined *Big Bang* in quite some detail in terms of how Sheldon's linguistic patterns contribute to his exemplification of the nerd stereotype. He "instantiates" a nerd/geek schema (p. 223). On the positive side, Li and Orthia (2016) found that viewing episodes of the show could help viewers understand the "nature of science." In the world of 2000s TV, where sitcom popularity was declining, *Big Bang* stood out as an exemplary success.

274 APPENDIX B

Bednarek, M. (2012). Constructing 'nerdiness': Characterisation in *The Big Bang Theory. Multilingua, 31*(2–3), 199–229.

Li, R., & Orthia, L. A. (2016). Communicating the nature of science through The Big Bang Theory: Evidence from a focus group Study. *International Journal of Science Education, Part B, 6*(2), 115–36.

December 16, 2009 *The New Adventures of Old Christine* (2006–10), "It's Beginning to Stink a Lot Like Christmas"

Christine has been avoiding her neighbors for five years. Finally, she agrees to go to their Christmas party. Initially she is pleasantly surprised, as they seem like her kind of people. When she discovers the husband kissing another woman, she tells the wife, her new friend, about it. That leads to some uncomfortable moments, but the wife says not everything means something. Christine needs to learn what the neighborhood is all about. Eventually, she discovers that the entire neighborhood is filled with swingers. She retreats to her home, vowing not to come out ever again.

Many sitcoms feature "the neighbor," who is always visiting and being nosy. In past days, some neighbors seemingly had free rein in the house, coming and going at they pleased, taking food, and so forth, à la Norton or Kramer. Putnam (2000) documented declines in civic life, which includes less frequent interactions with neighbors as we spend more time with media. Howley et al. (2015) argue that such interaction would have beneficial effects, should we choose to engage in it.

Howley, P., Neill, S. O., & Atkinson, R. (2015). Who needs good neighbors? *Environment and Planning A: Economy and Space, 47*(4), 939–56.

Putnam, R. D. (2000). *Bowling alone: The collapse and revival of American community.* Simon and Schuster.

December 9, 2010 *It's Always Sunny in Philadelphia,* "A Very Sunny Christmas"

Nothing is sacred when *Always Sunny* partakes in the "joy" of Christmas, despite past disappointments. Highlights like stealing the neighbors' toys and getting into Santa's sex life bring the perverse holiday spirit in a way that can only be enjoyed by this antifamily. "Merry Christmas, bitches!"

This is arguably the most unlikable show on television. In spite of this, Nutile (2018) demonstrates its ratings resilience, showing a barely declining ratings trend compared to *Modern Family* or *The Simpsons*.

Nutile, M. (2018). The gang beats the odds: *It's Always Sunny in Philadelphia's* consistent popularity. *Cinesthesia, 8*(1), 4.

October 18, 2011 *Last Man Standing*, "Grandparents Day"

Mike makes a comment about a boy dressed as a fairy princess when he visits his grandson's preschool. That comment gets the grandson kicked out. So, Mike has to take him to work for a few days.

Mike is an unreconstructed *guy*. The world around him is going "woke." He is surrounded by women. Mike does not "validate" feelings. For him, words are only words. But he also takes pride in being the male center of a female universe, as was the case in many sitcoms before him. Chozick (2011) identified that in the 2011 TV season, a variety of sitcoms were trying to deal with what it is to be "a man." Most of them fell by the wayside.

Chozick, A. (2011, June 10). A New Generation of TV Wimps. *Wall Street Journal*.

May 27, 2012 *Veep* (2012–19), "Baseball"

The Veep learns that she might be pregnant. The staff must find pregnancy tests and manage the story lest it gets out in the press. A visit to a baseball stadium reveals the Veep's lack of baseball knowledge. As the episode ends, the Veep is singing songs with schoolchildren while also learning that she is definitely pregnant.

Ever since the days of Lucy's pregnancy, how the "condition" is covered on TV has been an issue. In the case of *I Love Lucy*, it was a much-welcomed event, even if the wording and presentation of it were somewhat stilted (Bor, 2013). On the *Veep* episode, it is treated as a personal and political disaster, something entirely unwelcome that could ruin a career.

Bor, S. E. (2013). Lucy's two babies: framing the first televised depiction of pregnancy. *Media History, 19*(4), 464–78.

March 3, 2013 *The Office*, "The Farm"

Dwight must go home for his mother's funeral. It appears that his family is some sort of Appalachian religious cult. Meanwhile, at the office, Todd comes back to apologize for having insulted everyone. He gives everyone cupcakes, but they are actually spiked with drugs and laxatives. At first Pam convinces

276 APPENDIX B

everyone that they should not eat these cupcakes, because Todd is not sincere. Eventually, they cannot resist the cupcakes, and they all have weird and terrible nights. The next day, Kevin finds one uneaten cupcake. He starts to eat it, but Pam says he should not, because Todd is the "worst person in the world." Kevin replies, "In other words, normal." This is the message of *The Office*. To conclude, Dwight has accepted the challenge to run the family "worm farm."

Beeden and De Bruin (2010) explore differences in the American and British versions of *The Office*. While it was suspected that an American version could not work, it did. As it turns out, people are horrible on both sides of the ocean.

Beeden, A., & De Bruin, J. (2010). *The Office*: Articulations of national identity in television format adaptation. *Television & New Media, 11*(1), 3–19.

November 19, 2014 *The Goldbergs* (2013–), "A Goldberg Thanksgiving"
Erica wins a Jazzercise bet, allowing her to skip the family Thanksgiving. Uncle Marvin comes, annoying Murray because he relates so strongly to Adam. He encourages Adam to pursue a "career" in video games. The family Thanksgiving collapses. Fortunately, Pops intervenes with the wisdom of the aged, and the holiday is saved.

Thanksgiving never starts well in a sitcom, but it always ends well. Do we learn how to celebrate holidays from TV? Katz (1998, p. 232) goes even further: "Exaggerating only slightly, one can say that television has the power to declare holidays and to invite ritual participation in them. Usually acting in collusion with establishments, television has the extraordinary power to command a moratorium, reshuffle roles, and focus every eye and ear for hours, sometimes days and weeks, on the progress of a ceremonial event."

Thanksgiving, the quintessential American holiday, seemingly crosses almost every ethnic boundary, on TV and in real life.

Katz, E. (1998). Broadcasting holidays. *Sociological Inquiry, 68*(2), 230–41.

May 11, 2015 *Mike and Molly* (2010–16), "'Near Death Do Us Part"
Mike and Molly are two cute people who meet at Overeaters Anonymous. They get together and try to get healthy. Otherwise, things proceed along the lines of a typical sitcom. Carl and Mike almost die while on duty as police. Carl tells Mike he's going to propose to Victoria. Mike tells Molly; she tells Victoria and Joyce. Carl changes his mind, deciding not to propose. They break up.

Sitcom Syllabus   277

"Should Fatties Get a Room?" was an online *Marie Claire* blog post that has since been taken down. In response to *Mike and Molly*, the writer thought that the protagonists were too overweight to inspire any sort of romantic interest on the part of viewers. Many people objected to the article. In the sitcom world, many male stars had been overweight, but it was much more unusual for female stars. *Roseanne* changed that equation slightly, but *Mike and Molly* made membership in Overeaters Anonymous a premise of the show. It is a lagging cultural indicator for the growing obesity problem in the US.

October 31, 2016 *Two Broke Girl$* (2011–17), "And the College Experience"

Caroline and Max have come a long way to achieve their drive toward financial success. They started as waitresses, and now they own their own dessert bar. After a local magazine checks out the place, Caroline gets invited to talk to a business class at Wharton, her old school.

Sometimes sitcoms take a complex comedic persona and do damage to it. Audissino (2019) sees such a phenomenon with the actress-comedian Kat Dennings in *Two Broke Girls*. The show did have good comedic chemistry between its two main stars, and overall its run could be considered a success. But many of the episodes are painfully sophomoric, with an overreliance on sexual humor that does not always seem organic. The show mines a hipster Brooklyn esthetic, but it is greatly sanitized for the network audience in a period when networks are still making some efforts to have broadly accessible sitcoms for older demographics as well as young.

Audissino, E. (2019, June 14). 2 *Broke Girls*: Flattening Kat Dennings into Max Black: Screenwriting and Character Complexity in the Sitcom Format. Writing for Screens Symposium, University of Portsmouth, UK.

February 1, 2018 *Young Sheldon* (2017–23), "A Sneeze, a Detention and Sissy Spacek"

Young Sheldon is germophobic. He goes to enormous lengths to avoid being exposed in school, which results in a detention and then finally self-isolation at home. Only his beloved Meemaw can entice him to return to the world.

Sheldon's neuroses are comic in nature. But it is worth wondering whether the portrayals have any destigmatizing effect on perceptions of mental illness. Rajan (2021) is not completely approving of the humor-only images of Asperger's but still sees them as a step forward from a condition that was previously symbolically annihilated.

278 APPENDIX B

Rajan, B. (2021). Popular culture and the (mis)representation of Asperger's: A study on the sitcoms Community and The Big Bang Theory. In J. Smith (Ed.), *Normalizing Mental Illness and Neurodiversity in Entertainment Media* (pp. 66–82). Routledge.

October 31, 2019 *The Good Place* (2016–20), "Chip Driver Mystery"
Characters find themselves in an experimental "bad place."
Few sitcoms are explicitly based on philosophical premises, but *The Good Place* has an actual moral philosopher as a main character. Professional philosophers approved, as explored in Engels and Richards' (2020) volume on the show's philosophy.

Engels, K. S., & Richards, T. (Eds.). (2020). *The good place and philosophy: Everything is forking fine!* New York: Wiley-Blackwell.

February 25, 2020 *Schitt's Creek* (2015–20), "Presidential Suite"
Jonny and Moira are trying to have a romantic night in the presidential suite they have built in the motel. *Schitt's Creek* is a fish-out-of-water modern *Green Acres*. Rich folks are forced to live among a basket of deplorables. In this version, though, there is character development, as the Rose family comes to accept their new environment.
Chisholm (2021) sees the show as part of a third stage in the development of sitcoms, with the first stage being the traditional family sitcom and the second stage being an ironic rejection of that norm in workplaces. The third stage is influenced by ideas like *nicecore*, where responses to situations alternate between sincerity and irony. The third stage is a dialectic synthesis of the two previous generations.

Chisholm, A. (2021). 'An evolution of a combo': the current state of the North American sitcom, and its influence from both prior stages of the genre, and contemporary narrative trends through an examination of *Schitt's Creek*. *Comedy Studies, 12*(2), 215–26.

NOTES

1. Polsby uses the term to indicate a family configuration, most of which (the nontraditional ones) he disapproves of.
2. Luckie (2015).
3. White (2021).

BIBLIOGRAPHY

Acham, C. (2004). *Revolution televised: Prime time and the struggle for Black power.* Minneapolis: University of Minnesota Press.

Acland, C. (1990). The "space" behind the dialogue: The gender-coding of space on *Cheers. Women and Language, 13*(1), 39.

Albig, W. (1937). The content of radio programs, 1925–1935. *Social Forces, 16,* 338.

Anderson, S. (1919). *Winesburg, Ohio.* New York: Modern Library.

Andrews, T. (2018, May). Bob Newhart's "quietly revolutionary" sitcom ended 40 years ago. But it changed TV. *Washington Post.*

Armstrong, J. (2013). *Mary and Lou and Rhoda and Ted.* New York: Simon and Schuster.

Association of American Medical Colleges. (2021, February 2). *Nation's physician workforce evolves: More women, a bit older, and toward different specialties.* https://www.aamc.org/news-insights/nation-s-physician-workforce-evolves-more-women-bit-older-and-toward-different-specialties

Attalah, P. (2003). The unworthy discourse. In J. Morreale (Ed.), *Critiquing the sitcom* (pp. 91–115). Syracuse, NY: Syracuse University Press.

Audissino, E. (2019). *2 Broke Girls*: Flattening Kat Dennings into Max Black: Screenwriting and character complexity in the sitcom format. Paper presented to Writing for Screens Symposium. University of Portsmouth, UK.

Austerlitz, S. (2014). *Sitcom: A history in 24 episodes.* Chicago: Chicago Review Press.

Bakhtin, M. (1984). *Rabelais and his world.* Bloomington: Indiana University Press.

Barnouw, E. (1966). *A tower in Babel.* New York: Oxford University Press.

Barnouw, E. (1970). *The image empire.* New York: Oxford University Press.

280 BIBLIOGRAPHY

Barnouw, E. (1978). *The sponsor.* Oxford, UK: Oxford University Press.

Barthes, R. (1967). *Elements of semiology.* New York: Hill and Wang.

Baser, M. S., Weiskopf, K., & Wiser, B. (Writers), & Kenwith, H. (Director). (1977, November 29). Barbara's friend (Part 1) [TV series episode]. In N. Lear (Executive Producer), *One day at a time.* Los Angeles: TAT Communications Company.

Battles, K., & Hilton-Morrow, W. (2002). Gay characters in conventional spaces: *Will and Grace* and the situation comedy genre. *Critical Studies in Media Communication, 19*(1), 87–105.

Bednarek, M. (2012). Constructing 'nerdiness': Characterisation in *The Big Bang Theory. Multilingua, 31*(2–3), 199–229.

Beeden, A., & De Bruin, J. (2010). *The Office*: Articulations of national identity in television format adaptation. *Television & New Media, 11*(1), 3–19.

Bergson, H. (1914). *Laughter.* New York: Macmillan.

Berry, D. M. (2012). *Understanding digital humanities.* London: Palgrave Macmillan.

Bettie, J. (1995). Class dismissed? *Roseanne* and the changing face of working-class iconography. *Social Text, 45*, 125–49.

Blankenhorn, D. (1995). *Fatherless America: Confronting our most urgent social problem.* Scranton, PA: HarperCollins.

Bodroghkozy, P. (2003). Is this what you mean by color TV?. In J. Morreale (Ed.), *Critiquing the sitcom* (pp. 129–49). Syracuse, NY: Syracuse University Press.

Bogle, D. (2001). *Toms, coons, mulattoes, mammies, and bucks: An interpretive history of Blacks in American films.* London: Bloomsbury.

Bogle, D. (2001a). *Prime-time blues.* New York: Farrar, Straus & Giroux.

Bor, S. E. (2013). Lucy's two babies: Framing the first televised depiction of pregnancy. *Media History, 19*(4), 464–78.

Braxton, G. (2022, June 29). *Friends'* lack of diversity 'embarrassed' its co-creator. So she made a $4-million decision. *Los Angeles Times.* https://www.latimes .com/entertainment-arts/tv/story/2022-06-29/friends-diversity-marta-kauffman -brandeis-university

Brooks, L. (2020). Kafka's Seinfeldian humor. *Comparative Literature: East & West, 4*(1), 1–14.

Brooks, T. (2020). *The blackface minstrel show in mass media.* Jefferson, NC: Macfarland.

Brooks, T., & Marsh, E. F. (2009). *The complete directory to prime-time network and cable TV shows, 1946-present.* New York: Ballantine.

Brown, B. (1982). Family intimacy in magazine advertising, 1920–1977. *Journal of Communication, 33*(3): 173–83.

Brown, P. (2020, January 13). How The WB became a hub for Black entertainment in the '90s. *Vibe.* https://www.vibe.com/features/editorial/how-the-wb-became -a-hub-for-black-entertainment-in-the-90s-672439

BIBLIOGRAPHY 281

Brunsdon, C., & Spigel, L. (2007). *Feminist television criticism: A reader*. London: McGraw-Hill Education.

Bryant, J., Carveth, R. A., & Brown, D. (1981). Television viewing and anxiety: An experimental examination. *Journal of Communication*, 31(1): 106–19.

Bryson, L., Free, L., Gorer, G., Lasswell, H., Lazarsfeld, P., Lynd, R., & Waples, D. (1940). *Research in mass communication: A Rockefeller committee memorandum*. New York: Rockefeller Foundation.

Buerkel-Rothfuss, N. L., Greenberg, B. S., Atkin, C. K., & Neuendorf, K. (1982). Learning about the family from television. *Journal of Communication*, 32(3), 191–201.

Bulloc, K. (2018). Orientalism on television: A case study of *I Dream of Jeannie*. *ReOrient*, 4(1), 4–23.

Bullock, K. (2015). Visible and invisible: An audience study of Muslim and non-Muslim reactions to Orientalist representations in *I Dream of Jeannie*. *Journal of Arab & Muslim Media Research*, 8(2), 83–97.

Burch, T. K. (1967). The size and structure of families: A comparative analysis of census data. *American Sociological Review*, 32(3): 347–63.

Burns, G. (1955). *I love her, that's why!* New York: Simon and Schuster.

Butsch, R. (1992). Class and gender in four decades of television situation comedy: Plus ça change . . . *Critical Studies in Media Communication*, 9(4), 387–99.

Butsch, R. (2000). *The making of American audiences*. Cambridge, UK: Cambridge University Press.

Butsch, R., & Glennon, L. M. (1983). Social class: Frequency trends in domestic situation comedy, 1946-1978. *Journal of Broadcasting & Electronic Media*, 27(1), 77–81.

Cameron, S. (2014, October 1). "All in the Family": THR's 1971 Review. *Hollywood Reporter*.

Campbell, A., & Converse, P. E. (1972). *The human meaning of social change*. New York: Russell Sage Foundation.

Cards against Humanity (2018). Cards against Humanity's Pulse of the Nation Poll: Public Issues Survey Wave 7, Question 11 [31115222.00010]. Survey Sampling International. Cornell University, Ithaca, NY: Roper Center for Public Opinion Research.

Carley, M. (1981). *Social measurement and social indicators*. London: George Allen & Unwin.

Carveth, R. & Alexander, A. (1985). Soap opera viewing motivations and the cultivation hypothesis. *Journal of Broadcasting & Electronic Media*, 29, 259–73.

Cassidy, D. (1994). *C'mon get happy: Fear and loathing on the Partridge Family bus*. New York: Warner Media.

Chen, Y., Peng, Z., Kim, S., & Choi, C. (2023). What we can do and cannot do with topic modeling: A systematic review. *Communication Methods and Measures*, 17(2):1–20.

Chisholm, A. (2021). 'An evolution of a combo': the current state of the North American sitcom, and its influence from both prior stages of the genre, and contemporary narrative trends through an examination of *Schitt's Creek*. *Comedy Studies*, 12(2), 215–26.

Chozick, A. (2011, June 10). A New Generation of TV Wimps. *Wall Street Journal*.

Christie, A. (1920). *Elements of situation comedy*. Los Angeles: Palmer Photoplay.

Collier, E. (1973, June 17). Sanford and son is white to the core. *The New York Times*. https://www.nytimes.com/1973/06/17/archives/sanford-and-son-is-white-to-the-core-eugenia-collier-is-coeditor.html

Collins, R. L., Elliott, M. N., Berry, S. H., Kanouse, D. E., & Hunter, S. B. (2003). Entertainment television as a healthy sex educator: The impact of condom-efficacy information in an episode of Friends. *Pediatrics*, 112(5), 1115–1121.

Cooke-Jackson, A., & Hansen, E. K. (2008). Appalachian culture and reality TV: The ethical dilemma of stereotyping others. *Journal of Mass Media Ethics*, 23(3), 183–200.

Cooks, L. M., & Orbe, M. P. (1993). Beyond the satire: Selective exposure and selective perception in *In Living Color*. *Howard Journal of Communications*, 4(3), 217–33.

Cooper, E. (2003). Decoding *Will and Grace*: Mass audience reception of a popular network situation comedy. *Sociological Perspectives*, 46(4): 513–33.

Cosby, W. (1976). An integration of the visual media via *Fat Albert and the Cosby Kids* into the elementary school curriculum as a teaching aid and vehicle to achieve increased learning. Doctoral dissertation. University of Massachusetts at Amherst.

Craig, M. A., Rucker, J. M., & Richeson, J. A. (2018). Racial and political dynamics of an approaching "majority-minority" United States. *ANNALS of the American Academy of Political and Social Science*, 677(1), 204–14.

Crane, D., & Kauffman, M. (Writers), & Bright, K. S. (Director). (2001, October 11). The one where Rachel tells (Season 8, Episode 3) [TV series episode]. In K. S. Bright, D. Crane, & M. Kauffman (Executive Producers), *Friends*. Los Angeles: Warner Bros. Television.

Crotty, M. (1995). Murphy would probably also win the election. *Journal of Popular Culture*, 29(3): 1–15.

Cullen, J. (2020). *Those were the days*. New Brunswick, NJ: Rutgers University Press.

Dalton, M. & Linder, L. (Eds.). (2016). *The sitcom reader*. Albany, NY: SUNY Press.

Dave Thomas Foundation for Adoption (2002). Dave Thomas Foundation for Adoption Poll: January 2002, Question 78 [USHARRIS.02ADOPT.R705CF]. Harris Interactive. Cornell University, Ithaca, NY: Roper Center for Public Opinion Research.

BIBLIOGRAPHY 283

David, L. (Writer). (1995). The Soup Nazi [TV series episode]. In David (Producer), *Seinfeld*. Los Angeles: Castle Rock Entertainment.

Davis, J. M. (2014). From the romance lands: Farce as life-blood of the theatre. In Zenia S. Da Silva & Gregory M. Pell (Eds.), *At Whom Are We Laughing? Humor in Romance Language Literatures* (pp. 3–18). Newcastle, UK: Cambridge Scholars.

Derrida, Js. (1998). *Of grammatology*. Baltimore, MD: Johns Hopkins University Press.

Dillard, J. P., & Shen, L. (2005). On the nature of reactance and its role in persuasive health communication. *Communication Monographs, 72*(2), 144–68.

Douglas, W., & Olson, B. M. (1995). Beyond family structure: The family in domestic comedy. *Journal of Broadcasting & Electronic Media, 39*(2), 236–61.

Dow, B. (1996). *Prime-time feminism*. Philadelphia: University of Pennsylvania Press.

Doye, D., & Brorsen, B. W. (2011). Pasture land values: A "Green Acres" effect? *Choices, 26*(2). https://www.choicesmagazine.org/UserFiles/file/cmsarticle_25.pdf

Duncan, O. (1969). *Towards social reporting: Next steps*. New York: Russell Sage Foundation.

Eco, U. (1979). *A theory of semiotics*. Bloomington: Indiana University Press.

Engels, F. (2021). *The origin of the family, private property and the state*. London: Verso.

Engels, K. S., & Richards, T. (Eds.). (2020). *The Good Place and philosophy: Everything is forking fine!* New York: Wiley-Blackwell.

Falbo, T., & Polit, D. F. (1986). Quantitative review of the only child literature: Research evidence and theory development. *Psychological Bulletin, 100*(2), 176.

Fast, E., Chen, B., & Bernstein, M. S. (2016). Empath: Understanding topic signals in large-scale text. Proceedings of the 2016 CHI conference on human factors in computing systems.

Ferguson, M. & Ford, T. (2008). Disparagement humor: A theoretical and empirical review of psychoanalytic, superiority, and social identity theories. *Humor, 21*(3): 283–312.

Flesch, R. (1948). A new readability yardstick. *Journal of Applied Psychology, 32*(3), 221.

Forbes, K. (1943). *Mama's Bank Account*. New York: Harcourt, Brace.

Frazer, J. M., & Frazer, T. C. (1993). *Father Knows Best* and *The Cosby Show*: Nostalgia and the sitcom tradition. *Journal of Popular Culture, 27*, 163–172.

Freedman, C. (1990). History, fiction, film, television, myth: The Ideology of *M*A*S*H*. *The Southern Review, 26*(1), 89.

Freud, S. (1905). *Jokes and their relation to the unconscious*. New York: Norton.

Fry, R. & Parker, K. (2021, October 5). *Rising share of U.S. adults are living without a spouse or partner*. Pew Research Center's Social & Demographic Trends Project.

https://www.pewresearch.org/social-trends/2021/10/05/rising-share-of-u-s
-adults-are-living-without-a-spouse-or-partner/

Fuller-Seeley, K. H. (2015). Becoming Benny: The evolution of Jack Benny's character comedy from vaudeville to radio. *Studies in American Humor, 1*(2), 163–91.

Gates, H. (1989, November 12). TV's Black world turns. *New York Times.*

Generic Radio Workshop. (n.d.). *The Jack Benny Show: The Women.* https://www
.genericradio.com/show/9713A8ZSVLW

Genzlinger, N. (2020, October 15). Bob Shanks dead. *New York Times.*

George Gerbner Archive. (n.d.). *The George Gerbner archive.* The Annenberg School for Communication. https://web.asc.upenn.edu/gerbner/archive.aspx?sectionID=1

Gerbner, G. (n.d.). *Casting and fate: Women and minorities on television drama, game shows, and news.* The Annenberg School for Communication. https://web.asc.upenn.edu/gerbner/Asset.aspx?assetID=1074

Gerbner, G. (1958). On content analysis and critical research in mass communication. *AV Communication Review, 6,* 85–108.

Gerbner, G. (1969). Toward 'cultural indicators': The analysis of mass mediated message systems. In G. Gerbner, O. R. Holsti, K. Krippendorf, W. J. Paisley, & P. Stone (Eds.), *The Analysis of Communication Content: Developments in Scientific Theories and Computer Techniques* (pp. 123–132). New York: John Wiley & Sons.

Gerbner, G. (1970). Cultural indicators: The case of violence in television drama. *Annals of the American Academy of Political and Social Science, 388*(1): 69–81.

Gerbner, G. (1973). Cultural indicators: The third voice. In G. Gerbner, L. P. Gross, & W. H. Melody (Eds.), *Communications technology and social policy* (pp. 555–73). New York: John Wiley & Sons.

Gerbner, G. (1977). Television: The new state religion? *ETC: A Review of General Semantics, 34*(2): 145–50.

Gerbner, G. (1987). Television's populist brew: The three Bs. *Et cetera, 44*(1), 3.

Gerbner, G. (1998). Cultivation analysis: An overview. *Mass Communication and Society, 1*(3–4), 175–94.

Gerbner, G., & Gross, L. (1976). Living with television: The violence profile. *Journal of Communication, 26*(2), 172–99.

Gerbner, G., Gross, L., Morgan, M., & Signorielli, N. (1980). The 'mainstreaming' of America: Violence Profile No. 11. *Journal of Communication, 30,* 10–29.

Gerbner, G., Gross, L., Morgan, M., & Signorielli, N. (1980a). Aging with television: images on television drama and conceptions of social reality. *Journal of Communication, 30*(1), 37–47.

Gerbner, G., Gross, L., Morgan, M., & Signorielli, N. (1982). Charting the mainstream: Television's contributions to political orientations. *Journal of Communication, 32*(2), 100–27.

Gerbner, G., Gross, L., Morgan, M., & Signorielli, N. (1994). Living with television: The dynamics of the cultivation process. In J. Bryant and D. Zillmann (Eds.), *Media effects. Advances in theory and research* (pp. 7–24). Hillsdale, NJ: Erlbaum.

Gillota, D. (2010). Negotiating Jewishness: *Curb Your Enthusiasm* and the *schlemiel* tradition. *Journal of Popular Film & Television, 38*(4), 152–61.

GLAAD. (2021). *Where we are on TV report—2021.* https://www.glaad.org/whereweareontv21

Gladden, J. (1976). Archie Bunker meets Mr. Spoopendyke. *Journal of Popular Culture, 10*(1): 167–80.

Glennon. L., & Butsch. R. (1982). The family as portrayed on television. In D. Pearl, L. Bouthilet, & J. Lazar (Eds.). *Television and behavior: Ten years of scientific progress and implications for the eighties* (Vol. 1). Washington, DC: US Department of Health and Human Services, Public Health Service, Alcohol, Drug Abuse, and Mental Health Administration, National Institute of Mental Health.

Goldman, R. (1982). Hegemony and managed critique in prime-time television: A critical reading of *Mork and Mindy. Theory and Society, 11*(3), 363–88.

Goostree, L. (1988). *The Monkees* and the deconstruction of television realism. *Journal of Popular Film and Television, 16*(2), 50–58.

Gouldner, A. W. (1979). *The future of intellectuals and the rise of a new class.* New York: Seabury Press.

Gouldner, A. W. (2019). *The future of intellectuals and the rise of the new class.* New York: Seabury.

Gray, H. (1986). Television and the new Black man: Black male images in prime-time situation comedy. *Media, Culture & Society, 8*(2), 223–42.

Gray, J. & Lotz, A. (2019). *Television studies.* Cambridge, UK: Polity.

Gray, T. (2021, January 12). Looking back on the legacy of *All in the Family* 50 years later. *Variety.* https://variety.com/2021/tv/spotlight/all-in-the-family-50-year-anniversary-1234878168

Green, M. J., Sonn, C. C., & Matsebula, J. (2007). Reviewing whiteness: Theory, research, and possibilities. *South African Journal of Psychology, 37*(3), 389–419.

Grice, H. P. (1975). Logic and conversation. In P. Cole & J. Morgan (Eds.), *Speech Acts* (pp. 41–58). New York: Academic Press.

Gross, L. (1984). The cultivation of intolerance: Television, blacks, and gays. In G. Melischeck, K. E. Rosengren, and J. Strappers (Eds.), *Cultural indicators: An international symposium* (pp. 345–63). Vienna: Verlag der Österreichischen Akademie der Wissenschaften.

Gross, L. (2001). *Up from invisibility: Lesbians, gay men, and the media in America.* New York: Columbia University Press.

Gruenberg, S. (1955). The challenge of the new suburbs. *Marriage and Family Living*, 17(2): 133–37.

Gruner, C. (1997). *The game of humor: A comprehensive theory of why we laugh*. New Brunswick, NJ: Transaction.

Harris, H. (1975). Mark Twain's Response to the Native American. *American Literature*, 46(4), 495–505.

Hart, R. P. (2022). Why Trump lost and how? A rhetorical explanation. *American Behavioral Scientist*, 66(1), 7–27.

Hatfield, E. F. (2010). "What it means to be a man": Examining hegemonic masculinity in *Two and a Half Men*. *Communication, Culture & Critique*, 3(4), 526–48.

Hein, J. (2003). *Jump the shark*. New York: Plume.

Hemingway, E. (1952). *The old man and the sea*. New York: Scribner.

Henderson, F. D. (2011). The culture behind closed doors: Issues of gender and race in the writers' room. *Cinema Journal*, 50(2), 145–52.

Hermann, E., Morgan, M., & Shanahan, J. (2021). Television, continuity, and change: A meta-analysis of five decades of cultivation research. *Journal of Communication*, 71(4), 515–44.

Hermann, E., Morgan, M., & Shanahan, J. (2022). Social change, cultural resistance: A meta-analysis of the influence of television viewing on gender role attitudes. *Communication Monographs*, 89(3), 396–418.

Hilmes, M. (1993). Invisible men: *Amos 'n' Andy* and the roots of broadcast discourse. *Critical Studies in Media Communication*, 10(4), 301–21.

Hilmes, M. (2013). *Only connect: A cultural history of broadcasting in the United States*. Boston: Cengage Learning.

Hitchens, C. (2007, January). Why women aren't funny. *Vanity Fair*. https://www.vanityfair.com/culture/2007/01/hitchens200701

Hirsch, P. (1980). The 'scary world' of the nonviewer and other anomalies: A reanalysis of Gerbner et al.'s findings of cultivation analysis. *Communication Research*, 7(4), 403–56.

Holbert, R. L., Shah, D. V., & Kwak, N. (2003). Political implications of prime-time drama and sitcom use: Genres of representation and opinions concerning women's rights. *Journal of Communication*, 53(1), 45–60.

Howley, P., Neill, S. O., & Atkinson, R. (2015). Who needs good neighbors? *Environment and Planning A: Economy and Space*, 47(4), 939–56.

Hundley, H. L. (1995). The naturalization of beer in *Cheers*. *Journal of Broadcasting & Electronic Media*, 39(3), 350–59.

Hunt, D. & Ramon, A. (2022). *Hollywood Diversity Report*. Los Angeles: UCLA.

IMDb. (n.d.). *Betty and the jet pilot*. https://www.imdb.com/title/tt1482570/

Innis, L., & Feagin, J. (2002). *The Cosby Show*: The view from the Black middle class. In R. Coleman (Ed.), *Say it loud: African-American audiences, media, and identity* (pp. 187–204). New York: Routledge.

Iyengar, S., Lelkes, Y., Levendusky, M., Malhotra, N., & Westwood, S. J. (2019). The origins and consequences of affective polarization in the United States. *Annual Review of Political Science, 22*(1), 129–46.

Jacewicz, E., Fox, R. A., O'Neill, C., & Salmons, J. (2009). Articulation rate across dialect, age, and gender. *Language Variation and Change, 21*(2), 233–56.

Javna, J. (1988). *The critics' choice: The best of TV sitcoms.* New York: Harmony.

Jhally, S. & Lewis, J. (1992). *Enlightened racism:* The Cosby Show, *audiences, and the myth of the American dream.* Boulder, CO: Westview.

Johnson, W. (1944). Studies in language behavior: I. A program of research. *Psychological Monographs, 56,* 1–15.

Jones, R. A., (1986). *Emile Durkheim: An introduction to four major works.* Beverly Hills, CA: Sage.

Jowett, G. S., Jarvie, I. C., & Fuller, K. H. (1996). *Children and the movies: Media influence and the Payne Fund controversy.* Cambridge, UK: Cambridge University Press.

Kahneman, D., Diener, E., & Schwarz, N. (Eds.). (1999). *Well-being: The foundations of hedonic psychology.* New York: Russell Sage Foundation.

Karp, J. (2018). The roots of Jewish concentration in the American popular music business, 1890–1945. In S. Ross et al. (Eds.), *Doing Business in America: A Jewish History* (Vol. 16, pp. 123–43). Lafayette, IN: Purdue University Press.

Katz, E. (1998). Broadcasting holidays. *Sociological Inquiry, 68*(2), 230–41.

Katz, J. (1999). Death of a sitcom. *Entertainment Weekly.* Retrieved from https://ew.com/article/1999/04/16/death-sitcom

Katz, E., & Katz, R. (2016). Revisiting the origin of the administrative versus critical research debate. *Journal of Information Policy, 6,* 4–12.

Kennedy, G. (2014). *An introduction to corpus linguistics.* London: Routledge.

Kenton, G. (2016). The 1960s magicoms. In Dalton, M. & Linder, L. (Eds.), *The sitcom reader* (pp. 75–90). Albany, NY: SUNY Press.

Kim, J. L., Lynn Sorsoli, C., Collins, K., Zylbergold, B. A., Schooler, D., & Tolman, D. L. (2007). From sex to sexuality: Exposing the heterosexual script on prime-time network television. *Journal of Sex Research, 44*(2), 145–57.

King, L. N. (2017). "A Show about Language": A Linguistic Investigation of the Creation of Humor in *Seinfeld.* Master's thesis: East Tennessee State University.

Kins, E., & Beyers, W. (2010). Failure to launch, failure to achieve criteria for adulthood? *Journal of Adolescent Research, 25*(5), 743–77.

Koblin, J. (2018, May 19). 'Roseanne' canceled by ABC after star's racist tweet. *The New York Times.* https://www.nytimes.com/2018/05/29/business/media/roseanne-barr-offensive-tweets.html

Konstan, D. (1988). The premises of comedy: Function of dramatic space in an ancient and modern form. *Journal of Popular Film and Television, 15*(4), 180–90.

Krippendorff, K. (2018). *Content analysis: An introduction to its methodology.* Beverly Hills, CA: Sage.

Kwak, H., Zinkhan, G. M., & Dominick, J. R. (2002). The moderating role of gender and compulsive buying tendencies in the cultivation effects of TV shows and TV advertising: A cross cultural study between the United States and South Korea. *Media Psychology, 4*(1): 77–111.

Kypker, N. (2012). One right-on sister: Gender politics in *Maude*. *Comedy Studies, 3*(2), 139–49.

Kypker, N. (2017), Laughter and ideology: A critical discourse of changing representations of rape in Norman Lear's sitcoms. *Comedy Studies, 8*(1), 13–21.

Land, K. (1983). Social indicators. *Annual Review of Sociology, 9*, 1–26.

Land, K. (2000). Social indicators. In E. Borgatta (Ed.), *Encyclopedia of Sociology*, Vol. 4 (pp. 2682–89). MacMillian: New York.

Landay, L. (2016). *I Love Lucy*. In M. Dalton & L. Linder (Eds.), *The sitcom reader* (pp. 31–41). Albany, NY: SUNY Press.

Lang, A. (2013). Discipline in crisis? The shifting paradigm of mass communication research. *Communication Theory, 23*(1), 10–24.

Lantz, H. R., Schmitt, R., Britton, M., & Snyder, E. C. (1968). Pre-industrial patterns in the colonial family in America: A content analysis of colonial magazines. *American Sociological Review, 33*(3), 413–26.

Larson, M. (1991). Sibling interactions in 1950s versus 1980s sitcoms: A comparison. *Journalism Quarterly, 68*(3), 381–87.

Lasch, C. (1977). *Haven in a heartless world*. New York: Basic.

Lasch, C. (1983). Archie Bunker and the liberal mind. In L. Brown (Ed.), *Fast forward: Television and American Society*, 165–170. Kansas City, MO: Andrews & McMeel.

Lasch, C. (1995). *Revolt of the elites*. New York: W. W. Norton.

Lasswell, H. D. (1948). The structure and function of communication in society. In L. Bryson (Ed.), *The communication of ideas* (pp. 37–51). New York: Harper and Row.

Lazer, D., et al. (2018). The science of fake news. *Science, 359*(6380), 1094–96.

Levine, E. (2006). *Wallowing in sex: The new sexual culture of 1970s American Television*. Durham, NC: Duke University Press.

Lewis, S. (1922). *Babbitt*. New York: Harcourt and Brace.

Li, R., & Orthia, L. A. (2016). Communicating the nature of science through *The Big Bang Theory*: Evidence from a focus group study. *International Journal of Science Education, Part B, 6*(2), 115–36.

Lipsitz, G. (2003). The changing face of a woman's narrative. In J. Morreale (Ed.), *Critiquing the sitcom* (pp. 7–24). Syracuse, NY: Syracuse University Press.

Livingston, G. (2018, September 24). *Stay-at-home moms and dads account for about one-in-five U.S. parents*. Pew Research Center. https://www.pewresearch.org

/fact-tank/2018/09/24/stay-at-home-moms-and-dads-account-for-about-one
-in-five-u-s-parents/

Lowery, S. & De Fleur, M.(1988). *Milestones in mass communication research*. New York: Longman.

Lu, Y., Amory, K., & Shi, L. (2021). Social change and gendered reaction to the threat of victimization, 1973–2016: An age-period-cohort analysis. *Sociological Quarterly*, 63(4): 1–27.

Luckie, M. (2015, October 26). I went to an HBCU because of *A Different World*. *BuzzFeed News*. https://www.buzzfeednews.com/article/marksluckie/i-went -to-an-hbcu-because-of-a-different-world

Lynd, R., & Lynd, H. (1929). *Middletown: A study in contemporary American culture*. New York: Harcourt and Brace.

Macrae, D. (1985). *Policy indicators: Links between social sciences and public policy*. Chapel Hill: University of North Carolina Press.

Mara, J., Davis, L., & Schmidt, S. (2018). Social animal house: The economic and academic consequences of fraternity membership. *Contemporary Economic Policy*, 36(2), 263–76.

Marc, D. (1997). *Comic visions*. Malden, MA: Blackwell.

Markert, J. (2004). *The George Lopez Show*: The Same Old Hispano? *Bilingual Review/La Revista Bilingüe*, 28(2): 148–65.

Mastro, D. (2009). Effects of racial and ethnic stereotyping. In Bryant, J. & Oliver, M. (Eds.), *Media Effects* (pp. 341–57). London: Routledge.

Mastro, D. E., & Tropp, L. R. (2004). The effects of interracial contact, attitudes, and stereotypical portrayals on evaluations of Black television sitcom characters. *Communication Research Reports*, 21(2), 119–129.

Matabane, P. W., & Merritt, B. D. (2014). Media use, gender, and African American college attendance: The *Cosby* effect. *Howard Journal of Communications*, 25(4), 452–71.

McCann, A. (2020). "Bewitched:" Between housewifery and emancipation. *Studia Universitatis Babeș-Bolyai-Dramatica*, 65(1), 245–59.

McCrohan, D. (1987). *Archie & Edith & Mike & Gloria*. New York: Workman.

McIntosh, W. D., Schwegler, A. F., & Terry-Murray, R. M. (2000). Threat and television viewing in the United States, 1960–1990. *Media Psychology*, 2(1), 35–46.

McLeland, S. (2016). "Roseanne, *Roseanne*, reality and domestic Comedy." In Dalton, M. & Linder, L. (Eds.), *The sitcom reader*. Albany, NY: SUNY Press.

Means Coleman, R. (1998). *African American viewers and the Black situation comedy*. New York: Garland.

Media Education Foundation. (n.d.a). *Mean world syndrome discussion guide*. https://www.mediaed.org/discussion-guides/Mean-World-Syndrome -Discussion-Guide.pdf

Media Education Foundation. (n.d.b). *Mean world syndrome: Transcript.* https://www.mediaed.org/transcripts/Mean-World-Syndrome-Transcript.pdf

Mitz, R. (1980). *The great TV sitcom book.* New York: R. Marek.

Monod, D. (2020). *Vaudeville and the making of modern entertainment.* Chapel Hill: University of North Carolina Press.

Moore, M. (1992). The family as portrayed on prime-time television, 1947–1990: Structure and characteristics. *Sex Roles, 26*(1), 41–61.

Morgan, M. (1983). Symbolic victimization and real world fear. *Human Communication Research, 9,* 146–57.

Morgan, M. (1984). Heavy television viewing and perceived quality of life. *Journalism Quarterly, 61,* 499–504, 740.

Morgan, M. (2012). *George Gerbner: A critical introduction to media and communication theory.* New York: Peter Lang.

Morgan, M., Leggett, S., & Shanahan, J. (1999). Television and family values: Was Dan Quayle right? *Mass Communication and Society, 2*(1–2), 47–63.

Morgan, M., & Shanahan, J. (1996). Two decades of cultivation research: An appraisal and a meta-analysis. In B. Burleson (Ed.), *Communication yearbook 20* (pp. 1–45). Thousand Oaks, CA: Sage.

Morgan, M., Shanahan, J., & Signorielli, N. (2015). Yesterday's new cultivation, tomorrow. *Mass Communication and Society, 18*(5), 674–99.

Morreale, J. (Ed.). (2003). *Critiquing the sitcom: A reader.* Syracuse, NY: Syracuse University Press.

Morreale, J. (2012). *The Donna Reed Show.* Detroit, MI: Wayne State University Press.

Moyer-Gusé, E. (2008). Toward a theory of entertainment persuasion: Explaining the persuasive effects of entertainment-education messages. *Communication Theory, 18*(3), 407–25.

Moyer-Gusé, E., Mahood, C., & Brookes, S. (2011). Entertainment-education in the context of humor: Effects on safer sex intentions and risk perceptions. *Health Communication, 26*(8), 765–74.

Neale, S. & Krutnik, F. (2018). Popular film and television comedy. In Marx, N. & Sienkiewicz, M. (Eds.) *The comedy studies reader.* Austin, TX: University of Texas at Austin.

Newcomb, H. (1976). *Television: The critical view.* New York: Oxford University Press.

Newcomb, H. (1978). Assessing the Violence Profile of Gerbner and Gross: A humanistic critique and suggestions. *Communication Research, 5*(3), 264–82.

Newcomb, H. (1979). Appalachia on television: Region as symbol in American popular culture. *Appalachian Journal, 7*(1/2), 155–64.

Newman, E. L. (2016). From *That Girl* to *Girls*: Rethinking Anne Marie/Marlo Thomas as a feminist icon. *Journal of American Culture, 39*(3), 285–97.

Nisbet, E. & Myers, T. (2012). Cultivating tolerance of homosexuals. In Morgan, M., Shanahan, J. & Signorielli, N. (Eds). *Living with television now*. New York: Peter Lang.

Nutile, M. (2018). The gang beats the odds: *It's Always Sunny in Philadelphia's* consistent popularity. *Cinesthesia, 8*(1), 4.

NYU Furman Center. (n.d.). *Upper West Side neighborhood profile.* https://furmancenter.org/neighborhoods/view/upper-west-side

Ogburn, W. (1922). *Social Change.* New York: B. W. Huebsch.

Ogburn, W. F. (1933). *Recent social trends in the United States. Report of the President's Research Committee on Social Trends, 2,* 10–18.

Olson, B., & Douglas, W. (1997). The family on television: Evaluation of gender roles in situation comedy. *Sex Roles, 36*(5), 409–27.

Oppenheimer, J. (1996). *Laughs, luck—and Lucy: How I came to create the most popular sitcom of all time.* Syracuse, NY: Syracuse University Press.

Oxford English Dictionary. (n.d.). *Oxford English corpus: Lexicography and beyond.* University of Oxford. https://digital.humanities.ox.ac.uk/oxford-english-corpus-lexicography-and-beyond

Paolillo, J. C. (2019, July). Against 'sentiment'. In Proceedings of the 10th International Conference on Social Media and Society (pp. 41–48).

Parsons, T. (1955). The American family: Its relations to personality and to the social structure. *Family, socialization and interaction process.* New York: Free Press.

Patterson, E. (2016). The *Golden Girls* Live: Residual television texts, participatory culture, and queering TV heritage through drag. *Feminist Media Studies, 16*(5), 838–51.

Pew Research Center. (2021, November 9). *The progressive left: A political and demographic profile.* https://www.pewresearch.org/politics/2021/11/09/progressive-left

Polsby, D. D. (1994). Ozzie and Harriet had it right. *Harvard Journal of Law & Public Policy, 18,* 531.

Proust, M. (1928). *Swann's way.* New York: Modern Library.

Putnam, R. D. (2000). *Bowling alone: The collapse and revival of American community.* New York: Simon and Schuster.

Quail, C. (2011). Nerds, geeks, and the hip/square dialectic in contemporary television. *Television & New Media, 12*(5), 460–82.

Quayle, D. (1992). *Remarks on family values and Murphy Brown.* Voices of Democracy. https://voicesofdemocracy.umd.edu/quayle-murphy-brown-speech-text-2

Railey, J. (2022). *Andy Griffith's Manteo.* Charleston, SC: History Press.

Raine, A. J. (2011). Lifestyles of the not so rich and famous: Ideological shifts in popular culture, Reagan-era sitcoms and portrayals of the working class. *McNair Scholars Research Journal, 7*(1), 13.

Rajan, B. (2021). Popular culture and the (mis)representation of Asperger's: A study on the sitcoms *Community* and *The Big Bang Theory*. In M. Johnson & C.

Olson (Eds.), *Normalizing Mental Illness and Neurodiversity in Entertainment Media* (pp. 66–82). London: Routledge.

Redbook (1994). Redbook Poll: August 1994, Question 3 [USEDK.94AUG.R03]. EDK Associates. Cornell University, Ithaca, NY: Roper Center for Public Opinion Research.

Reeves, R. V. (2022). *Of boys and men: Why the modern male is struggling, why it matters, and what to do about it*. Washington, DC: Brookings Institution.

Reich, R. B. (1992). *The work of nations: Preparing ourselves for 21st century capitalism*. New York: Vintage.

Rhym, D. (1998). An analysis of George Jefferson and Heathcliff Huxtable. *Journal of African American Men, 3*(3): 57–67.

Richards, B. (1987). Type/token ratios: What do they really tell us? *Journal of Child Language, 14*(2), 201–09.

Rosa, A. F., & Eschholz, P. A. (1972). Bunkerisms: Archie's suppository remarks in *All in the Family. Journal of Popular Culture, 6*(2), 271.

Rosenkoetter, L. (1999). The television situation comedy and children's prosocial behavior. *Journal of Applied Social Psychology, 29*(5): 979–93.

Rosenthal, P. (2018, May 3). Bob Newhart looks back on his second sitcom 40 years later. *Chicago Tribune*. https://www.chicagotribune.com/entertainment/tv/ct-bob-newhart-sitcom-40th-anniversary-20180503-story.html

Schaffer, G. (2010). *Till Death Us Do Part* and the BBC: Racial politics and the British working classes 1965–75. *Journal of Contemporary History, 45*(2), 454–77.

Scharrer, E. (2001). From wise to foolish: The portrayal of the sitcom father, 1950s-1990s. *Journal of Broadcasting & Electronic Media, 45*(1), 23–40.

Schneider, M. (2022). Peak TV Tally: According to FX Research, A Record 559 Original Scripted Series Aired in 2021. *Variety*. Retrieved from: https://variety.com/2022/tv/news/original-tv-series-tally-2021-1235154979/

Schiappa, E., Gregg, P. B., & Hewes, D. E. (2006). Can one TV show make a difference? *Will & Grace* and the parasocial contact hypothesis. *Journal of Homosexuality, 51*(4), 15–37.

Schulman, N. M. (1992). Laughing across the color barrier: *In Living Color. Journal of Popular Film and Television, 20*(1), 1–7.

Seinfeld. (1989). The pilot (Season 1, Episode 1) [TV series episode]. In J. David (Producer), *Seinfeld*. Castle Rock Entertainment.

Seinfeld. (1992). The keys (Season 3, Episode 23) [TV series episode]. In J. David (Producer), *Seinfeld*. Castle Rock Entertainment.

Seinfeld, J. (1993). *SeinLanguage*. New York: Bantam.

Seinfeld. (1995). The hot tub (Season 7, Episode 5) [TV series episode]. In J. David (Producer), *Seinfeld*. Castle Rock Entertainment.

Seinfeld. (1996). The rye (Season 7, Episode 7) [TV series episode]. In J. David (Producer), *Seinfeld*. Castle Rock Entertainment.

Shales, T. (1977, December 7). A programmer's maxims. *Washington Post*.

Shanahan, J. (1991). *Argentine television and the problem of democracy*. Dissertation: University of Massachusetts Amherst.

Shanahan, J. (2004). A return to cultural indicators. *Communications*, 29(3), 277–94.

Shanahan, J. (2021). *Media effects*. Cambridge, UK: Polity.

Shanahan, J. & Jones, V. (1999). Cultivation and social control. In D. Demers & K. Viswanath (Eds.), *Mass media, social control, and social change* (pp. 1–50). Ames: Iowa State University Press.

Shanahan, J., & Morgan, M. (1999) *Television and its viewers: Cultivation theory and research*. Cambridge, UK: Cambridge University Press.

Shanahan, J., Nisbet, E. C., Diels, J., Hardy, B., & Besley, J. (2005). Cultural Indicators: Integrating measures of meaning with economic and social indicators. New York: International Communication Association.

Shankman, A. (1978). Black pride and protest: The *Amos 'n' Andy* crusade of 1931. *Journal of Popular Culture*, 12(2), 236.

Shapiro, M. & Jicha, T. (2015). *The top 100 American situation comedies: An objective ranking*. New York: McFarland.

Sheehan, S. T. (2010). "Pow! Right in the Kisser": Ralph Kramden, Jackie Gleason, and the emergence of the frustrated working-class man. *Journal of Popular Culture*, 43(3), 564–82.

Shorter, E. (1975). *The making of the modern family*. New York: Basic.

Showalter, D. (1975). Archie Bunker, Lenny Bruce, and Ben Cartwright: Taboo-breaking and character identification in *All in the Family*. *Journal of Popular Culture*, 9(3), 618.

Sienkiewicz, M. & Marx, N. (2022). *That's not funny*. Oakland: University of California Press.

Signorielli, N. (1989). Television and conceptions about sex roles: Maintaining conventionality and the status quo. *Sex Roles*, 21(5–6), 341–60.

Signorielli, N. (1990). Television's mean and dangerous world: A continuation of the cultural indicators perspective. In N. Signorielli & M. Morgan (Eds.), *Cultivation analysis: New directions in media effects research* (pp. 85–106). Newbury Park: Sage.

Signorielli, N. (2009). Race and sex in prime time: A look at occupations and occupational prestige. *Mass Communication and Society*, 12(3), 332–52.

Signorielli, N., Gross, L., & Morgan, M. (1982). Violence in television programs: Ten years later. In D. Pearl, L. Bouthilet, & J. Lazar (Eds.), *Television and behav-*

ior: Ten years of scientific progress and implications for the 80's, Volume II (pp. 158–73). Rockville, MD: NIMH.

Signorielli, N., Morgan, M., & Shanahan, J. (2019). The violence profile: Five decades of cultural indicators research. *Mass Communication and Society, 22*(1), 1–28.

Smith, D. S. (1993). The curious history of theorizing about the history of the Western nuclear family. *Social Science History, 17*(3), 325–53.

Smith, S. L., & Granados, A. D. (2009). Content patterns and effects surrounding sex-role stereotyping on television and film. In Bryant, J. & Oliver, M. (Eds.), *Media Effects* (pp. 358–77). London: Routledge.

Smith, T. W. (1990). Liberal and conservative trends in the United States since World War II. *Public Opinion Quarterly, 54*(4), 479–507.

Snow, C. P. (1959). *The two cultures*. London: Cambridge University Press.

Spigel, L. (1992). *Make room for TV*. Chicago: University of Chicago Press.

Statista. (n.d.). *Average size of a family in the U.S.* Statista. https://www.statista .com/statistics/183657/average-size-of-a-family-in-the-us

Sterritt, D. (2009). *The Honeymooners*. Detroit, MI: Wayne State University Press.

Stowe, H. B. (1852). *Uncle Tom's cabin*. London: J. Cassell.

Surlin, S. & Bowden, E. (1976). *The psychological effect of television characters: The case of Archie Bunker and authoritarian viewers*. ERIC Document ED150612.

Sussman, M. B. (1958). The isolated nuclear family: Fact or fiction. *Social Problems, 6*(4): 333.

Tagliamonte, S., & Roberts, C. (2005). So weird; so cool; so innovative: The use of intensifiers in the television series *Friends*. *American Speech, 80*(3), 280–300.

Tahmahkera, D. (2008). Custer's last sitcom: decolonized viewing of the sitcom's "Indian." *American Indian Quarterly, 32*(3), 324–51.

Tajfel, H., & Turner, J. C. (2004). The social identity theory of intergroup behavior. In J. T. Jost & J. Sidanius (Eds.), *Political Psychology: Key Readings* (pp. 276–93). New York: Psychology Press.

Tan, A., Fujioka, Y., & Lucht, N. (1997). Native American stereotypes, TV portrayals, and personal contact. *Journalism & Mass Communication Quarterly, 74*(2), 265–84.

Thomas, D. (1991). *Make room for Danny*. New York: Putnam.

Thomas, S., & Callahan, B. P. (1982). Allocating happiness: TV families and social class. *Journal of Communication, 32*(3), 184–90.

Tidhar, C. E., & Peri, S. (1990). Deceitful behaviour in situation comedy: Effects on children's perception of social reality. *Journal of Educational Television, 16*(2), 61–76.

Todd, A. M. (2011). Saying goodbye to *Friends*: Situation comedy as lived experience. *Journal of Popular Culture, 44*(4), 855.

Tönnies, F. (1887). *Gemeinschaft und Gesellschaft: Abhandlung des Communismus und des Socialismus als empirischer Culturformen*. Leipzig: Fues.

BIBLIOGRAPHY

Tucker, L. (1997). Was the revolution televised?: Professional criticism about "the Cosby show"; and the essentialization of Black cultural expression. *Journal of Broadcasting & Electronic Media, 41*(1), 90–108.

Twenge, J. M., VanLandingham, H., & Keith Campbell, W. (2017). The seven words you can never say on television: Increases in the use of swear words in American books, 1950–2008. *Sage Open, 7*(3).

UNESCO Institute for Statistics. (2024). Initial launch of the SDG Indicator 11.4.1 Survey on cultural and natural heritage expenditure. http://uis.unesco.org/en/news/initial-launch-sdg-indicator-11-4-1-survey-cultural-and-natural-heritage-expenditure

U.S. Census Bureau. (n.d.). Households and persons per household. https://www.census.gov/quickfacts/fact/note/US/HSD410219

U.S. Census Bureau. (2016, June 30). *America's age profile told through population pyramids.* Random Samplings. https://www.census.gov/newsroom/blogs/random-samplings/2016/06/americas-age-profile-told-through-population-pyramids.html

U.S. Census Bureau. (2022, May 25). 20.6 Million People in the U.S. Identify as Asian, Native Hawaiian or Pacific Islander. https://www.census.gov/library/stories/2022/05/aanhpi-population-diverse-geographically-dispersed.html

van Oosten, J. M., Peter, J., & Vandenbosch, L. (2017). Adolescents' sexual media use and willingness to engage in casual sex: Differential relations and underlying processes. *Human Communication Research, 43*(1), 127–47.

Vargo, C. J., Guo, L., & Amazeen, M. A. (2018). The agenda-setting power of fake news: A big data analysis of the online media landscape from 2014 to 2016. *New Media & Society, 20*(5), 2028–49.

Vazquez, L. (2014). Cultural Indicators. In Michalos, A.C. (Ed.), *Encyclopedia of Quality of Life and Well-Being Research.* Dordrecht: Springer. https://doi.org/10.1007/978-94-007-0753-5_644

Vidmar, N., & Rokeach, M. (1974). Archie Bunker's bigotry: A study in selective perception and exposure. *Journal of Communication, 24*(1), 36–47.

Wallace, B. C. (2015). Computational irony: A survey and new perspectives. *Artificial Intelligence Review, 43*(4), 467–83.

Walsh, K. R., Fürsich, E., & Jefferson, B. S. (2008). Beauty and the patriarchal beast: Gender role portrayals in sitcoms featuring mismatched couples. *Journal of Popular Film and Television, 36*(3), 123–32.

Wasylkiw, L., & Currie, M. (2012). The *Animal House* effect: How university-themed comedy films affect students' attitudes. *Social Psychology of Education, 15*(1), 25–40.

Watkins, M. (1994). *On the real side.* Chicago: Lawrence Hill.

Weaver, J., & Wakshlag, J. (1986). Perceived vulnerability to crime, criminal victimization experience, and television viewing. *Journal of Broadcasting & Electronic Media, 30,* 141–58.

Whisnant, D. E. (1973). Ethnicity and the recovery of regional identity in Appalachia: Thoughts upon entering the zone of occult instability. *Soundings, 56*(2), 124–38

Whitaker, M. (2014). Why comedians still think Bill Cosby is a genius. *The Daily Beast.* Retrieved from https://www.thedailybeast.com/why-comedians-still-think-bill-cosby-is-a-genius

White, A. (1985). How green were our acres. *Film Comment, 21*(3): 76–77, 80.

White, B. (2021, April 7). 'The Nanny' is a crucial gay text that must be preserved for future generations. *Decider.* https://decider.com/2021/04/07/the-nanny-on-hbo-max-is-a-crucial-gay-text/

Wieselman, J. (2014). Jerry Seinfeld on diversity in comedy: "Who Cares? Are You Making Us Laugh Or Not?" *Buzzfeed.* https://www.buzzfeed.com/jarettwieselman/jerry-seinfeld-on-diversity-in-comedy-who-cares-are-you-maki#.nfLMLDAm6

Williams, L. (2001). *Playing the race card. Melodramas of Black and white from Uncle Tom to OJ Simpson.* Princeton, NJ: Princeton University Press.

Williams, R. (1954). *Preface to film.* London: Film Drama Limited.

Williams, R. (1973). Base and superstructure in Marxist cultural theory. *New Left Review,* (82)3, 16.

Wilson, B. J., Kunkel, D., Linz, D., Potter, J., Donnerstein, E., Smith, S. L., & Gray, T. (1998). *National Television Violence Study. Vol. 2.*

Wilson, E. O. (1978). *On human nature.* Cambridge, MA: Harvard University Press.

Woods, J. (1995). "Leave It to Beaver Was Not a Documentary": What educators need to know about the American family. *American Secondary Education, 24*(1), 2–8.

Worland, R. & O'Leary, J. (2016). The rural sitcom from *The Real McCoys* to relevance. In Dalton, M. & Linder, L. (Eds.), *The sitcom reader* (pp. 59–74). Albany, NY: SUNY Press.

World Bank. (n.d.). *Fertility rate, total (births per woman).* Gender Data Portal. https://genderdata.worldbank.org/en/indicator/sp-dyn-tfrt-in#data-table-section

Yamane, T., & Nonoyama, H. (1967). Isolation of the nuclear family and kinship organization in Japan: A hypothetical approach to the relationships between the family and society. *Journal of Marriage and the Family, 29*(4): 783–96.

Yang, G., & Ryser, T. A. (2008). Whiting up and Blacking out: White privilege, race, and White chicks. *African American Review, 42*(3/4), 731–46.

Yan, Y., Woo, S. & Shanahan, J. (Forthcoming). Cultural indicators and gender.

YouTube. (n.d.). *Gilligan's Island show creator Sherwood Schwartz* [Video]. https://www.youtube.com/watch?v=yXHotrIbCMo

Zappa, F. (1966). *More trouble every day* [Song]. On *Freak Out!* Santa Monica, CA: Verve Record.

Zillmann, D. (1983). Disparagement humor. In *Handbook of Humor Research: Volume 1: Basic Issues* (pp. 85–107). New York: Springer.

Zook, K. B. (1999). *Color by Fox: The Fox network and the revolution in black television.* Oxford, UK: Oxford University Press.

AUTHORS CITED INDEX

Acham, C., 105–106, 117
Acland, C., 260
Albig, W., 10
Alexander, A., 12
Amazeen, M., 22
Amory, K., 217
Anderson, S., 101
Andrews, T., 255
Armstrong, J., 254
Attalah, P., 53
Audissino, E., 277
Austerlitz, S., 246

Barnouw, E., 42, 45, 48, 102
Barthes, R., 15
Baser, M., 257
Battles, K., 116
Bednarek, M., 273–274
Beeden, A., 276
Bergson, H., 165–166
Berry, D., M., 22
Bettie, J., 264
Beyers, W., 265
Blankenhorn, D., 266
Bodroghkozy, A., 252

Bogle, D., 100, 197
Bor, S., 275
Bowden, E., 104
Brooks, L., 267
Brooks, T., 122, 246
Brorsen, B., 251
Brown, B., 92
Brown, D., 12
Brown, P., 68
Brunsdon, C., 21
Bryant, J., 12
Bryson, L., 19
Buerkel–Rothfuss, N., 115
Bullock, K., 250
Burns, G., 46, 241
Butsch, R., 38, 40, 93

Callahan, B., 94
Cameron, S., 104
Campbell, A., 8
Campbell, W., 27
Carley, M., 7
Carveth, R., 12
Cassidy, D., 254
Chisolm, A., 287

AUTHORS CITED INDEX

Chozik, A., 275
Christie, A., 47
Collier, E., 107
Collins, R., 115
Converse, P., 8
Cooke–Jackson, A., 248
Cooks, L., 112–113
Cooper, E., 116
Craig, M., 218
Crotty, M., 115
Cullen, J., 57, 253
Currie, M., 258–259

Dalton, M., 117
David, L., 160
De Fleur, M., 80
deBruin, J., 276
Derrida, J., 158
Dillard, J., 25
Dominick, J., 12
Douglas, W., 95
Dow, B., 257
Doye, D., 251
Duncan, O., 7

Eco, U., 15
Engels, F., 80
Engels, K., 278

Falbo, T., 82
Fast, E., 181
Ferguson, M., 224
Ford, T., 224
Foster, S., 40
Frazer, J., 109
Frazer, T., 109
Freedman, C., 261
Freud, S., 224
Fujioka, Y., 199

Fuller–Seeley, K., 42, 241
Fürsich, E., 270

Genzlinger, N., 17
Gerbner, G., vii, 5, 11–14, 20–22, 24,
    124, 141, 190, 199, 207, 209–211
Gillotta, D., 269–270
Gladden, J., 42
Glennon, L., 93
Goldman, R., 260
Goostree, L., 249
Gouldner, A., 212
Granados, A., 117
Gray, H., 105
Gray, J., 19, 20, 117
Gray, T., 253
Green, M., 54
Grice, H., 161
Gross, L., 11, 14, 190, 199, 200, 207,
    209, 254
Gruenberg, S., 80
Gruner, C., 224

Harris, H., 224
Hart, R., 23
Hein, J., 256–257
Hemingway, E., 159
Henderson, F., 272–273
Hermann, E., 193, 209
Hilmes, M., 60, 240
Hilton–Morrow, W., 116
Hirsch, P., 20
Hitchens, C., 175
Holbert, L., 116
Howley, P., 274
Hundley, H., 260–261
Hunt, D., 192

Iyengar, S., 214

AUTHORS CITED INDEX

Jacewicz, E., 161
Javna, J., 122
Jefferson, B., 270
Jhally, S., 108, 262
Jicha, T., 242
Johnson, W., 157
Jones, R., 6
Jones, V., 205–206, 209

Kahneman, D., 5
Karp, J., 100
Katz, E., 118, 276
Katz, R., 118
Kennedy, G., 156
Kenton, G., 54
Kim, J., 270–271
King, L., 161
Kins, E., 265
Konstan, D., 255–256
Krippendorf, K., 10
Krutnik, F., 25
Kypker, N., 98–99

Land, K., 7–8
Lang, A., 19
Larson, M., 95
Lasch, C., 79, 90, 104, 212
Lasswell, H., 19
Lazer, D., 22
Levine, E., 258
Lewis, J. 108, 262
Lewis, S., 101
Li, R., 273–274
Linder, L., 117
Lipsitz, G., 239–240
Lotz, A., 19, 20, 117
Lowery, S., 80
Lu, Y., 217
Lucht, N., 199

Lynd, H., 101
Lynd, R., 101

Macrae, D., 7
Mara, J., 258–259
Marc, D., 89, 117, 243
Markert, J., 273
Marsh, E., 122, 246
Marx, N., viii, 61
Mastro, D., 116–117
Matabane, P., 109, 263
McCann, A., 248–249
McCrohan, D., 253
McIntosh, 247–248
McLeland, S., 64–65
Means Coleman, R., 21, 99, 109
Merritt, B., 109, 263
Mitz, R., 122
Monod, D., 38–39
Moore, M., 94
Morgan, M., vii, 5, 11–14, 20, 24,
    114, 115, 193, 198, 207–208, 210
Morreale, J., 117, 245
Moyer-Gusé, E., 25, 116
Myers, T., 200–201

Neale, S., 25
Newcomb, H., 19, 20, 248
Newman, E., 251
Nisbet, E., 200–201
Nonoyama, H., 80
Nutile, M., 274–275

O'Leary, J., 52
Ogburn, W., 7
Olson, B., 95
Oppenheimer, J., 240
Orbe, M., 112
Orthia, L., 273–274

AUTHORS CITED INDEX

Paolillo, J., 22
Parsons, T., 80
Patterson, E., 264
Peter, J., 265
Polit, D., 82
Polsby, D., 244–245
Putnam, R., 274

Quail, C., 266

Railey, J., 247
Raine, A., 262
Rajan, B., 277–278
Ramon, A., 192
Reeves., R., 194
Rhym, D., 259
Richards, B., 156
Richards, T., 278
Richeson, J., 218
Roberts, C., 268
Rokeach, M., 21
Rucker, J., 218
Ryser, T., 268

Schaffer, G., 103
Scharrer, E., 94, 272
Schiappa, E., 271
Seinfeld, J., 163, 164, 167, 169
Shales, T., 50, 121
Shanahan, J., 5, 13, 14, 19, 24,
  114, 153, 193, 205–206, 209, 210
Shankman, A., 100
Shapiro, M., 242
Sheehan, S., 241–242
Shen, L., 25
Shi, L., 217
Sienkiewicz, M., vii, 61
Signorielli, N., vii, 12, 13, 14, 22, 24,
  114, 127, 129, 153, 171, 193–194, 209

Smith, D., 81
Smith, S., 117
Smith, T., 57
Snow, C. P., 20
Spigel, L., 21, 79
Sterritt, D., 242
Sussman, M., 80

Tagliamonte, S., 268
Tahmakera, D., 266
Tajfel, H., 224
Tan, A., 199
Thomas, D., 243
Thomas, S., 94
Todd, A., 268
Tönnies, F., 80
Tropp, L., 116
Tucker, L., 108
Turing, A., 26
Turner, J., 224
Twenge, J., 27

Van Landingham, 27
Van Oosten, J., 265
Vandenbosch, L., 265
Vargo, C., 22
Vazquez, L., 8–9
Vidmar, N., 21, 104

Wakshlag, J., 12
Walsh, K., 270
Wasylkiw, L., 258–259
Watkins, M., 40
Weaver, J., 12
Weiskopf, K., 257
Whisnant, D., 248
White, A., 250–251
Wieselman, J., 175
Williams, L., 40

AUTHORS CITED INDEX

Williams, R., 207, 219
Wilson, B., 24
Wilson, E. O., 81
Wiser, B., 257
Woods, J., 244
Worland, R., 52

Yamane, T., 80
Yan, H., 171
Yang, G., 267–268

Zillman, D., 225
Zook, K., 113

SUBJECTS INDEX

'Till Death, 103
$%^! My Dad Says, 145
2 Broke Girls, 277

ABC, 67, 126, 253
Addams Family, The, 55
Adventures of Ozzie and Harriet, The, 45, 102, 192, 244, 245
age portrayals in sitcoms, 129–153
age, period, cohort analysis, 216–220
Aldrich Family, The, 45, 50, 139
ALF, 63
Alice, 60, 152, 203
All American Girl, 227
All in the Family, 2, 3–4, 18, 56–57, 59, 66, 72–74, 92, 96, 99, 112, 170, 218, 252–253, 262; and race, 103–107
Allen, Gracie, 45–46, 232, 241
Altman, Robert, 58
Always Sunny in Philadelphia, 215, 274–275
Amen, 63
Amos 'n' Andy, 41, 42, 48, 52, 99–100, 105–107, 197, 226, 240, 247
Amos, John, 1, 120

Andy Griffith Show, The, 24, 52, 54, 55, 58, 83, 90, 92, 102, 203
Annenberg School for Communication, 126–127
Archie Bunker's Place, 63, 74
Arnaz, Desi, 78, 242
Arthur, Bea, 98, 119, 157, 230

Bachelor Father, 102
Ball, Lucille, 44, 49, 56, 78, 117, 258, 271
Barber of Seville, The, 37, 38
Barney Miller, 160, 199, 255–256
Barr, Roseanne, 63–65
Baywatch, 24
Becker, 213
Benny, Jack, 42–44, 48, 55, 241
Beulah, 55, 100
Beverly Hillbillies, The, 17, 52–53, 247–248
Bewitched, 54, 58, 160, 188, 248–249
Bhutan, 5
Big Bang Theory, The, 69, 92, 123, 153, 213, 273–274, 278
birth and birth rate, 74, 84–86, 204, 217, 246, 259

306   SUBJECTS INDEX

Bishop, Joey, 222, 245–246
Black characters in sitcoms, 39, 42, 44,
    54–55, 59–60, 61, 63, 73–74, 101, 102,
    116, 117–118, 120, 204, 218, 224–226,
    240, 246, 247, 252, 253, 259, 262, 263,
    256–260, 267–268, 269, 272, 277;
    1970s, 105–107; 1990s, 67–68; after
    The Cosby Show, 111–113; Black-led
    sitcoms, *112*; *The Cosby Show*, 107–111;
    Cultural Indicators data, 129–152;
    prejudice, 99–100; race and minority,
    197–202; race and minstrelsy, 39–41;
    in *Seinfeld*, 177–178
Black-ish, 36
blackvoice, 41, 99, 240
Bless This House, 169
Blondie, 42, 45
Bob Crane Show, The, 146
Bob Newhart Show, The, 36, 91,
    92, 255
Bono, Sonny, 3
Brady Bunch, The, 3, 90, 170, 203
Brooks, Mel, 267
Bruce, Lenny, 224
Bunker, Archie, 4, 21, 56, 62–63, 74, 96,
    104, 105, 107, 116, 252–253
Burns, George, 45–46, 48, 241

Carlin, George, 168, 169–170, 224
Carney, Art, 3
Carroll, Diahann, 252
catchphrases, 44, 99, 164–165,
Cavemen, 124
CBS, 3, 57, 67, 100, 104, 126, 144,
    153, 246, 248, 250
Chayefsky, Paddy, 48
Cheers, 62–63, 75, 93, 204, 232, 233,
    260–261
Cher, 3
Clemens, Samuel, *see* Twain, M.

coarse dialogue, 27–28, 129, 152, 167,
    170, 206
Conners, The, 145
content analysis, 9–11, 12–13, 26–28,
    93–95, 121–124
corpus and corpora, 155–156
Cosby Show, The, 44, 61, 62, 63, 74,
    107–111, 112, 121, 152, 232, 259, 261–262,
    263
Cosby, Bill, 44, 61, 109, 236, 259, 262, 286
Courtship of Eddie's Father, The, 83, 199
critical studies, 111–113
cultivation analysis, 13, 209
Cultural Indicators data, 124–139,
    192–193, 199; characters, 129–139;
    character features, 136–139; coding,
    127; demographics, 131–133; method,
    125–127; multivariate comparisons,
    134–136; results, 128–139; sitcom
    genres, *126*
Cultural Indicators Project (CI), 11–13,
    20–21, 23–24
cultural indicators, 5–6, 8–9, 14–17;
    sitcoms as, 17–18
cultural studies, 19–20
Curb Your Enthusiasm, 70, 216, 226–227,
    269–270
CW, The, *112*, 126

Danny Thomas Show, The, 51, 243
Danson, Ted, 63
Darwin, Charles, 157–158
David, Larry, 70, 269
December Bride, 242
Degeneres, Ellen, 68
Delaware, University of, 126–127
Delta House, 258
Dennis the Menace, 51
Derrida, Jacques, 157–159
Desilu Productions, 240, 242

SUBJECTS INDEX

307

Dick Van Dyke Show, The, 43, 55, 57, 66, 83, 246
Diff'rent Strokes, 204, 263
Different World, A, 61–62, 109, 263
Disjointed, 145
disparagement humor, 224–228
divorce, 16, 82–83, 90, 96, 101, 115, 203; divorce rates, 83
Donna Reed Show, The, 56, 197
Doyle, Arthur Conan, 157–158
Drew Carey Show, The, 69

economic indicators, 5, 14–15, 17
Ellen, 68
EMPATH, 181–184
Evans, Mike, 2
Everybody Hates Chris, 169, 272
Everybody Loves Raymond, 69, 197, 213, 268–269

F Troop, 199
Family Matters, 265, 266
family structure, 79–100; 1970s families, 56–60; demography of, 82–86, 121–153; four-person "families", 90–93; marriage, 203–206; neo-traditional families, 60–63; non-nuclear families, 86–89; nuclear, 81–82, 89–90; nuclear families in 1950s, 45–51; rural families, 52–54; in *Seinfeld,* 163, 165; size, 84–86; size, 85; sociology of, 79–82; whiteness and nuclear families, 54–56, 100–103
Family Ties, 61–62, 74, 262
fantasy sitcoms, 54
farce, 37–38
Father Knows Best, 45, 48, 51, 55, 58, 61, 89, 94–95, 102–103, 109, 160, 177, 186, 206, 243, 262

fatherlessness, 90, 106, 254, 266
FBI, 6, 208
female-led sitcoms, 97–98
Fibber McGee and Molly, 45
Flintstones, The, 55, 123
Flip Wilson Show, The, 3
Flo, 60
Floyd, George, 110, 216, 218
Fonzie, 75, 164–165, 256, 266
Forbes, Katherine, 239
four-character sitcoms, 90–93
FOX, 68, 111–113, 126, 126, 169, 197
Fox, Michael J., 61
Foxx, Redd, 106–107, 168
Frank's Place, 109–110, 113, 197
Frasier, 38, 213
Fresh off the Boat, 199
Fresh Prince of Bel-Air, The, 266
Friends, 36, 65–66, 69, 74, 92, 94, 110–111, 115–116, 117, 152, 160, 177, 183–184, 205, 213, 217, 268
Full House, 203

gay, images of, 57, 64, 68, 116, 185, 200, 201, 204, 226, 228, 252, 254, 255, 258, 269, 271; images in Seinfeld, 179–181; marriage, 204
gemeinschaft, 80
gender, 129–153, 190–195, 209–210, 227, 260–261, 263, 264, 270, 272–273; portrayals in sitcoms, 190–197; in *Seinfeld,* 171–177
General Social Survey, *191*
George Burns and Gracie Allen Show, The, 45–46, 48, 87, 241
George Carlin Show, The, 169
George Lopez Show, The, 273
Gerbner, George, vii, 5, 11–14, 20–24, 108, 117, 121–125, 127, 128, 190, 198, 205–215, 220

SUBJECTS INDEX

gesellschaft, 80
Get a Life, 264
Gilligan's Island, 79, 206
Girl with Something Extra, 146
GLAAD, 179, 200
Gleason, Jackie, 34, 241–242
Goldbergs, The, 41, 46, 71, 88–89, 100, 273, 276
Golden Girls, The, 63, 92, 98, 264
Gomer Pyle, USMC, 54
Good Place, The, 278
Good Times, 41, 60, 74, 106, 120, 146, 164
Goodman, Benny, 40
Green Acres, 54, 215, 228, 247, 250–251, 278
Griffith, D. W., 40
Growing Pains, 74, 148

Happy Days, 56, 60, 74, 75, 165, 199, 234, 256, 260, 268
Harris, Joel Chandler, 52
Hazel, 55
Hein, Jon, 256–257
Here's Lucy, 56
Hispanics and Latinos, 89, 129, 134, 136, 218–219, 273
Hogan's Heroes, 56, 267
Hollywood Diversity Report, 192, 217
Home Improvement, 197
Homeboys in Outer Space, 123
Honeymooners, The, 34, 46–48, 51, 63, 69, 71, 87–88, 94, 95, 108, 227, 241–242
households and household size, 14, 46, 84–86

I Dream of Jeannie, 36, 54, 168, 249–250
I Love Lucy, 17–18, 36, 45, 47, 49, 50, 64, 65, 68, 71, 78, 83, 86–87, 91, 167, 216, 226, 240

IMDB, 122–124, 139–151; age data in, 141; main characters, 145–147; ratings, 147–151; gender and age, 141
In Living Color, 111–113, 116, 197
Indiana University, vii, 223
indicators, theory of, 13–17
institutional process analysis, 12, 30, 207
irony, 26–28, 176, 184, 186, 278
It's Always Sunny in Philadelphia, 215, 274–275

Jack Benny Program, The, 42–44, 48, 241
Jamie Foxx, 68
Jeffersons, The, 18, 59–60, 74, 105, 218, 259
Jews, 39–41, 46, 52, 88, 100, 175, 178, 185, 225–227, 247, 267, 269–270
JJ (*Good Times* character), 41, 74, 106, 164
Joanie Loves Chachi, 124
Joey Bishop Show, The, 222, 245
John Read Middle School, 4
Jolson, Al, 41
Joyce, James, 157–158
Julia, 54, 83, 102, 252
Just Shoot Me, 213, 270–271

King of Queens, 69, 88, 144, 270
Kirk, 148
Klein, Paul, 50, 121
Kramden, Ralph, 164, 241–242, 270

Last Man Standing, 215, 275
Laverne and Shirley, 146
Lear, Norman, 18, 58–60, 72, 96, 104, 147, 259
least objectionable programming, 50, 121
Leave it to Beaver, 80, 90, 95, 102, 117, 243, 244
lexical diversity, 157–161

SUBJECTS INDEX

Life with Luigi, 50, 52, 71, 100
Living Single, 68, 113, 205
Love, Sidney, 68

M*A*S*H, 18, 56, 58–59, 60, 74, 254, 261
mainstream(ing), 114, 209, 211–212,
   214–220
Make Room for Daddy, 51, 123, 243, 246
Mama, 50, 71, 88–89, 100, 239
Man with a Plan, 217
Marcus Welby, M. D., 24, 56
marital status, 30, 83, 129–153, 203–206
marriage rates, *83*
Married with Children, 17, 113, 170
Martin, 68, 113
Mary Tyler Moore, 56–58, 92, 97, 98, 99,
   121, 146, 147, 218, 254
mass communication research, 18–23,
   80–81
Maude, 96–99, 107, 116, 146, 230
McGovern, George, 4
Meadows, Audrey, 34
mean world syndrome, 11–12
media effects, 5, 19–20, 81, 113–118,
   171–172, 200
metoo, 216, 218
Middle America, 47, 63, 71, 89, 101–103,
   104, 108, 118, 211, 213, 246, 255
Mike and Molly, 45, 276–277
minstrelsy, 38–43, 44, 57, 74, 99, 106, 197,
   253, 259, 267
mirroring, sitcoms as social reflection,
   6, 21, 124, 189–190, 196, 201, 205
Modern Family, 69, 144, 204, 213, 274
Mom, 213
Monkees, The, 72, 92, 249
Montgomery, Elizabeth, *188*
Moore, Mary Tyler, 57–58, 246
Moorehead, Agnes, *188*
Morita, Pat, 199

Mork and Mindy, 259–260
Munsters, The, 55
Murphy Brown, 114–115, 264
My Three Sons, 56, 91, 102, 123, 203
My World and Welcome to It, 149

Nabors, Jim, 54
NBC, 67, 116, 126, 246
Nelson, Frank, 44
Nelson, Ozzie, 48, 102, 192
New Bill Cosby Show, The, 146
new class, 212–214
new state religion, theory of TV,
   210–212
New York, 34, 65, 87, 88, 94, 105, 177,
   178, 251
Newhart, 63
Newhart, Bob, 44, 63, 255
Nixon, Richard, 4

O. Henry, 241
O'Connor, Carroll, 2
Obergefell v. Hodges, 204
Office, The, 69, 148, 275–276
One Day at a Time, 60, 96, 152, 203,
   218, 257
Oppenheimer, Jess, 240
Orwell, George, 157–158
Our Miss Brooks, 45, 50
Oxford English Corpus (OEC), 161–163

Parks and Recreation, 69
Partridge Family, The, 72, 90, 253–254
Patty Duke Show, The, 56
Payne Fund studies, 11
peak TV, 139
persuasion, 19, 25
prejudice, 18, 40, 99–100, 103, 109, 111,
   117, 196, 199, 248
Presley, Elvis, 40

SUBJECTS INDEX

Private Secretary, 51
Pryor, Richard, 169, 224

race, 129–153; portrayals in sitcoms,
197–203; racism in sitcoms, 3–4
radio, golden Age of, 37, 42–45
Ranch, The, 215
ratings; 1950s, 51; 1960s, 53; 1970s,
59; 1980s, 62; 1990s, 64; 2000s, 70;
1950–2000, 73
reactance, 25
reading level, readability, 157–161
Reagan, Ronald (and Reaganism), 56,
61–62, 262
Real McCoys, The, 51, 52
Reed, Donna, 48
Reiner, Carl, 232, 246
relevance, 4, 18, 56–60, 66, 72, 74, 75,
135, 144, 195, 253, 255, 256, 259, 261
repetition in humor, 163–167
retardation, of social change,
205–206, 209
Rhoda, 146, 254
Ricardo, Lucy, 36, 48, 71, 86–88,
170, 226, 234, 240, 275
Ricardo, Ricky, 36, 86–88, 91, 170,
226, 240
Richard Pryor Show, The, 169, 224
Rickles, Don, 169, 224
Roc, 108, 113, 204
Rogers, Will, 52
Rolle, Esther, 106, 120
Roseanne, 63–65, 80, 95, 117, 145, 169,
264, 277
Rossini, Giacchino, 37
rural-coms, 52–54
Rutherford Falls, 199

Sanford and Son, 59, 106–107, 168
Schitt's Creek, 70, 215, 228, 278

Scorsese, Martin, 60
Seinfeld, 30, 36, 66–67, 68, 70, 74, 75, 91,
155–187, 199, 215–216, 265, 267, 269; as
data, 155–156; gay issues in, 179–181;
gender in, 171–177; most-used words
in, 161–167; profanity in, 167–171;
progressivism in, 185–186; race in,
177–179; textual analysis of, 155–187;
word frequencies in, 156–171; topic
modeling, 181–184
semiotics, 15–16; signifier and
signified, 16
seven dirty words, 27, 168, 170
Sex and the City, 92
Simpsons, The, 48, 94–95, 113, 123, 274
Sinbad Show, The, 113
situation comedies, 1950s, 45–51; 1960s,
52–56; 1970s, 56–60; 1980s, 60–63;
1990s, 63–68; 2000s, 67–71; roots,
36–37
social change in sitcoms, 206
social indicators, 5, 6–8, 14–15, 17
social science, 19–20
Sonny and Cher Comedy Hour, The, 3
Soo, Jack, 199
standard of living in US, 48–49
stereotypes, 223–228
Steve Harvey Show, The, 67–68
Still Standing, 272
structure of feeling, 219
Suddenly Susan, 69

Taxi, 60, 62–63, 204
textual analysis, 155–187; most frequent
words in sitcoms, 123
That Girl, 58, 251
Thomas, Danny, 243, 251
Thomas, Marlo, 251
Three's Company, 17, 60, 168, 170, 257–258
Tinker, Grant, 58

SUBJECTS INDEX

Trump, Donald, 218
Twain, Mark, 3, 52, 61, 185, 224, 260
Twitter, see *X*
Two and a Half Men, 69, 92, 153, 213, 271–272
type-token ratio, 156–158

Umeki, Mitoshi, 199
Uncle Tom's Cabin, 40
UNESCO, 9
UPN, 111, 113, 126, 197

vast wasteland, 207
vaudeville, 38–39
Veep, 275
Veronica's Closet, 69
Violence Index (VI), 12–13

Walker, Jimmie, 41
Wayans Brothers, The, 67, 267
WB, The, 67–68, 111, *112*, 113, 126, 197
Webster, 262–263
Whiteman, Paul, 40
whiteness, 54–55, 100–103
Wikipedia, 122–124; corpus, 156
Will & Grace, 68, 114, 160, 179, 213, 271
Wilson, Flip, 3
Winkler, Henry, 164–165
word token, 156–157
word type, 156–157

X, 29

York, Dick, *188*
Young Sheldon, 277

James Shanahan is Professor in the Media School at Indiana University, where he was Founding Dean from 2015 to 2021. He is author of *Media Effects: A Narrative Perspective,* (with Michael Morgan) of *Television and Its Viewers: Cultivation Theory and Research,* and (with Katherine McComas) of *Nature Stories: Depictions of the Environment and Their Effects.* He is editor (with Janet McCabe, Kimberly A. Novick, and Gabriel M. Filippelli) of *Climate Change and Resilience in Indiana and Beyond* (IUP, 2022), (with Michael Morgan and Nancy Signorielli) of *Living with Television Now: Advances in Cultivation Theory and Research,* and of *Propaganda without Propagandists?: Six Case Studies in U.S. Propaganda.*

For Indiana University Press

Lesley Bolton, Project Manager/Editor

Allison Chaplin, Acquisitions Editor

Anna Garnai, Production Coordinator

Sophia Hebert, Assistant Acquisitions Editor

Samantha Heffner, Marketing and Publicity Manager

Katie Huggins, Production Manager

Dan Pyle, Online Publishing Manager

Pamela Rude, Senior Artist and Book Designer